Immigrants, Markets, and States

IMMIGRANTS, MARKETS, AND STATES

*The Political Economy
of Postwar Europe*

JAMES F. HOLLIFIELD

Harvard University Press
Cambridge, Massachusetts
London, England 1992

This book is printed on acid-free paper, and its binding materials
have been chosen for strength and durability.

Library of Congress Cataloging-in-Publication Data

Hollifield, James Frank, 1954–
    Immigrants, markets and states : the political economy of postwar Europe /
James F. Hollifield.
        p. cm.
    Includes bibliographical references and index.
    ISBN 0-674-44423-X
    1. Europe—Emigration and immigration. 2. Europe—Emigration and
immigration—Government policy. 3. Alien labor—Europe. 4. Alien
labor—Government policy—Europe. I.Title.
JV7590.H65 1992
304.8′094—dc20
91-44717
        CIP

For Machiko, who persevered

Preface

The subject of immigration easily inflames the emotions. Rags-to-riches stories of immigrant grandparents can bring forth tears of nostalgia. Too often, however, the presence of foreigners draws out nationalist passions and racial hatred. The conflict between territorial norms of community and authority, bounded by the nation state, and modern notions of the free, rational individual, an ideal of liberal democracy, continues to play itself out in the advanced industrial societies.

My purpose in this book is to explain why immigration has become a prominent feature of industrial societies, and why liberal democracies in particular have difficulty in controlling immigration. The principal focus is immigration in postwar Europe, specifically in France and Germany—two states that have struggled to cope with largescale migrations. The European experience is compared with the American to highlight some of the differences between the Old World and the New, and to explore the convergence of policies that affirm freer markets for migrant labor and greater protection of the civil rights of aliens.

Immigration has played and continues to play a crucial role in the political economy of postwar Europe and the United States, providing an essential supply of labor during periods of rapid economic growth. But the rise in immigration in the second half of the twentieth century cannot be understood purely in economic terms. The spread of market relations and the demand for cheap labor in the industrial democracies were necessary but not sufficient conditions for the surge in immigration. People are not just commodities: can an individual reside and work in a liberal society without enjoying the rights that are accorded, in principle, to every member of society? The extension of rights to an ever larger number of individuals and groups is a central feature of the story of immigration in the United States and Europe. Both of these developments—markets and rights—I argue, are profoundly liberal.

Developing the ideas and carrying out the research for this book has taken many years. Along the way pieces of the study have been published in one form or another, and I should like to thank the publishers for their permission to use the revised versions here. Parts of chapters 3 and 4 originally appeared in a special issue of *The Annals of the American Academy of Political and Social Science* (May 1986), edited by Martin and Barbara Heisler. Some of the sections on France in the same chapters were published in *Searching for the New France* (New York: Routledge, 1991), edited by George Ross and me. Chapter 6 is a revised version of an article which appeared in *Comparative Political Studies* (April 1990) and in the *Revue Française de Science Politique.* Finally, portions of chapter 8 were taken from an article in a special issue of the *Revue Européenne des Migrations Internationales* 6 (1990), edited by Yves Charbit and me.

It is impossible to thank every person and institution that contributed in some way to this work. However, I feel I owe a special debt of gratitude to certain people and places.

First of all, I thank my friends and colleagues of the Institut National d'Etudes Démographiques and the Institut d'Etudes Politiques in Paris. Every scholar should be so fortunate to receive the kind of intellectual and material support in his or her endeavors that was afforded me during numerous stays in France. Thanks are due to Didier Blanchet, Philippe Bourcier de Carbon, Yves Charbit, Jean-Claude Chesnais, Thérèse Franjou, Jacqueline Hecht, Riva Kastoryano, Georges Lavau, Claude Lévy, Hervé Le Bras, Rémy Leveau, Alain Parant, Emmanuel Todd, Michèle Tribalat, Jacques Veron, and Catherine de Wenden. I am especially grateful to Georges Tapinos, without whose support this work might not have been possible.

Many other European and American colleagues contributed either directly or indirectly to the making of the book. I should like to thank especially Rogers Brubaker, James Caporaso, R. Taylor Cole, Wayne Cornelius, Jacqueline Costa-Lascoux, William Field, Lawrence Fuchs, Jean-Pierre Garson, Craufurd Goodwin, Peter Hall, Barbara and Martin Heisler, Stanley Hoffmann, Peter Katzenstein, Charles Kindleberger, André Lebon, Mark Miller, Eric Nordlinger, Alejandro Portes, Rosemarie Rogers, Ronald Rogowski, George Ross, Peter Schuck,

Peter Schwanse, Myron Weiner, Heinz Werner, and several anonymous reviewers of my publisher. I am most deeply indebted to Seyom Brown, Peter Lange, and Sidney Milkis, for their encouragement, expertise, and friendship.

I also gratefully acknowledge the support provided, at various stages of research, by the Department of Political Science of Duke University, the Shell Foundation, the National Institute of Mental Health, the French-American Foundation, and the Center for European Studies at Harvard University.

Above all, I thank Machiko Tadokoro Hollifield, who has been so much more than a wife to me and a mother to our children.

Contents

I. THE LIBERAL PARADOX

1. Regulating Immigration in the Liberal Polity   *3*
2. The Political Economy of International Migration   *19*

II. IMMIGRATION IN POSTWAR EUROPE

3. Guestworkers and the Politics of Growth   *45*
4. Foreigners and the Politics of Recession   *74*

III. POLICIES AND MARKETS

5. Immigration Policy and Labor   *99*
6. Immigration and the French State   *124*
7. Immigration and Industrial Policy in France   *141*

IV. MARKETS AND RIGHTS IN EUROPE AND THE
    UNITED STATES

8. Citizenship and Rights   *169*
9. Immigration and the Principles of Liberal Democracy   *214*

Selected Bibliography   *235*

Notes   *251*

Index   *297*

Figures

4.1 Foreign populations in France, Germany, and Switzerland   89
4.2 Immigration in France, Germany, and Switzerland   89
4.3 Foreign workers in France, Germany, and Switzerland   90
5.1 Long-run demand curve for labor   108
5.2 Four labor market situations   112
5.3 The political-economic model of the policymaking process   119
6.1 The political-economic model of policy implementation   128

Tables

5.1 Average annual percentage increase in real GDP in five labor-importing countries, 1960–1981   103
5.2 Average annual percentage increase in real consumer prices in five labor-importing countries, 1960–1981   103
5.3 Average annual unemployment rates in five labor-importing countries, 1960–1981   103
6.1 Estimates of the political-economic models of immigration and foreign employment in France, 1950–1987   137
7.1 Foreign workers in selected economic sectors in France, 1950–1980   144
7.2 Foreign workers in French industry, 1967–1979   146
7.3 Employment, productivity, and investment in French industry, in periods of growth (1967–1973) and crisis (1974–1979)   148
7.4 Foreign employment in selected industrial sectors in France, 1967–1979   151
7.5 Foreign and national employment in France, 1967–1979   152
7.6 Estimates of the political-economic model of worker immigration by four sectors, 1946–1980   162
7.7 Estimates of the political-economic model of foreign employment by economic sector   163

I • THE LIBERAL PARADOX

1 ◆ Regulating Immigration in the Liberal Polity

For thence—a paradox
Which comforts while it mocks—

—ROBERT BROWNING

In Switzerland in 1974 I watched a televised debate between two solemn-looking Swiss citizens over immigration. One was Swiss German whose ancestry went back many centuries. The other was a banker from Geneva whose parents had immigrated from Tunisia. The debate concerned a referendum that would decide the fate of thousands of foreign residents: it called for drastic measures to curb "overforeignization" *(Überfremdung)*. The Swiss German, a confident member of Helvetic society, took a liberal stand against the referendum, while the banker of Tunisian origin, a beneficiary of immigration, took the nationalist position in favor.

The story illustrates a problem which strikes at the heart of liberalism as a political philosophy. The free, rational individual not tightly bound by authority is a principal tenet of liberalism. Freedom of movement, some would argue, is a fundamental "human" right. But immigration comes into direct conflict with older norms of community and nationhood.[1] Despite the historical tension between immigration and nationalism, the extension of rights to aliens and the global spread of market relations have led to a surge in immigration in postwar Europe and the United States.

The Swiss experience again serves to illustrate the point. Switzerland was among the first countries in postwar Europe to experience largescale immigration. The influx of foreigners, most of whom were

3

viewed as guestworkers *(Gastarbeiter)*, was politically sanctioned and economically beneficial. Foreign workers contributed significantly to Swiss economic growth by helping employers avoid labor shortages while keeping wages in check. Indeed, the argument has been made that the postwar economic miracle *(Wirtschaftswunder)* in Europe could not have occurred without immigration, which provided "unlimited supplies of labor" during crucial periods of economic expansion in the 1950s and 1960s.[2] Yet many in Switzerland, as in France, Germany, and other European states came to question the benefits of foreign labor and to justify their opposition to immigration by pointing out that foreign workers were no longer needed because of slow growth of the economy and high unemployment among *citizen* workers. Others opposed immigration for sociocultural reasons, arguing that it threatened national identity and weakened the civic culture. The former is a specious argument, which, as I hope to demonstrate, is contradicted by the evidence. The latter, while perhaps equally specious, is a more complex position that appeals to nationalist and culturalist instincts. While these arguments are made with great frequency in the course of partisan debates, neither is helpful in understanding immigration—a movement which, since 1945, has become a prominent feature of European and U.S. societies.

Reactions against immigration in Europe in the 1980s underscore a dilemma for politicians of the right (many of whom have become, if they were not already, economic liberals) as well as politicians of the left (who espouse worker solidarity). Because foreign workers are viewed by the national rank and file as competitors for scarce jobs and social services such as housing, education, and health care, leaders of trade unions and leftwing parties in Europe are under pressure to take a hard line against immigration. Yet party leaders have hesitated to oppose immigration outright, feeling compelled to show solidarity with foreign workers while pushing for tighter controls on the use of foreign labor.

Immigration poses a more difficult dilemma for parties of the liberal right, whose electoral base is threatened by anti-immigrant and ultranationalist movements. Yet rightwing parties represent business interests and are committed to liberal, free market policies: they are thus faced with the incompatibility of economic liberalism and political nationalism. In the 1980s, the liberal right in Europe and the United States condemned state intervention in the marketplace. The two most celebrated examples of "neoliberalism" were Thatcherism in Great Britain and Reaganism in the United States. Both movements shared a commitment to such liberal causes as free trade, that is, the unrestricted movement of capital, goods, and services, and deregulation of everything from airlines to telecommunications. Implicit in their attacks against the state was a broader attack on collectivist politics and regulation in general. In the United States, the attack targeted certain types of New Deal legislation, entitlement programs, and other rights-based legislation, all of which were viewed as strengthening the state and organized interests at the expense of the individual and the market. In Britain, trade unions were the target of Conservative attacks because of the perceived role of unions in contributing to inflation. In France, the state and the bureaucracy came under fire for stifling the entrepreneurial spirit of individuals and the creativity of "civil society."[3]

In the face of neoliberal efforts to promote free markets, immigration remained highly controlled, at least in principle. Most of the industrial democracies, which include roughly the membership of the Organization for Economic Cooperation and Development (OECD), took steps to slow or stop immigration, especially after the severe recessions of the 1970s and early 1980s. Immigration policy in the United States was a partial exception to this generalization. Both the 1986 Immigration Reform and Control Act and the 1990 reform raised levels of *legal* immigration. But, as was the case in Europe, the spirit of immigration reform in the United States was to accommodate (undocumented) aliens already in the country, while tightening control over future immigration. In spite of the growing interdependence of national economies—a trend which has helped to change the nature of international relations by weakening the sovereignty and autonomy of states—and sweeping technological changes that facilitate transportation and communication, the industrial democracies have been committed to slowing the international mobility of people. The reasons for this "restrictionism," as I hope to demonstrate in the pages that follow, are political and to a certain extent symbolic. Even though immigration has proved to be economically beneficial,[4] there is a strong desire among the public and politicians in the industrial democracies to control migration, for what seems to be a simple reason. The control of borders (territorial closure) is the essence of state sovereignty. Hence international migration is seen, not surprisingly, as an issue of national security, and governments (of the left and the right) are fearful of a nationalist backlash against immigration. Appearances, however, can be deceptive. We must look beyond public opi[n]ion, partisan politics, and simplistic notions of sovereignty to understand immigration and the success or failure of policy.

Immigration is a test of economic and political liberalism. I define political liberalism as the ongoing extension of civil, political, and social rights to every member of society, whereas economic liberalism can be defined in terms of the creation and protection of relatively free markets. With the rise of liberalism and the development of the welfare state in the West since 1945, political theorists such as John Rawls and Michael Walzer have reexamined the contractarian assumptions of classical liberalism of John Stuart Mill and others. This rethinking put a new emphasis on rights and social justice.[5] Through the study of immigration we can explore the subtleties, paradoxes, and contradictions of the new liberalism. By the same token, we cannot understand immigration without a clear conception of political and economic change in postwar Europe and the United States. We must examine the way in which each organizational and ideological sphere, the polity on the one hand and the marketplace on the other, affects the structure of incentives and constraints that influence immigration and the state's capacity for regulating it. But before we look at the relationship between liberalism and immigration in postwar Europe and the United States, let us review some of the principal questions that animate this study and provide its theoretical agenda.

First, given public opposition to immigration and the attempt by states to gain greater control over the entry of foreign nationals, *how can we explain the persistence of immigration?* Even in those states where public opposition to immigration has been high, such as Germany, France, and Switzerland, immigration has continued to play an important role in society and the economy. In the United States, despite efforts to restrict illegal immigration, undocumented aliens have continued to enter at historically high levels. It is debatable whether we should put the United States in the same category with more restrictionist European states or whether trying to control illegal immigration should be considered restrictionist. But people coming into the United States and Europe without documents should not be excluded from a comparative study of immigration. Indeed, in the United States as in Europe, Japan, and the "dominions" (Canada, Australia and New Zealand), *illegal* immigration has become the focus of policy debates. In turn, these debates have helped to give greater legitimacy to *legal* immigration.

Why have liberal states had difficulty controlling immigration? Are there hidden constraints that prevent governments from implementing restrictionist policies? If so, what are the constraints, and what do they tell us about the relation among immigrants, markets, and states? Regulating immigration in the liberal polity is the central topic of this book. What better way to study the limits of politics and markets than to look at the role of aliens in liberal societies, at what rights they have, and the role they play in the productive process?

A prominent critic of classical liberalism, Karl Polanyi, was among the first to recognize the fallacies that underlie a-political (and a-social) versions of the liberal argument.[6] Of particular interest are two precepts of classical liberalism: the notion that the market functions most smoothly in the absence of constraining regulations—the self-regulating market—which implies the theoretical and practical possibility of assigning politics and economics to separate spheres of influence; and the notion that labor is a commodity to be bought and sold as any other commodity. These two precepts reveal several aspects of a liberal paradox, which is particularly acute in the area of migration. Even the most liberal states seek to regulate labor markets by preventing competition between citizen and foreign workers—this is the practical effect of policies designed to control immigration. And foreign workers, who are among the most vulnerable individuals in any society, cannot be reduced to their economic function. These individuals are not pure commodities. Like other marginal groups in liberal societies, they have acquired rights.

Since the economic downturn in the 1970s, when a number of governments in Europe attempted to suspend (worker) immigration as a way of controlling unemployment, a debate has been joined by policymakers and politicians over the role of immigrant labor in advanced industrial societies. Economist Michael Piore argued that foreign workers contribute to duality in the labor markets of industrial societies.[7] From this perspective, foreign workers are seen as a necessary component of labor supply in capitalist economies because they are easier to hire and fire than citizen workers. Foreign workers are likely to be hired in greater numbers during periods of economic growth and laid off in greater numbers during periods of recession. Thus foreign labor allows firms to avoid regulatory entanglements that govern the labor markets in welfare states. In short, foreigners are more easily exploited.

My second question follows from this argument: *can foreign workers be used as "shock absorbers" in industrial economies?* The implications of Piore's argument are that by hiring foreigners firms can control their workforce and introduce greater flexibility into the production process. From this it follows that states, by carefully regulating immigration, can use foreign workers to manage the labor market, adjusting supply to demand. I shall examine these arguments in light of the difficulties that France and Germany have encountered in controlling immigration in the postwar period. Explaining the role of foreign labor in industrial societies is one of the principal objectives of this book. Yet we must be careful not to reduce immigration to an issue of economics and thereby to ignore its important political dimensions.

Governments in Western Europe and the United States have come under pressure, particularly in the 1970s and 1980s, to stop or at least curtail immigration. Much of the pressure in Europe has been from nationalist groups, usually on the right of the political spectrum, which view immigration as a threat to national identity. The national front parties in Britain in the 1970s and France in the 1980s, rightwing parties in Germany such as the National Democrats (NPD) in the 1960s and the Republicans in the 1980s, the *Überfremdung* movement in Switzerland, and nativist lobbies (such as FAIR) in the United States have brought pressure to bear on governments to stop immigration. In most of these countries—again with the partial exception of the United States—policies in the late twentieth century have shifted in the direction of more stringent administrative controls on all types of migrant flows: skilled and unskilled workers, family members, seasonal workers, as well as refugees and asylum seekers. Yet despite policy shifts that reflect anti-immigrant sentiments, governments have had little success in controlling immigration. These problems of control cannot be attributed solely to a lack of political will; nor can policy failures be explained purely in terms of the ever-present demand for cheap labor, as the dual labor market theory would suggest. Other political and economic factors are at work to constrain governments in their efforts to control immigration. One especially important political factor is the accretion of rights for aliens and the emergence of adversarial legal cultures that afford greater protection (for many minority groups) from arbitrary powers of the state and employers.

This study focuses primarily on domestic rather than international political economy, although the two levels of analysis are not mutually exclusive. It is important to look at international efforts to regulate migration, particularly in the European Community, which has created an international migration regime and a regional labor market. Treaties governing migration exist, and some international organizations—such as the United Nations and the International Labor Office (ILO)—have tried to set standards for dealing with refugees and migrant workers. But with the exception of the European Community, international agreements for regulating migration have not been very effective. Why have fewer attempts been made by international organizations to control the flow of *people* than to regulate trade and capital flows?

The third question, with which I begin this study, is: *what weight should be given to domestic and international factors in explaining immigration, and how has migration affected the sovereignty and autonomy of democratic states?* If an international market for labor exists, to what extent is this market regulated by states that participate in it? We might be tempted to argue that international migration is simply an indicator of economic interdependence, which contributes to the convergence of international and domestic political economies and the construction of international regimes.[8] But we must avoid this temptation. International regimes rarely exist in the absence of domestic regulation, even in the European Community, which has by far the most sweeping multilateral arrangement for controlling migration, both among the member states and, if current trends towards political and economic union continue, between the Community and other states. Unlike trade and monetary "regimes," which limit the power of states to pursue independent economic policies, few international constraints on the sovereignty and autonomy of states exist in the area of migration. Again, the European Community is an exception. Yet states are constrained in their efforts to regulate immigration by liberal norms and principles at the domestic level.

My fourth question is the most difficult to answer: *is immigration driven primarily by political or economic factors?* The question would be a nonstarter were it not that it has become a central feature of policy debates in most of the industrial democracies. For students of political economy, it is a theoretical and empirical nightmare. Few would deny that international migration is influenced by political as well as economic factors, but trying to draw a line and distinguish between the two is another matter. At first blush, it may seem that the question turns on a false distinction between politics and economics, which so many theorists of late have labored long and hard to debunk.[9] After all, did I not just agree with Polanyi that any attempt to understand economics apart from politics is naive at best? But for policy purposes we must be prepared to tell which aspect of migration derives its meaning from the polity, and which one stems from the "logic" of the market. To put it another way, are Haitians who flood into south Florida political or economic refugees? Do Salvadorans come to the United States primarily because of the economic opportunities that exist, or because of the political freedoms and rights from which they hope to benefit? In exploring this question, we must bear in mind that political and social principles are "embedded" in market relations, and any attempt to tear them apart, even for analytical (or policy) purposes, is a risky business.

Issues in the Political Economy of Immigration

The study of immigration affords a unique perspective on the interaction of states and markets and thence a way to view some of the age-old problems of liberalism (rights versus markets) and nationalism (sovereignty versus cultural and economic interdependence). In addition, international migration, along with trade, is one of the quintessential features of the modern world order. Even more than the movement of goods and services, migration is a defining characteristic of the postwar international political economy.

A look at European and American history since the industrial revolution tells us that immigration involves four issues, each of which poses a problem for the nation-state. From the standpoint of national security and international relations, the first and most obvious problem is that of *sovereignty*. The legitimacy of the state would be threatened were it unable to exercise control of its borders. Control implies the legal right of the state to regulate the entry of individuals into its territory. All states exercise this right of control, and many extend sovereignty to include control over exit as well as entry.[10] Already we can see a distinction between liberal and nonliberal states: the former generally allow freedom of exit, whereas the latter seek to restrict both entry and exit. The reasons for these restrictions are many, but they derive essentially from the beginnings of the nation-state system in early modern Europe. Notions of a commonwealth or social contract would be weakened were the state unable to distinguish between citizens and noncitizens. One of the dilemmas that migration poses for the liberal state is to decide whether individuals should be free to choose to identify (or not) with the nation. Every state restricts entry, yet the nature of these restrictions varies considerably, even within the community of liberal democracies.

A second issue in the political economy of immigration is *citizenship*. Political struggles over immigration from the middle of the nineteenth century to the present have revolved around the issue of citizenship. Membership in liberal societies involves not only legal definitions of who can or cannot be a citizen, but also questions of assimilation, ethnicity, race, and culture. Few issues reflect political cultures and the traditions of nationhood as well as citizenship.[11] Looking at debates over immigration in Europe and the United States, especially in the 1980s, we might be tempted to conclude that immigration can be reduced to issues of citizenship and national identity.[12] Such a conclusion would be premature and historically inaccurate. Immigration in postwar Europe and the United States has been driven by demographic and economic concerns as much, if not more, as by concerns with citizenship. Yet citizenship has become a central issue in the political economy of immigration, especially in Europe.[13]

A third issue in the political economy of immigration is *labor*, which has been the principal concern of immigration policy in the industrial democracies during the postwar period. International labor migration presents economic liberals with a paradox. The notion that foreign workers are commodities that can be used to boost labor supply in periods of economic growth or perform jobs that are unattractive to citizen workers belies the fact that foreigners are individuals entitled to rights under the aegis of liberal constitutions. Nonetheless, in Europe and to a lesser extent in the United States, efforts to regulate immigration have been predicated upon the assumption that foreign or guestworkers are expendable commodities.

The fourth issue in the political economy of immigration is *humanitarian*. Many migrants are able to enter liberal states by virtue of family ties or because they request political asylum. Both types of migrants—family members and refugees—appeal to humanitarian sensibilities in liberal regimes. It is difficult to oppose family reunification or to refuse entry to an individual who is in personal danger. Nevertheless, the humanitarian issue has been less prominent in the political economy of immigration during much of the postwar period because groups concerned with refugees and asylum have been smaller and less powerful politically than those concerned with labor and citizenship. The humanitarian dynamic has come to the fore in the 1980s because labor immigration was officially suspended in Europe in the 1970s. Refugee migration and asylum seekers have increased in every liberal democracy in the 1980s, thus fueling debates over the political and economic dimensions of immigration. Whether this upsurge in refugee migration is the result of a more hostile political environment in certain areas of the world or of attempts by migrants to find new avenues of migration is open to debate.

Thus immigration in the modern era is multifaceted, and states have attempted to regulate it by creating categories of migrants (workers, seasonals, family members, frontier workers, and refugees), each of which requires a special policy or set of policies to control. It is important to note, however, that migrants are highly motivated individuals, whose primary objective in moving from one country to another is to find employment and improve their and their families' standard of living and quality of life. This fact alone makes it difficult for liberal states to control immigration, a state of affairs that is counterintuitive because foreigners are among the most (politically) vulnerable members of liberal societies. Traditionally, they have had fewer rights than citizens, and are often compelled to seek employment in a black market for labor. Given this common trait and the abundant supply of potential migrants, what prevents liberal states from simply being overwhelmed by utility-maximizing aliens? Does demand for cheap labor in these states determine levels of immigration? Or are liberal states institutionally and administratively capable of controlling migrant flows? If so, are some liberal states culturally or institutionally better equipped than others to cope with immigration?

The prominence of illegal immigration in postwar Europe and the United States might lead us to conclude that immigration is largely an affair of markets, as employers seek to hire cheap labor and migrants are willing to undergo enormous hardships to fill the demand. This is a tribute to the economic attractiveness of liberal systems and to the tenacity and ingenuity of individual migrants. Yet politics and the state are not absent from the story. Political controls range from administrative efforts to regulate "stocks and flows," usually as a way of managing labor supply, to nationalist appeals of extremist politicians seeking to eliminate immigration in order to rid society of foreigners, preserve some type of mythical national identity, and win elective office.

I have chosen to focus on policy and process in liberal political systems, which offer protections and opportunities for aliens in the form of rights. As we shall see, these rights vary from one system to another, depending on formal-legal arrangements (whether the system for adjudicating rights is driven by abstract considerations of due process, as in the United States, or by somewhat more concrete considerations of administrative procedure, as is often the case in Europe) and elements of political culture (whether the subject, substance, basis, and purpose of rights are driven by considerations of citizenship and nationality, or by broader and more abstract considerations of human rights and individual worth).

In short, I argue for a comparative political-economic approach to the study of immigration, and I make three claims for my subject. The first is that the study of immigration serves as a window through which we can view the working of liberal systems and gain insights into the interaction of states, markets, and rights. My second claim is that immigration offers us a rich set of comparisons that can help us to see differences and similarities in regimes, which we might otherwise overlook. My third claim is that by seeking to understand the role of foreign labor in the industrial democracies we shall be in a better position to understand the successes and failures of immigration and employment policies.

The Comparative Study of Immigration

Framing the question and settling upon a theoretical approach does not solve the methodological problems associated with the comparative study of immigration. Some of the classical methods of social and political science, such as survey research, are of limited utility. It would be difficult to get an adequate representative sample of immigrants in France, Germany, and the United States that would allow us to explore the relationship between liberalism and immigration. A better, although far from perfect, alternative is to look at national data on immigration with an eye to understanding how migrant stocks and flows have been influenced by political and economic change. The pitfalls of this strategy, especially the reliability of national immigration statistics, will become clear as we move into the historical and empirical analysis.

Data problems aside, the most difficult task in designing a comparative study of immigration is the selection of cases. Almost every country in the world is affected in one way or another by immigration.

The present study is limited to a subset of liberal democracies—France, Germany, and the United States. Each of these states has relied heavily on immigration to fuel economic growth, but each has taken a different approach to regulating immigration, consistent with longstanding national traditions and policy objectives. For much of the postwar period the French state was concerned with population decline, while the German state was concerned with labor supplies and economic growth. Since the early 1950s, the American state has been preoccupied with all of the issues listed above—sovereignty, citizenship, labor, equity, and justice. The French and German states, in turn, have been compelled to confront the same range of issues in the political economy of immigration as they moved away from demographic and economic concerns. From the standpoint of comparative political economy, the question we must ask is whether institutional and cultural differences among these states have led to different outcomes. If, as I argue, outcomes (that is, levels of immigration and the use of foreign labor) have been remarkably similar, how can we explain the convergence?

It should be obvious by now that I am not working within the rubric of "push-pull" theories of migration. This study looks only at a few receiving countries. How then, one might ask, is it possible to generate and test a theory of immigration without giving attention to the sending countries? My assumption is that current inequalities within the international system are such that a large and highly elastic supply of labor is available and ready to migrate from less developed to more developed countries. Hence constraints on migration—apart from transportation costs and information—are closely linked to the political and economic performance of the industrial democracies, and outcomes (levels of immigration) are a function of the interaction of markets and rights in these societies. Barring some radical change that would reduce inequalities in the international system, thus improving living standards and the quality of life in the Third World, political and economic conditions in the industrial democracies will continue to have a dominant influence on the magnitude and direction of migration flows.

Whether or not they have a long experience of immigration, the principal receiving countries in the postwar period have tried to use immigration for specific national purposes. Britain, France, and to a lesser extent the United States have been constrained in their efforts to control immigration by historical and geographical circumstances.

Britain and France have had to cope with a colonial legacy, which for much of the postwar period has meant extending rights of residence (if not citizenship) to migrants from former colonies. The United States, which has its own neocolonial history in various areas of the world, particularly in Latin America and Southeast Asia, also has been compelled for moral, cultural, and foreign-policy reasons to accept large numbers of immigrants qua refugees from the Third World. The situation of the United States is compounded by its sharing a long common border with Mexico—a major sending country—whereas Britain (and Japan) are aided in their efforts to control immigration because they are island-nations. Not surprisingly, the British government has been reluctant to support European Community efforts to eliminate internal border controls, precisely because it would mean giving up this geographical advantage and entrusting a crucial aspect of British sovereignty to states such as Greece, Italy, and Spain that have yet to prove their effectiveness in controlling illegal immigration from the Third World.

In addition to France and Britain, European states that have experienced largescale migration in the postwar period include Germany, Switzerland, Sweden, Belgium, and the Netherlands. More recently, Italy and Spain have become countries of immigration with influxes of people primarily from North Africa and the Middle East. Among these states, Germany and Switzerland stand out as examples of countries that have tried to use foreign workers for national economic purposes. France also has been an importer of labor, although French governments have defined foreign workers not simply as guests, but as immigrants *(travailleurs immigrés)* who will bolster a declining population. Finally, it is important to mention three other members of the "club" of liberal democracies: Canada, Australia, and Japan. Of these, only Canada and Australia have been countries of immigration. Recent reports, however, show that the foreign worker population in Japan has been growing, as a result of the economic boom of the 1980s, the aging of the Japanese population, and the demand for cheaper unskilled labor, especially in the construction and service industries. Yet Japan remains an anomaly. It is the only industrial democracy that has not relied heavily on foreign labor to fuel economic growth in the postwar period, if we discount the resident Korean and Chinese populations.

To generalize the experience of immigration in postwar Europe and the United States, it is essential for us to understand the political and economic similarities (and differences) of the cases at hand. Economically, there is one important distinction among the countries of immigration. Some have tried to use foreign labor for specific economic purposes, hoping that it would be possible to repatriate guestworkers when they were no longer needed. The most prominent examples of guestworker programs are those of Germany and Switzerland. At the other extreme is the United States, where, with few exceptions (such as the *bracero* program with Mexico), migrations have been treated as permanent or settler migrations. Unlike many Germans, most Americans readily accept the legitimacy of immigration, which is seen as a normal feature of an advanced industrial society. Between these two extremes lie the other countries of immigration, with France representing the most ambiguous case. As a country with a relatively long tradition of immigration, dating from the latter half of the nineteenth century, France has demonstrated an openness to settler migration.[14] Yet in the interwar and postwar periods immigration has been treated alternately as a major political and economic problem (the cause of unemployment and a threat to French national identity) and as a boon for the economy and society.

In terms of the political system and culture, the countries of immigration can be divided along several lines. One of the most important distinctions is to be found in citizenship law and the terms of membership in society. The biggest difference in this regard arises from two legal traditions: *jus soli* and *jus sanguinis*. The former (soil) grants citizenship to individuals born within the national territory, whereas the latter (blood) confers citizenship to the offspring of citizens. These traditions are linked in turn to the political and social history of each country. Germany follows the tradition of *jus sanguinis* in keeping with the history of the German nation, which has a strong ethnocultural tradition. The United States grants citizenship according to *jus soli* and *jus sanguinis*, which reflect a more expansive view of membership. These national legal distinctions point to differences in political culture, and they are crucial in determining how states have attempted to control immigration. Once again, France falls somewhere in the middle of a liberal continuum. Like the American, French political culture (since 1789) has been characterized by a universalist, revolutionary discourse. The French state has tended to be quick in extending citizenship to foreign residents through liberal naturalization policies. France also practices *jus soli* and *jus sanguinis*. But in other respects France resembles more closely the

German case, with a Roman and statist tradition of jurisprudence. In the following chapters the importance of these cultural, institutional, and legal distinctions, particularly the opposition between a more national-statist and liberal-pluralist tradition, will be made clear.

Even though this study focuses on immigration policy and process, it assumes that migrants are prototypical economic actors, particularly resistant to regulation of any kind. Attempts to control immigration for national purposes have proved difficult, in part because of the nature of the actors. Immigration has a strong *economic and humanitarian* dynamic, and the ability of governments to override this dynamic can tell us much about the strength and autonomy of the state.[15]

Since immigration is a defining characteristic of liberal democracy, it should lend itself easily to comparative analysis. Yet truly comparative works on immigration are few. In the field of migration studies, the tendency has been to collect national case studies, bind them together, and call the study *comparative*. Such compendia are useful sources of information, but they rarely yield theoretical insights.[16]

What is needed, and what this work seeks to provide, is a study of immigration which begins with a clearly defined set of questions and a theoretical agenda. This is a necessary, but not sufficient, condition for building a theory of immigration. We must look at policy outcomes (levels of immigration and foreign employment) across a range of carefully selected cases and seek to determine how political and economic differences among these states have influenced outcomes.

The first two chapters of the book are devoted to a discussion of alternative perspectives on international migration. In chapter two, the liberal thesis is developed and refined through an examination of issues of sovereignty and a look at the relationship between migration and international relations. This chapter also examines attempts by the European Community to regulate the movement of people, and the emergence of a liberal regime for international migration in Europe. Chapters three and four explore the liberal argument through a study of immigration and foreign worker policies in France and Germany, with some references to Switzerland. These chapters look at the role of foreign labor in Europe's postwar growth. Chapters five, six, and seven explore the relationship between immigration, employment, and industrial policy in Europe, with special attention to the French case. Finally, chapter eight is devoted exculsively to a comparative analysis of citizenship and immigration in France, Germany, and the United States. The conclusion summarizes the argument and reviews the major empirical findings of the book.

At one level, the book can be read as a comparative history of immigration and citizenship in postwar France, Germany, and the United States. Chapters three, four and eight cover most issues in the political economy of immigration, from the role of foreign labor in economic growth to the politics of citizenship. But the central puzzle of the book is to explain the persistence of immigration in the liberal democracies. My argument is developed in three stages, beginning in chapter two, which looks at changes in the international system and their impact on migration. In the context of international relations, migration can be seen as a reflection of the globalization of markets and an indicator of interdependence. However, migration cannot be understood simply as a function of increases in international exchange. It is also the result of a new (rights-based) liberalism in the industrial democracies.

The second stage of my argument is outlined in chapter five, which seeks to explain how policy interacts with markets to fix levels of immigration. A political-economic model of the policymaking process is used to explore the strength and autonomy of the state—especially the administrative capacity of states for intervening in labor markets. The ability to regulate immigration (and the market for foreign labor) serves as a test of statist, liberal, and Marxist theories of immigration.

The third stage of my argument is spelled out in chapter two and more fully developed in chapter eight, which explains how guest-workers were transformed from expendable commodities into objects of political conflict. The rise of a politics of citizenship and the advent of a more intensive, rights-based liberalism, first in the United States and subsequently in Europe, reinforced the political and humanitarian dimension of migration.

The conclusion summarizes the argument and seeks to explain why immigration has become a defining characteristic of liberal democracy. The movement of individuals across national boundaries forces a constant redefinition of the relationship between the individual and the state, thus opening for debate the concept of citizenship itself, which lies at the heart of liberal regimes.

2 ✦ The Political Economy of International Migration

After all that has been said of the levity and inconstancy of human nature, it appears evidently from experience that a man is of all sorts of luggage the most difficult to be transported.

—ADAM SMITH, *The Wealth of Nations*

From his perspective in eighteenth-century England, Adam Smith hardly could have anticipated the rapid and dramatic changes that would occur in the international political economy over the next two centuries. Given the cultural and political barriers to international migration—not to mention the dangers and difficulties of travel—it may have been perfectly reasonable to assume that individuals, unlike goods or capital, would remain tied to the nation-state, if not to the village. In England the Enclosure Acts had swept away the last vestiges of feudalism, permanently uprooting the English peasantry and creating something like a *national* market for labor that would grow and diversify in the eighteenth and nineteenth centuries. Colonization, well under way by the middle of the eighteenth century, remained part of the process of empire building or, as often as not, an avenue of escape or exile for adventurers, dissenters, and criminals. David Ricardo and John Stuart Mill sought to rationalize international migration as a natural and necessary step in the building of a larger *British* community. Both theorized about the relationship between trade and the international mobility of capital and labor.[1] But the prospect of massive population movements from one society to another was still distant. The first round in the liberal battle for freer trade was not won until 1846, with the repeal of the Corn Laws, and the Bank of England had not yet succeeded in creating and controlling

19

an integrated system of international finance. In short, *Pax Britannica* was just beginning to emerge in the late eighteenth century, and the great transatlantic migrations would not begin until later in the nineteenth century.[2] It was too early to foresee that migration would become such a prominent feature of the international political economy.

With the benefit of hindsight, we know that just as capital became more mobile and trade expanded, helped in part by the development of international regimes for finance and trade, labor too began to move.[3] One could expend a good deal of time and energy to explain why labor, which is only one segment of an internationally mobile population, began to move in large numbers toward the middle of the nineteenth century. Certainly colonization played an important role in the growth of international migration. Natural disasters, such as the Irish potato famine, and technological improvements in transportation and communication also played a role. But at some point we must recognize the emergence of an international labor market, which has a *political* as well as an economic dimension.

The central purpose of this chapter is to look at the relationship between international migration and changes in the international system in the postwar period. I am especially interested in theories of international political economy and the explanations they offer for changes in levels of international migration. Many scholars of migration take the realist view that states are sovereign and thereby have the power to protect and defend their territorial integrity. The notion of sovereignty includes the legal right of the state to regulate entry into (if not the departure of) any individual from its national territory. For reasons I shall make clear as we move into the comparative-historical chapters, I am skeptical of realist views that states can regulate immigration in the national interest.[4]

Clearly, migration is affected by domestic and international politics. But we must seek to understand what weight should be given to domestic as opposed to international factors in explaining it. We must be able to distinguish between the two levels of analysis in order to specify international systemic factors that affect migration and how they interact with domestic structures and policy to influence migration. One question to ask is why no regime has developed for regulating migration comparable to liberal regimes for trade, money, and finance that have emerged in the postwar period. To some, the answer to this question may seem obvious. States have few incentives to cooperate in controlling migration, because states (and employers) can obtain what they want, namely foreign labor, without cooperation. Moreover, the political-economic characteristics of labor, as a factor of production, are so different from those of capital, goods, and services as to prohibit most types of international regulation.[5] It would be hard to disagree with these commonsense observations. Yet we must push beyond the obvious, to explore some of the differences among international markets for labor, capital, goods, and services. By comparing the characteristics of these markets, we shall be in a better position to explain the absence of an international migration regime in the postwar period. Without such a regime, which, according to Steven Krasner, should act as an intervening variable, how much conflict and cooperation in international relations have resulted from the growth of migration in the postwar era?[6]

Migration and International Relations

Four theories of international relations inform our thinking about migration. Before developing my version of the liberal argument, I want to review them briefly and give a short critique of the principal assumptions of each.

The Realist Theory

The first perspective is realism. The realist argument (which has many statist features) is that governments must regulate international migration to protect the national interest. Defining (and defending) the national interest is the stuff of which politics are made, especially in liberal democratic states. To take but one example: the state has an interest in assuring an adequate supply of labor. A disproportionately large outflow of workers might result in an increase in wages; conversely a large inflow of workers could undermine wages and lead to a deterioration in the standard of living of citizen workers.[7] From this perspective, states are the relevant units of analysis and our attention should be focused at the level of domestic politics, for it is here that crucial decisions are made (about the rights of aliens, for example) that will affect all types of international exchange, including migration.

The state must regulate trade and other types of international exchange to promote the national interest and protect national security. This is the position taken by many governments, parties, and interest groups in democratic as well as nondemocratic states. In the postwar period, liberal states have pursued restrictionist policies with respect to migration, while showing greater willingness to allow international markets for capital, goods, and services to operate more freely. Yet migration has become a dominant feature of the international political economy. How do we explain the gap between the objective of statist policies (to control and curtail migration) and outcomes (increases in levels of immigration)? One popular answer is that policies for regulating migration have not been implemented well: states are lax in controlling their borders, therefore immigration simply has got out of control. As I hope to demonstrate, this is a wholly inadequate answer to an interesting question.

The Marxist Theory

Marxism is grounded in a dualist logic. Marx conceived of population movements in terms of the impact of primitive accumulation—the rationalization of agricultural production along capitalist lines, which created a new class of landless laborers. This surplus population became an "industrial reserve army," to be mobilized during periods of growth and disbanded during periods of crisis. The argument in *Capital* is more complex than this, but the central point is that capitalism, as a system of production, needs an industrial reserve army to overcome cyclical fluctuations in the process of accumulation.[8] Marx does not go far in translating this argument from the domestic to the international level, even though he offers a critique of colonization at the end of Volume I of *Capital*.

It is left to later Marxist theorists to explain international migration. The most celebrated among them are Rosa Luxemburg and Otto Bauer. Following Marx and Lenin, they suggest that emigration and colonization are a natural consequence of capitalist development. Lenin argued in *Imperialism, the Highest Stage of Capitalism*, that ever-expanding markets were needed to alleviate periodic crises of underconsumption and excesses of savings over investment. A corollary of this theory of international relations is that imperialist expansion can provide an outlet for surplus populations, as well as a source of labor during periods of growth in capitalist economies.[9] It is but a short step from these arguments to dependency and world systems theory, which also view migration in terms of imperialism, unequal exchange, dependence, and exploitation.[10] With the end of the colonial period in the 1950s and 1960s, the attention of Marxist theorists of migration turned to explaining the role of immigrant labor in advanced capitalism. Although there are many subtleties in these arguments, they all essentially rely on the original Marxist insight that capitalism needs an industrial reserve army to surmount periodic crises. Thus far from eliminating dualism, as liberals would have it, international exchange perpetuates it.[11]

The Marxist literature on migration is quite extensive, and it would be impossible adequately to review it here. Nonetheless, the implications of Marxist theories for the political economy of international migration are clear: authority relations in liberal states (and in the international liberal order) are so skewed in the direction of capital as to make labor dependent on the actions of capital, that is, decisions to trade, invest, hire, or fire. In *Birds of Passage,* Michael Piore focuses on inequalities and duality in the labor market; whereas Alejandro Portes and John Walton are more concerned with explaining labor migration in the context of an inherently unequal capitalist world system of exchange. In each case, however, the basic units of analysis are social classes. Immigrant workers are viewed in terms of a capitalist division of labor. They are subservient to the interests of capital and the state, and they are an essential feature of advanced capitalist societies, helping employers overcome "inefficiencies" that are the result of market regulation. In this framework, states are generally seen as political organizations that represent the interests of the capitalist class, and migration is the direct consequence of inequalities that result from the process of capital accumulation and class differences, within and among nations. Migration allows employers to avoid inefficiencies in the process of accumulation and to dilute the power of citizen workers who demand higher wages, better working conditions, and so on.

According to the dual labor market variant of Marxist theory, industrial societies are divided into a primary sector with good jobs, high wages, and job security, and a secondary sector with poor jobs, low wages, and no security. The reasons for the bifurcation of labor markets are related to the variability and uncertainty associated with industrial capitalism. Fluctuations in demand mean that every economy needs a flexible element in the production process, which can be forced to absorb insecurity. It is the secondary sector, according to the argument, that fulfills this function. Other marginal groups in society, such as youth, ethnic minorities, and women also contribute to the secondary labor market. The political and economic assumptions that underly the dual labor market argument are close to those of Marxist theory that capitalism needs an industrial reserve army to survive.[12]

The Marxist argument assumes that employers (with the support of the capitalist state) can use foreign workers, first, to keep wages down in periods of high growth, and second, to increase the tractability of the work force during periods of slow growth and adjustments to changing market situations.[13] If these assumptions are correct, then the state (and employers) in advanced capitalist societies have an effective weapon with which to combat some of the most difficult problems relating to industrial development and the business cycle. Marxist theories rely on structural factors, especially class, for explaining changes in levels of migration, and the argument turns on the exploitability of foreign workers, who are useful to employers because they can be easily hired and fired.

The Liberal Theory

From the liberal perspective the expansion of markets and the drive to eliminate inefficient sectors in national and global economies lead first to greater mobility of the factors of production, including labor, then to a decline in mobility, the growth of factor endowments, and factor-price equalization.[14] In the classical version of this theory, from Adam Smith to John Stuart Mill, there is a tendency to fall back on mercantilism to account for international migration, because of the recognition that the movement of people is different from other types of international exchange (see the quote from Smith at the beginning of this chapter).

Not until the twentieth century, with the attempt to construct a more deductive theory of international exchange, do we see an effort to overcome this mercantilist ambiguity. The result is to eliminate politics from the argument altogether, and downplay the importance of migration (in the long-term).[15] Trade theory contends that in the longterm economic growth will reduce transnational factor mobility. Under the most rigorous assumptions, Paul Samuelson demonstrates that any differences in the marginal productivities of labor and capital from one economy to another will disappear as trade increases. Trade and economic growth will eliminate inefficient sectors and reduce dualities in international and domestic economies. This is the theorem of factor-price equalization.[16] The (policy) implications of the theory are that states should not interfere with trade and the operation of markets. By promoting international economic exchange, political difficulties that might arise as the result of the inequality of factor endowments (and migration) will be eliminated.[17]

We would be hard-pressed to find examples of states that have pursued this type of liberal (economic) policy with respect to migration. Trade and foreign investment are seen by the more developed (liberal) states as a way of reducing the pressures for emigration in less developed states. Japan, for example, has pursued this strategy of bringing "capital to people" as a way of avoiding tensions in the labor market at home, and pressures for emigration in less developed neighboring countries (especially the one billion Chinese just next door). A number of European states, as well as the European Community, also consider trade and foreign investment as the best solutions to the problem of migration. The liberal theory conforms to a simple push-pull logic whereby stopping migration is viewed as a matter of reducing economic inequalities within the international system.[18]

The Theory of Hegemonic Stability

This hybrid of the realist and liberal arguments offers a fourth perspective on the political economy of international migration. Although the theory has gained wide currency in the field of international relations, migration as an issue has not been studied within the rubric of hegemonic stability.[19] This is surprising, since the argument offers some insights into international migration, even if, as I shall argue, it falls short of providing a satisfactory explanation. Robert Gilpin (paraphrasing Charles Kindleberger whom he views as the originator of this theory) states that "an open or liberal world economy requires the existence of a hegemonic or dominant power."[20]

The theory of hegemonic stability represents an important break from realism. Rather than looking at issues of exchange in terms of the interests of the state in an anarchic system, hegemonic stability posits the existence of an international order that is closely linked not only to the interests of a dominant state or states, but to (liberal) ideas and institutions that help to shape the international order. Following this line of reasoning, we would expect rules governing the movement of people to reflect the interests of dominant states. In the postwar period, the rise in levels of international migration can be seen as a function of the (liberal) interests and values of the United States and its allies. Another version of this argument is the theory of complex interdependence, which is closely associated with the work of Robert Keohane and Joseph Nye.[21] Keohane and Nye make a strong argument that a liberal-institutional order came into being after Bretton Woods, with transnational actors and new types of exchange fundamentally altering the basis of international relations. In areas such as trade, money, and finance, the new liberal order was institutionalized by the creation of regimes that acted to constrain state policies. Thus states no longer operated in an anarchic system where military force was the primary measure of power. Governments were no longer the sole guardians of the national interest, because they were tied (via international regimes) to a world order that reduced the range of policy options, leading to higher levels of cooperation. Therefore, in the area of migration, one would expect states to be constrained by a liberal logic, only if this liberalism has been sufficiently institutionalized, as in the areas of trade (General Agreement on Tariffs and Trade, or GATT) and finance (International Monetary Fund, or IMF).

John Ruggie, following Karl Polanyi, makes the important point that any international order (or regime) contains within it the values or social purpose of the hegemonic state(s); hence the notion of an "embedded liberalism in the postwar economic order." Ruggie's argument is complementary to the theory of complex interdependence, because it is hard to conceive of an international system (or regime) in the absence of a unifying set of principles and norms.[22]

The concept of embedded liberalism is helpful for understanding international migration, because in addition to recognizing the importance of markets in international relations, it offers a more sophisticated theory of international politics. It takes into account the role of power as well as ideas, principles, and norms in the international system. Embedded within the postwar order are liberal notions of rights. Admittedly these rights are a reflection of the politics of the hegemonic states, principally the United States; as property rights are among the most sacred liberal rights, capital (or business) tends to enjoy a privileged position in the international as well as the domestic political economy.[23] If we stopped with this critique of classical liberalism, which is oriented primarily to property rights and capital, we would be ignoring other rights that are extended to individuals (qua workers) in liberal societies—rights which spill over into international relations. Such simple constitutional protections as equality before the law and due process are important constraints on the power of liberal states. Rights are doubly important for aliens, who, as noncitizens, are among the most vulnerable individuals in liberal societies. Thus embedded liberalism can help to explain the prominence of international migration as a feature of the postwar international order. But we should keep in mind that liberal outcomes in the area of international migration and embedded liberalism in the international system are reflections of domestic political developments in the hegemonic states, principally the OECD countries. We must therefore look carefully at domestic struggles over *policy and rights* in these states, as well as the spread of market relations, in order to understand how and why international migration has increased since Bretton Woods.

A Reformulation of the Liberal Argument

I argue that international migration is closely tied to changes in the international system, which reflect the development of a new rights-based politics in democratic states. My argument is liberal in at least three respects: (1) it accepts the possibility of relatively free markets; (2) it gives primacy of place to rights in the political sphere; and (3) it takes individuals and states as the primary units of analysis.[24] I call this type of system a *rights-based regime*, which places an emphasis on human rights and social justice.[25]

At the domestic level, rights are expressed in legal and procedural terms. Norms and principles (such as equality before the law, due process, and so on) are statements about rights. The individual and her relationship to the state become the focus of policy debates. At the international level, rights are expressed in terms of embedded liberalism. A crucial difference between a realist and a liberal view of migration is that in the latter rights can act to constrain the behavior of states. Rights are especially influential in international and domestic labor markets, where the interaction of supply and demand can determine the fate of individuals in society, that is, their life-chances and personal development. The operation of labor markets brings into play Karl Polanyi's self-protective mechanisms (and John Ruggie's embedded liberalism), and individuals invoke rights to insulate themselves from the vagaries or injustices of unregulated markets and the arbitrary power of states.

The classic example of rights-based politics in the postwar period is the civil rights movement in the United States, whereby the state is compelled by law to intervene on behalf of marginal groups to assure equal protection and equal treatment. This type of low politics (at the domestic level) spills over into high politics (at the international level), and migrants are the indirect beneficiaries. Even though migrants (aliens) are not citizens, they are entitled by virtue of their humanity to many of the same protections.[26] The increase in the number of refugees in the 1970s and 1980s and the use of asylum procedures as a way for economic migrants to gain protection from deportation by liberal states illustrates the growing importance of rights in international politics.[27] The confluence of open (unregulated) international markets for labor and rights-based politics in domestic regimes explains the surge in immigration in the postwar period, and it has created the conditions for the emergence of international migration regimes. Such regimes, which are evolving at a regional level in Europe and North America, are confronted with the task of resolving the liberal tension between rights and markets. In these regimes, legitimacy is derived both from ideas of justice and from the legal protections of due process and equal treatment guaranteed through the judicial systems of liberal democracies.[28]

At the international level, rights-based politics is expressed in the form of embedded liberalism, which reflects the principles of the hegemonic states. The primacy of rights leads states to exercise caution and restraint in dealing with migrants. Unsuccessful attempts in 1990 by the British government to expel large numbers of Vietnamese refugees from Hong Kong provides a classic example of the importance of embedded liberalism. Realist or Marxist theories of migration would have difficulty in accounting for this type of state behavior. In the postwar period, international migration has developed a stronger political and humanitarian as well as an economic dynamic, making it difficult for states with liberal pretensions to regulate migration purely in terms of national security.

But we must be careful not to overstate the case for embedded liberalism. It provides only a partial explanation for increases in international migration in the face of statist and restrictionist policies. In the case of guestworkers in Germany who take advantage of liberal asylum laws or illegal aliens in the United States who are protected from deportation by constitutional provisions of due process, both states are constrained in their actions by liberal norms and principles. How these norms are applied and how migrants are treated in each country depends heavily upon the nature of the political system, particularly institutional arrangements such as the role of courts and bureaucracies, as well as the degree to which immigration has become a partisan issue. The rights-based, liberal argument simply helps us to understand the connections between low (domestic) and high (international) politics. If immigration and refugee issues have surged onto the agenda of world politics in the 1970s and 1980s, it is precisely because of the advent of rights-based politics which spill over into the international arena; subsequent attempts to resolve the liberal paradox (rights versus markets) become a primary concern of the international community.[29]

If international migration can be explained in terms of the interaction of unregulated markets and politics as rights, is this true of other types of international exchange? To understand regimes for money, finance, and trade, we must recognize that relations of power are more important in some arrangements (or regimes) than in others, and rights may be more embedded in some regimes than in others. By virtue of its historical scarcity as a factor of production, capital (qua business) has greater power to regulate exchange through cartels or other oligopolistic arrangements, or to seek regulation by the state.[30] Hence norms and principles are less important in capital markets, because business has the power to protect itself from the vagaries of unregulated markets. Certain liberal rights, particularly property rights, help to sustain capitalist arrangements, but it is important to note that rights in liberal societies pertain to individuals (or groups), not to inanimate commodites (land or capital). The rights of labor were achieved through struggle by trade unions and political parties— a struggle which resulted in the partial incorporation of workers into decisionmaking processes in the private and public sectors in some of the industrial democracies.[31] But, it is hard to find evidence of the political influence of organized labor at the international level, except in a negative sense. Many international investment decisions of firms are driven by considerations of labor costs.[32]

With respect to monetary and trade regimes, limits on the actions of governments and firms are economic and institutional. They are imposed (via rules governing competition, banking, and the like) by states, at both domestic and international levels. This type of regulation helps firms to avoid cutthroat competition, while regulation of trade and finance helps states (and firms) to avoid conflicts that might lead to confrontation. International markets for capital, goods, and services are regulated through a variety of treaty arrangements. The most prominent among these are the GATT and the IMF. In addition to the legitimacy provided by institutional arrangements, international regimes need the power of a hegemon to sustain them; hence the notion of a hegemonic regime or hegemonic stability.[33] While there may be some importance attached to norms, principles, and ideas in an international economic regime (for example, a commitment to free trade), the legitimacy of the arrangement depends upon the consent of contracting parties to a treaty, which is not the equivalent of a fully institutionalized, domestic social contract. States reserve the right to withdraw from such arrangements for reasons of national security.[34]

Immigration and the International System

It might be tempting to conclude that migration, like trade and finance, is a function of the openness of the international system and the presence of a liberal hegemon. The first great waves of international labor migration ground to a halt in the 1920s and 1930s with the advent of the Great Depression, the collapse of the international economic order, and the ensuing war, which marked the end of *Pax Britannica*. The second great wave of international migration, which began as an exodus of refugees from Europe in the 1930s and 1940s, took place in the post–World War II period under a new world order sometimes described as *Pax Americana*. But the Cold War and the bipolar nature of the international system that emerged in the 1950s helped to constrain East-West migration, while in some instances it stimulated South-North migration. This was particularly true in areas of the world such as Central and South America, Southeast Asia, and southern Africa where there were low-level conflicts and proxy wars between the superpowers. With the end of the Cold War and the disappearance of bipolarity in 1989–90, migration might be expected to increase dramatically, as new avenues of exchange open up between East and West as well as North and South. The revolutions of 1989 and the collapse of communism in Eastern Europe may be the harbinger of a new world order, based more than ever on the liberal (rights-based) principles of the hegemonic states. If this change in the international system is enduring, then migration should become a more prominent feature of the international political economy.

However, the argument that international migration depends upon hegemonic stability may be spurious. The first problem with such an argument is that no specific regime for labor (with the possible exception of the EC) has emerged in the postwar period. Second, liberal states have continued to pursue restrictionist policies, despite (or perhaps because of) the advent of a more interdependent world order and the end of the Cold War. Thirdly, there is considerable evidence of international migration in various parts of the world even during the darkest days of the 1930s and 1940s. Finally, according to liberal trade theory (particularly the theorem of factor-price equalization), the expectation is that as trade increases (during a period of international stability), factor mobility will decline. If we cannot explain changes in levels of migration in terms of systemic theories of international relations and political economy, where do we turn?

John Ruggie's theory of embedded liberalism suggests that the spread of market relations provokes a self-protective reaction. With respect to international migration, this reaction takes one of two forms: liberalism or nationalism. It is difficult for states to steer a middle path between the two. The liberal response to migration is to maintain relatively open borders and regulate the flow of people in such a way that the basic human rights of individuals (citizens or denizens) are respected, thus mitigating to some extent the adverse impact of unregulated (illegal) migration. The statist/realist reponse is to regulate migration in such a way that national interest and security concerns are respected. Here, "national interest" could mean anything from reducing unemployment by expelling foreign workers, to protecting the identity of the nation by excluding certain types of ethnically and culturally undesirable groups.

In Europe and the United States in the postwar period the liberal position has prevailed, despite statist policies and nationalist reactions against migration. To substantiate my liberal thesis, however, we must show (1) that outcomes in the area of migration have in fact been liberal, in economic as well as political terms; (2) that statist policies with respect to migration have been ineffective; (3) that markets provide important incentives for migration; and (4) that market incentives for migration have been reinforced by rights-based politics, which help to deter the development of unregulated (black) markets for migrant labor.

My agument deals only with migration in the industrial democracies, which nonetheless accounts for a substantial portion of international migration in the postwar period. The liberal thesis is relevant for other regions of the world such as the Middle East or South Asia, which have experienced important migrations, only to the extent that rights-based liberalism is embedded in the politics (and foreign policies) of these states. The various countries of the Persian Gulf and the Asian subcontinent historically have not been constrained by liberal norms and principles. Yet they may be constrained by markets, insofar as the potential for international labor migration is always present. Likewise the policies of nonliberal states may be constrained by liberal norms, expressed in the "court of world opinion" and international human rights conventions.[35]

Statist Policies and Liberal Politics in Europe and the United States

Among the liberal democracies, the principal countries of immigration in the postwar period are to be found in North America, Europe, and Australia. If we look at the experiences of these countries with respect to migration, a common pattern emerges. To quote the European reporter to an OECD conference on the future of migration: "Economic, political and social considerations, in turn or together, dictated immigration policies which were fairly *liberal* at the outset, but which became more restrictive before culminating in steps to enforce a ban; *flows continued nevertheless.*"[36] Immigration has gone through several distinct phases in postwar Europe. The first phase is associated with a period of economic reconstruction and expansion, accompanied not by liberal (as the OECD reporter said), but by statist policies that were designed to manage labor markets, using foreigners as guestworkers. From the 1950s until the late 1960s, governments in Europe, particularly those of France, Germany, and Switzerland, actively recruited foreign workers to avert labor shortages. The second phase began with the mild recession of 1966–67 and the boom which followed when large numbers of Third World migrants replaced European migrants. Italy, Spain, Portugal, Yugoslavia, and Greece became less important as suppliers of labor, giving way to Turkey and the various countries of North Africa. During this period (1968–73) most of the labor-importing states of Western Europe began to rethink policies of recruitment—which in fact had amounted to open-door policies for many migrants—in favor of greater selection and control. The third phase of migration in postwar Europe began with the oil shock of 1973 and the deep recession which followed. It was at this point that labor-importing states throughout Western Europe attempted to suspend most types of migration, and encourage return migration. The fourth phase of migration began in the early 1980s, and was marked by increases in family and refugee migration.

By contrast, in the United States it is difficult to identify such distinct phases of migration in the postwar period, in part because of the lack of reliable data on flows of undocumented aliens. We only have indirect measures of illegal flows from the record of those actually caught trying to cross the border. One trend is clear, however. After the relatively quiet period of the 1950s and early 1960s, immigration (both legal and illegal) began to rise, slowly at first, but with increasing intensity in the 1970s. The trend began after 1965, when American policy was altered to favor family reunification, and it abated temporarily in the late 1970s and early 1980s. By the mid-1980s the trend was rising again, despite efforts to control illegal immigration (such as sanctions against employers who knowingly hire undocumented workers) spelled out in the 1986 Immigration Reform and Control Act.[37] Yet despite efforts to restrict immigration in Europe and the United States, outcomes, as measured in terms of migrant flows, continued.

In Europe, scholars have identified a "migratory chain" in which the initial economic, temporary, or guestworker migration becomes progressively more permanent, and hence more political.[38] Their argument is that once started, worker migration is self-perpetuating because family members inevitably follow individual workers. Indeed, the efforts by governments in Europe to stop worker immigration accelerated the rise in foreign populations: freezing the migrant flows led many temporary migrants to settle and seek family reunification.[39] By attempting to regulate worker migration, governments thus actually encouraged new forms of (family and seasonal) migration. Yet governments were under pressure to respond to popular anti-immigration (and anti-immigrant) sentiments to avoid the appearance of encouraging migration in periods of recession and unemployment during the late 1970s and early 1980s.

The history of settler immigration in the United States is different from the history of labor migration in postwar Europe, but this truism is not entirely true.[40] Focusing on the postwar period, we find that immigration in the United States is driven politically and economically by the tension between legal and illegal immigration. This is not to say that the migratory chain is unimportant in the American case. Since 1965 legal immigration has been dominated by family immigration, much to the chagrin of human capital theorists, who prefer that immigration be tied more closely to the needs of the American economy and the skills of potential immigrants.[41] Illegal migrations have helped to create a large black market for labor in the United States, which has no equivalent in Europe.[42] There is no fiction of temporary migrations (or guestworkers) in the United States; because the marginal/foreign work force—which is undocumented—does not officially exist.[43] A greater sense of the inevitability of illegal immigration persists in the United States, whereas in Europe the emphasis in immigration policies since the mid-1970s has been on stopping both legal and illegal immigration, and on the need to assimilate second-generation immigrants. A final difference between Europe and the United States is the tone of the debate over immigration in the 1980s. In Europe the debate has focused on citizenship, which in turn has led to politicization of immigration and the rise of anti-immigrant political parties on the right, particularly in France and Germany. In the United States the debate has been couched largely in terms of interest group politics and how to protect the rights of minorities, particularly Hispanics, while at the same time regulating immigration without damaging the interests of employers.[44]

Given these many differences in the postwar history of immigration in Europe and the United States, how can we compare the political economy of immigration in the two regions? And how can we explain the similarities in outcomes? The first basis for comparison is precisely in terms of *outcomes:* immigration in the postwar period has increased at historically high rates, despite efforts by liberal states to curtail entries and (in the case of Europe) reduce the size of the foreign population. While the foreign worker population has stabilized in the major labor-importing states of Europe since the recession of 1973–74, other forms of immigration have risen, especially family, seasonal, illegal, and refugee migration.[45] As a result, the foreign populations in Europe and the United States have remained at historically high levels (see chapters 3 and 4).

Statist policies for closing the doors in Europe were designed to protect labor markets and placate anti-immigrant sentiments among the public. But opening the window (to family members, seasonals, and refugees) represented a concession to liberal, political ideals of social justice, especially civil and human rights. German and French governments in the late 1970s tried to implement draconian statist policies to stop immigration by restricting family reunifications. These policies were struck down by courts on constitutional and legal grounds—an unusual occurrence in political systems that have strong statist traditions, where administrative discretion is wider than in political systems (such as the American) that are characterized by a rigid separation of powers and judicial review. Likewise, attempts in France and Germany to place tighter restrictions on refugee flows and political asylum have failed in the face of liberal pressures. In the German case, closing the refugee valve would have meant a change in the Constitution (Basic Law), which contains a liberal provision for refugees. Even though this constitutional provision was made with ethnic German refugees in mind, it is difficult in a liberal system, which guarantees equality before the law, to discriminate openly against non-German asylum seekers. Especially the Turks have sought protection in large numbers under the liberal Constitution of the Federal Republic.[46] In the late 1980s, with a new openness to emigration in Eastern Europe and the Soviet Union, ethnic Germans (the *Aussiedler*) began to arrive in great numbers to the chagrin of politicians, who were under pressure from rightwing groups to alleviate the tensions in housing, education, and urban labor markets that are partially caused by immigration.

France—which has a long republican tradition and places great stock in naturalization and strict assimilation of immigrants—has more liberal nationality laws than Germany. As in the United States, in France citizenship derives either from *jus soli* (place of birth) or *jus sanguinis* (line of descent); whereas citizenship in Germany is largely contingent upon *jus sanguinis*.[47] In liberal polities individuals can remain marginalized only for so long, before they invoke or acquire the rights and privileges of other members of society. Even in Germany and Switzerland, which have had the most rigid statist controls on immigration and naturalization, foreigners have achieved permanent resident status—the first step on a long road to integration. Legal and political mechanisms came into play in these liberal societies to lift the aliens out of their strictly economic existence, giving them rights. Laws enacted in France (1981), the United States (1986 and 1990), and Germany (1990) have broadened the rights of resident aliens, while trying to assert greater control over future migrations (see chapter 8).

In the United States, the contrast between the politics and economics of immigration is more stark than in Europe. The cause is the tension between legal and illegal immigration. The rhetoric of some politicians concerning immigration, particularly at the state and local level, has been statist and nationalist; and the history of immigration policy includes the illiberal Chinese Exclusion Act and the National Origins Quota System. Yet the United States has been compelled to live up to its liberal creed by the civil rights revolution, the growth of a hemispheric labor market, and by human rights activists who encourage immigration by individuals fleeing oppression from friendly regimes of the right and not-so-friendly regimes of the left. In the postwar period immigration policy has come to focus on issues of rights and equity, which is not surprising since American political development in the postwar era reflects a struggle for the extension of rights to minorities and the political-economic incorporation of marginal groups via affirmative action programs.[48]

Administrations in the United States have made fewer (and less ambitious) attempts to regulate immigration for the purpose of managing labor markets. As a result, markets have played a greater role in determining outcomes. Yet precisely because of the openness of labor markets in the United States, which has contributed to the often harsh conditions of immigrant life, the political struggles to guarantee the rights of immigrant workers have been more intense in the United States than in Europe. Numerous interest groups have formed in the United States (particularly in the postwar period) to protect the rights of immigrants and minorities in general. These groups operate through the Congress and the courts to influence immigration and refugee policies. In terms of the political process, the courts are a major avenue through which undocumented aliens and refugees seek protection.[49] With few exceptions, the goal of these individuals is to remain in the United States, not as second-class citizens who fulfill only an economic role, but as legal members of society. Once an alien has succeeded in achieving this adjustment of status, the road to naturalization and citizenship is a relatively smooth one.[50]

The history of postwar immigration in both Europe and the United States has been characterized by the development of an unregulated international market for labor, followed by statist and administrative attempts to reassert control over national labor markets. These statist reactions to international migration brought into play embedded liberalism, which led governments to alter policies to conform to the constitutional norms and principles by which these societies are governed. In the United States in the 1970s and 1980s the backlash against immigration has been less dramatic than in Europe, because of the strength of ethnic/cultural pluralism and the prominence of civil rights as a cornerstone of American politics. Political liberalism has been more deeply embedded in American society and economy since the civil rights movement of the 1950s and 1960s. In Europe the principal labor-importing states also have seen the rise of a new politics of civil rights in the 1980s, which has been closely associated with increases in immigration since the 1950s and 1960s. The political struggles over immigration have pitted liberal and republican groups of the left and right against nationalist, racist, and xenophobic elements of the extreme right, particularly in France.

It is hard to overlook the influence of liberal politics on immigration at the domestic level. Even though we do not find much evidence of liberal international regimes for migration, domestic liberalism has tended to spill over to the international level, providing some political protections for migrants, but without becoming fully institutionalized. Still the prospect for regulating international labor markets is greater in the European context, because of the Treaty of Rome (1957) and subsequent European Community policies, which guarantee freedom of movement for most of the citizens of member countries. By contrast, in North America, regulation of international migration has depended almost entirely on the one bilateral relationship between the United States and Mexico. Both states have been negotiating a free trade agreement in the 1990s, which could have a major impact on migration. The impending moves toward greater political and economic unity in 1992 also hold out the promise of greater *regionalization* of labor markets and a common immigration policy in the European Community. But there is no guarantee that these regional regimes will reflect embedded liberalism, which has remained strong at the domestic/national level.

Migration and the European Community: A Liberal Regime?

The European Community functions as an international regime for migration at a regional level. Sovereignty with respect to the population of member states has been ceded to the Community, since ratification of the Treaty of Rome. Within the Community, most of the citizens of member states have freedom of movement. Only Spain and Portugal have yet to be included as full members whose citizens can live and work anywhere in the EC. These two states are currently in a transition period, and all restrictions on their citizens will expire in January 1993. In effect, "citizens" of the Community benefit from the same basic rights with respect to employment.[51] Yet the consolidation of a European labor market has not led to the massive movement of workers from less to more developed countries. Instead, migration from lower-wage countries of the South, such as Italy and Greece, has decreased markedly with the advent of freedom of movement. The drop in intra-European immigration can be attributed to the stimulative effects of trade and economic integration, which have raised living standards and increased employment opportunities in the less developed countries of the South. In this instance, at least, liberal trade theory appears to have been vindicated. Trade has substituted for migration, thereby reducing pressures for emigration from less developed countries of the South to the more developed countries of the North.

Historically, the main feature of postwar immigration in Europe was a South-North movement within Europe itself. In the 1950s and much of the 1960s the principal sending countries were Italy, Spain, Greece, and Portugal; and the principal receiving countries were France, Germany, Belgium, the Netherlands, and Britain (which of course did not join the Community until 1973). This South-North movement within the Community quickly gave way in the late 1960s to a South-North movement within the larger Mediterranean context.[52] But the development of a European labor market with the participation of the populations of the twelve member states is not negligible. Within the Community, France has the largest "European" population (1,577,900), followed by Germany (1,364,700), Great Britain (754,000), and Belgium (583,900).[53] These internal migrations lend impetus to the need for greater coordination of social and fiscal policy. Greater mobility of labor has contributed to the need for the harmonization of a range of social policies. Yet international migration, particularly the elimination of border controls, also has proved to be an obstacle to European integration. It is not the internally mobile European population that is the problem, but a potentially mobile foreign population.

In 1988 there were 7,259,400 resident aliens in the Community, which represented 2.2 percent of the total European population. Of the 12 member states, Germany (4,630,200) and France (3,752,200) had by far the largest foreign populations, followed by Great Britain

(982,000), Belgium (853,200), and the Netherlands (591,800).[54] Even though considerable variation exists within Europe concerning immigration and naturalization policies, members of the EC are struggling to reach agreement on how to deal with international migration. The Schengen Agreement provides more evidence of movement toward internal liberalization, with externally protectionist overtones: it was approved by five European states (France, Germany, Belgium, Luxembourg, and the Netherlands) in June 1990. The agreement calls for the elimination of internal border controls, the harmonization of visa and asylum policies, and the coordinated policing of external borders, leading to the construction of a symbolic "ring fence" around the common territory. The Agreement is viewed as a prototype for an EC agreement under which all border controls would be eliminated after 1992. Human and civil rights groups in Europe have denounced the Schengen Agreement and plan to fight its implementation, because they consider it overly restrictionist and at odds with more liberal asylum and human rights policies of member state governments.

The issue of a regional regime for labor will have to be resolved to the satisfaction of the British, and others, before all internal border controls are relaxed. Britain's principal objections to the elimination of border controls, as spelled out in the Schengen Agreement, is the effect that such a move could have on illegal immigration within the member countries of the Community. The negative reaction of the British government to the Schengen proposals represents a nationalist response to what is seen as a damaging infringement of British sovereignty; whereas the opposition of European human rights groups to Schengen constitutes a liberal response to what could be a highly restrictionist and statist arrangement, damaging to civil and human rights.

The new impetus given to European integration by the Single European Act of 1985 has the potential for stimulating third country (non-EC) immigration. Some of the reasons for this projection—increased economic growth in the Community, stable and in some cases declining populations, coupled with a gradual increase in the demand for labor—have been spelled out in various studies.[55] But quite apart from the economic stimulus provided by the creation of a single market for goods, services, capital, and labor in 1992, the political consequences of creating a single territory with a community-wide jurisprudence will create new (political and legal, as well as economic) spaces for aliens. The question that must be asked, but cannot yet be answered, is whether the emergence and consolidation of a regional regime for labor in Europe will draw more workers from the economically underdeveloped but demographically expansive South (especially Africa) or from the traditional sending countries of Central and Eastern Europe, which are once again free to export labor to Western Europe. In the absence of a common immigration and refugee policy giving preference to certain nationalities, what we are likely to witness is a steady growth of more or less legal immigration from the former communist countries (especially Poland and the new republics of the former Soviet Union), and a continuing influx of largely clandestine migrants (false tourists, economic refugees, and the like) from Africa, entering the Community via the "soft underbelly" of Europe: Italy, Greece, Spain, and Portugal.

Certainly the building of a regime for migration in Europe (with both liberal and statist overtones) will proceed slowly, because of the politically explosive nature of immigration. At the moment, most states in Europe want desperately to control immigration, but without adopting the illiberal tactics proposed by rightwing groups. The 1980s have witnessed a surge in xenophobic, nationalist, and anti-immigrant parties and movements in France, Germany, and Italy. Hence any move by member states to cede autonomy to the Community on the issue of immigration will be done most carefully to avoid stimulating extremist political movements. Yet given the size of the foreign population in the Community, there is a potentially new category of "citizens" who could invoke their rights and seek protection at the European level, bypassing unresponsive national governments and institutions and appealing to the European Court of Justice and/or the Court of Human Rights at Strasbourg. As of 1991, no European jurisprudence has developed in this area. The first and foremost concern of many national politicians is that foreigners not be given freedom of movement within the Community. How this could be prevented, if these individuals are legally resident in member countries, is unclear.

Conclusion

Above I have developed a framework for understanding international migration in postwar Europe and the United States. I began by asking why no international regime exists for governing migration comparable to liberal regimes for trade, money, and finance. To answer that liberal states have not felt the need to cooperate in the area of migration because it has not been in their interest to do so is facile and tautological; moreover, the European Community seems to be well on its way to creating the first regional labor market within the world economy—a development which has many politically and economically liberal features.

With the growth of international exchange and increasing economic interdependence in the postwar period, migration has come to play an important role in the international political economy. In the absence of a fully developed international regime, the movement of individuals across national boundaries has been driven by a liberal dynamic with a strong economic dimension. The *economic* dimension is directly related to the supply of labor in the world economy, which is highly elastic, and the demand for labor in the industrial democracies, which has been high throughout most of the postwar period. In short, the globalization of markets has engendered higher levels of international migration. The *political* dimension is linked to the uncoordinated attempts by states to regulate migration. But to understand the political dimension, we must *compare* the politics and policies of immigration in the industrial democracies. We must examine the way in which states have attempted to use foreign workers to regulate national labor markets, and look at the liberal reaction against statist policies. Finally, we must study the issue of citizenship, to understand how foreign workers have been transformed in each country from expendable commodities (guestworkers) into objects of political conflict (potential citizens).

Immigration represents a critical dilemma for the governments of liberal states. The expansion of civil and social rights since 1945 (for citizens as well as noncitizens) has contributed to increases in migration. Governments, especially in Europe, have struggled to cope with immigration and the challenge to state autonomy and sovereignty that it represents. Nothing short of a major political-economic upheaval that would roll back the liberal gains of the past forty years or eliminate current international inequalities is likely to arrest the movement of individuals across national boundaries.

II • IMMIGRATION IN POSTWAR EUROPE

3 ◆ Guestworkers and the Politics of Growth

International migration can be said to be a good thing on the basis of revealed preference: employers hire foreign workers, and workers migrate to jobs abroad.

—CHARLES P. KINDLEBERGER, *Europe's Postwar Growth*

Every state must face the difficulty of regulating the entry of individuals into its national territory. Likewise, the state must establish the conditions of residence for aliens and the methods by which noncitizens can become citizens. Decisions to control a population within a given territory are *not* simply technical, economic, or demographic choices; they are profoundly *political* choices that often must be made in moments of crisis and in the midst of highly charged national debates. They can affect the lives of millions of people; and they can reveal in pristine form the innermost workings of the political system and the key philosophical assumptions upon which the system is based. Surely Charles Kindleberger is right to say that international migration is a *good* thing on the basis of revealed preference. But, as with any social or economic choice, such things are the result of the actions of many individuals, acting within the constraints of a political system.

The next two chapters trace the history of immigration policy in France and Germany, from the immediate postwar period through the 1970s,[1] a time when these states were actively involved in fostering a market for foreign labor. I will look closely at some of the successes and failures of the "guestworker" approach to regulating immigration and address the question of whether foreign labor can be used as a "shock absorber" in industrial capitalist societies. Both chapters deal

45

almost exclusively with France and Germany, with occasional references to Switzerland, because of the prominence of guestworker (or rotation) policies for foreign labor in Swiss strategies for economic development.

Immigration in Prewar Europe

Perhaps because of the large numbers of Europeans who have emigrated to the four corners of the earth, especially to the Americas, we have tended to overlook the important role that immigration has played in European history. Students of English history are aware of the role played by the Irish in building England into the "workshop of the world."[2] What is less apparent, however, is the role that foreigners have played in the economy and society of France and Germany. In addition to the fact that many Europeans emigrated to the New World, strong ethnocultural and nationalist traditions in Europe help to explain the lack of historical attention to immigration. Histories of Prussia and the German Reich have focused on the ethnocultural dimension of nation-building, but they seldom mention the influx of Poles into Eastern Germany and the crucial role that Polish migration played in the political-economic compromises that gave birth to the Second Reich. Until recently, the extraordinarily important role of Belgians, Swiss, Germans, Italians, and Poles in the making of the French working class has been overlooked by historians of France. As in the German case, political, economic, and social histories of France have tended to focus on themes of national identity and struggles between tradition and modernity.[3]

Before plunging into the study of the political economy of immigration in postwar France and Germany, it behooves us to look, however briefly, at the prewar history of immigration in these two states. Among the states of Western Europe, France stands out as a country which has benefited most from immigration, a process that dates roughly from the middle of the last century. Unlike other European states, France never became a major country of emigration. Transoceanic migrations of French nationals were limited both in scope and duration. Major exoduses are associated with the persecution and expulsion of Protestants in the seventeenth century and with the development of the French Empire.[4] Conversely, by 1876 there were more than 800,000 foreigners in France. Increases in levels of immigration, particularly during the Second Empire, clearly were related to the declining population and the beginning of industrialization. The rural exoduses that provided labor for English and German industrialization in the eighteenth and nineteenth centuries did not begin in earnest in France until the twentieth century, due in part to the strength of traditional society and the persistence of smallscale agriculture. Thus French capitalism was forced to *invent* a working class, in view of the unwillingness of rural workers to leave their farms, by importing labor from abroad.[5]

By contrast, Germany, which only emerged as a sovereign and unitary state in the latter half of the nineteenth century, was for much of modern history a country of emigration. Ethnic Germans helped to settle both the American and Eurasian frontiers in the eighteenth and nineteenth centuries. But foreign ethnic groups equally contributed to the building of Germany itself. The Poles are by far the most important group, providing labor initially for the large rural estates of Prussia and the mining industry of upper Silesia.[6] In spite of or perhaps because of the precarious situation of Poland in nineteenth-century Europe, the Polish Question and the availability of foreign labor were issues in the political maneuverings between industrialists of western Germany and the landed aristocrats (Junkers) of Prussia, which led to the so-called "marriage of iron and rye."[7] Junker support for industrialization, particularly the growth and protection of the steel industry and the naval buildup under Bismarck, was contingent upon liberal migration policies. In addition to providing labor for Prussian agriculture during the Bismarckian period, Poles were a crucial source of surplus labor for German industry during the First World War.

From the end of the nineteenth century until the Second World War, the number of foreigners in France and Germany steadily increased. Even though German authorities periodically deported large numbers of foreigners, especially Poles, in the last decades of the nineteenth century, by 1918 there were over 700,000 Poles living in Germany. While many of these immigrants worked the land in eastern Germany, increasing numbers were to be found in cities and in the industrial sector. Industrialists were given a relatively free hand to recruit foreigners to work in the factories of western Germany whenever the need arose.[8] Reliance on foreign labor increased dramatically during the First World War, which caused important labor shortages. The interwar period in Germany, however, was not a period of intense immigration, in consequence of the economic difficulties of the Weimar Republic. The use of foreign labor grew apace with the coming to power of Hitler and the Nazis. Following the outbreak of the Second World War, the Nazis quickly resorted to the use of forced foreign labor, which rose to a high of 6 million by 1944–45. To this number must be added another 2 million prisoners of war and countless inmates of concentration camps. Many of these foreign workers were assigned to military industries, which could not have operated very efficiently without this pool of surplus labor.[9]

In Third Republic France, unlike in interwar Germany, foreign workers were fairly quickly assimilated into French society. This was due in part to liberal naturalization and citizenship laws in France, and also to the Jacobin notion of citizenship, which had served since the Revolution as a political and ideological counterweight to the regional and ethnic diversity of France. Jacobinism has been a powerful ideal for the assimilation and socialization of ethnic minorities within, and foreigners from without.[10]

In addition to imposing a republican order on an essentially traditional, nonindustrial society, one of the most important problems of political development during the Third Republic was how to incorporate ethnically distinct groups. The most significant event in this regard was the Dreyfus Affair, which ended in a reaffirmation of Jacobin ideals of citizenship and equality before the law, regardless of ethnic identity.[11] At the time of the Dreyfus Affair, which helped to consolidate the republican model of integration, immigration began to play a more important role in the social and economic life of France. Just as they were to do after the Second World War, immigrants helped to meet the demand for labor created by relatively late but rapid industrialization, and the weakness (or in some areas the absence) of a French working class. In sectors such as coal and steel, immigrants from Belgium, Italy, and Poland formed the backbone of the labor force.[12] During the first decades of the Third Republic the state was not centrally involved in controlling immigration, as firms, starved for labor, took the lead in recruiting workers from neighboring countries where there was an excess labor supply, especially Italy. These new immigrant workers were rather quickly assimilated, with schools, trade unions, and the new Communist party taking the lead in the socialization process.

Political opposition to immigration was not long in coming. In the heated political climate of the 1920s, foreigners were viewed with suspicion. Reactions from the right were especially severe, and immigrants were denounced as a source of labor unrest and communist agitation. The state took the first tentative steps in the 1920s to regulate immigration, largely in response to political pressures.[13] The onset of the Great Depression in the 1930s and stagnation of the economy resolved the immigrant problem, at least temporarily. Despite the Depression, the foreign population in France reached a high of 6.6 percent in 1931, before falling back to 4.1 percent during the turbulent decades of the 1930s and 1940s. Italians and Belgians together with Spaniards, Poles, and Germans were the largest groups entering between 1921 and 1931.

During the First World War, the French state tried to assert control over immigration by requiring all foreigners over the age of fifteen to obtain a residency permit *(carte de séjour)*. At the same time, however, French employers took an increasingly active role in recruiting immigrant workers. In 1924 the Société Générale d'Immigration (SGI), a private organization, was established for the purpose of helping firms locate sources of foreign labor. Not until the late 1920s and 1930s did the state take stronger steps to control immigration. Regulatory measures initially were a response to political pressure, but they found their ultimate justification in the deteriorating economic conditions of the Depression years.[14]

Like France and Germany, Switzerland also has a long tradition of using foreign workers to industrialize and solve problems of labor shortage during periods of rapid economic growth. As early as 1900 the Federal Council expressed concern over the rapidly increasing foreign population, which numbered 550,000 in 1910, or 10 percent of the total population.[15] In the last decades of the nineteenth century Switzerland was rapidly transformed from a country of emigration to a country of immigration. Already during the First World War Swiss authorities adopted restrictive migration policies, which were continually refined until a comprehensive federal immigration policy was enacted in 1931. The 1931 statutes have remained virtually unchanged, with the exception of a few liberalizing amendments in 1948. Levels of immigration and the size of the foreign population declined during the interwar period, reaching a low of approximately 4 percent in 1941 before accelerating in the postwar period.[16] The vast majority of immigrants to Switzerland during the late nineteenth and early twentieth centuries came from Italy, with foreign workers concentrated heavily in the industrial and construction sectors.[17]

Even though historians have not focused attention on the role of immigration in the social and economic development of Western Europe, foreigners have contributed prominently to industrialization and the formation of working classes in France, Germany, and Switzerland. In the post-World War II period immigration resurfaced as a central feature of state-led strategies for economic growth. As we move into a discussion of the political economy of immigration in postwar Europe, it is important to keep in mind how the foreign workers were treated in each of these states during the first half of the twentieth century. Despite outbursts of xenophobia during the 1920s and 1930s, French policies toward immigration and foreign workers were relatively liberal, and the recruitment of foreign workers was largely in the hands of private business. In Germany the use of foreign labor was linked to the harsh treatment of Polish workers during the Second Reich, and the brutal, racist, and exploitative policies of the Nazi regime. The premise of immigration policies in Germany during the first half of the century was that foreigners were an expendable and exploitable commodity to be used at the discretion of the state, and expelled when no longer needed. Every effort was made to prevent foreigners from settling and obtaining German citizenship. Yet despite these harsh policies and very restrictive naturalization and citizenship laws, a substantial number of Poles managed to immigrate.[18] The history of immigration in Switzerland seems to follow a political-economic cycle whereby foreign workers are let in during periods of rapid economic growth, immigration increases, and the foreign population rises. These periods of immigration are then followed by xenophobic politics, as the native Swiss population becomes fearful of being submerged by foreigners, hence the expression *Überfremdung*. The cycle is particularly volatile in Switzerland because of the smallness of the country and its population.[19]

Migration and State-Led Strategies for Growth

The history of immigration in postwar Europe must begin with a discussion of economic reconstruction and attempts by states to use foreign workers to regulate labor supply, to avoid the pitfalls of rapid economic growth (especially inflation), and to adjust to an increasingly interdependent European and world economy. Immigration made it possible for Switzerland to sustain high rates of growth in the absence of an adequate supply of Swiss labor. German and French strategies for reconstruction, industrialization, and economic modernization in the 1950s and 1960s also required new supplies of labor in order to avoid the inflationary consequences of relative full employment. Without foreign workers and immigrants, these states would have been forced to alter their strategies for economic growth.

Statist approaches to managing foreign worker populations are indicative of broader patterns of political and economic development. The Germans employed a mix of legalistic and corporatist policies with a strong bureaucratic orientation in the *Gastarbeiter* program, which was administered in the late 1950s and 1960s in a statist fashion. The French economic planners made a concerted effort during the Fourth Republic to provide sufficient inputs of labor for a rapidly modernizing industrial sector, while an old pronatalist lobby pushed for immigration as a way of stemming a century-and-a-half long decline in the French population. The Swiss had a long history, dating from the turn of the century, of coordinated control of foreign worker and immigration policy. Federal, cantonal, and local officials worked closely to monitor the foreign population, making sure that migrants did not violate the terms of their contracts. Somewhat surprisingly, the confederal Swiss state has been more effective in its attempts to use foreigners for the purpose of regulating labor markets than the unitary and bureaucratic French state.

Migration and Reconstruction

At the conclusion of the Second World War, both France and Germany faced the enormous task of economic reconstruction. Germany's efforts to rebuild its economy were complicated by the political uncertainties surrounding the occupation and eventual partition of the country. The Germans could not begin to focus on strategies for rebuilding their war-torn economy until an international political settlement was reached. The creation of the Federal Republic of Germany in the western zones of occupation in 1949 was the first step in a process of political and economic rehabilitation that would continue for the next decade under the leadership of Konrad Adenauer and the Christian Democratic party (CDU). Immigration did not figure prominently in German strategies for reconstruction, which were driven largely by the free-market policies of the liberal Minister of Economics, Ludwig Ehrhard. During the 1950s the young Republic faced no real problems of labor shortages, despite the takeoff of the economy and high levels of employment. Ethnic German refugees from the Soviet occupied countries of Central and Eastern Europe provided an immediate injection of labor. Over seven million refugees and expellees arrived in the Federal Republic in the immediate post-war period. At the same time, during the eleven years from the founding of the Federal Republic to the construction of the Berlin Wall in 1961, two and a half million refugees fled from East to West Germany. In total, some twelve million persons arrived in the Federal Republic during the decade of the 1950s, which proved to be an adequate supply of labor for economic expansion. Thus authorities in the new German state were able to focus their attention on rebuilding the industrial infrastructure, establishing a consumer economy, and controlling inflation. Labor market policy was confined to establishing corporatist-style cooperation (and codetermination) between the Federation of German Trade Unions (Deutscher Gewerkschaftsbund, or DGB), business (Bundesvereinigung Deutscher Arbeitgeberverbände, or BDA), and the state.[20]

The political-economic agenda in postwar France was very different, and immigration figured prominently in the policies of the first postwar governments. The provisional tripartite government headed by General de Gaulle, as well as the first governments of the Fourth Republic, targeted immigration as a priority issue. Given the traditional weakness of the French population[21] and ambitious policies of economic modernization set forth by the state, immigration came to be seen almost immediately as a necessary ingredient for economic growth. The problem which confronted economic policymakers was to construct a political consensus for recruiting immigrant workers. Not surprisingly, major interest groups—trade unions in particular—looked to the experiences of the interwar period for policy guidance. During the 1920s and 1930s, immigration and the recruitment of foreign workers were largely the private concern of big business.

With Liberation and the end of the Second World War, the dominant French trade unions, including the Confédération Générale du Travail (CGT) and the Confédération Française des Travailleurs Chrétiens (CFTC), argued forcefully for the creation of a neutral state agency for controlling immigration. They had made the same demands unsuccessfully in the 1920s, when the SGI had a virtual monopoly over the recruitment of foreign workers. The hope was that French workers' interests would be served better by public rather than private control of immigration. The unions wanted to limit the number of foreign workers employed in industry and, wherever possible, to avoid competition between French and foreign workers. The state was under pressure to regulate immigration in such a way as to avoid damaging the interests of labor or capital. Yet it was another group whose counsel the authorities would follow from the beginning of the postwar period—the *populationnistes,* a group of academics and politicians associated with the old pronatalist Alliance Nationale pour l'Accroissement de la Population Française, which had been very active during the Third Republic in publicizing the dangers of a declining population and promoting measures to increase birth rates.[22] In the wake of economic devastation caused by the war, two prominent members of the pronatalist group, Robert Debré, a physician and father of a future prime minister, and Alfred Sauvy, an economist and demographer, argued forcefully that one of the central problems facing liberated France was to find workers to supplement a depleted population and to rebuild the country. Immigration, they argued, was the answer to France's perennial demographic problem of low birth rates and a declining population.[23] French pronatalism, linked closely with Vichy and Pétainisme during the war, found a sympathetic echo among the nationalist leaders of the immediate postwar period, particularly the Gaullists. Germany, in contrast, had not suffered such population decline, and its politicians and policymakers were uninterested in natalist policies that might be linked to the immediate nationalist and fascist past.

The first order of business for French politicians was to pick up the pieces of republicanism and reestablish the legitimacy of the state, in the wake of defeat, occupation, and liberation.[24] Although the disruptions of politics and society caused by the war provoked a crisis of legitimacy, they also created the conditions for modernization of the economy, which had for so long lagged behind other industrial economies of Europe.[25] This was the era of industrial planning on a national scale. With the creation of a National Planning Commission (CGP) and the adoption of the first five-year plan (the Monnet Plan), the state took an active role in shaping the economic future of the country. Little was to be left to the uncertainties of the marketplace. The drive to rationalize capital and labor markets was as much the result of fear of political disruptions that might be caused by the collapse of small business and farming sectors as of fear that industrial development could not succeed without the intervention of the state.[26]

The selective allocation of capital to cooperative firms was not the only weapon in the French planners' arsenal. The planners recognized that achieving economies of scale in industrial production also would require new sources of labor. Fearing that new industries could not attract enough labor from the agricultural sector to sustain high rates of growth,[27] state officials took steps early in the postwar period to recruit foreign workers and place them in those sectors where they would be most needed. To this end the new Office National d'Immigration (ONI) was created to regulate the influx of immigrant workers. Foreign labor, it was hoped, would prevent severe occupational and geographical dislocation of workers, particularly in traditional sectors such as farming. At the same time, the additional labor would help to prevent labor shortages that might lead to increased wages and lower investments. In many respects the French economy was repeating the pattern of development of earlier periods of industrialization, with one major difference—the state was leading the effort to recruit foreign labor and modernize the economy, rather than following the lead of the private business sector.

Imbued with an *étatiste* and Cartesian tradition, as well as a new sense of mission to rebuild the war-torn French economy, administrative elites (and the planners in particular) hoped to use immigrants and foreign workers for clearly defined national purposes, most often delineated in the economic plans. Throughout the Fourth Republic, immigrant workers were defined as "factors of production" and tools for managing population and labor supply. By creating the ONI, the provisional government under de Gaulle hoped to establish a state monopoly over the recruitment and placement of foreign workers. The ONI was put under the control *(tutelle)* of the Ministry of Labor; and the agency was given a neocorporatist character. A twenty-four member administrative council was established to oversee the activities of the ONI. The council included representatives from major trade unions and employer groups, as well as from various ministries concerned with immigration matters—namely Labor and Population, which competed for control of the ONI. This arrangement was in keeping with the corporatist ambitions of the provisional government—ambitions which can be attributed to the desire to achieve consensus as quickly as possible and get on with the task of rebuilding the economy.[28] Here we can see a direct analogy with the German experience, where the Labor Ministry in the late 1950s brought together major economic groups concerned with foreign worker policy, and the Bundesanstalt für Arbeit (BA) like the French ONI, was set up to be a socially representative board of directors. In Germany as in France, however, human rights and church groups were not a part of these policymaking bodies.

Two groups dominated immigration policymaking at this early stage in France. First were the *populationnistes* who controlled the Ministry of Population. Led by Sauvy and Debré, the *populationnistes* were prime movers in setting an intellectual agenda for immigration. Trade unions were the other group that was initially successful in influencing immigration policy. The CGT went so far as to push for restrictions on immigration that would screen (Italian) workers according to their partisan affiliations in the home country. To this end, there was cooperation between the CGT and its Italian counterpart. Such screening was opposed by the other major trade union, the CFTC, which saw screening as a blatant attempt by the Communist party to use immigration for partisan purposes.[29]

Undoubtedly, the loser in struggles over immigration policy during the period of the tripartite government was the employer. Employers lost the considerable influence they had enjoyed during the interwar period.[30] As in other policy areas, the administrative state enjoyed great leeway in setting policy goals. Thus from the beginning of the postwar period, immigration policy was controlled by policymakers with specific objectives, while employers were denied unrestricted access to cheap foreign labor. This was also the case in Germany. Once the German authorities committed themselves to a policy of recruiting foreign labor, the bureaucracy was given great leeway in implementing policy and managing migrant flows.[31] In France, at the urging of the *populationnistes*, the decision was made to push for a *permanent* immigration of Catholics, primarily Italians, who would be culturally and ethnically compatible with the French population. This decision clearly distinguishes migration policy in France during the 1950s from the German *Gastarbeiter* policies of the 1960s. From the beginning, German authorities were insistent on maintaining a policy of rotation, whereby foreign workers would be brought into the labor market on a contractual basis for a limited period of time.[32] A major problem with the French strategy of recruiting ethnically and culturally compatible populations from southern Europe was that the French state (and employers) had to compete with the Swiss, and eventually with the Germans, for excess Italian labor.

The selective nature of immigration policy in France and the opposition of trade unions to opening the labor market to foreign workers helped to keep immigration down in the early years of the Fourth Republic. In Germany too worker immigration continued to be low by comparison with the influx of refugees from the East.[33] One factor that contributed to low levels of immigration in France in the early 1950s was the still uncertain economic climate. Employers were reluctant to expand their work force, and there is evidence that they viewed domestic labor supplies as adequate for anticipated increases in aggregate demand.[34] In the area of employment, as in the area of investment, the state was doing everything possible to convince employers of the virtues of expanding production. The Monnet Plan estimated that the economy would require approximately 430,000 new immigrants in 1946–47 alone.[35] At the time, many experts saw these figures as wildly exaggerated. Yet the French planners were convinced that if their ambitious goals of modernization were to be realized, a large influx of immigrant labor would be necessary. The problem was to convince employers to think big, in terms of investment *and* in terms of employment.[36] The rate of entry of immigrant workers did not begin to increase substantially until 1956 (see chapter 4). But thanks to the efforts of the state, immigration was soon to play a crucial role in the economic boom of the 1960s.

Despite longterm economic planning, the French economy was plagued with stop-and-go fluctuations in demand that led to inflationary pressures. The first sustained period of growth in the postwar period did not begin until 1953. The expansion of industrial production that followed and the increased confidence of employers in the new *dirigisme* were reflected in the labor market. Demand for labor soared during the period from 1953 to 1957, and, as the planners had predicted, immigrant labor became one of the most important productive factors in a rapidly expanding economy. The domestic supply of labor was quickly exhausted, and the policies of recruitment put in place by the tripartite planners must have seemed prophetic to many employers. The principal users of foreign labor in the early years of the Fourth Republic were mining, manufacturing (principally steel but also chemical and glass industries), and construction.[37]

It would be wrong, however, to attribute too much foresight to the planners. Marshall Plan aid and wars in Korea and Indochina played an important part in economic growth and industrial development in all of Europe. In addition, the departure of the Communist party from government helped to clear the way for closer cooperation between the French state and employers. By 1953 the confidence of businessmen in the planning process was increasing, as employers chose to accept the commitment of the Monnet planners to a relatively free market and ignore the socialist implications of *dirigisme*. In the area of immigration policy, employers' influence increased with the departure of the Communist Minister of Labor, Ambroise Croizat, in 1947. Firms began to recruit foreign workers directly in the sending countries, thus bypassing the ONI and normal institutional channels for hiring foreigners.[38]

Immigration soared in the final years of the Fourth Republic, surpassing 120,000 in 1956, a floor that would not be broken again until 1987. The *taux de régularisation* (legalization rate), which is a measure of immigration not controlled by ONI, jumped in 1956–57 from 20 to 50 percent, as the state progressively lost control of immigration. The geographical and occupational mobility of French workers also increased during this period.[39] These changes in the labor market were indicative of rapid industrial expansion that began in the mid-1950s. Although worker immigration controlled by the ONI remained relatively low, if we count Algerian immigration, which was not controlled by ONI, net immigration more than doubled during the 1950s.[40] Until the granting of independence in 1962 Algeria was considered to be part of Metropolitan France, and Algerian workers and their families were allowed to move freely into and out of France.[41]

Despite increases in immigration and the central role of the state in helping to recruit foreign workers, there was no political reaction in France to the growing foreign presence, as in the 1920s and later the 1980s, even though public opinion surveys showed the public to be skeptical of the benefits of immigrant labor and to express a general sense of opposition to immigration.[42] Georges Tapinos attributes these negative attitudes to three factors: a Malthusian fear of unemployment that might result from immigration; a xenophobic reaction *(la France aux français)*; and a general ignorance of the economic benefits of immigration.[43] Another important historical factor that explains negative public attitudes was the heightened tension caused by the colonial wars in Vietnam and Algeria and the beginning of the end of the French Empire. The public's preoccupation with the violent process of decolonization helps to explain why there were so few recorded outbursts of racial violence or demonstrations against immigration during this period. (In Germany, in contrast to France and Britain, immigration and the use of foreign workers in the 1960s were not linked to a colonial past.[44]) The full impact of decolonization on the politics of immigration in France, however, would not be felt until the end of the Algerian conflict and the granting of independence to the various colonies of North and West Africa.

The important point to retain from this look at immigration, labor market policy, and reconstruction in France in the 1950s is that the administrative elite, acting first under the authority of the provisional tripartite government and subsequently under various governments of the Fourth Republic, took the lead in formulating and implementing a *recruitment* policy—a statist approach to managing immigration that would be repeated in Germany in the 1960s. The policies of the Fourth Republic set the parameters for the use (and abuse) of foreign labor during the 1960s and 70s. French employers became dependent on immigrant labor, eventually taking almost complete control of the recruitment process in the 1960s; whereas trade unions (and the French Communist party) came to oppose immigration because of the competition that foreign workers represented, and because of the problems of caring for and housing immigrants in crowded working-class urban areas. Despite the impending political crisis of 1968 and the economic crises of the 1970s, which focused attention on immigrants as scapegoats for the problems of industrial change, the pronatalists succeeded in bolstering the French population and helping the economy overcome a potentially severe labor shortage. In the 1960s, however, the supply of highly assimilable Southern European Catholics began to exhaust itself (with the notable exception of Portugal), and non-European, largely Muslim immigrants began to take their place.

Migration and the Social Market Economy in Germany

Beginning in the late 1950s, Germany entered the European market for foreign labor with a vengeance. Almost immediately the foreign population began to rise and by the early 1960s German authorities had committed themselves to a policy of recruiting foreign workers. The Germans were following the lead of the Swiss and the French, who had turned to the use of foreign labor over a decade earlier. The impulse to recruit foreign workers came not so much from a fear of population decline or labor shortages, as was the case in France during the Fourth Republic, but from a concern that the German economy would be unable to sustain its high rate of growth at full employment without inflation. Also there was a clear hope among German policymakers that recruiting foreign labor would allow Germany to maintain export-led growth without the necessity of moving production abroad as a way of keeping wage costs down. The use of foreign labor allowed German industry to keep its production facilities at home and avoid globalization of production, which was occurring at an increasingly rapid pace in some other industrial economies, most notably in the United States.[45]

The first sector of the German economy to press the state for access to greater supplies of foreign labor, in mid to late 1950s, was the agricultural sector. The lobbying activities by German farmers, who, like their French counterparts, were looking primarily for seasonal labor, set the stage for industry's demands for greater access to foreign labor. The abundant supplies of easily assimilable, skilled ethnic German workers from the East was beginning to dry up. With the construction of the Berlin Wall in 1961 and the sealing of the Iron Curtain, the flow stopped altogether. Ironically, employers' associations in Germany, as in France during the first years of the Fourth Republic, were skeptical of the need for foreign labor.[46] Nevertheless, business groups and government were aware of the possible inflationary consequences that might result from severe labor shortages. In such good economic times, it was not difficult to convince the major interest groups to support a new, intensive policy of recruitment of foreign workers. Not surprisingly, the one group that showed some reluctance were the trade unions.[47]

Unlike their French counterparts in the 1950s (principally the CGT), the DGB did not object stringently to the policies of recruiting foreign workers.[48] The first and most obvious reason for the union's willingness to acquiesce in these policies was that times were good. The economy was growing, employment was expanding, and wages were rising. The second reason—more revealing of differences between the French and German political economies—is that the DGB was closely involved in the formulation and implementation of the new policies. The involvement of the unions in migrant worker policy was yet another indication of the highly consensual approach in postwar Germany to the formulation and implementation of economic policy. Such cooperative strategies in the politics of growth coalesced into what came to be known as the Social Market Economy, whereby the enlightened self-interest of the citizenry would guide the German economy and society away from cutthroat capitalism on the one hand and statist planning or socialism on the other. Foreign workers were in some respects left out of this new consensus, however. They were more directly subject to the power of the federal state than citizens, and they were not covered by all the protections and guarantees provided to German workers through social market arrangements.[49]

In terms of the policymaking process, neocorporatist practices such as codetermination allowed the DGB to lobby successfully for incorporation of provisions into recruitment policies that would protect the interests of German workers. The most important provisions in this regard were that foreigners be paid wages equivalent to their German counterparts, and that preference in hiring always be given to German workers. As a result of this willingness of business and the state to take into account the interest of trade unions, they were able to agree on policies of recruitment. It is important to note, however, that during this period of the late 1950s and early 1960s the government was (and had been since the creation of the Federal Republic) in the hands of the right. The Christian Liberal coalition under Adenauer was favorable to the interests of business. The opposition Social Democrats (SPD), while expressing skepticism and some criticism of the policies, agreed to go along for the sake of avoiding a slowdown in the economy or inflation.[50]

In the first years of the program, by far the most important institution for managing the foreign worker program was the Bundesantalt für Arbeit (BA). Like its French counterpart the ONI, the BA was given administrative powers to recruit and place foreign workers with German firms. Also like the French, the German state set up recruitment offices in the major sending countries, which at this point were Italy, Greece, Turkey, and Yugoslavia. The BA was to act as a conduit for establishing contact between interested and qualified workers and German firms. It was given the responsibility for issuing labor and residence permits, which from the beginning of the *Gastarbeiter* program were firmly linked, in contrast with French policy, which made no legal connection between employment and rights of residence. Work permits were viewed as contracts not only between the worker and the employer, but also between the worker and the state. Permits were issued only for well-defined jobs with specific time limits. The granting of residence permits also was contingent upon having a valid work permit, while family reunification was discouraged. The BA acted as guarantor of the contract established with force of the law between the employer and the foreign worker.[51]

This institutional arrangement gave the federal German authorities administrative autonomy for managing the foreign worker population in the 1960s. By the end of the decade, over 70 percent of all recruiting went directly through the BA. (In France the trend was in exactly the opposite direction). The administrative capacity and bureaucratic authority of the German state in the area of foreign worker policy was more in keeping with the political and regulatory traditions of previous German regimes, especially the Third Reich, than with the decentralized, federal pattern of policymaking of the Bonn Republic and its social market economy. In fact other policy areas, such as industrial relations and social welfare, displayed a more society-centered and cooperative pattern, with less state autonomy. Only in this policy area did the federal government rely so heavily on administrative discretion.[52]

Immigration and Gaullist Modernization

The rise to power of the Gaullists in 1958, with their nationalist and Jacobin designs for the economy and a commitment to turn France into a military-industrial power, reinforced the interventionist role of the French state. Several events, however, made the necessity of intervening in the labor market less pressing. The settlement of the Algerian conflict and the decolonization of North Africa brought an influx not only of white colonists—*pieds noirs*—but of nonwhite Frenchmen (such as the *harkis*) and Africans (from the franc zone) seeking employment in a rapidly expanding economy. The period of decolonization from 1958 to 1962 was the beginning of a massive and largely uncontrolled immigration. Average annual immigration jumped from 66,400 in the period from 1946 to 1955 to 248,800 in the period 1956 to 1967. At the same time, the legalization rate went from roughly 50 to 80 percent. In effect, migration flows were exploding, while administrative control over foreign labor was decreasing. This development was in stark contrast to the German experience, where the bureaucracy increased its control of worker migration in the 1960s.

Despite the political crises surrounding the Algerian conflict, economic stabilization already had begun by the end of the Fourth Republic. Policymakers had succeeded in creating a favorable climate for growth. Monetary stability was restored in 1958, and the confidence of investors was on the rise.[53] If the political situation inherited by the Gaullists was chaotic, the economy was nonetheless in fairly good shape. The Gaullists brought a distinctive pro-big-business philosophy to government. This did not mean that there was less economic planning, but rather a much greater degree of cooperation between business and government in the making of economic policy.[54]

In the area of migrant worker and labor market policy, employers had great freedom to recruit, hire, and fire foreign as well as French workers. Conversely, the political power of labor declined, and hence fewer left political parties as well as trade unions were represented in the Fifth Republic. At the ONI the input of trade unions was restricted, while employers were given a freer hand to recruit workers directly abroad.[55] The new system of administering worker migration was in fact similar to the system that existed during the interwar period, when employers through the SGI were allowed to recruit abroad. The major difference is that the ONI retained a measure of administrative control over legalization (or *régularisation*).

The decline in the unions' position was accentuated by the rapid rise in uncontrolled immigration. Employers succeeded in boosting the overall supply of workers, while putting pressure on real wages.[56] The political risks of this strategy for increasing output and productivity were not apparent until 1968, when the May events together with a general strike led the government to intervene in the market on behalf of workers.

During the first decade of the Fifth Republic (1958–1968), the power of the administrative state was consolidated in the hands of the executive, making the government more powerful in a formal-legal sense, but also more vulnerable and more partisan.[57] Despite these institutional reforms, the major instruments for intervening in the economy were still operative. Planning remained a central feature of economic policymaking. The Third Plan (1958–1961) called for continued recruitment of foreign labor and estimated the levels of foreign manpower needs to be on the order of 175,000 for the period covered by the plan. If we count Algerian immigration during this period, immigration met and surpassed levels forecast by the plan.[58] Nonetheless, immigration was not high on the agenda of the first Gaullist governments. The Interministerial (Standing) Committee on Immigration did not meet from the end of the Fourth Republic until 1965. Only the left—the CGT and the PCF—sought to focus attention on the issue of immigration. Yet there were noticeable signs of splits within the leadership of the left, which was trying to walk an ideological tightrope by arguing for international proletarian solidarity in the face of growing opposition to immigration among the national rank and file.[59]

The rise in immigration in France during the 1960s can be attributed to the process of decolonization and to the rapid growth of the economy, which kept the demand for labor high. But what had begun as an effort by the state to secure an adequate supply of labor and boost the population in the 1950s rapidly became an open process whereby employers had virtually unlimited access to new supplies of foreign labor. Although the recruitment responsibilities of the ONI were extended through a variety of treaties concluded in 1963 with Morocco, Tunisia, and Portugal, and Yugoslavia and Turkey in 1965, employers continued to usurp powers of recruitment. Private recruitment was easier in sending countries that still had a neocolonial relationship with France, particularly Algeria and various countries of the franc zone of West Africa (Senegal, Ivory Coast, Togo). Algerians were required only to pass a medical examination after 1963, whereas the West Africans were not subject to control. Residency and work permits, which were required for all other nationalities, were not required for the Algerians and the West Africans.[60]

In 1965 the Interministerial Committee on Immigration was convened to study the problem of the private recruitment of foreign workers and recommend ways of dealing with what came to be called "immigration from within." The Committee decided that the government should take a more active role in setting levels of immigration and that the ONI should be reorganized and given a new mandate. However, the belief was still widespread, as late as 1966, that industry was in danger of running out of labor. J. M. Jeanneney, then Minister of Social Affairs, was quoted as saying that "clandestine immigration itself is not useless, because if we stick to a strict application of international regulations and agreements, we will perhaps be short of labor."[61] Partly as a result of this preoccupation with the possibility of labor shortages, the Fifth Plan estimated that the economy would require 325,000 foreign workers for the period 1966–1970.[62] Since the plan also predicted considerable unemployment for the same period, trade unions saw immigration policy as a blatant attempt on the part of the state and employers to suppress wages by maintaining an "industrial reserve army." Both the CFDT (Confédération Française Démocratique du Travail) and the CGT denounced employment of foreigners as a mechanism for exploiting the working class.[63]

As a means of legitimizing new immigration, the administrative reorganization of the ONI again brought trade unions into the decisionmaking process. However, this did not silence the criticism of the policymaking process by the leaders of the trade union movement. Their attacks followed the argument that foreign workers were a more attractive source of labor because, unlike French workers, they were not covered by expensive and cumbersome social welfare protections. Thus it was much easier to exploit foreign workers, to pay them lower wages, to avoid social security and other payments, and to use foreign workers to divide and weaken the working class itself.[64] The trade unions argued that by abandoning Italian labor, which was now covered by the Rome Treaties, in favor of a vulnerable and more tractable supply of African workers, employers were able to circumvent regulations designed to protect all workers.

Among the effects of the growing hostility of workers toward immigration was an upsurge in feelings of racism and xenophobia among the general public.[65] By the end of the Gaullist decade, public opinion held that immigration was contributing to a rapid deterioration in urban living standards and conditions. Many immigrant workers were living in urban enclaves in the worst housing, and this confused the public as to cause and effect. Immigrants came to be viewed as different and inferior because of poor housing conditions and lack of education, and even though the national leadership of trade unions and leftwing political parties sought to promote harmony between French and foreign workers, race and ethnic relations in the 1960s began to worsen and spill over into the political arena.[66] The state was not oblivious to the situation. One indication of the awareness of social problems associated with largescale immigration was the creation in 1966 of a Ministry of Social Affairs, which included a Department of Population and Migration (Direction de la Population et des Migrations, or DPM). The DPM was given the responsibility of taking care of immigrants at each stage of the migratory process, from recruitment and placement to naturalization and assimilation. The creation of the DPM marked the beginning of a new effort by the government to regain control of the migratory process.[67]

The minor recession of 1966–67 brought a slowdown in hiring in France and Germany, but after a brief respite the rate of immigration in both countries continued to climb. Following this minor blip in economic activity in the two countries, the levels of foreign employment and the foreign populations soared (see chapter 4). In France the upheaval of 1968 changed the nature of the labor market and altered the relationship between state and economy. The events of May 1968 increased labor market regulation via the Grenelle Agreements, and at the same time brought to power a more pro-business faction of the Gaullist party. The Pompidou government put a new emphasis on the role of the market in determining patterns of growth. The plan as an instrument of intervention in the economy was weakened, and the recommendations of the CGP became pro forma. The net effect of the events of 1968 was, paradoxically, to increase the power of both labor and capital and reduce the interventionist capacity of the state.

In 1968 the state paid the price for conducting a policy of unrestrained economic growth that had damaged the interests of traditional classes, while postponing a more equitable distribution of wealth in favor of workers and consumers. The events of May 1968 marked the end of statist Gaullism, in the sense of using the power of the administrative state to solve the political conflicts associated with economic modernization. The compromises that had been worked out in the decade since 1958 favored business. Unrestrained access to foreign labor was but one example of the pro-business philosophy of the period, which was justified in terms of national grandeur. The student strike was an opportunity for workers to regain a measure of influence in the political process, even though the parties of the left remained incapable of winning elections. As most observers of the events of 1968 have pointed out, however, the workers had few revolutionary designs and little sympathy with the radical leaders of the student movement.[68] The trade unions wanted a share of the profits from the economy they had helped to build. The upheaval ended with the Grenelle Agreements, negotiated by Prime Minister Pompidou, who convinced employers to accede to some of the demands of the trade unions. The issue of immigration was not part of these negotiations. In some respects, immigration would become the Achilles heel of the workers' movement, because employers were able for a time to use foreign labor to circumvent some aspects of new labor market regulations imposed by the Grenelle Agreements.[69]

The economy rebounded quickly from the political uncertainty of 1968. The demand for labor soared in 1969–70, as the new Pompidou government placed a greater emphasis on full employment and manpower policy in general.[70] All indications are that the neo-Gaullist *pompidoliens* were determined not to repeat the mistakes of their predecessors in the area of immigration policy. Economic policy relied more on market forces to solve the problems of resource allocation, while the state set about to minimize the sociopolitical costs of renewed growth. Centralized planning was no longer an objective of government but rather a tool for the private sector. Earlier Gaullist governments had struck an agreement with business, but there was little doubt that the state was the senior partner in the alliance. Under Pompidou the situation was reversed, with government doing everything politically possible to foster the growth of a free market. The result was that traditional interests were undercut, and industry became more concentrated than ever.[71]

The free market orientation of the Pompidou government initially gave employers greater access to foreign labor, as levels of immigration climbed from an average annual rate of 248,800 during the period from 1956 to 1967, to a rate of 341,100 for the period from 1968 to 1973. Yet at the same time the administrative state was trying to reassert control over the migratory process through the ONI, which was struggling to fulfill its primary mission of recruitment and placement of foreign workers. The legalization rate dropped from 80 to 60 percent while the rise in immigration of so-called permanent workers was accompanied by substantial increases in family and seasonal immigration. Family immigration was most frequent among those who had immigrated in the previous decade, primarily from Italy, Spain, and Portugal. The new foreign workers were coming from North and West Africa, Yugoslavia, Turkey, and Portugal (the latter continued to be a major supplier of foreign labor). Algerian immigration also increased markedly during the period from 1968 to 1973. Looking at these numbers, many policymakers and students of immigration came to the conclusion that foreign workers were a permanent and necessary feature of advanced capitalist society. Indeed, conditions for immigration and the use of foreign labor were never more favorable than in the early 1970s, as both demand for labor and state policies seemed to encourage recruitment and hiring of foreign workers.[72]

Nevertheless, as the political economy reached the end of the *Trente Glorieuses*,[73] the focus of the debate over immigration shifted from economic and demographic issues to the sociological and political problems of assimilation. The hope of the *populationnistes* for a permanent immigration of Southern European Catholic workers and their families had been realized. The older Italian and Spanish migrations of the 1950s and early 1960s gave way at first to Portuguese immigration, and eventually to a largescale immigration from Africa.

The distinguishing feature of this new immigration was the cultural distinctiveness of the Muslims from North Africa. From the 1970s through the 1990s the state struggled to cope with the presence of millions of ethnically and religiously distinct individuals. A new debate over French national identity and the meaning of citizenship was starting to take shape.

The role of the administrative state was increasingly ambiguous. Even though the plan continued to calculate inputs, such as the number of foreign workers that would be needed to fulfill growth targets, the planners became more cautious in their estimates. The Sixth Plan, which covered the period 1971–1975, predicted a net annual immigration of 75,000, compared with 130,000 for the period of the Fifth Plan.[74] These estimates were easily surpassed by actual levels of immigration, which is further evidence of the increasing irrelevance of the planning process, except as a device for forecasting growth and providing information and support for industry.

The principal instrument for controlling immigration remained the Office National d'Immigration. Yet from its creation after the war ONI was given a hopeless task. It was charged with the responsibility of making the supply of foreign workers correspond to demand, within the limits of immigration law and policy. Given the availability of foreign labor and the reticence of employers to avail themselves of the services of the ONI, it is not surprising that business continued to circumvent the official channels of recruitment. Right up until the cutoff of immigration in 1974, employers continued to undermine policy measures designed to regulate the use of foreign labor. The normal procedure was to hire workers first, then seek *régularisation*.[75]

In 1967 the Ministry of Social Affairs took steps to limit noncontractual immigration. A large number of exceptions to the new rules, however, made a crackdown on unofficial immigration ineffective. The Portuguese and foreign workers in all categories of skilled labor that could not be filled with French workers were exempt. New sanctions against employers of undocumented workers were adopted in 1968, but it is difficult to measure the effect of these sanctions, which required employers to reimburse the state for any payments made to foreign workers who had not passed the medical exam administered by ONI. The legalization rate declined in 1968, so it would seem that the sanctions had some effect. However, even though employers' control over the migratory process decreased, levels of immigration increased dramatically.

The rapid rise in immigration in the early 1970s provoked a change in policy. The *circulaire Fontanet* (basically an administrative memorandum, named for its author and having the power of an executive order) was disseminated through a bulletin of the Ministry of Social Affairs early in 1972.[76] This *circulaire* and others that followed sought to eliminate all forms of noncontractual immigration. The stated purpose of these measures was to prevent the exploitation of foreign workers and reestablish public control of the migratory process.[77] The *circulaire Fontanet* created a complex bureaucratic procedure for the recruitment and placement of foreign workers, including long delays between actual recruitment and starting work. The employer was charged with the responsibility of finding housing for the new immigrant—all in all, a bureaucratic nightmare. The Ministry of Labor was bombarded by criticism from employers' associations, particularly those representing sectors such as construction (Fédération Nationale du Bâtiment, or FNB) that relied heavily on foreign labor.[78] The result of these appeals was to convince the Ministry of Labor to issue a new *circulaire* that liberalized the procedure for *régularisation*. At the same time the CFDT brought the question of the legality of these new regulations to the Conseil d'Etat, which declared them illegal in 1975. The uncertainty surrounding the legalization procedure is reflected by fluctuations in the legalization rate, which dropped from 63 percent in 1971 to 49 percent in 1972, before jumping back up to 60 percent in 1973.

The state was actively pursuing other ways to influence levels of immigration, particularly by controlling it at the source, that is in the sending country. This could be done only with the cooperation of the government of the sending countries. In 1971 the French and Portuguese governments signed a protocol which gave French authorities greater control over what had been a quasi-clandestine flow of workers. In exchange the French government agreed to raise levels of Portuguese immigration, thus granting Portugal "most-favored nation" status as a supplier of labor for the French market. Similar agreements were signed with Algeria, in an attempt to gain control of the flow of Algerian workers and their families into France. In 1969–70 Algerians in France were required to obtain a single permit that gave them the right to live and work in France. These agreements slowed the rate of increase of the Algerian population in France. However, they became moot in September 1973, when the Algerian government unilaterally suspended all emigration to France because of hostile reactions there against Algerian immigration. Attempts were made to extend control over West African immigration, which was quite small in comparison with other flows. In 1970–71 all workers from the countries of the franc zone were required to obtain work permits. But immigration of West Africans continued in the form of false tourism.[79]

Overall, the Pompidou years were marked by a high degree of inconsistency in immigration policy, as various attempts were made to increase public control over the migratory process, with mixed results. One of the reasons for the ineffectiveness of immigration policy was that the Pompidou government's approach to economic management was decidedly liberal in comparison with the statist philosophy of earlier Gaullists. Employers reacted to this new liberalism by recruiting and hiring record numbers of foreign workers, making it more difficult to use foreign labor as an instrument for regulating labor supply. Administrative attempts to reassert control over the migratory process in the early 1970s were met with resistance from almost every sector of society, including trade unions (which distrusted the government), immigrant associations (which sought to protect their rights), and employers (who wanted to maintain access to cheap foreign labor).

Efforts to stem the rising tide of immigration clearly were linked to the general unpopularity of Third World immigration. Uncontrolled migration was blamed for a host of social problems, as immigrant enclaves turned into urban slums in many cities. Although public control over the migratory process was greater than before, the problem of assimilating a growing foreign population was more severe. Public sentiment was running heavily in favour of suspending immigration. During this period, 1972–1974, the first rumblings of a nationalist reaction against immigration were heard.[80] Amid the rising controversy, the government attempted to deal with the problem through the various *circulaires* (Fontanet, Marcellin, and Gorse). But these new regulations only added to administrative confusion, while intensifying political conflicts over the issues of immigration and unemployment. Employers, particularly in the construction and agricultural sectors, were skeptical of attempts to regulate immigration, since foreign workers were seen as an essential source of labor. Many of these heavy users of foreign labor preferred the established patterns of recruiting directly in the sending countries and seeking legalization for their foreign workers (via ONI) after the workers were firmly established in the workplace. Trade unions wanted the government to reassert control, but not at the expense of isolating and alienating the already large foreign work force in France. The onset of the worldwide economic recession, following the oil shock of 1973, set the stage for a protracted political battle over immigration, which was destined to become one of the most important partisan issues of the 1980s and 90s.[81] In 1973–74 the economic crisis was compounded by a political crisis in the interval between the death of Georges Pompidou and the election of Valéry Giscard d'Estaing as President of the Republic. This brief period of political uncertainty succeeded in delaying by several months administrative efforts to cut off immigration, which already had begun in other countries of Western Europe, notably in Germany.

Reasserting State Control

The impact of public opinion on changes in immigration policy cannot be underestimated. Resentment against foreigners, which all too often took the form of violent outbursts of racism and xenophobia, convinced German and French authorities that something had to be done to regain control of immigration. Well before the oil shock in 1973 and the economic crisis that followed, French and German governments took steps to curb uncontrolled migrations. There was a growing awareness of the political and social consequences of large-scale immigration. To avoid further backlashes against foreigners, authorities felt compelled to regain control of the migratory process (the recruitment, placement, and integration of foreigners), and to create a better social infrastructure to house, educate, and care for the resident foreign population.

New regulations were put into effect governing the recruitment and placement of foreign workers. In Germany prior to 1972 it had been possible for employers to recruit foreign workers privately. This option was eliminated by the Social Democratic government of Willy Brandt in November 1972, thus forcing employers to go through official recruitment commissions to hire foreign workers. The new regulations for the most part met with the approval of employers, and they were applauded by the trade unions.[82]

The Pompidou administration took similar steps in the early 1970s to eliminate the private recruitment of foreign workers. The decision in France, however, proved to be much more controversial, since for the first time the proposal was made to link work permits with residence permits. This provision was opposed by the trade unions, because it was seen as giving the employer much greater power over the worker. By threatening to fire a worker, an employer could effectively jeopardize the right of the worker to remain in the country. Employers for their part were concerned that the new regulations would hamper their freedom to recruit and hire foreign workers.

Another important policy change during the peak period of immigration in the early 1970s was a new obligation for employers to provide adequate housing for workers. Both France and Germany adopted measures to force employers to contribute to the development of the infrastructure that would be needed to maintain a foreign workforce. In Germany, the government increased the recruitment fees *(Anwerbepauschale)* that were to be paid by firms employing foreigners. In France such measures were criticized by employers' associations, which viewed the new regulations as a threat to their ability to recruit foreign workers at a time when the overall demand for labor was high and wages were increasing.[83] Eventually, pressure from both trade unions and employers' associations convinced the French government to back down and liberalize the procedure for admitting foreigners to the work force. In Germany, on the other hand, there was a growing consensus among major interest groups that the uncontrolled recruitment of foreign workers had to be stopped.[84]

Even though federal authorities in Germany managed to retain control of worker migration, there was a spurt in the number of foreign workers entering the labor market in the late 1960s and early 1970s. The election of a Social Democratic government under Willy Brandt in 1969 did not change the prominent role of foreign labor in the German political economy. The Social Democrats had been quite critical and skeptical of Christian—Liberal governments' willingness to resort to foreign labor as a means of managing the labor market and avoiding the inflationary effects of full employment. Yet the more Keynesian approach to economic policy of the SPD required an equal vigilance on the inflation front; and it was not possible to cut back on the use of foreign labor in the heated economic environment of Europe in the early 1970s.[85]

Conclusion: Market Failures?

Immigration played a crucial role in the economic growth of Europe during the 1950s and 1960s. French and German governments were able to mobilize a much needed supply of foreign labor to avoid the inflationary consequences of near full employment. By the late 1960s the balance altered as the national and ethnic composition of immigrant flows changed rapidly from European and Catholic to largely Muslim, Turkish, and North African workers. Governments were struggling to regain control of immigration, which was driven increasingly by market forces. As the economies slowed and the prospects of unemployment loomed in the wake of the first oil shock in 1973, a political/administrative reaction against immigration began to build. In France the first in a series of backlashes against immigration came from the left of the political spectrum. What had been a tremendous economic advantage in the 1950s and 1960s was transformed virtually overnight into a political liability, for which the state and the rightwing parties of government would be held responsible in the eyes of public opinion. The rise in Muslim immigration and an economic downturn in the mid-1970s sowed the seeds for a more volatile, xenophobic, and nationalist politics in the 1980s and 1990s. Yet if the first popular reactions against immigration came from the left, it was the extreme right that rose to exploit the sociocultural antagonisms of class and race. The turbulent years of the 1970s began with debates over the economic virtues of immigration, only to end with bitter conflicts over race and ethnicity. The tone of the debate became ever more partisan in the 1980s, as the issue of immigration surged onto national agendas in almost every state in Western Europe.

Guestworker programs throughout Europe created the illusion that immigration was really an economic matter, and that the state could easily intervene in the marketplace to close the immigration valve. Foreign labor was considered to be an important factor of production (or input), and it was treated as such by French and German authorities through statist policies that were designed to meet a rapidly rising demand for labor in the 1950s and 1960s. French policymakers took a somewhat more expansive (and less economic) view of worker migration than German authorities, mainly because immigration was seen in France as a way of stemming a long process of population decline. Nonetheless, as immigration began to spin out of control in the late 1960s, taking on an increasingly Third World and Muslim character, the French administrative elite reacted in a fashion quite similar to that of German and Swiss policymakers. It was determined to be in the national interest to slow down the influx of foreigners and to regulate more carefully the market for foreign labor. In France new restrictionist policies were touted as a way of protecting the interests of the immigrant workers themselves, who had become increasingly vulnerable to exploitation and poor working and housing conditions. One thing seemed clear in both France and Germany: the market could not be allowed to operate. This would have complicated the task of administrative authorities, and made it more difficult for the state to regulate immigration in a period of rapidly rising unemployment.

Despite the political and economic pressures to stop the recruitment of foreign workers and close the immigration valve following the oil shock in 1973, the real test of the capacity of the French and German states for controlling immigration did not come until the late 1970s and early 1980s, when immigration became a partisan and political issue. The deep recessions and the rise in unemployment in the 1970s seemed to make it imperative that states stop all forms of immigration and reduce the size of foreign populations. Policy was the logical mechanism for administering what were still considered to be guest or foreign worker programs. Where markets had failed correctly to channel migration, states were bound to succeed.

4 • Foreigners and the Politics of Recession

The Keynesian dream of stable economic growth, full employment, and low inflation came abruptly to an end in 1973, when the political-economic climate in Western Europe and throughout the industrialized world changed dramatically. Rising energy costs as a result of the Arab oil embargo contributed to inflation, provoking a recession and increases in unemployment. Foreign workers were among the early victims of these changes in the political economy of Western Europe in the 1970s. Confronted with the first dramatic increase in unemployment since the period immediately following the end of World War II, labor-importing states like France and Germany moved quickly (1) to suspend immigration and the recruitment of foreign workers, (2) to encourage as many workers as possible to return to their countries of origin, and (3) to integrate into society those foreigners and their families who had been working and living in the country for specific periods of time.[1] These were the main objectives of policy change, first in Switzerland following the *Überfremdung* initiatives, then in Germany in 1973 and France in 1974.[2] The new immigration policies in Western Europe were designed to eliminate competition between foreign and citizen workers for increasingly scarce jobs, and to counter popular reactions against immigrants by assimilating foreigners who could not be expelled for legal or humanitarian reasons.

We shall take a close look here at the *politics* of restrictionism in France and Germany. Consistent with statist approaches to controlling migration, governments tried to intervene in the labor market and solve the growing problem of unemployment by stopping worker immigration. It was deemed to be in the national interest to move quickly to suspend recruitment of foreign workers and to repatriate as many foreigners as possible. As a result of these policies, foreign workers were transformed (in a short period of time) from fictitiously expendable commodities to objects of political conflict.

Immigration and Unemployment: The Administrative Reflex

By the end of the 1960s the memories of war and the postwar reconstruction were fading in Western Europe. Germany and France had succeeded in building mass-based consumer societies and stable democratic regimes. The tasks of reconstruction and modernization appeared to be completed. In France Pompidolian and Giscardian liberalism held out the promise of less ideological politics and a more market-based economy, which was to be the beginning of the fulfillment of the Radicals' dream of a liberal political order based on laissez-faire economics.[3] In Germany a new left-liberal coalition under Willy Brandt and the SPD had come to power, but the change in government did little to alter the consensus in favor of the "social market economy," which had been created by previous Christian-Liberal governments. Germany proved that capitalism could be run in a liberal but organized fashion, in keeping with the broader humanist values of social democracy and the welfare state. But the new liberalism in France and Germany was to be sorely tested by the oil crisis of 1973–74 and the global recession that followed. The role of immigrants, which was changing in step with the political economy of Western Europe, was uncertain. Immigrant and foreign workers had served their economic purpose, and it was politically expedient to stop immigration, especially from the Muslim countries of Turkey and North Africa.

The energy crisis struck a severe blow to the economies of Western Europe, a region that had become accustomed to prosperity and relative full employment. Among the first casualties of the economic crisis were foreign workers. A halt in further immigration was decreed in Germany in November 1973 and in France in July 1974. This was the initial (statist) response to falling growth rates and increasing unemployment. Governments felt a new urgency to control immigration, in order to protect the jobs of citizen workers and to promote equilibrium in the labor market. The policy shift is consistent with the Marxist analysis of capitalism: if foreign workers constitute an industrial reserve army with few political protections, then states (and employers) would be expected to discriminate against them during hard times. Likewise, it would seem to be in the national interest of these states to get rid of an economically superfluous, socially expensive, and politically controversial labor force.

Despite similarities in the policy responses to recession and rising unemployment, there were some notable differences in the French and German approaches. First, in keeping with the tradition of administrative control of foreign worker programs, the suspension of migration in Germany was more categorical and severe than in France. German authorities insisted that at no time had any commitment been made by the state to allow the permanent settlement of guestworkers.[4] At first German authorities saw no inconsistency in unilaterally halting migration and "exporting" unemployment by simply refusing to renew the work permits of foreign workers. The decision to suspend migration was viewed largely as an administrative act and was supposed to be categorical. No exemptions to the new policy were to be granted. In France, however, it was argued that certain industries could not survive without access to cheap labor. The mining and construction industries were perhaps the most prominent examples. Agriculture also was allowed to continue to use seasonal labor for harvesting crops—*la vendange* could not proceed without foreign assistance. As a result, the French ban on worker migration was more flexible and less categorical than in Germany. French authorities continued to see foreign labor as a necessary component of labor supply and were thus willing to grant exemptions to the ban.[5]

Exemptions notwithstanding, we might have expected the French state to have an advantage in making and implementing policy because of the unitary nature of the political system and the relative autonomy of the administration from pressure groups.[6] The German state, however, had some advantages in policy implementation, which were more structural than institutional. Interest groups in Germany were linked to the state through a variety of neocorporatist arrangements, making it more likely for them to support a change in policy.[7] This is important, especially in the area of immigration policy, because without the compliance of key groups like employers, it is difficult to enforce a ban on worker immigration. The more highly organized nature of interest group politics should have made it easier for the federal German state to gain the support of employers in banning the recruitment of foreign workers. These differences in state-society relations in France and Germany also reflect differences in the two economies. In France production traditionally has been decentralized in small firms; whereas in Germany production has been concentrated in much larger firms. Controlling the use of foreign labor in large manufacturing industries is easier than controlling it in small shops.

Despite strong evidence of an administrative reflex in immigration and foreign worker policy, both the German and French political systems were moving away from bureaucratic and regulatory traditions. In Germany, changes in the political system following the Second World War were designed to create a more decentralized form of authority and decisionmaking, and the *Länder* (states) were given a greater role in social and economic policy than had been the case in previous German regimes.[8] As pointed out in the previous chapter, the *Gastarbeiter* program was a glaring exception to the trend away from administrative and regulatory politics. In France, the administrative or *étatiste* tradition was more in evidence during the Fourth and the first decade of the Fifth Republic. However, the election of Giscard d'Estaing in 1974 brought to power a government that was committed, rhetorically at least, to dismantling the more overtly interventionist institutions of the French state.[9] Still, the new economic and political liberalism in France and Germany did not extend to foreigners. Only months after taking office, a series of *circulaires* were adopted by the Council of Ministers of the Giscard government, headed by the young neo-Gaullist premier, Jacques Chirac. These executive orders were supposed to result in a suspension of further immigration.[10] Such drastic measures were not unexpected, since most other labor-importing countries in Western Europe, including Germany, already had adopted similar measures.

None of these measures was sufficient to stop immigration. Any hopes of using immigrants as guestworkers to manage labor supply and solve problems of unemployment were dashed by the failure of repatriation policies in the late 1970s. The same experience was repeated in Germany, where the state tried to prevent family immigration and induce foreign workers to return home through various incentives. Such heavyhanded administrative attempts to control immigration set the tone for debates over immigration in the 1980s, contributing to the politicization of the issue and the rise of nationalist movements such as the Front National in France, and the Republikaner in Germany.

Group Politics and Restrictionist Policies

Restrictionist policies were generally accepted as necessary, given the growing unpopularity of high levels of immigration, the social costs of uncontrolled family migration, and rising unemployment. Public opinion was favorable, and major trade unions offered little resistance. French trade unions showed more ambivalence over the issue of immigration than did their German counterparts. The leaders of the Communist union, the CGT, were trying to promote greater solidarity among national and foreign workers. They were afraid that the rightwing government and employers would use foreign workers to divide the working class.[11] They were reluctant to support the government's policy of stopping immigration for fear of alienating foreign workers, whose support they needed to fight plant closings in declining industries. At the same time, conflicts between citizen and foreign workers inside and outside the factories were indicative of the tensions that existed among the national rank and file.

French trade unions and left political parties, particularly the CGT and the PCF (French Communist party), were critical of the selective and ad hoc allocation of foreign labor, which was seen as an underhanded way for the government to deal with problems of industrial adjustment. The relationship between trade unions and immigrant workers was more complex after the suspension of immigration. The main reason for difficulties was that immigration and the employment of foreigners were now highly politicized and emotionally charged issues. Many French workers were convinced that immigration was a principal cause of unemployment. The leadership of the unions unwittingly promoted this view, while at the same time speaking out for greater solidarity in the wake of the economic crisis.

On the shop floor, foreign workers were suspicious of attempts to organize them; and their decision to join or not to join a union usually depended on what services the union could offer, rather than ideological affinities. Throughout the 1970s the CGT and the PCF were more involved than the Socialists in immigrant issues, for two simple reasons: immigrant labor was more highly concentrated in the old industrial sectors, (steel and automobiles) where the CGT was strongest, and immigrants were housed near the factories in Communist neighbourhoods. With the beginning of industrial restructuring at the end of the decade, the CGT made an effort to enlist immigrant workers in the fight to save jobs in declining sectors. This strategy was an explicit recognition of the important role of immigrant workers in the labor market, and of the necessity of preventing the state and employers from using immigrants to diffuse opposition to closing unproductive firms.[12]

Immigrant workers had other reasons to distrust the Communists. On a number of occasions there were outbursts of racial violence in working-class neighborhoods, especially in the so-called red belt around Paris. Government housing policies for immigrants led to greater and greater concentrations of foreign workers in dormitories in largely Communist towns, such as Bobigny and Ivry-sur-Seine. These immigrant enclaves not only led to increased ethnic conflict; they also strained the social infrastructure set up to house and educate foreign workers. Incidents such as a Communist mayor's directing a bulldozer to block the entrance of an immigrant dormitory cast a shadow over relations between immigrants and the left.[13]

The main concern of trade unions in both France and Germany was to promote a policy that would reinforce state control of worker immigration. Such a policy would insure that citizen workers were protected, while at the same time it would stabilize levels of foreign employment. The German unions initially took a tough stance against the settlement of guestworkers. By the end of the 1970s, however, the DGB fully supported policies for stopping worker immigration, encouraging return migration, wherever possible, and integrating into German society those workers and their families who could not be repatriated.[14]

While trade unions in France and Germany ultimately were pleased to see the government taking steps to stop the recruitment of foreign workers, employers were more diffident. Officially, the decision to suspend worker migration was welcomed by employers. In France, however, the position of the major employers' associations, the Conseil National du Patronat Français (CNPF) and the Confédération Générale des Petites et Moyennes Entreprises (CGPME) was ambiguous. Even though the leaders of these organizations were in favor of the ban, some of the member groups, such as the FNB, were reluctant to give up an important source of cheap labor.[15] Some employers intervened in the policymaking process to plead their case with the new Secretary of State for Immigrant Workers, Paul Dijoud. The FNB was the most vociferous in its objections to the new policy.[16] Dijoud seemed to accept immigrant workers as a structural component of labor supply.[17] Likewise, German authorities showed some ambivalence about the freeze on hiring foreign workers and future need for foreign labor. A report by a special government commission released in 1977 outlined the reasons for suspending further recruitment of foreign workers, pointing out that Germany is not a country of immigration—*Wir sind kein ein Wanderungsland*—while holding out the prospect of future demand for foreign labor, and arguing in favor of the assimilation of foreign workers into German society.[18]

The French and German governments' motives for attempting to suspend immigration were closely related to the changed context of growth after the oil shock. Acting independently of public opinion and interest group pressures, both states decided that the social costs of immigration were too high, especially when domestic labor supplies appeared to be more than adequate for future growth. The governments moved quickly to legitimize the new policies. In France the Conseil Economique et Social (CES) issued a report calling for the elimination of all uncontrolled migration.[19] In Germany a coordinating committee (Koordinierungskreis) within the Ministry of Labor was convened to help establish a consensus for implementing the ban on immigration. Both the CES and the coordinating committee brought together major groups concerned with the issue of immigration. Within these neocorporatist settings, groups were able to voice their support for or opposition to restrictionist policies.

The decision to suspend immigration, however, failed to take into account the structural role of foreign labor in European labor markets. Because of the increase in French wage rates brought on by the Grenelle Agreements, employers in some sectors had come to rely on immigrant workers to cut production costs. Efforts were made in these sectors to retain foreigners wherever possible. Before the suspension, the turnover rate among foreign workers was much higher.[20] Likewise, those firms that were heavily dependent on foreign labor (particularly in the construction and service sectors) turned to immigrant family members to replace foreign workers who had returned home or were expelled. Moreover, both undocumented and seasonal migrants helped to maintain the structural role of foreign labor in the labor market.[21] There is also evidence that seasonal workers were moving out of the agricultural sector and into the small business sector.[22] A sectoral study of the impact of restrictions on employment of foreigners in the construction industry concluded that such policies would impose hardships and severely limit the capacity of the industry to adapt to new economic realities. The same study conducted a survey of executives in the construction industry, which revealed that employers did not expect the ban on recruitment to last.[23]

The effect of employers' lobbying appears to have been limited, at least so far as a formal change in policy is concerned. The government allowed some exemptions to the restrictions on recruitment and hiring of foreign workers. But these exemptions were few and circumscribed by a variety of administrative requirements that made it difficult for most employers to escape the new controls.[24] When a request for hiring a foreign worker was made by an employer to the DPM (Direction de la Population et des Migrations), it was often made through an intermediary, such as the employer's union or a Member of Parliament. Presumably, a request made in this way would carry more weight than if the employer went directly to the Ministry. In her study of employers' attitudes toward immigration, Marie-Claude Hénneresse found that over 90 percent of the requests for exemptions submitted to the DPM by employers in 1974–75 were approved. These exemptions, however, account for only 14 percent of total worker immigration controlled by the ONI.[25] It seems unlikely, therefore, that there was any overt collusion between employers and the state to keep immigration high.

Some sectors, however, appear to have received more favorable treatment than others. Mining, which was in full decline, accounts for more than 40 percent of all exemptions in 1974–75, while the employers in the small business sector represented by the CGPME were denied access to foreign labor by the DPM. In this respect, the French government was pursuing a strategy for economic development that dated from the Fourth Republic—favoring big over small business. Unlike the "national champions," the traditional sector of small businesses in France was denied legal access to foreign labor. Yet the influx of family members and seasonal workers, many of whom became immigrant workers, provided a new source of labor for employers in the traditional sector.[26]

In Germany there was much less public dissent among employers over the suspension of immigration. The principal employers' association, the BDA, backed the new policy; but, like the DGB, the BDA initially opposed the settlement of guestworkers and assimilation of foreigners into German society.[27] This stance by German employers ran counter to their market interests in maintaining an unlimited supply of cheap labor. However, as was the case in France, it was politically difficult for any group openly to oppose the stopping of worker immigration during the recessionary period of the late 1970s. Employers in both France and Germany were able to count on an adequate supply of foreign labor even after the suspension, because of the increase in family immigration and the entry of second and third generation immigrants into the labor market. In France most of these new immigrants would go into the service sector, whereas in Germany the manufacturing sector continued to be the heaviest user of foreign labor.[28]

Return Policies and Repatriation

Throughout the 1970s France and Germany sought to reinforce the suspension of worker immigration by cooperating with the principal sending countries. Numerous bilateral agreements, diplomatic conventions, and protocols were worked out with the major sending countries in an effort to regain control of international migration and assist in the repatriation of migrants who chose to return. In France four cases are of particular interest. The Portuguese continued to enjoy a somewhat privileged status there because of agreements that made Portugal a most favored supplier of labor (note that Portugal was not yet a member of the EC). These agreements helped to eliminate the clandestine flow of Portuguese workers and their families into France. Similarly, migrants from the *franc zone* of West Africa benefited from a special status. Movement between France and its former colonies in West Africa continued to be relatively free of administrative restrictions. Moroccans received special consideration because of their importance as a source of manpower for the mining industry. Finally, Algeria, which used to be one of the most important sending countries, unilaterally suspended emigration in 1973 because of violence against Algerian nationals in France. Before this date, Algerians had been able to move more or less freely into and out of France. Much later, the Franco-Algerian accords of 1980 brought renewed cooperation between the authorities of the two countries, primarily on the question of repatriation and training for returnees.[29]

The suspension of legal worker migration proved to be insufficient either to stop immigration or reduce the size of the foreign population. As a result, stricter measures were taken to limit family immigration and repatriate as many foreigners as possible. Financial incentives were offered to foreigners if they would return to their countries of origin. These return policies were modestly successful in France, where 54,631 foreigners actually received some aid to repatriate over the period 1977–1981. In total, 86,019 foreign workers and their families took advantage of the program.[30]

The policy of paying foreigners to return was first proposed in France in early 1976. The objective was to provide incentives for those foreigners who wanted to leave but could not afford to make the move. In addition to a one-time payment of a modest sum of money, foreigners could participate in retraining programs set up in cooperation with the sending countries, especially Portugal, Spain, and Algeria. More than two thirds of the total returnees were from Spain and Portugal, while most of those who entered the retraining programs were from North Africa, particularly Algeria.[31] By 1980, over 1,000 foreign workers were benefiting annually from these training programs.

The unilateral suspension of immigration by Germany abrogated most prior agreements worked out with the sending countries. Starting in 1973, however, German authorities placed great emphasis on assisting the sending countries with the repatriation of migrants, and certain types of economic aid (for example, military aid to Turkey) were tied to cooperation on repatriation. Agreements also were signed with Greece and Turkey to set up a special fund in those countries to aid returnees. Not until November 1983 did the German government formally approve a return policy offering substantial monetary incentives to induce foreigners to repatriate: this policy only lasted one year. Unlike the French policy, which remained in effect until 1981, German return policy did not stress job training. Neither the French nor German return policies proved very effective, as more and more foreign workers chose to settle and seek family reunification.[32]

Family Immigration and Assimilation

Apart from stopping immigration and encouraging foreigners to repatriate, policies were set in motion in France and Germany that would assist in the assimilation of immigrants.[33] However, the new plans were quickly overwhelmed by waves of family, seasonal, and clandestine immigration that were the result of the suspension.[34] Problems associated with the integration of large foreign populations in France and Germany are too numerous to be discussed in detail here. For our purposes it is helpful to divide assimilation policies of the 1970s and

1980s into three basic categories, each of which has important socio-political ramifications: (1) family reunification and the problems of the second and third generations; (2) social welfare; and (3) the rights of foreign workers, including civil and political rights, such as voting.

Certainly the biggest challenge to the restrictionist policies of the 1970s was the increase in family immigration. Both France and Germany experimented with regulations to limit family immigration. For example, each tried to prevent foreigners, who had been in the country for less than a specified period of time, to bring family members into the country. German authorities tried to refuse work permits to family members, or grant them only after a specified period of residence. Likewise, attempts were made to restrict family immigration unless the head of household was in a position to provide adequate housing for all family members. These regulations changed frequently in both countries, often as the result of pressure from human (and civil) rights organizations. Some groups, particularly in Germany, opposed these restrictionist policies on humanitarian and constitutional grounds. Church groups and organizations for the support of foreign workers lobbied successfully for better working conditions for foreigners and for extensions of residence and work permits. In the end, the most restrictive and illiberal regulations—limits on mobility, exclusion from the labor market, and denial of family reunification—were struck down by administrative or constitutional courts.

With the drop in departures of foreigners after the suspension of immigration, family arrivals rose significantly in both France and Germany. This was a natural consequence of suspending immigration, which accelerated the settlement of workers, who then sought to reunite their families in the host country. In the late 1970s and early 1980s, the problems of housing, educating, and providing health care for the second and third generation of immigrants became more acute as a result of family reunification. The development of immigrant enclaves in large cities contributed to the severity of the "immigrant problem" and led to a deterioration in ethnic relations. The presence of large, ethnically and culturally distinct populations in the cities focused public attention on immigration. In Germany the state tried to shift the burden of caring for immigrants and their families to parapublic institutions, especially churches. Because of the decentralized and federal nature of social policy, local governments were forced to deal with issues ranging from the housing and education of immigrants to health care—a situation not unlike that in the United

States, where state and local governments bear the brunt of problems of assimilation. As early as June 1973, the German government saw the impending crisis in social services for migrants and their families, and began to seek ways of coping with the new influx.[35]

The distinction between residence and work permits for family members became increasingly important in light of the rise in family immigration after 1973.[36] German authorities hoped to prevent the spouses and children of foreign workers from entering the labor market by granting them temporary residence permits, while denying them work permits. Administrative restrictions were also imposed on the geographical mobility of foreign workers and their families. As pointed out above, these regulations did not survive the scrutiny of administrative and constitutional tribunals. In the French case, the government admitted substantial numbers of new immigrants, including family members, into the labor market within a year of the suspension of worker immigration in 1974.[37]

The entry of second-generation immigrant children into the school system in France and Germany in the 1970s and early 1980s, and immigrant-related unrest, such as the SONACOTRA rent strikes in France and the strikes at Ford in Cologne, brought the problem of immigration closer to home for many. The public became increasingly conscious of the social costs of immigration, and public opinion brought pressure to bear on governments to maintain official policies of suspension.[38]

One of the initial responses of the French government to public pressures for action was to commission a study by the CES. The report made several recommendations, the most important of which was a call for the elimination of illegal immigration. To accomplish this, the government needed to adopt more radical measures for controlling worker and family immigration. In both France and Germany a major area of public concern was the impact of immigration on welfare and unemployment programs. Anti-immigrant groups argued that too many immigrants were becoming wards of the state and, as such, a drain on public finances. These groups were especially concerned about unemployment among foreign workers and the possibility that foreigners might benefit from the dole.[39]

In the 1970s unemployment of foreigners was actually lower or on a par with unemployment of citizen workers, but by the 1980s it had risen above the rate for citizen workers. If we compare unemployment rates between the two groups since 1973, we find that unemployment of foreigners in France reached a high of almost 10 percent in the early 1980s, which was slightly higher than that for French workers. In Germany, the unemployment rate among foreign workers fluctuated between 4 and 5 percent until 1980, when it rose significantly, surpassing 12 percent in 1982, two to three points above the unemployment rate for German workers.[40] In the late 1980s foreign unemployment was significantly higher than unemployment among citizen workers. Apart from the deterioration of the job market in both countries during the 1980s, part of the rise in unemployment among foreigners was due to the entry of family members and second-generation migrants into the work force. Unemployment statistics notwithstanding, studies of the use of social services by immigrants in France and Germany have shown that immigrants contribute more to the budget in taxes because of higher activity rates than they take out in the form of unemployment benefits, health care, education, or social security. As the second (and third) generations came to be of school and working age, the problem of integrating immigrants into society grew more complex and expensive. The housing situation in crowded urban areas, such as Berlin, became a flash point of controversy.[41]

The decision was made in 1977 to try to inhibit the development of immigrant enclaves in Germany by imposing numerical limits on the number of foreign workers living in administratively defined districts *(Kreise)*. The limit was set at 12 percent of the population of the district, and the residence and work permits of foreigners contained a reference to the district to which the individual was assigned. The objective of these controls was to "rationalize" the spatial distribution of the foreign population within the country and to maintain control of the use of foreign labor in the economy. In fact these measures remained in force for only a short period of time, as a result of legal and constitutional challenges to the administrative power of federal authorities. In France no administrative restrictions were placed on the mobility of foreigners, and the granting of residence permits was not linked to the social and economic status of the migrant. The French socialist governments of the 1980s took various measures in the areas of housing, education, and civil rights to insure greater integration and participation of immigrants in French society.[42] The granting of social rights to immigrants in France in the 1980s became a rallying cry for anti-immigrant groups, especially the Front National.

In both France and Germany the political activities of foreigners have been circumscribed by legislation that limits rights of association and occupational and geographical mobility. This situation has contributed to the insecurity of foreigners inasmuch as their rights are subject to administrative discretion rather than constitutional procedure. Legislation concerning rights of association was designed to maintain public order and allow the expulsion of foreigners who threaten that order. Many of these restrictions were dropped in France after the election of the socialists in 1981.[43] Foreigners in both France and Germany have been allowed to form associations to promote their interests and to consult with national and local authorities on policy questions that affect them.

In 1990 in the midst of the turmoil over unification, the German Bundestag passed a new law governing the situation of foreigners residing in the Federal Republic. This law superseded a 1965 law, which gave broad powers to the *Länder* concerning the "rights of residence" of foreigners.[44] The German authorities were anxious to revise the 1965 law before the completion of the unification process. The most important change was to expand considerably the rights of residence for foreigners who held an unlimited residency permit, as well as for their immediate families. Thus the German state took a crucial step in recognizing the permanent settlement on German territory of a large foreign population. The 1990 law opened the possibility for restarting the *Gastarbeiter* policies that were terminated in 1973, if the economic situation warranted such a move. In addition, the law created greater opportunities for family reunification, by removing the powers of the *Länder* to make decisions about the resident status of family members, on a case-by-case basis. The German statute still retains the distinction between residence and work permits, thus allowing German authorities (in principle) to refuse the right to work to foreigners legally residing in the country. Although the law does not embrace the French and American conceptions of citizenship and naturalization—which are based on *jus soli* as well as *jus sanguinis*—it does liberalize the rules governing naturalization, to make it easier for long-term resident foreigners (and their children) to obtain citizenship. This is yet another step in recognizing the political and social reality of immigration in postwar Germany.[45]

Neither France nor Germany have been willing to extend the franchise to foreigners. Obtaining the right to vote is contingent upon naturalization. Thus participation in political parties is difficult for foreigners in both countries. Yet foreigners have the right to participate in trade union activities, including the right to vote and stand as candidates in union elections, and the right to strike. Evidence indicates that foreigners have had some success in making their voices heard on the shop floor.[46] In recent years, with second-generation immigrants in the labor market and with first-generation immigrants having been residents of long duration, foreign workers have become more militant. They are often in the vanguard of striking workers in declining industries, such as steel and automobiles. Strikes at Ford in Cologne and Renault in Paris in the 1970s were notable for the militant role played by foreign workers. The rate of unionization of foreign workers in Germany has been higher than in France. By the mid-1980s, 10 percent of the DGB membership was foreign; whereas the number of foreign workers who are members of the three main trade unions in France (the CGT, CFDT, and FO) has remained quite low.[47]

The Limits of Policy

Given the political consensus in France and Germany for suspending immigration, why did it prove difficult for these states to implement restrictionist policies? The pitfalls of using immigration to solve problems of unemployment soon became clear. After the economic crisis of the 1970s, the French and German governments feared that unemployment among foreigners would contribute to tensions between foreign and citizen workers—a fear which proved to be well-founded. Politicians hoped that suspending immigration would solve some of the problems of unemployment among citizen workers by creating more vacancies. However, they failed to foresee the full consequences of a complete suspension of immigration, particularly the difficulty of controlling family, seasonal, and clandestine migration. They also failed to take into account the cultural and institutional constraints that prevent their liberal governments from treating individuals as commodities.

From figures 4.1–4.3 we can see one dimension of the impact of restrictionist immigration policies in France, Germany, and Switzerland. Figure 4.1 shows the differences in the evolution of the foreign populations in France and Germany prior to 1961, when only the French and Swiss governments were actively promoting the recruit-

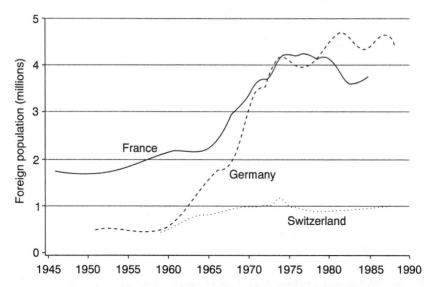

Figure 4.1. Foreign populations in France, Germany, and Switzerland

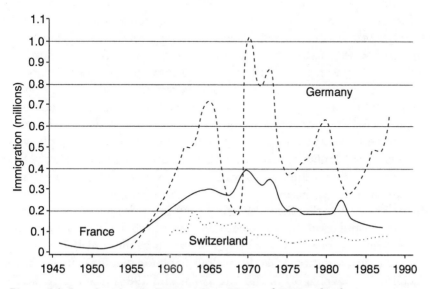

Figure 4.2. Immigration in France, Germany, and Switzerland

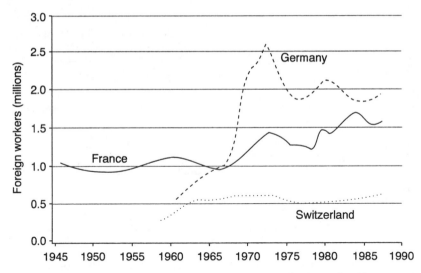

Figure 4.3. Foreign workers in France, Germany, and Switzerland

ment of foreign labor. The construction of the Berlin Wall sealed the iron curtain and cut Germany off from its traditional supply of labor in central Europe. In 1961–62 the German government began to promote the recruitment of foreign workers. During the 1960s the foreign population in Germany grew rapidly, eventually surpassing 7 percent of the total population in 1980, where it has remained. In France the foreign population reached a peak of 8 percent of the total population in 1977, before falling back to the 7 percent range in the 1980s (see Figure 4.1).[48] Similarly, with respect to numbers of foreign workers Germany started at much lower levels proportionately than France but quickly caught up with and surpassed it in the late 1960s (see Figure 4.3). The percentage of foreign workers in the Swiss labor force has hovered at or above the 15 percent level for most of the postwar period. The number of foreign workers in the German labor force has fluctuated around the 9 to 10 percent level since the beginning of the 1970s. In France, the number has been in the range of 5 to 7 percent since the end of the Second World War.[49] Even though the size of the foreign populations in each country has remained relatively stable since the suspension of worker immigration in the mid-1970s, levels of legal immigration (that is, inflows of foreigners) gradually have declined or leveled off in the late 1970s and 1980s (see Figure 4.2).[50] But there was no dramatic drop in levels of immigration, despite the implementation of restrictionist policies. In both Germany and Switzerland levels of immigration have recovered in the late 1980s, whereas in France legal immigration has dropped below 150,000 per year. The rise in immigration in 1981–82 (see Figure 4.2) was the result of the amnesty granted to illegal immigrants in the first years of the Mitterrand era.

The upward trend in the size of the foreign worker population was reversed in France, Germany, and Switzerland in 1973 (see Figure 4.3). It continued to fall in France until the late 1970s. In Germany and Switzerland the downward trend lasted from 1973 to 1979. Certainly some of the lowering of levels of foreign employment may be attributed to changes in policy. However, economic (and labor market) conditions deteriorated (more so in France than in Germany or Switzerland) as a result of the global recession. Thus, much of the change in the size of the foreign worker population may be attributed to a decline in the overall demand for labor in these economies.

The foreign worker population dropped significantly in each country, but especially in France and Germany. This drop is all the more impressive if we take into account that the number of workers from member states of the EC was higher as a percentage of the total foreign worker population after 1974, as employers began to turn to more regulated and expensive sources of labor. But changes in the national composition of foreign worker stocks notwithstanding, total immigration (and the size of the foreign population) remained at historically high levels throughout the 1970s and 1980s (see figures 4.1 and 4.2). Much of the difference (between levels of immigration and foreign worker stocks) can be accounted for by increases in family and seasonal immigration, which picked up rapidly as worker migration declined. This lends some weight to the dual labor-market argument that foreign labor had become a structural component of labor supply in capitalist economies (that is, a necesary pool of surplus labor that could be more easily hired and fired in times of crisis).[51] In effect, family and seasonal immigration replaced worker immigration as the principal source of foreign labor in Western Europe. In France, from 1978 to 1980, the number of family members admitted to the labor market by the Ministry of Labor surpassed the total number of family members admitted to residency through the ONI. The discrepancy between family immigration statistics of the ONI and admissions to the labor market, as recorded by the Ministry of Labor, is evidence of the use of kinship rules by some migrants to gain access to the labor market. Spanish, Portuguese, Moroccan, and Tunisian immigrants made up the bulk of this new flow. Hence the new immigration policies were not successful in controlling immigration—in the words of one official of the French Ministry of Labor, "*On ferme la porte et on ouvre la fênetre.*"

With respect to the foreign populations, the restrictionist policies seem to have had the opposite effect from the one intended (see Figure 4.1). Although they may have helped to stabilize the foreign population in the short term, in the long term the suspension of immigration contributed to an increase in the foreign population. By stopping the inflows of workers, the new policy inadvertently created a larger inflow of family members and, in the case of France, seasonal workers.[52] It has been suggested, although it is difficult to prove, that the cut-off also led to increases in illegal immigration.[53] Because of its sociodemographic complexity, immigration does not lend itself easily to statist regulation. Once started, it has its own dynamic and is to a certain extent self-perpetuating.[54]

Several other factors that were beyond the state's control also contributed to increases in the foreign population. These include: (1) natural growth of the resident foreign population; (2) entry and settlement of workers from member countries of the European Community; (3) political refugees; and (4) clandestine immigration. Concerning the first factor, the demographic profile of immigrants shows them to have higher birth rates and lower mortality rates than the indigenous population.[55] Hence the foreign populations in France and Germany have been growing of their own accord. Regarding the second point, since 1968 most workers who are nationals of EC states have had freedom of movement. The policies discussed above do not apply to European migrants, even though they are counted as foreigners.[56]

The third contributing factor is that a significant number of foreign workers who legally entered France and Germany since 1973 have become political refugees. Although the inflow of refugees cannot compare with inflows of workers prior to 1973, refugee immigration has become increasingly important in the 1980s. In France, which has long been a country of asylum, most of the refugees have come from Southeast Asia, sub-Saharan Africa, Central and Latin America, and the Middle East. The annual number of asylum seekers, however, has climbed steadily since the suspension of immigration in 1974, approaching 30,000 by the mid-1980s.[57] Germany has had a larger influx of political refugees, primarily from Turkey. The increase in the number of applications for political asylum in the late 1970s and early 1980s led to the adoption of a series of measures designed to stop abuses. Among the steps taken by the German government was to deny applicants for asylum work permits during their first year of residence.[58] Various German governments have been constrained in their attempts to control refugee immigration by the very liberal asylum provisions of the Basic Law (Articles 16 and 113), which were intended to benefit ethnic German refugees from Central and Eastern Europe.

Lastly, as in all of the labor-importing regions of the industrial North, clandestine immigration has been a problem in Western Europe both before and after the adoption of restrictionist policies in the 1970s. Although the numbers in Western Europe pale by comparison with those in the United States, illegal immigration is by no means nonexistent. Estimates of the number of undocumented workers in the United States range from 3.5 to 5 million.[59] In Germany in 1975 there were estimated to be 200,000 undocumented workers, and in France the number of undocumented migrants who took advantage of the amnesty program of the first Mitterrand government in 1981–82 was on the order of 100,000.[60] During the 1970s the French and German governments imposed sanctions on employers who hired undocumented workers. Even though it is difficult to measure the impact of employer sanctions in deterring illegal immigration in Western Europe, available evidence indicates that such policies had only minimal success in helping states control illegal immigration.[61]

By far the most dramatic effort to deal with the problem of illegal immigration was the amnesty offered by the first Mitterrand government in France in 1981 to foreign workers and their families living in an irregular situation. The objective of this policy was to reduce the insecurity of foreigners residing in France, while at the same time maintaining a strict ban on new immigration. At least two preconditions limited the effectiveness of the amnesty: only foreigners who had entered the country before January 1, 1981 could apply, and all applicants had to present evidence of employment, preferably a contract to prove that they had been employed for at least one year.[62] Under these conditions, 82,493 workers obtained adjustments of status *(régularisations)* under the amnesty by the end of 1982.[63] The increase in immigration in France in 1981–82, which was quite modest, is directly attributable to the amnesty (see Figure 4.2).

Conclusion: Policy Failures?

The history of immigration in France and Germany in the postwar period provides tantalizing evidence of the difficulties that liberal states must face in their attempts to regulate international migration. Specific policies showed limitations, shortcomings, and failures. The inability of French and German governments to use immigration policy as a mechanism for regulating labor supply and for making employment policy is an indication of constraints on the autonomy of the administrative state. The more formal explanation of these constraints and a test of the liberal thesis follow in chapters 5–7. We will look at the interaction of market conditions and policy change to gain a better understanding of the role of foreign labor in advanced industrial societies.

To this point, we have explored two of the principal issues in the political economy of immigration: sovereignty and labor. We found that France and Germany were unable to regulate immigration to pursue statist objectives. The reasons for policy failures have less to do with the inadequacies of the policies or the governments—better implementation, tougher employer sanctions, more stringent border controls would not have made an appreciable difference in outcomes—than with liberal constraints. The first of these constraints is economic: an international market for labor exists in Europe, and it is extremely difficult for the state to prevent firms and employers from participating in this market, even when the "national interest" and politics dictate greater restrictions. Does this mean that the Marxist and dual labor-market assumptions are correct? Has foreign labor become a necessary component of labor supply in advanced capitalist economies? To answer these questions we must look more closely at the evidence, and especially at the ability of the state (via policy) to use immigrants as shock absorbers to cushion the fluctuations in demand that are associated with relatively open industrial economies.

The second liberal constraint is associated with the rights of individuals in these societies. Part III of the book is devoted to an examination of the issue of citizenship and the political economy of immigration in France, Germany, and the United States. What are the liberal, procedural devices that prevent the administrative authorities from treating foreign workers as commodities? What discourages politicians in these countries from enacting legislation to expel all foreigners during recessionary periods? The politics of citizenship and nationalism—which have come to the fore in Europe in the 1980s—must be taken into account. It is not sufficient simply to look at the problem of regulating immigration in the liberal polity from the standpoint of policy and markets; we must also look at the expansion of rights.

In the last two chapters we have seen how much more difficult it is to stop immigration than to start it. Little doubt remains that the influx of foreign workers into the French and German labor markets in the 1950s and 1960s helped to sustain phenomenally high growth rates and combat wage-push inflation during that period. The motives for recruiting guestworkers were primarily economic and, in the French case, demographic. The decision to suspend worker migration, however, was motivated largely by political and social considerations. The utility of foreign labor for many firms did not cease even after the recession of the 1970s, but it was no longer politically acceptable to have high levels of immigration at a time of unemployment among citizen workers.

In terms of policy and the political process, most major interest groups in France and Germany agreed with the government's decision to suspend immigration. But certain types of firms in both countries continued to hire foreign workers. The service sector in particular benefited from the new flow of labor, composed primarily of family members, refugees, illegal immigrants, and seasonal workers. The complexity of the migratory process, from the recruitment to the settlement of the temporary workers and their families, posed serious problems for the implementation of restrictionist policies designed to stop the influx of foreign workers. Immigrants who arrived in the late 1970s and early 1980s saw job prospects in France, Germany, and Switzerland as being good enough to warrant the move. Again, to quote Charles Kindleberger, "immigration is a good thing on the basis of revealed preference." At the same time, regulations designed to stop new rounds of immigration had to be abandoned in the face of constitutional and humanitarian constraints. It proved impossible to prevent the reunification of families of workers who chose to settle in the host country, to expel workers *en masse,* or to prevent family members from entering the labor market.

The history of immigration policy in France and Germany since the 1960s shows how difficult it is to use immigrant workers as shock absorbers. Immigration is not a very effective tool for dealing with unemployment. While it may be possible and desirable to use foreign or guestworkers to solve problems of manpower shortages, it is not possible simply to get rid of them when they are no longer needed. In the words of one Swiss official, "we asked for workers and we got people instead." The evidence tends to contradict both the dual labor-market and classical Marxist arguments. However, to evaluate competing theories of immigration more thoroughly, we must look more closely at the interaction of policy and markets.

III ✦ Policies and Markets

5 • Immigration Policy and Labor

Aside from the difference between despotic and libertarian governments, the greatest distinction between one government and another is in the degree to which market replaces government or government replaces market.

—CHARLES LINDBLOM, *Politics and Markets*

In both France and Germany the market for foreign labor outstripped the ability of the state to manage it. With the recession in 1973–74, it seemed imperative for states to regain control of migration, to ease the social costs of immigration and head off a political reaction against immigrants. But political and economic developments gave rise to distributional conflicts and a new politics of rights, closely linked to welfare states and liberal constitutions. In this chapter we shall look at the impact of changes in immigration policy on labor markets and at the interaction of policy, group politics, and markets.

Regulating Capital and Labor Markets

In market economies, where the process of growth depends heavily on an adequate supply of credit, it is not surprising that capital is the first target of regulators. Control over capital and the allocation of credit have been primary goals of governments since the beginning of the industrial era. Every capitalist state has an elaborate financial system that regulates and structures capital markets. The involvement of governments in capital markets has been the hallmark of industrial capitalism. The long history of central banks and national financial systems is a testimony to the importance of market regulation.

If capital markets have been regulated by the state since the beginning of the modern era, national labor markets have tended to be more open and competitive, except in those systems where trade unions were strong enough to compel the state to intervene on behalf of workers. One explanation for the different history of regulation in these two markets is that capital (qua business) has had a privileged position. The relative scarcity of capital has made it—and those who own it—more powerful than labor, which historically has been more abundant. Struggles over regulation between the owners of capital and the state have been characterized by a series of compromises in which each side recognized that it could not survive without the other. The margin of action of firms was determined by institutional and structural constraints.[1]

The development of trade unions and socialist parties gave workers the power to negotiate with employers and the state. As a result, despite the abundance of labor, workers succeeded in altering the structure of labor markets in their favor. Just as capital succeeded in gaining protections from the market (through banking regulation, public insurance schemes, and the like), labor also succeeded in getting the state to regulate labor markets (through child labor laws, the forty-hour week, health and safety laws, and so on). The workers achieved political and economic gains, especially with the advent of Keynesian macroeconomic policies in the 1950s and 1960s. Up until the late 1970s, it looked as though the Keynesian synthesis had solved some of the more intractable problems of economic growth. By demonstrating how governments could use fiscal policy to promote growth and full employment, Keynesian theory and policy provided the industrial democracies with the means to solve some of the more intractable problems associated with economic change.[2]

Following the oil shock in 1973 the context of growth changed, with a simultaneous rise in inflation and unemployment and the contraction of economic activity. This change brought an end to the dominance of Keynesian policies, as states moved quickly to stop the expansion of credit and slow the rate of government spending, thus reversing policies designed to promote full employment. The thrust of economic policy in the industrial democracies was to force *adjustment* and *flexiblity* in capital and labor markets. The role of the state in this transformation varied widely.[3] In the United States and Britain trade unions came under attack, and attempts were made to deregulate labor markets. In France the government initially fell back on statist and regulatory responses to recession to confront the new economic realities.[4]

Some political systems have an advantage in compelling workers to accept the sacrifices necessary for adjustment to new economic realities. For example, the fragmented position of organized labor in Japan and the United States has made it easier for governments and employers in those countries to obtain wage concessions or to shift labor from one sector of the economy to another. In Britain, Germany, and France, on the other hand, labor is stronger, better organized, and less willing to accept such sacrifices.[5] Trade unions in Western Europe are more capable of protecting the position of their members in the labor market than are their American or Japanese counterparts.

In the labor-importing countries of Western Europe foreign workers became targets for economic adjustment. Foreign workers in France and Germany were thrust into political and industrial conflict because of the vulnerable position they occupied in the economy and society. Whether one speaks of Algerians at Talbot or Turks at Volkswagen, foreign workers have been at the center of the controversies over market regulation and industrial adjustment in Europe. Because of technological innovation and a changing international division of labor, some firms opted to move production abroad in search of cheap labor to cut production costs. The watchword of the 1980s was flexibility, meaning the ability of the firm quickly to shift its resources from one sector or product to another in order to take advantage of new markets.

Governments responded to new economic realities in the 1980s by encouraging firms to adapt. Economic policies among OECD countries varied from the most overt forms of state intervention, such as nationalizations in France, to privatization in Britain, and deregulation in the United States. But in each case the goal was to force greater flexibility in capital and labor markets by increasing the mobility of productive factors within and across economic sectors. Much has been written on capital mobility and the organization of credit markets. Investment and industrial policies also have attracted much attention as key factors in restructuring, and several countries, particularly France and Japan, have intervened directly in credit markets to implement national industrial policies.[6] Certainly the allocation of capital (and credit) is crucial in determining which firms will expand and which will decline. Such decisions on the allocation of scarce resources are ultimately political decisions with real human consequences. The degree of politicization of markets varies considerably within the OECD group. Some governments have intervened directly at the level of the firm (more characteristic of the French and Japanese experiences), and others have opted for the indirect approach of manipulating fiscal and monetary aggregates (more characterisitic of the U.S. and British experiences).

Technically, it is easier for governments to intervene in capital markets than in labor markets, because of the strength of national financial systems. Institutions for controlling finance have evolved over a period of centuries. Labor markets are more difficult to structure, however, because moving people is problematic. Workers in traditional manufacturing industries such as steel, automobiles, and textiles are reluctant to move elsewhere and accept job changes. Individuals become attached to their communities and their jobs, and when organized into trade unions they are capable of resisting attempts by government or employers to force them to move or change jobs.

These differences in capital and labor markets do not detract from the importance of investment decisions, which directly affect labor mobility. However, we must keep in mind the organizational differences that exist between capital and labor markets, which make it technically and politically difficult for governments to formulate labor-market as opposed to investment policy. Governments interfere with the price mechanism in both markets, but the gap between policy outputs and outcomes is much greater in the labor market, because of the political difficulties of regulating labor supply and demand.

Immigration, Productivity, and Employment

With the decline in demand for labor after the oil shock, unemployment increased in each of the labor-importing countries, except Switzerland (see Tables 5.1–5.3). How did this change in the economic climate affect immigration and the role of foreign workers in the industrial democracies? According to the dual labor-market (and Marxist) hypotheses, we would expect foreign workers to be laid off, because they play the role of shock absorber. If foreign labor served to maintain levels of economic growth during the period of reconstruction in Western Europe, should it not also serve as a flexible

Table 5.1 Average annual percentage increase in real GDP in five labor-importing countries, 1960–1981

Country	1960–1968	1968–1973	1973–1979	1960–1981
F.R.G.	4.2	4.9	2.4	3.6
France	5.4	5.9	3.1	4.4
Switzerland	4.4	4.5	−0.4	2.9
U.S.A.	4.5	3.3	2.6	3.3
U.K.	3.1	3.2	1.4	2.1

Source: Organization for Economic Cooperation and Development, *National Accounts of the OECD countries* (Paris: OECD, 1954–1981).

Table 5.2 Average annual percentage increase in real consumer prices in five labor-importing countries, 1960–1981

Country	1960–1968	1968–1973	1973–1979	1960–1981
F.R.G.	1.2	4.2	5.0	3.5
France	1.3	5.1	9.9	5.6
Switzerland	3.1	3.8	2.5	3.4
U.S.A.	1.5	5.6	10.0	5.6
U.K.	1.1	6.1	10.0	8.6

Source: Organization for Economic Cooperation and Development, *Main Economic Indicators* (Paris: OECD, 1954–1981).

Table 5.3 Average annual unemployment rates in five labor-importing countries, 1960–1981

Country	1960–1968	1968–1973	1973–1979	1960–1981
F.R.G.	0.6	1.0	3.3	1.9
France	1.7	2.5	5.1	3.5
Switzerland[a]	—	—	—	—
U.S.A.	4.2	4.6	6.8	5.5
U.K.	2.5	3.4	6.3	4.5

Source: Organization for Economic Cooperation and Development, *Historical Statistics, 1960–1981* (Paris: OECD, 1981), p. 41.

a. Unemployment in Switzerland during the period was insignificant.

component of labor supply (and a cheap source of labor) during periods of recession?[7]

The liberal economic argument offers us another way of generalizing the experiences of states with respect to the use of foreign labor. The Lewis model of growth with unlimited supplies of labor, which describes the importance of labor supply in economic growth, is a good example of this argument.[8] Charles Kindleberger recognised the importance of this model for explaining economic growth in postwar Europe.[9] Kindleberger pointed specifically to immigration and foreign labor as key factors in Europe's economic recovery.

The Lewis-Kindleberger model of growth can be summarized as follows: unlimited supplies of labor keep the firm's wage bill down and profits up, thus creating a favorable environment for investment, increased productivity, low inflation, and higher consumption. The higher rate, Kindleberger points out, is the result of raised wages, which are made possible by greater profits and increasing employment. Thus wages remain a constant share of national income.[10]

The Lewis-Kindleberger model offers an optimistic scenario that holds so long as labor supplies are unlimited and *demand is increasing*. It is easy to understand why Kindleberger's analysis is optimistic, given the period in which he was writing. Until the early 1970s, the major economic problem facing most countries in postwar Europe was how to sustain phenomenally high rates of growth (see Table 5.1) and avoid the inflationary consequences of full employment or a shortage of credit.[11] Importing labor was at least a partial solution to the problem associated with high rates of growth and full employment, especially in countries like Switzerland, France, and Germany, all of which faced more or less severe problems of labor shortage.[12]

Despite the political reaction against immigration in the 1970s and 1980s, foreign labor continued to play an important role in European economic development. But, foreign workers and immigrants were singled out as a cause of rising unemployment. The notion that immigration causes unemployment shows a lack of knowledge of economic history and of the overall contribution of immigrants to economic growth in the industrial West.[13] Yet it was relatively easy for politicians (of the left and the right) to seize upon immigration as a way of diverting attention from the economic recession.

The official justification for suspending immigration was that foreign workers were no longer needed, given increases in unemployment and greater participation of women in the labor force.[14] Only in

Switzerland was it difficult to make the argument that immigration causes unemployment, because of the inadequacy of domestic labor supplies in many sectors. Even in Switzerland, however, there was a strong antiforeigner movement that pushed for the suspension of immigration and the repatriation of foreign workers. It is important to note that the Swiss state never succumbed to these pressures, preferring instead to regulate migrant flows and stabilize the foreign population at levels that would be generally acceptable.[15]

Two factors contributed to the continuation of international labor migration after 1973. (1) Even during periods of recession and unemployment, the supply curve for labor will be inelastic or even backward bending, because it is difficult for firms to attract additional labor in the short term.[16] Hence access to an outside supply of labor is one way for a firm to avoid this short-term problem. (2) The dual labor-market argument suggests that the continuing demand for foreign labor can be explained by the high degree of regulation of the domestic labor market, which guarantees high wages, safe working conditions, and job security for citizen workers. Such regulation creates incentives for employers to look outside traditional labor markets for cheaper, more tractable labor. Foreign workers, women, and other marginal groups are ideal sources of such labor. The persistent demand for foreign labor even after the onset of the recession in 1973 can be explained in terms of the degree of regulation in the domestic labor market, short-term demand for cheap labor, and relative factor costs. We must be careful to remember, however, that in liberal societies marginal groups (women, minorities, aliens, and so on) have obtained rights over time, as a result of political struggles. Group entitlements must therefore be taken into account in any discussion of markets and regulation.

A simple way to explain the demand for foreign labor is to relate alternative combinations of productive factors to final output of goods and services. Such a relationship, or production function, is widely used to derive a firm's demand for labor.[17] The combination of factors used in the production process depends on the marginal physical product of each factor. Therefore a firm will hire foreign labor until the marginal cost of the factor (equivalent to the wage rate) is equal to the marginal revenue it produces. This is a basic principle of economic theory for profit maximization under competitive conditions.[18]

Jean-Louis Reiffers's analysis of the role of foreign labor in the

German economy, using Cobb-Douglas production functions, shows that foreign workers were less productive in the short term than citizen workers. This short-term difference between the productivity of foreign and citizen workers in Germany was explained in part by differences in training and skill levels. Such differences in the marginal productivity of foreign workers tended to disappear in the long term, however, as foreigners become more skilled. But if foreign workers were less productive than citizen workers, why did employers in Western Europe and the United States continue to hire foreign workers throughout the postwar period? Reiffers found that hiring foreign workers was the best way for the firm to achieve desired levels of production during periods when other productive factors, namely citizen labor and new (capital-intensive) technologies, were in short supply.[19] Like Kindleberger's study, however, Reiffers's analysis was carried out prior to the recession of 1973. Therefore it tells us little about the demand for foreign labor during periods of recession.

Estimating the demand for foreign labor over a short period of time in one country, as Reiffers did for Germany from 1958 to 1968, does not help us to answer the broader comparative questions posed in this book. The reason is that other factors affecting the demand for foreign labor, such as changes in market conditions and relative factor costs, are highly variable across time and across countries. These are exogenous factors that cannot be incorporated easily into a long-term comparative analysis. Nonetheless, the production function offers a number of insights and can help us make some generalizations with respect to the use of foreign labor in relatively open industrial economies, even if, as I shall argue, it falls short of providing a fully satisfactory explanation. Since costs and the marginal productivity of productive factors are constantly changing, firms must be aware of the utility of foreign labor to minimize production costs. This consideration is even more important during periods of rapid economic change. Moreover, the implications of the firm's choice of factors will affect an industry's ability to compete in international markets. One fear of governments is that if a firm chooses to use cheap foreign labor rather than a capital-intensive technology or more highly skilled citizen labor, the strategic position of the industry (and comparative advantage) may be lost in the long run. Whether this fear is justified depends upon the role of foreign labor in industrial development.[20]

Because the use of foreign labor can affect comparative advantage, governments have an additional incentive to regulate immigration.

But considerations of comparative advantage notwithstanding, under competitive conditions the major problem for the *firm* is to choose the most efficient combination of productive factors to maximize profits. In economies where the state is a major player and conditions of competition do not always obtain, the choice of productive factors and their contribution to the final product may be as dependent on policy and the regulatory environment as upon profit maximization.[21]

At the level of the firm the use of foreign labor is easy enough to understand: every firm must compare the possibilities for purchasing factors with its production possibilities. This process is complicated when, because of regulation or shortage of a particular factor, the firm cannot fulfill its productive potential. Prior to 1967, the production possibilities of European firms were constrained by a shortage of citizen labor. In some countries government and business cooperated to recruit foreign workers; employers were thus able to solve their problems as governments helped them find new sources of cheap labor abroad. In effect, national labor markets were restructured by the state to create conditions favorable to continued economic growth.

A market model can help us understand the impact of foreign labor on national labor markets: (1) a drop in the price of labor means that more of that factor will be used in the production process, even if the level of output remains unchanged; (2) if the price of output changes after a decline in production costs, the firm will increase profits by expanding output. A drop in the cost of labor due to an influx of cheap foreign labor will in the long run cause the quantity of labor demanded to increase, because of increases in the (value) marginal product of labor (VMP_L), and because of increases in output. This process can be illustrated in a standard long-run demand curve for labor with a decrease in the price of labor (see Figure 5.1). In this model foreign labor lowers the price of labor in general and increases the elasticity of labor supply. With a shift in the supply curve from S_1 to S_2, wages will decline and the quantity of labor demanded will increase from L_1 to L_2.

As for the substitution of capital for labor, microeconomic theory tells us that increased use of labor as an input in the production process does not necessarily imply a decreased demand for capital, because increases in output may also require additional capital. The substitution effect reduces the amount of capital demanded, but the scale effect increases it. Predicting which effect is more powerful is

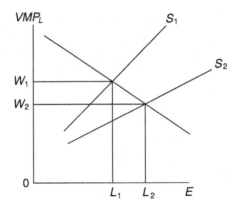

Figure 5.1. Long-run demand curve for labor

difficult, and it requires detailed knowledge of the cost and productive characteristics of each factor for the firm in the long run. Likewise, the substitutability of citizen and foreign labor depends in part on wage differentials and the productive characteristics of the two groups, which are constantly changing, in part as a result of the extension of civil and social rights to aliens (see chapter 8). The strengthening of legal and cultural protections for aliens makes it exceedingly difficult to generalize about the production characteristics of foreign workers. There is no constant elasticity of substitution between the two factors. Consequently, our ability to test hypotheses concerning the impact of immigration (and immigration policy) on labor markets is limited (1) by the paucity of wage data for foreign workers, making it difficult to estimate the cost of this factor, and (2) by limited knowledge of the skill levels and qualifications of foreign workers.[22]

Problems with the liberal economic argument arise with regard to some of the assumptions that underlie the market model. It is assumed that wages are flexible and labor is homogeneous—important assumptions that limit the usefulness of microeconomic reasoning in the study of immigration. Wages in the advanced industrial democracies are "sticky." Labor markets do not operate in a regulatory vacuum, and labor is not homogeneous with respect to its productive characteristics. This type of market analysis thus cannot resolve some of the principal policy issues that we raised earlier, namely the fear of governments (1) that foreign labor causes unemployment among citizen workers, and (2) that the use of foreign labor impedes the substitution of new technologies for labor and is damaging in the long run to the competitive position of those industries that are heavy users of foreign labor.

The absence of reliable national data on wages and marginal productivity of foreign workers makes it difficult to predict demand for foreign labor using a production function. To explain aggregate levels of immigration and the use of foreign labor, we must look at changes in policy and the regulatory environment in national labor markets, which in turn will help us to understand employers' hiring practices. With the changed context of growth after 1973, governments in Europe and the United States sought to limit immigration for political reasons, derived in the first instance from realist perceptions of the national interest (for example, immigration is no longer necessary to sustain economic growth), and in the second instance from the effects of interest group and partisan politics, which were pulling the state simultaneously in liberal and nationalist directions. Nonetheless, restrictionist policies placed severe constraints on the production possibilities of some firms. We have seen how, in some cases, employers lobbied to maintain access to foreign labor or to obtain exemptions to the restrictions on importing labor. In France these attempts to influence policy were marginally successful. In Germany governments were more adamant about enforcing the suspension of immigration. In the United States employers, particularly in the agricultural sector, simply chose to ignore restrictions on immigration, and hired undocumented workers.[23]

Immigration and Regulation of Labor Markets

To understand the changing role of foreign labor in the industrial democracies, we must be able to isolate the effects of policy change and market conditions on levels of immigration. The dual labor-market argument stresses the importance of the regulatory environment and the hiring of foreign workers to inject greater flexibility into the labor market. Certainly firms distinguish between foreign and citizen workers based on the marginal productivity of these inputs. It may be cheaper to hire a foreigner and easier to fire him or her. But it is unlikely that discrimination in employment is by itself sufficient to explain changing levels of immigration or the use of foreign labor. Foreign and citizen workers are equally vulnerable to changes in the business cycle, but neither the state nor any group of firms can use foreign workers to combat the effects of economic downturns. The reasons for this, as we shall see, are related to the rise of a new rights-based politics in the industrial democracies (see chapter 8).

Some European states tried to solve problems of unemployment by repatriating foreign workers. To evaluate the economic impact of these policies, we must look at the sectoral distribution of foreign labor before and after the suspension of immigration (this is done for the French case in chapter 7). Here I am concerned with the effect on the labor market of a change in immigration policy.[24]

My objective is to explore alternative hypotheses (liberal, statist, and Marxist) about the changing role of immigration and foreign workers in the political economy of advanced industrial democracies. My purpose is not to develop a comprehensive theory of international migration. Developing and testing such a theory would require evidence of the conditions for emigration in the sending countries. The models and hypotheses presented in this chapter seek rather to explain the ability of governments to intervene selectively in the labor market to suspend immigration and curtail the use of foreign labor. The success or failure of such intervention depends ultimately on the autonomy of the administrative state vis-à-vis international market forces and groups. We must specify the political and economic constraints that make it difficult for states to use immigrants for restructuring labor markets. One of the most important constraints is the development of rights and entitlements for marginal groups, including foreign workers.

In an industrial democracy, four labor market situations are possible: (1) high demand for labor with elastic labor supplies; (2) high demand with inelastic supplies; (3) low demand with elastic supplies; and (4) low demand with inelastic supplies. Since 1945, each labor-importing state in Europe has had to face one or more of these situations. Depending on the willingness and ability of governments to intervene in the market, they either recruited foreign workers when more labor was needed, or suspended immigration when they perceived an oversupply of labor.

Before looking at the interaction of policy and markets, one caveat is in order. Many factors prevent labor markets from reaching equilibrium. Some of these factors are political, relating to the nature of industrial democracy, such as trade union activities that keep wages high or other pricing policies that prevent wage rates from responding to changing conditions of supply and demand. Others are more technical or economic: for example, information about employment opportunities is often limited, which prevents workers from moving quickly from one area or sector to another in response to changes in market conditions. Whatever the explanation for market inefficiencies, short-run inelasticities of demand and supply have been the norm in the labor markets of the industrial democracies in the postwar period. The questions this analysis seeks to answer are: how have governments used foreign labor to deal with market inefficiencies? How has the market responded to such intervention? And how has the role of foreign labor changed in these economies?

The model presented in Figure 5.2a depicts two possible market responses to an increase in the demand for labor. In the first situation, the supply of labor is inelastic, that is S_1 equals only citizen workers. This was essentially the situation in France in the 1950s and in Germany in the 1960s.[25] If firms do not have access to additional supplies of labor, then there will be an excess demand for labor equal to L_1-L_3; wages will tend to rise from W_0 to their equilibrium value W_1. If wages rise, then excess demand will be reduced to L_2-L_3 and employment will rise by L_1-L_2. The area under the demand curve for labor (d_2) can be divided between wages and profits. In this case, with a two-factor model, the distribution of income will be changed in favor of labor: wages are equal to 0-W_1-W_1-L_2 and profits, after the shift in demand and the rise in wages, are equal to W_1-d_2-W_1. Here, the incentives for government intervention in the labor market are strong.

In Europe the 1950s and 1960s were decades of intensive economic activity with very high rates of growth at or near full employment (see Tables 5.1–5.3). Many of the economic successes of this period have been attributed to state-led strategies for growth and the efficient use of productive resources.[26] For these economies to continue to expand, it was essential to increase labor supply (from S_1 to S_2, as depicted in Figure 5.2a). Reasons for adopting a policy of recruitment of foreign labor under these conditions are compelling. Society as a whole benefited by maintaining high rates of growth.

In the second labor market situation, also depicted in Figure 5.2a, levels of immigration and the use of foreign workers increase, thus increasing aggregate labor supplies from S_1 to S_2. This was the situation in France and Switzerland in the 1950s and in Germany in the 1960s. At constant wages W_0, and with an increase in the demand for

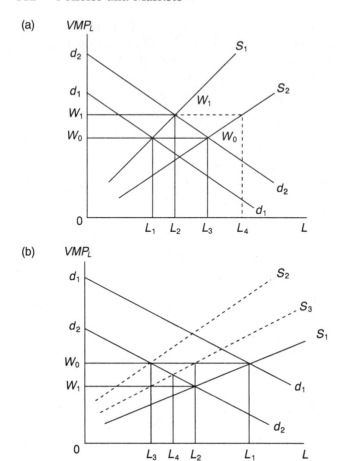

Figure 5.2. Four labor market situations

labor due to industrial expansion from d_1 to d_2, employment will rise from L_1 to L_3. Most of this increase in employment was due to an influx of foreign labor.[27] Assuming that wages remain constant, the distribution of income will be changed in favor of capital. Wage rates remain unchanged, but the wage bill increases to $0\text{-}W_0\text{-}W_0\text{-}L_3$. Returns to capital (profits) also increase to $W_0\text{-}d_2\text{-}W_0$. It is difficult to predict the magnitude of the changes in the distribution of income, for reasons outlined by Kindleberger.[28] We know, however, that conditions in the labor-importing countries were favorable for investment, especially during the 1960s. The fact that investments were increasing so dramatically during this period implies a pareto-optimal distribution of income, perhaps slightly skewed in favor of capital.

In France the events of May 1968 led to the Grenelle Agreements, which forced employers to accept much higher wage rates, increased job security for workers, provided for better working conditions, and so on.[29] In general, the rise in real wage rates throughout the advanced industrial countries in the late 1960s and early 1970s increased rigidities in the labor market, further stimulating immigration as employers turned to foreign workers as a way of cutting labor costs. This is one aspect of the dual labor-market hypothesis described by Michael Piore in various works.[30] Also during this period, there was a decline in activity rates of citizen workers, especially among the young, who were now entering the labor market at a later age; this made it more difficult to maintain the elasticity of labor supply.[31] One explanation for the delayed entry is that as educational levels increase, citizen workers are less inclined to accept menial, low-paying, and low-skill jobs.

These trends add up to increased demand for foreign labor, due less to an increase in demand for goods and services than to structural changes in the labor market. From Figure 5.2a we can see that with a rise in the wage rate to W_1, for example, the supply of foreign labor, which is highly elastic, will increase by the amount L_3-L_4. As countries became increasingly wary of dependence on foreign labor and the sociopolitical effects of immigration, employers nonetheless continued to hire foreign workers at a rapid pace. It was during this period in the late 1960s and early 1970s that many states in Europe progressively lost control of immigration and the market for foreign labor.

With the changed context of growth after 1973, a major policy problem in the industrial democracies was how to adjust to a drastic drop in the demand for goods and services. The process of adjustment meant that employment would decline, particularly in traditional manufacturing industries such as steel and automobiles. How to increase investments in the industrial sector and avoid bottlenecks in the supply of productive factors were no longer at the top of the agenda for economic policymakers in the industrial democracies. After the oil shock in 1973, the problem was how to allocate sacrifices among competing groups, each of which could lay claim to rights and entitlements that offered protection from the vagaries of the marketplace. Since traditional Keynesian policies for reestablishing growth were ineffective, increasing aggregate demand through fiscal measures was ruled out by most states. Another way of adjusting to changing demand was to allow wage rates to fall to their equilibrium level. As we know, however, this was not a viable option for most states because of social democratic arrangements and the power of trade unions to prevent a decline in real wages.[32]

The decline in overall demand, together with rigid wages and a highly elastic labor supply, created problems of unemployment throughout Western Europe, with the notable exception of Switzerland (see Table 5.3). In Figure 5.2b, we can see the effects of these economic changes on the labor market. At constant wages W_0, and with a decline in demand from d_1 to d_2, there will be an excess supply of labor (unemployment) equal to L_3-L_1. If wages were allowed to fall to their equilibrium value of W_1, then unemployment could be reduced to L_3-L_2. In any event, society as a whole loses, and the question becomes how to allocate losses among competing groups. The absence of pareto-optimal choices brings into play a variety of liberal constraints, which can prevent states from acting and prevent markets from clearing. If wage rates decline to W_1, then the distribution of income will remain relatively favorable to capital in this two product model. Wages will be equal to 0-W_1-W_1-L_2, and profits will be equal to W_1-d_2-W_1. But unions could not accept this solution because it would have meant a decline in the real income of workers. Governments also could not pursue this option because of the political risks involved. Employers, however, had an interest in keeping labor supplies elastic so as to keep pressure on wages and maximize profits.

At this point (after the 1973 crisis) governments were crucial players in the labor market. The decision was made to suspend immigration and stop the recruitment and hiring of foreign workers. We already have discussed the political reasons for this statist decision, which was taken in a situation of high unemployment among citizen workers and in the face of xenophobic reactions among the general public. The perception of the public and policymakers alike was that immigration causes unemployment, especially among low-skilled or semi-skilled workers, already hard hit by the recession.

The decision to hire foreign workers depends in part on the marginal physical product of foreign labor, compared to alternative factors of production. The evidence indicates that unemployment among foreign workers after 1973 was not significantly higher than unemployment among citizen workers (at least not until the mid to late 1980s, when second-generation immigrants were entering tight labor markets in large numbers). It would seem that employers in certain industries were continuing to use foreign labor because it had a higher marginal physical product than citizen labor. Another explanation for the continued demand for foreign workers is offered by the dual labor market hypothesis, which states that certain categories of jobs exist primarily, if not solely, for foreign workers. If governments pursue a policy of return migration or repatriation to alleviate problems of unemployment, it is unclear whether the low-skill jobs occupied by foreign workers would be filled by citizen workers or simply eliminated. Citizen workers may be unwilling to accept low-paying, difficult, and dangerous jobs; and employers may not be able to pay the wages necessary to attract them to these jobs.

The effect of immigration on employment is a hotly debated issue in the industrial democracies, as interest groups line up for or against open borders. Many of these groups, especially trade unions, have an interest in curtailing immigration, but foreign and citizen workers may share many of the same political goals, such as increasing entitlements and rights for marginal groups. The issue also has profound social and political implications in countries that have relied heavily on immigration in the past to fuel economic growth. In addition to their contribution to expanding industrial production, immigrants in Europe and the United States have contributed to the social mobility of citizen workers. While immigrant workers may have displaced some citizen workers, primarily in the low-skill jobs, the unemployment that resulted has tended to be frictional in nature. Prior to 1973 such unemployment was solved by the marketplace in relatively short periods of time, as citizen workers moved to higher-paying jobs in other sectors of the economy and often in other regions of the country (see Table 5.3). Unemployment among immigrants themselves also was rare, since they were among the more motivated members of the labor force and tended to adjust quickly to new opportunities.

Since the mid-1970s the supply of labor has tended to be greater than the capacity of industrial economies for creating jobs. The resulting high unemployment makes the utility of foreign labor less obvious to citizen workers and the state. As Figure 5.2b showed, the goal of suspending immigration was to reduce aggregate labor supplies. By suspending immigration, encouraging repatriation, and penalizing employers for hiring foreign workers (through employer sanctions), it was hoped that employment would fall from L_1 to L_3, thus creating a situation of equilibrium in the labor market. In France and Germany statist policies of suspension were accompanied by social policies for assimilating migrants who could not be induced to return.[33]

These restrictionist policies appeased trade unions because they were designed to eliminate foreign competition for low-skill jobs, and they reduced market pressures for lower wages. However, such policies are not pareto-optimal. Wages may remain constant, but the wage bill for firms increases to $0\text{-}W_0\text{-}W_0\text{-}L_3$, while returns to capital are reduced to $W_0\text{-}d_2\text{-}W_0$. In effect the suspension of immigration created more problems than it solved. For example, the hope that lowering the supply of foreign workers would lower unemployment turned out to be a false hope (see Table 5.3). It is difficult to get employers to accept political evaluations and constraints on labor supply. They are more likely to hire undocumented workers, than to accept a dramatic increase in labor costs. In addition, with wages still relatively high, few immigrants will return to their home countries and some new immigrants will enter the labor market, legally or illegally. Thus we are likely to see a surplus of foreign (and citizen) labor equivalent to $L_3\text{-}L_4$, at a wage rate of W_0. The supply curve for labor in this situation will be S_3, if policies for suspending immigration do not succeed in lowering supply to the desired level (S_2). Migrants will use every legal (and illegal) means at their disposal in order to remain in the host country until the economic situation improves, knowing that if they leave with an immigration stop in effect, they will not be allowed to reenter the country.

Hence immigration tends to become more permanent after an immigration stop is imposed, and the foreign population is likely to increase. As more migrants decide to stay, family immigration will inevitably rise. Since the foreign worker cannot return home to visit his (or her) family, family reunification in the receiving country is more desirable. The arrival of family members will increase the supply of foreign labor even more, as spouses, children, and other relatives enter the labor market. This is precisely what happened in Germany and France. At first, German and French authorities were surprised by the new wave of immigration, and they attempted to stop family members from entering the labor market. The problems of family and refugee migrations have plagued policymakers in Europe since the suspension of immigration. In Europe and the United States, illegal immigration is one of the unintended consequences of restricting worker migration.[34] This is the result of employers continuing to use foreign labor, either because they cannot hire citizen workers for certain jobs, as we have seen, or because using foreign labor is an efficient way of cutting costs, even during a recession.

Regulation of labor markets is difficult in an industrial democracy. The effectiveness of immigration policy in each of the labor market situations described above depends to some extent on state-society relations. In a neocorporatist setting where groups are highly organized and where the process of consensus-building is institutionalized, employers may be less likely to circumvent regulations for controlling worker migration. In a unitary political system such as France, where the state has a tradition of autonomy and where the administrative elite has a strong influence in the policymaking process, employers may also be less likely to hire undocumented aliens. In a pluralist setting such as the United States, firm-level decisions are less dependent on the state; but rights and entitlements have been extended to protect many marginal groups, including foreigners, and this legislation has impeded statist or restrictionist policies. Yet despite these important differences in state-society relations in each of our three cases (France, Germany, and the United States), outcomes have tended to be liberal. Straightforward market and institutional analyses (along the familiar pluralist-corporatist continuum) cannot account for the similarity in outcomes. We must look to the rise of rights-based liberalism in all of these industrial democracies for an explanation of the convergence of policy outputs and outcomes.

Because of existing inequalities in the international system, migrant workers always will be available for hire in the wealthier industrial societies. How this resource is used and whether it is considered an asset or a liability depends on the political process, the nature of the political system, and how states make and implement immigration policy. Any discussion of policy and process must recognize, however, the importance of rights and liberal constraints on political and economic actors. Policymakers, politicians, employers, workers, and others in the industrial democracies are subject to the norms and principles of liberal constitutional regimes. Markets never operate in a cultural or institutional void.

Markets, Groups, and the Policy Process

In a democratic political system the outcome of public policy depends on the ability of government to achieve consensus among competing groups, each of which may have a claim to rights and entitlements.

To understand immigration and the role of foreign labor in the industrial democracies, we must therefore look at the activities of groups that have the power to change market and policy outcomes.[35] The nature of competition between groups and individuals and the rules governing the competition depend on the history of political-economic conflict in society, the struggle over civil, social, and political rights, and institutions that have been created to defuse conflict and protect the rights of marginal groups. The policymaking process in advanced industrial democracies is thus a reflection of the history of distributional conflicts and struggles over rights in society; whereas the effectiveness of policy is a measure of the strength and autonomy of the state and its ability to manipulate or change social and market conditions to achieve a specific outcome.

Employers, workers, and the state all have an interest in immigration policy. Workers, represented by their trade unions, want to protect wages and working conditions, so they will try to control the number of foreign workers and the conditions under which these workers will be employed. Employers need foreign labor when it becomes difficult or impossible to recruit citizen workers for menial jobs. The question arises, therefore, to what extent can the government design and implement immigration policies that either incorporate the demands of interest groups (respecting rights and entitlements), bypass them in favor of some higher national interest, or simply allow the market to solve (or aggravate) the problem?[36]

The effectiveness of immigration policy is a measure of the autonomy of the state, which consists in its ability to prevent employers from hiring undocumented workers, and to change the structure of the labor market.[37] The smaller the gap between policy outputs and outcomes, the greater the ability of the state to control the hiring practices of employers and change market outcomes.[38] At least three factors can affect the making of immigration policy: (1) group pressures, which could take the form of adversarial legal actions to protect rights and entitlements or lobbying on the part of employers to maintain access to supplies of cheap foreign labor; (2) public opinion, which may be expressed through social unrest in the form of riots and collective or individual violence against foreigners and immigrants, or through traditional institutions such as political parties; and (3) the relatively independent assessment by policymakers of the need for immigration. The influence of each of these factors will depend on institutional arrangements. For example, the influence of interest groups depends on their access to a variety of institutions, ranging from traditional institutions such as parties, legislatures, courts, and bureaucracies, to neocorporatist institutions such as the CES in France or the Beirat (standing advisory councils) in Germany.

Figure 5.3 represents a political-economic model of the policymaking process in industrial democracies. The three factors that influence policy outcomes are depicted in this model: group politics (including a panoply of interests, rights, and entitlements), public opinion, and the relatively autonomous actions of the state. Note that there are two ways in which groups can affect policy outcomes: either through institutional channels (voting, lobbying, legal action), or through direct action. Workers may organize demonstrations or strikes in opposition to the hiring of foreign workers; employers may go directly to

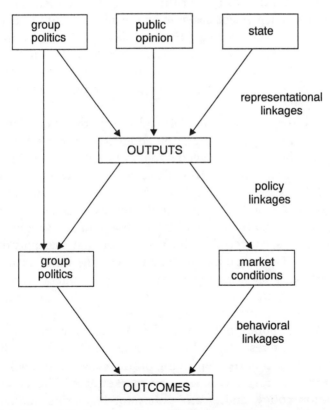

Figure 5.3. The political-economic model of the policymaking process

the black market for labor and hire undocumented workers rather than lobby the government to increase levels of immigration.

Public opinion can influence immigration policy through a wide variety of institutional mechanisms. In Europe in the 1980s extreme right-wing parties have emerged (or reemerged) and formed new constituencies organized primarily around the issues of immigration and race. These are the National Front parties in Britain and France and the Republican Party in Germany. In Switzerland popular initiatives against immigration in the early 1970s were organised into an ad hoc group calling itself the National Action against the Over-Foreignisation of People and Country *(Überfremdung)*. The much heralded reactions of the French Communist party and the CGT to the rent strikes in Paris in 1975, as well as the Brixton riots in London, are examples of outbursts of xenophobia that directly influenced the making of immigration policy.

Another factor that can affect the making of immigration policy is the relatively independent decision by the government (in its bureaucratic or administrative guise) to encourage or discourage immigration (see Figure 5.3). For example, just after World War II the French economic planners decided to recruit immigrant workers. The decision was based on projections of demographic trends and future demand for labor.

These are some of the sociopolitical factors that can affect policy outputs. The history of immigration policy (see chapters 3–4) showed that each of these factors played a role in bringing about the suspension of immigration in the 1970s. The economic downturn in Western Europe after the oil shock led to the first real rise in unemployment in the postwar period. This sent trade unions scrambling to protect jobs and wages, and foreign workers were among the first casualties. Some employers, conversely, felt a need to maintain a supply of cheap foreign labor. They therefore lobbied to keep the immigration valve at least partially open. At the same time, governments came under increasing pressure from public opinion to stop immigration and protect the jobs of citizen workers from foreign competition.

Even though policy outputs in the area of immigration may be similar in certain respects, policy outcomes can be radically different from country to country, depending on the capacity and willingness of governments to intervene in the marketplace. The outcome of immigration policy, and of any policy for regulating markets, is a political choice that reflects fundamental assumptions about the scope and role of government in the lives of individuals and individual firms.

Conclusion: The Formal Argument

The liberal argument suggests that immigration (I) and foreign employment (E) are a function of market conditions X_1, group politics X_2, and state policy X_3. In a liberal regime, neither market conditions nor policy alone will determine levels of immigration and the use of foreign labor. Interest group politics, which in the postwar period has been bound up with the politics of civil rights and entitlements, is a determinative factor. Yet one of these political and economic factors will have a greater impact than the other, depending on the power of the state to control and structure markets and on the extent of rights-based politics. What is of primary interest is the weight of each of these factors for explaining levels of immigration and foreign employment. The impact of rights-based politics on immigration is more difficult to measure and incorporate into the formal argument. As we shall see, the expansion of rights and citizenship only can be understood in comparative and historical terms. Nevertheless, it is necessary to look carefully at patterns of institutional and cultural development, as well as changes in policy and markets, to understand immigration and the changing role of foreign labor in the industrial democracies.

The liberal argument can be expressed as follows:

$$I_t = a + b_1 X_{1t} + b_2 X_{2t} + b_3 X_{3t} + u_t.$$

The same argument can be used to explain the use of foreign labor:

$$E_t = a + b_1 X_{1t} + b_2 X_{2t} + b_3 X_{3t} + u_t.$$

Note that these time-series models allow us to examine the changes in immigration and foreign employment over time. X_{1t} represents market conditions (supply and demand). X_{2t} represents group politics, ranging from employers and trade unions to human and civil rights groups. This concept obviously is more difficult to measure, in variable terms. Finally, X_{3t} represents the concept of state policy (for example, recruitment or suspension of immigration).

These additive models capture the effects of political and economic conditions on immigration and foreign employment over time. Again,

I stress the difficulty of incorporating (and measuring) the concept of rights-based politics. Before we look at some of the assumptions underlying these models and at the hypothesized direction and magnitude of the relationships, we must make one more important transformation. To improve the testing of the effects of political and policy change on immigration and foreign employment, we must introduce interactive terms into the equations. In this case the model for immigration would be

$$I_t = b_0 + b_1 X_{1t} + b_2 X_{2t} + b_3 Z_{1t} + u_t$$

where $Z_{1t} = X_{2t} X_{3t}$. This model assumes that the effects of group politics are dependent on the type of immigration policy in effect (for example, recruitment or suspension). The model for foreign employment also can be rewritten as

$$E_t = b_0 + b_1 X_{1t} + b_2 X_{2t} + b_3 Z_{2t} + u_t$$

where $Z_{2t} = X_{2t} X_{3t}$. Here, the assumption is the same with respect to the interaction of state policy and group politics. Market effects are assumed to be the same irrespective of policy (see the next chapter).

We can write the immigration and foreign employment functions for periods of expansive policy (recruitment in Europe, roughly 1946 to 1973) as follows:

$$I_t(E_t) = b_0 + b_1 X_{1t} + (b_2 + b_3) X_{2t} + u_t.$$

For periods of restriction (suspension), the immigration and foreign employment functions are

$$I_t(E_t) = b_0 + b_1 X_{1t} + b_2 X_{2t} + u_t.$$

Examining the direction and the magnitude of the relationships between immigration, market conditions, group politics, and policy change will allow us to explore more systematically the liberal argument (and by extension the statist and Marxist arguments as well).

I shall examine these arguments using French aggregate and sectoral data, to learn about the use of foreign labor in various economic sectors and thereby explain the role of foreign labor in the process of industrial change. What is of interest is how market changes, group politics, and policy have affected the use of foreign labor across sectors.

Foreign labor is a key factor in the process of industrial adjustment.

If it can be controlled by the state, then it may be possible for the state to structure or restructure the labor market according to whatever is politically or economically expedient. However, unlike capital markets or other markets for inanimate commodities, the labor market is more difficult to control and more volatile politically. The French, German, and Swiss states attempted to use foreign labor to achieve national goals. From the beginning of the postwar period until the late 1960s, immigrant workers were important actors in the politics of growth in Western Europe. By stopping immigration in the early 1970s and encouraging foreign workers to return to their countries of origin, it was hoped that unemployment among citizen workers could be reduced. Yet these policies were ineffective and many employers continued to use foreign labor. Governments were then confronted with a new politics of citizenship and civil rights.

The political-economic model of policymaking and the arguments outlined here have important implications for the nature of state-society relations in the advanced industrial democracies, for the capacity of states in these countries to intervene in the marketplace, and for distributional conflicts and struggles over rights that arise as a result of rapid economic change. If market forces play a larger role than the state in determining the allocation of foreign labor, then the distributional conflicts that arise over immigration and foreign employment may be more severe, and the state will come under increasing pressure to act. At the same time democratic states face many cultural and legal constraints, which can and do prevent them from intervening in the labor market.

6 ◆ Immigration and the French State

> *The essential French view . . . is that the effective conduct of a nation's economic life must depend on the concentration of power in the hands of a small number of exceptionally able people, exercising foresight and judgement of a kind not possessed by the average successful man of business.*
> —ANDREW SHONFIELD, *Modern Capitalism*

An evaluation of the strength and autonomy of the democratic state will help clarify some of the difficulties of implementing immigration policy. Specifically, we must be able to determine how effectively the state, as a bureaucratic and administrative power, can intervene in the marketplace to restrict immigration. Here I am less concerned with policymaking and group politics than with problems of policy implementation and the administrative capacity of the state. To explain why it is so difficult for democratic states to regulate immigration, it is necessary to have an adequate understanding not only of the history of immigration policy (and the workings of labor markets), but of the capacity of states to implement policy. State capacity in turn is contingent upon the nature of state-society relations and institutional arrangements.

When we link the study of state capacity with the study of immigration, we gain insights into theories of the democratic state as well as the difficulties that governments face in regulating migrant flows.[1] From the standpoint of theories of the state, immigration is an interesting problem because of the salience of this policy issue in the industrial democracies, particularly in postwar Europe and the United States, and because of the perceived threat to the sovereignty and autonomy of the state that uncontrolled migration represents.[2]

124

At a time of growing public demands to restrict immigration economic growth surged in Western Europe in the 1980s, creating jobs and making European labor markets more attractive to Third World migrants. This chapter discusses the problems of policy implementation and examines the extent to which immigration is a function of economic conditions, tied to the supply of and the demand for labor in France. The analysis sheds light on the political and economic determinants of immigration and on the possibility of using foreign workers as shock absorbers in an industrial democracy. Before presenting the French data, I shall review briefly some of the literature on theories of the democratic state, which has helped to shape our thinking about comparative public policy and political economy.

The State and Public Policy

A new literature in political science has attempted to reassess the role of the democratic state, in its bureaucratic and administrative guise, in areas ranging from political economy and political development to policymaking.[3] The reasons for the rather sudden rediscovery of the state remain somewhat obscure. The new emphasis seems to be linked to a resurgent interest in institutions and the belief that administrative and procedural arrangements can make a big difference in policy outcomes. Some scholars have gone so far as to attribute volition to the state, using such terms as state actors or actions and characterizing states as strong or weak.[4] Neoinstitutionalist arguments stand in contrast to models of politics and the policy process that seek to explain policy outcomes in pluralist terms, usually with a focus on group politics. For example, one of the principal explanations for the poor performance of democratic governments in the 1970s was that group conflict had got out of control, leading to overloaded government and a "crisis of democracy."[5] Mancur Olson, James Buchanan, and other economists placed the pluralist argument in a microeconomic framework by demonstrating how group activity (the accretion of rights and entitlements) can be detrimental to economic performance.[6] The thrust of these essentially pluralist arguments is that the state is subject to "capture" by groups that will push for policies that support the interests of their members, but are not necessarily in the national interest. For Olson this process can be detrimental to economic performance, whereas for Buchanan and other public-choice theorists such activities are the "logical foundations of constitutional democracy." The theoretical battle lines over the issue of the state and its relationship to society appear to have been drawn around the issues of public policy and the (largely economic) performance of government. The pluralist school argues for the importance of organized interests in determining policy outcomes, while the institutionalist school prefers to restore some balance to the analysis by "bringing the state back in."

My argument is that we must distinguish between state autonomy and strength. Some theorists have alluded to this distinction, but few have pursued it with any vigor.[7] By *autonomy* I mean the ability of governments to make or formulate policies without being subject to excessive demands of special interests.[8] One could conceive of any number of institutional arrangements that might facilitate state autonomy, ranging from strong party government and parliamentary supremacy, as in Britain, to a strong administrative state that is detached from the vagaries of electoral politics, as has been the case in France. Nevertheless, as any student of politics and policymaking should know, the ability to formulate policy is only half the game, at best. The real test of state strength (or capacity) comes at the level of policy implementation. Accordingly, *state strength* can be defined as the ability of governments to enforce policy decisions—to effect the desired change in the behavior of those groups or individuals that are the targets of regulation. This ability can be measured in terms of the gap that exists between policy outputs and outcomes (see Figure 5.3 above). In measuring state capacity in the area of immigration, our question must be: to what extent do the effects of immigration policy approximate the objectives of policy?

Obviously, the strength and autonomy of democratic states will vary across policy areas and over time. The best (and perhaps the only) way to assess the relative importance of political, social, and economic factors in explaining policy outcomes is to choose a case and examine the competing hypotheses. The French state is interesting because it is generally viewed as strong and autonomous, free to formulate policies in the national interest and having the administrative capacity for implementing those policies, even in the face of social opposition and adverse market conditions. Whether or not this is an accurate depiction of the French state is debatable. A number of studies question this conventional, étatiste view of French politics.[9]

Much of the success of the French state in managing economic resources and planning industrial production (during the Fourth Republic) has been attributed to a forward-looking civil service. The list of scholars who give credit to the French state for the economic successes of the 1950s and 1960s is quite long. Charles Kindleberger and Andrew Shonfield point to the ability of the planners to force industrialists to sacrifice some short-term gains for long-term economic growth and modernization.[10] They stress the importance of a competent civil service with a high degree of independence from group politics. Andrew Shonfield refers to "a conspiracy to plan" in which big business is pressured into cooperating with planners. John Zysman points to the strength and autonomy of the French state in the area of finance and industrial policy.[11]

When compared with other democratic states, the French state appears much stronger in view of the powerful instruments that were available to it, such as (in the Fourth and part of the Fifth Republic) a national planning agency, highly centralized control of banking and finance, and well-developed and centralized police organizations. More recently, one of these powerful institutions—the national planning agency or CGP—has declined precipitously.[12] The autonomy of the French state in the area of economic policy also has been weakened by the ongoing process of European economic integration.

My view of the problem of policy implementation is depicted in Figure 6.1. This is a two-stage process, where outputs are defined at the level of policy formulation and outcomes are *in part* the result of policy implementation. State autonomy (or lack thereof) will be most evident at the formulation stage, where groups and other actors in the political process have the chance to influence policy choice through normal institutional channels. State strength (or lack thereof) will be manifest at the implementation stage, where various groups and individuals who are the targets of regulation have the option of compliance or resistance. Here two factors mediate between policy outputs and outcomes in relatively open democratic political systems.

Public policy is always designed to affect the behavior of groups in society, be they large or small. Mancur Olson demonstrated that the size of the group is a crucial factor in determining outcomes.[13] I would add that not only is the size of the group important, but also the nature of the actors within the group. Migrants are a special group with political and economic characteristics that make them difficult targets of regulation. Although migrants are among the most vulnerable individuals in liberal societies, they are also prototypical eco-

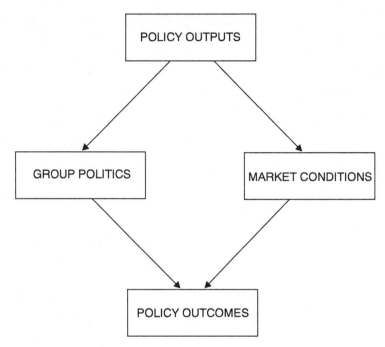

Figure 6.1. The political-economic model of policy implementation

nomic actors, capable of pursuing their interests, which usually include a desire to remain and work in the host country. For these and other reasons, migrants occupy a special position in the labor markets of the industrial democracies that makes them difficult targets for regulation. For many employers they represent an "irreplaceable" source of cheap labor, while for many trade unionists they are viewed as unwanted and unnecessary competition.

The objective of public policy is to restructure markets by changing the behavior of groups in the marketplace. According to Figure 6.1, however, the possibility of unintended consequences is great, especially in open, democratic societies where groups may choose to resist or circumvent regulation in a legal, quasi-legal, or illegal fashion. If policies are to achieve their objectives, the potentially distorting influence of intervening factors must be minimized. It is of course conceivable that market conditions and group activities could help rather than hinder the state in its efforts to implement policy.[14] Here I define politics and economics in terms of group politics and market condtions. The two factors are not wholly independent, because groups influence market conditions and vice-versa (see figures 5.3 and 6.1).[15] However, the principal distinction between group politics and market conditions is that the latter are likely to be more sensitive to changes in the international economy. The sensitivity of domestic economies to trade and other aspects of international markets associated with interdependence is certainly one of the more severe constraints on the democractic state.[16] Market conditions are more likely than group activities to have an independent effect on outcomes, because markets are less sensitive to policy change. Many other factors such as the international economic climate can affect national market conditions. Specific groups are more likely to alter their behavior in the short term to adjust to changes in policy. Hence the effect of policy and group politics on outcomes will be interactive, whereas market conditions are more likely to have an independent effect on outcomes. Policy only affects markets at the margins in most areas of a mixed economy. Often, however, this marginal influence is important, and the degree of marginality must be defined.

Consideration of the intervening effects of group politics and market conditions on outcomes provides tools to test the effectiveness of public policy and get a better picture of the strength of the state. We cannot simply assume that a state that appears strong and autonomous will have an effective policy in which outputs will approximate outcomes. In liberal political systems it is difficult to force compliance with policies that are detrimental to the interests of well-organized groups, such as employers, who occupy a privileged position vis-à-vis the state. Centralized authority in a unitary state does not necessarily give that state an advantage over another (federal) state in policymaking. Nor does the absence or presence of strong interest groups make it easier for the state to implement policy. The literature on interest groups and their effect on policy in the industrial democracies is contradictory. The pluralists (and free-market economists) tell us that highly organized group politics is detrimental to economic performance and to the ability of the state to respond to economic change.[17] According to corporatist literature, in contrast, strong (peak) interest groups can facilitate policy formulation and implementation, thereby making it easier for states to respond to economic change.[18] France has been described as a country with a strong state and weak interest groups; that is, its major interest groups, especially trade unions, wield less power than similar groups in the other industrial democracies.[19] But it is misleading to infer that a strong state and weak groups facilitate policymaking, especially if the state is incapable of implementing policy in the face of social opposition and adverse economic conditions. Likewise, it is dangerous to infer that a change in outputs is concurrent with a change in outcomes; that is, that the actions of the state were responsible for the outcomes—in this case raising or lowering immigration and foreign employment.

Immigration and State Autonomy

Few policy issues have so challenged the autonomy of the state and so incited the passions of political groups and public opinion in the postwar period as immigration. The reason it has become so controversial is because of the rapid shift in economic conditions that occurred after the oil shock of the mid 1970s, and because of the tight labor markets of the 1980s, particularly among low-skilled workers. Governments in most of the labor-importing countries reacted to these poor economic conditions and the growing hostility of many groups toward foreigners by attempting to stop or at least curtail immigration. Yet labor markets in general and the market for foreign labor in particular have been extremely difficult to control.

It proved difficult to stimulate aggregate demand after 1973 in order to maintain full employment. Most of the labor-importing countries adopted restrictionist policies in the 1970s as a way of easing tension in the labor market and heading off xenophobic political movements (the United States is the exception). However, far from solving the problems of unemployment and reducing immigration, these policies further politicized the issue as well as contributing to increases in the foreign population, at least in the short and medium term.

The positions of workers and employers varied across countries and over time. But, by and large, they have followed their market interests. Major interest groups in the industrial democracies have a stake not only in the formulation of immigration and labor market policy, but in the implementation of policy as well. Immigrants have been caught up in a struggle among groups over the allocation of the pains of sacrifice in periods of low growth—a struggle that extends beyond formulation to the implementation stage of the policy process. Given this bitter and highly divisive struggle, especially in Western Europe, the position of the state was crucial. Yet the liberal nature of these regimes countered the effective use of a narrow conception of the national interest.

Marxist theorists of immigration argue that foreign labor is necessary for the survival of advanced capitalism. If this argument is correct, it is not surprising that employers would do everything possible to maintain migrant flows, which contribute to the "industrial reserve army." Manuel Castells argued that market conditions are really unimportant in determining levels of immigration and foreign employment, because employers always will be eager to hire non-unionized and highly exploitable foreign workers rather than citizen workers. According to Castells, the addiction of many employers to cheap foreign labor is the reason that levels of immigration (and foreign employment) remained at historically high levels, even after the onset of the recession after the first oil shock in 1973.

In a different version of this argument Michael Piore contends that foreign labor introduces an element of flexibility in employment practices and duality in the labor market. He points out that it is less risky (and cheaper) for employers to hire foreigners because they can be more easily laid off in periods of low demand, and it may not be necessary for the employer to contribute to social security or other benefits for foreign workers. Thus foreign workers are important productive factors in an uncertain economic climate. What then should be the position of the state (or the government) with respect to immigration and the employment of foreigners?

In the pluralist view, the state must mediate between the demands of workers, employers, and immigrant groups, while trying to respond to increased pressure from public opinion to control immigration. From a statist (and realist) perspective, the state should use immigration to pursue national economic or demographic objectives. Immigration should be seen as a source of human capital and an important factor of production that can be used for regulating labor supply and economic growth. In all of the labor-importing countries, immigration has become an important policy issue and source of conflict. Yet it remains unclear whether immigration obeys some structural logic, as Marxist arguments imply, whether it can be reduced to questions of national interest, as the statist/realist theories suggest, or whether it is the result of a more subtle interaction of policy, markets, and rights.

My objective is to explore these arguments and the hypotheses that flow from them. By examining the effects of policy change, group activities, and market conditions on immigration and foreign employment, we get a clearer picture of the limits of politics and markets, and of the forces that influence levels of immigration. As I stated earlier, this analysis *cannot* provide a complete explanation of immigration or a definitive test of theories of the state. A complete model of immigration must include push as well as pull factors; and there is *no* definitive test of theories of the state. We must continue to build our knowledge of specific cases and policy areas in the hope that it will help us make informed judgments about the governing capacity of liberal democratic states.

The French Case

France is generally considered to have a strong state, capable of pursuing its national interest, and the country has a long and varied history of immigration. Used as a case study, it will allow us to explore and possibly impugn hypotheses derived from theories of migration. It should be kept in mind, however, that no state with relatively open borders, where tourists and other travelers are allowed to cross frontiers with some degree of freedom and where foreigners are protected from the arbitary powers of the state by constitutional provisions of due process and the like, can be expected to control completely the comings and goings of all foreign nationals. What is important in this analysis is the extent to which the state is capable of directly influencing migration flows through policy.

Policy effectiveness is taken as a measure of state capacity. Like other labor-importing states in Western Europe, France chose to suspend immigration in the mid-1970s. This decision came after a long period of public and private recruitment of foreign labor, which began almost immediately after World War II (see chapter 3). After the oil shock in 1973 and the recessions that followed, public pressure to suspend all forms of migration intensified (see chapter 4); hence policy shifted rather abruptly from relatively open borders to a suspension of immigration in 1974. Efforts to regulate immigration more closely actually began several years earlier with various decrees for tightening recruitment and admitting foreign workers to the work force.

A quick glance at changes in levels of immigration and foreign employment in postwar France, especially during the crucial period of the 1970s, indicates a decline and leveling off of the immigrant population and a gradual decline in levels of foreign employment (see figures 4.2 and 4.3). Total immigration, which is composed of several different flows, was highest during the five years (1968—1973) leading up to the suspension of immigration in 1974. The average annual rate of immigration was highest for seasonal and permanent workers (137 and 133 thousand annually respectively), while family immigration increased significantly, up to 70.5 thousand per year compared with 36.7 for the previous period. After 1974 we saw a substantial decline in immigration among workers, while seasonal and family migration remained relatively high. Presumably the state would have had greater control over resident alien workers, who must obtain work permits to remain in the country, than over family migrants, whose arrival and settlement was driven more by humanitarian than economic motives. Nonetheless, we can see that immigration to France did not cease after the policy of suspension was adopted in 1974.

Data on the foreign worker population, based on estimates from Ministry of Labor surveys, show a gradual decline in the foreign work force after 1973, but nothing dramatic appears to have happened in the market for foreign labor. The national labor market, however, deteriorated dramatically after 1973–74. (The ratio of excess supply of labor over excess demand, as measured by the Agence Nationale pour L'Emploi, went from roughly 2 in 1973 to 51 in 1986!) The analysis which follows seeks to determine what part of the variation in levels of immigration and foreign employment can be accounted for by policy as opposed to changes in labor market conditions. For this a simple examination of time-series data is not sufficient. We cannot, for example, begin to understand the relationship between policy outputs and outcomes without sophisticated analysis. To understand the effectiveness of immigration policy, we must be able to control for the intervening effects of group politics and economic conditions. We cannot simply assume that changes in levels of immigration and foreign employment result from policy shifts.

Two hypotheses flow from these arguments:

(1) Immigration and foreign employment are conjunctural phenomena related to the business cycle; market conditions rather than policy determine the rate of entry and employment of foreigners.

(2) The state is administratively and politically strong enough to override market influences and prevent employers from appealing directly to immigrants; policy rather than market conditions establishes the terms of recruitment and placement of immigrants.

Before testing these hypotheses, it is important to emphasize the complexity of immigration. Migrant flows are composed of perma-

nent (or resident alien) workers, family members, and seasonal workers, as well as refugees. Each category of immigration has its own
dynamic, but all forms of migration in postwar France (with the
partial exception of refugees, discussed in chapter 8) are subject to
similar political and economic conditions. But a foreign worker seeking a permanent job may respond to these conditions in a different
manner than an individual seeking temporary or seasonal employment, or the spouse (or child) of a worker who has decided to settle
permanently in the host country.

Despite the complexity and diversity of migration, French governments expected *inflows* of migrants as well as *stocks* of foreign workers and population to decline after the suspension of immigration.
The fact that migration is so complex and that it is such an intractable
policy issue makes it, in one sense, a weak test of the strength and
autonomy of democratic states. Nevertheless, immigrants (or resident
aliens) are generally viewed (incorrectly) as weak actors, with few
political rights and little power to influence policy. Moreover, the
history of the French state and the relative autonomy of administrative elites (vis-à-vis groups such as employers) leads one to assume
that the state has the upper hand in dealing with an intractable
problem like immigration. This expectation is problematic, as I
pointed out above.[20] Yet during the Fourth and early years of the Fifth
Republic the state was able to cajole or force employers into accepting
controversial economic policies. It remains unclear to what extent
the power of the administrative state in France has declined since the
beginning of the Fifth Republic. Yet despite Jacobin, statist, and administrative approaches to immigration, French governments of the
right and the left have had difficulty regulating immigration. How
can we explain this failure?

The Marxist, Statist, and Liberal Arguments

The proposition to be tested is that immigration and the employment
of foreign workers are a function of labor market conditions,
employers' hiring practices (as measured by the legalization rate, *taux
de régularisation*), and policy change. The models bring together the
concepts of policy, process, and markets presented in chapters 3, 4,
and 5. They show how policy and markets interact to influence levels
of immigration and the employment of foreign workers. These time-
series models cannot capture all of the subtleties of the Marxist,

statist, and liberal arguments, but the analysis will give us more insight into the difficulties of regulating immigration in a liberal polity.

For immigration (inflows) the model can be written as

$$I_t = a + b_1 lnMar_{t-1} + b_2 lnCon_{t-1} + b_3 Pol_{t-1} + u_t$$

and for levels of employment of foreign workers (stocks) as

$$E_t = a + b_1 lnMar_{t-1} + b_2 lnCon_{t-1} + b_3 Pol_{t-1} + u_t$$

where *lnMar* is a measure of market conditions, *lnCon* is a measure of legalization rates, and *Pol* is a measure of policy change. These two models capture the (additive) effects of economic and political change on immigration and the employment of foreign workers. They allow us to explore the hypotheses presented above. The time-series results tell us whether the French state is as strong as outward appearances would indicate. The analysis helps us to determine whether immigration in postwar France is a conjunctural phenomenon linked to the business cycle, or whether it is possible for the state to use immigration to regulate labor markets, lower unemployment, and keep wages low but profits high.

Measures of the endogenous variables are reasonably straightforward. Immigration flows (entries) can be divided into four categories: permanent worker immigration (I_{1t}), seasonal worker immigration (I_{2t}), family immigration (I_{3t}), and total immigration (I_{4t}). The French data do have a number of idiosyncracies: most important, the Algerians and certain West African nationalities are not included in the immigration statistics.[21] The other main endogenous variable, foreign employment (E_t), is more difficult to measure. The measure requires some rather sophisticated manipulation of Ministry of Labor survey data on foreign employment, together with estimates of departures based on data from the Ministry of the Interior.[22] Hence the measure of immigrant stocks, necessarily based on estimates, is less reliable than the entry data.

The exogenous variables measuring market conditions (*lnMar*), the legalization rate (*lnCon*), and policy change (*Pol*) are relatively straightforward measures that will allow us to interpret the effects of political, social, and economic conditions on outcomes (immigration and foreign employment). The market variable is a ratio measuring excess labor supply over excess demand. It is taken from statistics of the National Employment Agency[23] and gives a good picture of economic conditions as reflected in the labor market. The political/regulation variable is a measure of the control of employers (or else of the state) over the migratory process. It is simply a ratio of the number of migrants brought into the country by employers over the number brought in through the administrative procedures of the ONI. Finally, the system level policy variable is a dichotomous dummy variable measuring policy change. It is equal to 1 for periods of recruitment and 0 for periods of suspension.[24] Although some may object to this simplification of policy change, it is reasonable to dichotomize the two policy periods because there was a clear policy shift in 1973–74 from recruitment to suspension of worker migration. The attempt to restrict other forms of migration (family, seasonal, and eventually refugee) is less clear-cut; but it is nonetheless interesting to look at the effects of policy change on these (more or less artificial) categories. A more subtle analysis of the politics of rights and citizenship and their effects on immigration is done in chapter 8.

The two equations above can be used as tests of the effectiveness of immigration policy and of the administrative capacity of the state. To capture the complexity of the relationship between policy outputs and outcomes (as depicted in figures 5.3 and 6.1) we must transform both equations from simple additive models into interactive models. Specifically, we must be able to capture the interaction effect between policy change and the legalization rate. The multiplicative term $lnCon \times Pol$ is introduced on the assumption that the effect of policy change on immigration and the employment of foreign workers is dependent on the hiring practices of employers. But consistent with the relationship depicted in Figure 6.1, we are not assuming an interaction effect between policy change and market conditions. These conditions will be only marginally affected by a change in immigration policy, since labor market conditions are dependent on a wide variety of factors.[25]

We can therefore rewrite our two equations as follows:

$$I_{kt} = b_0 + b_1 I_{kt-1} + b_2 lnMar_{t-1} + b_3 lnCon_{t-1} + b_4 Pol_{t-1}$$

$$E_t = b_0 + b_1 E_{t-1} + b_2 lnMar_{t-1} + b_3 lnCon_{t-1} + b_4 Pol_{t-1}$$

where b_2 represents the partial coefficient for market effects, b_3 represents the partial coefficient for the effects of changes in the legalization rate, and b_4 is the partial coefficient representing the interactive effect of policy and the legalization rate.[26] This model incorporates a one-year lag, on the assumption that a change in the political, social and economic conditions of employment will not have an immediate effect on the behavior of immigrants.[27]

Table 6.1 gives the results for each model (each type of immigration plus foreign employment). The first column of standardized coefficients in parentheses (I_{1t}) gives the percentage change in permanent worker immigration for each unit change in the explanatory variable. Since it shows that *changes in market conditions have by far the largest impact on worker immigration,* the variant of the Marxist argument (Castells's thesis) that worker immigration is not affected by business cycles (or market conditions) is incorrect. It is interesting to note that the legalization rate (which captures the hiring practices of employers) (β_3) has a substantial impact on levels of worker immigration, whereas the system level policy variable (β_4) has only a marginal impact on worker immigration. The positive sign for the policy coefficient indicates that the state gained more control over

Table 6.1 Estimates of the political-economic models of immigration and foreign employment in France, 1950–1987 (βs are in parentheses)

	Immigration (I)				Employment (E)
	(I_{1t})	(I_{2t})	(I_{3t})	(I_{4t})	(E_t)
b_0	5.6581[a]	1.3512[a]	0.9496	3.3340[a]	2.5867
	—	—	—	—	—
b_1	0.2457	0.8800[a]	0.8403[a]	0.6975[a]	0.8584[a]
	(0.2343)	(0.9308)	(0.8388)	(0.66924)	(1.0421)
b_2	−1.2781[a]	−0.1773	−0.4658[a]	−0.6034[a]	−0.0328
	(−0.5738)	(−0.1242)	(−0.2114)	(−0.4065)	(−0.1073)
b_3	0.8818[a]	0.0591	0.3263	0.2673	−0.1483[a]
	(0.2906)	(0.0304)	(0.1087)	(0.1322)	(−0.2399)
b_4	0.0189	−0.0163	−0.0755	−0.0837[a]	0.0188
	(0.0374)	(−0.0501)	(−0.1508)	(−0.2482)	(0.3910)
adj r^2	0.7844	0.9407	0.8969	0.8355	0.9759
F	33.750	143.829	79.306	46.725	102.047
Prob	0.0001	0.0001	0.0001	0.0001	0.0001
df	36	36	36	36	10
d	1.185	2.083	1.644	1.860	2.394

a. Significant at .05 level or better, two tail test.

worker immigration after 1974; however, the smallness of the coefficient means that the effect of policy change was negligible, particularly in comparison with the effects of changes in labor market conditions.[28]

The second column of coefficients (I_{2t}) concerns seasonal migration, which is less sensitive than worker migration to changes in the political, social, and economic conditions of the receiving country. The findings indicate that both the legalization rate and labor market conditions had some effect on seasonal migration. Most interesting is that policy change (β_4) actually contributed to a *loss* of state control over seasonal migration. Although the effects of policy are marginal, they are still the opposite of those intended. In this regard the Marxist (industrial reserve army) and dual labor market arguments are more applicable. Employers still hire immigrants, although the supply of foreign labor in the form of seasonal workers and family immigrants is unstable (and perhaps clandestine).

Column three (I_{3t}) gives the results for family immigration. The effect of employers' hiring practices (as measured by the legalization rate) on this sector is quite high. Many migrants who enter as family members eventually become workers seeking to enter the labor market. It is not surprising, therefore, that this new flow of migrants would be sensitive to the hiring practices of employers. These results also indicate that family reunification is to a certain extent contingent upon social and economic conditions in the receiving country. As was the case with seasonal migration, policy change helped to increase the level of family migration after 1974. The analysis lends further support to the argument that any attempt to stop labor migration leads (at least in the medium term) to increases in other forms of immigration.

Looking at column four, which represents total entries (I_{4t}), we see that immigration in postwar France is largely a conjunctural phenomenon $(\beta_2 = 0.39)$ and that the effects of policy change have been marginal—another indication of the weakness of statist theories of migration. Suspending immigration did, however, give employers a greater incentive to intervene in the policy process in order to maintain access to foreign labor. Determining precisely which employers in which sectors may have tried to circumvent policy requires a detailed analysis of specific sectors, which is reserved for the next chapter.

The state had the greatest short-term success in the area of foreign worker stocks. The success is short term because increases in family and seasonal immigration (and in the stock of foreign population) in the long run offset the decline in foreign worker stocks. From column five, we can see that all factors contributed to a reduction of foreign worker stocks. Employers cut back on private recruitment and hiring of foreign workers (β_3 is negative), as they did with other categories of workers. In this case the objectives of the state and of the socio-economic actors appear to converge, resulting in the lowering of foreign worker stocks.[29]

Conclusion

In the course of the above exploration of the statist, Marxist, and liberal arguments, an important distinction was made between state autonomy and strength. Autonomy of a democratic state implies the independence of politicians and policymakers from special interests in formulating policy. State strength refers to the administrative capacity of the state and its ability to implement policy. For much of the postwar period the French state was autonomous in its ability to pursue aggressive policies of recruitment of foreign workers, in the face of opposition from trade unions and even some skeptical employers. However, it proved difficult to implement the suspension of immigration in 1974 and subsequent legislation with respect to family and return migration. The French state has fared no better than other democratic states in its efforts to restrict immigration, either before or after the official suspension of immigration in 1974. In many ways the statist/administrative approach to immigration has contributed to the rise of a new politics of citizenship.

The overall conclusion is that a large gap exists between policy outputs and outcomes. Several explanations are possible for the weakness of the state in this policy area. First, the French state is less powerful than history implies. The Colbertist and statist traditions remain largely ideological, with the state administratively incapable of implementing policy. Second, the evidence has shown that (labor) market conditions have a greater impact on immigration and foreign employment than policy change. This may be due to the special nature of migrants as a group. The market for foreign labor has an important clandestine dimension. Hence the restrictionist policies of the French state (suspending immigration, encouraging return migration, and so on) are largely symbolic, and their effectiveness is not important, since they were designed to placate xenophobic public opinion and have little hope of overriding market pressures. A third

(Marxist) explanation is that the state is in league with employers to maintain a reserve foreign workforce that can be mobilized to keep downward pressure on wages in periods of high demand, and disbanded when no longer needed in periods of low growth and unemployment.

Of these three explanations for the failure of the French state to regulate immigration, I find the second and to some extent the first to be most convincing. The second explanation points to the special character of migrants as actors in a liberal political economy. Liberal regimes attract foreigners, who become difficult to control because of the nature of the market *and* the polity in these systems. Migrants tend to be highly motivated economic actors with important claims to rights in the liberal polity, even though they are not citizens. These characteristics make it exceedingly difficult for liberal democracies to regulate immigration. Still, governments may be compelled by popular and/or partisan pressures to take some type of symbolic action.

The first explanation, that the French state is ideologically strong but administratively weak, is plausible, but a note of caution is necessary. The problem here is one of generalization. The state may appear weak in one policy area but be strong in another. Certainly the French state at various moments in its history and in specific policy areas has shown great administrative strength. As we have seen in this chapter, however, the record is mixed, and the state remains vulnerable in certain policy areas. Finally, I would reject the Marxist explanation because it fails to account for the difficulties the state and employers encounter in seeking to disband the industrial reserve army, once it has served its purpose. This difficulty, I suggest, is due in large part to the sheer tenacity with which many migrants have pursued their interests in a liberal political economy, and to constraints, such as due process, which limit the power of the administrative state. Migrants have stayed and continue to arrive and work, not only in France but in other democratic states as well.

It is the market and the open nature of the liberal polity that influence levels of immigration and foreign employment in France—a country much like other relatively open societies. The same factors are at work in other countries of immigration, such as the United States, where markets and rights play an even larger role in the migratory process. Before turning to a discussion of the politics of citizenship and civil rights, it is worth taking a closer look at immigration and industrial change in postwar France.

7 • Immigration and Industrial Policy in France

The state has an interest in knowing whether immigrants tend to concentrate in declining or expanding sectors, whether the availability of foreign labor helps the national economy adjust to changes in international economic conditions, which industries benefit from immigration, and what conditions determine the use of foreign labor in these industries. These issues of immigration and industrial policy in France are developed in the framework of the political-economic model we have used in chapter 5.

A Sectoral Analysis of Immigration

Immigration has been described as one of the major factors in the resurgence of the postwar French economy.[1] Recall that an unlimited supply of labor is essential in periods of rapid economic growth to keep wages down and profits up. The French planners were aware that adequate labor supplies were a prerequisite of industrialization. In the high growth years of the 1950s and 1960s they sought to recruit foreign workers and place them in those sectors where demand for labor was high.

Since the oil shock of 1973 demand for labor has been declining, particularly in the manufacturing sector. Some industries were threatened with collapse as a result of rising energy costs, declining demand, and the disappearance of domestic and foreign markets. The change in economic conditions in the late 1970s led governments in Western Europe to change their macroeconomic policies from expansive Keynesianism to restrictive monetarism, followed by deregulation of markets in the 1980s. The ban on recruitment of foreign workers was an important element in this new approach to governing the economy.

But the suspension was not in keeping with growing pressures for deregulation. In effect, the suspension was part of a short-lived statist reaction to the economic downturn of the 1970s. Governments in France, Germany, and Britain tried in the late 1970s to maintain some type of statist control of markets, primarily through subsidies to sectors of their economies that had been hit hardest by recession.

Without such intervention to shore up declining industries and to protect domestic labor markets, traditional manufacturing industries such as steel and textiles, to name but two, might have disappeared, and many jobs would have been lost. A sudden and dramatic increase in unemployment was politically and socially unacceptable.[2] The central question is, to what extent was the French state able to use foreign workers to ease the pains of industrial adjustment? From the employers' perspective, keeping wages down during a period of economic crisis may be as important or more important than during periods of rapid growth. However, the political and social consequences of using cheap and tractable foreign labor to accomplish this economic goal are more severe during times of recession.[3]

The aggregate levels of immigration and foreign employment were largely dependent on market conditions. Had foreign labor therefore been used in the same way across industries and sectors? More likely immigrants, foreign workers, and employers in each sector of the economy responded differently to changes in market conditions and policy. The French state tried to limit the use of foreign labor in some sectors, while permitting its use in others. This selective policy was partly attributable to group politics. Some employers had greater success than others in obtaining permission to use foreign labor, but on the whole their access was much diminished. Only decrepit industries such as mining, and recession-prone sectors such as construction were granted exemptions from the ban on hiring foreign workers.

For policy purposes, it is important to be able to gauge the impact of a change in immigration policy on different sectors of the economy, and to determine which industries were hurt more than others by cutting off access to cheap foreign labor. We must look closely at changes in the ratio of foreign to citizen workers in each sector to determine if one type of labor has been substituted for another. Finally, we must link our study of policy change and outcomes to the choice of productive factors and economic performance as measured by productivity, investment, and so on in each sector.[4] Such a sectoral analysis will help answer two of our principal questions: to what extent can foreign labor be used as a shock absorber in an industrial economy, and is immigration primarily a political or an economic phenomenon?

If, for example, foreign workers are employed in declining sectors,[5] and if the allocation of foreign labor is controlled primarily by employers, then immigration may well play some role in allowing firms in these sectors to cut costs and keep wages down. If, conversely, foreign workers are employed more frequently in high growth sectors, it may be that immigration continues to fulfill the function of providing a supply of additional labor in expanding markets, as the Lewis-Kindleberger model suggests.

This type of evidence is needed to understand the role of immigration and foreign labor in an industrial economy. In the advanced industrial democracies many political, social, and economic consequences are associated with the use of foreign labor. The policy of using foreign workers to cushion the shock of industrial decline may ease the pain of recession and lessen the political repercussions of unemployment. But thus far we have found little evidence (at the national level) that states can use foreign labor in such a controlled fashion. The liberal argument suggests that it is politically impossible to reduce foreign workers to the level of inputs. Yet the use of foreign labor may have some specific consequences for the strategic and competitive position of the national economy. Foreign labor may allow nonproductive firms to survive, thus retarding the development of more capital-intensive production technologies that would in the long run assure the international competitiveness of certain industries.

It is unwise to attempt to answer these questions using cost-benefit analysis, because of the danger of reducing foreign workers to economic inputs and of overlooking the political consequences of immigration, which are difficult to quantify but nonetheless crucial to understanding the role of immigration in advanced industrial societies. Cost-benefit studies were more common in the 1970s, when migration was still viewed largely in statist terms of input-ouput tables, cost-benefit, and so on.[6] With the advent of a new politics of citizenship in the 1980s and the recognition of liberal constraints on the power of states and the operation of markets, cost-benefit or input-output analyses of immigration are less significant.

Immigration and Industrial Policy

Immigration has figured prominently in the strategies for industrialization and economic modernization in postwar France. Beginning with the provisional tripartite government, planners recognized the need for immigrant labor if the ambitious goals of modernization and industrialization were to be met. The Monnet Plan targeted investments for such sectors as steel, mining, and electricity.[7] Each of these industries came to rely on foreign workers to meet the growing demand for labor and to fulfill the production goals set by the planners. Rapid (but unplanned) growth occurred in the automobile sector, which became a heavy user of capital and labor in the 1950s and 1960s.[8] By the 1970s the auto industry was one of the heaviest users of immigrant workers, second only to the construction industry.

As can be seen from Table 7.1, during the reconstruction period (1946–1955) the mining and construction sectors absorbed more than a third of all immigrants entering the labor force, well over 100,000. The percentage of immigrants going into the manufacturing sector during this period, although not negligible, was smaller (approximately 10 percent). These figures give some indication of the importance of immigrant/foreign labor during the first major period of industrial change in postwar France.

The real push to modernize French industry began in earnest with the creation of the European Economic Community in 1957. The opening of the French economy to international competition in the

Table 7.1 Foreign workers in selected economic sectors in France, 1950–1980

Sectors	1946–1955	1956–1967	1968–1973	1974–1980
Mining	56,614	41,823	9,906	4,593
(% of total)	(17.4)	(3.5)	(1.2)	(2.4)
Manufacturing	31,236	198,596	116,505	23,265
(% of total)	(9.6)	(16.5)	(14.5)	(12.1)
Construction	56,880	452,391	269,818	33,249
(% of total)	(17.5)	(37.5)	(33.7)	(17.2)
Services	—	169,736	152,846	56,899
(% of total)	—	(14.1)	(19.1)	(29.5)

Source: OMI (formerly ONI).

late 1950s provided a stimulus for industrial growth and an incentive for restructuring.[9] It was during this period of rapid growth that immigration shifted heavily into manufacturing (16.5 percent), construction (37.5 percent) and services (14.1 percent). Such rapid expansion was unprecedented in French economic history.[10]

Large inputs of labor were needed to build and maintain the new industrial infrastructure. Since the "baby boom" generation of workers had not yet entered the work force, immigrant workers were the only source to meet the increased demand for labor under conditions of near full employment. Without this additional resource the French economy would have been unable to expand productive capacity so rapidly; inflation would in all likelihood have been worse than it was; and many of the goods and services produced domestically to meet rising demand would have had to be imported.[11]

Using immigrant/foreign labor to facilitate industrialization during the expansionary period of 1958 to 1967 posed no insurmountable political problems for the Gaullists. The Debré government in particular, which was decidedly pronatalist, welcomed the influx of immigrant workers from Italy, Spain, and Portugal. The only real opposition to immigration came from the communists.[12] Even this opposition was tempered by the fact that times were good and employment plentiful for both citizen and foreign workers. The main concern of the left was that foreign workers not be used by employers to keep wages down and to divide the working class.[13]

The second phase of industrialization began in 1968, after the May revolt and the increase in wages as the result of the Grenelle Agreements. The rapid rise in wages contributed to a boom in consumer demand. This boom was essentially noninflationary because of the thriving international economy, which allowed the French to pay for the wage increase by increasing exports.[14] The new economic climate had a dual effect on the use of immigrant labor. First, the rapid expansion of industrial production to meet rising domestic and international demand contributed further to the demand for labor. As a result, the yearly rate of immigration in manufacturing jumped from 16,500 in the previous period to 19,500 for the period 1967–1973 (see Table 7.1). The increase was slightly less in the construction sector mainly because housing needs were by then being met. The biggest increase in the use of immigrant/foreign labor came in the service sectors. They absorbed one fifth of total immigration, as more immigrant workers were needed to maintain the existing industrial infrastructure and as demand for services rose due to increased affluence. The other effect of the Grenelle Agreements, which radically altered the regulatory environment in the labor market, was to increase employers' preferences for cheaper and more tractable foreign labor.[15] This is the period in which the dual labor market argument became one of the most widely accepted explanations for increases in immigration and the use of foreign labor.

Politically, however, importing labor as a strategy for maintaining industrial growth became problematic, not because of any change in the marginal productivity of foreign labor, but because of public opinion, which was increasingly hostile to immigration.[16] Thus by the end of the Pompidou period (1973) the first tentative steps were taken to control and limit the use of foreign labor.[17] By this point, however, foreign workers had become a structural component of labor supply in some sectors, and it was exceedingly difficult to gain control of the situation.[18] The decision of the Fourth Republic's planners to recruit foreign workers had little effect until the French economy began to expand. At that point, in the mid-1950s, immigrant workers poured into the labor market. Turning off the flow and exporting foreign workers proved to be difficult, despite the administrative capacity of the state.

Table 7.2 gives an indication of the importance of immigrant labor in the industrial work force. During the Pompidou period (roughly

Table 7.2 Foreign workers in French industry (average annual percentage change in two periods)

Sectors	1967–1973	1974–1979
Intermediate goods		
Foreign workers	7.8	–3.8
(% of total)	(11.3)	(12.4)
Capital goods		
Foreign workers	9.1	–3.6
(% of total)	(10.5)	(11.4)
Consumer goods		
Foreign workers	4.8	–3.3
(% of total)	(6.9)	(7.8)
Construction		
Foreign workers	4.3	–4.7
(% of total)	(21.8)	(22.3)

Source: Ministry of Labor.

1967–1973) immigrant labor accounted for an annual average of over 10 percent of employment in the intermediate and capital goods sectors, while in the consumer goods sector it averaged slightly less than 7 percent of employment. By far the largest user of foreign labor was the construction industry, where immigrant workers accounted for 21.8 percent of employment over the period 1967–1973.

One of the most interesting aspects of the distribution of immigrant workers in the economy is the extent to which immigrants had penetrated almost every sector. Even after the recession of 1973–74, immigrant labor as a percentage of total employment in each sector remained high. There was a slight increase in the share of foreign workers in the work force of each sector.

The growth in immigrant/foreign employment during the boom years of the Pompidou period was reversed after the recession, with immigrant labor falling most rapidly in the construction sector (4.7 percent). The decline in levels of foreign employment after 1973 was a reflection of the general decline in employment in the industrial sector. Table 7.3 gives the average annual percentage change in industrial employment, productivity, and investment. The most radical drop in employment occurred in intermediate and consumer goods, and in the construction sector.[19] The capital goods sector fared somewhat better, in part because of higher productivity. Investment declined in all sectors, with the most rapid decline occurring in the capital goods sector.[20] If we compare Tables 7.2 and 7.3, we see that there is very little difference between overall economic performance in the industrial sector and the use of immigrant/foreign labor. In fact, one could argue that changes in levels of immigrant employment are a good indicator of industrial performance. During the period of rapid growth in employment, productivity, and investment, foreign employment increased in all sectors. During the period of economic decline from 1974, immigrant employment declined at only a slightly higher rate than total employment.[21]

These findings reinforce the conclusions of previous chapters, namely that immigration and the use of foreign labor are closely tied to the business cycle. The evidence presented here tends, however, to refute Marxist arguments that foreign workers will be laid off in greater numbers than citizen workers. It completely contradicts the argument that immigration is not related to economic cycles. The data indicate that very little restructuring of industry actually took place in France. Every indicator of economic performance dropped in the post-1973 period. It is therefore unreasonable to argue that im-

Table 7.3 Employment, productivity, and investment in French industry in periods of growth (1967–1973) and crisis (1974–1979) (average annual percentage change)

Sectors	1967–1973	1974–1979
Intermediate goods		
Employment	1.7	−2.0
Productivity	1.9	1.1
Investment	7.8	−1.6
(Exports/imports)	(0.87)	(0.96)
Capital goods		
Employment	3.4	−0.5
Productivity	2.6	1.6
Investment	9.5	−2.0
(Exports/imports)	(1.17)	(1.32)
Consumer goods		
Employment	−0.2	−2.6
Productivity	2.1	1.2
Investment	7.8	−5.4
(Exports/imports)	(1.38)	(1.05)
Construction		
Employment	0.8	−2.3
Productivity	1.2	1.0
Investment	3.7	−1.7

Source: INSEE.

migrants played a prominent role in the adjustment of French industry to changes in the international economy. The numbers in parentheses in Table 7.3 give the ratio of exports to imports. From this statistic we can see that the intermediate and capital goods sectors, where the ratio is higher, made some adjustment to changing international conditions. However, in the former the improvement was quite marginal, whereas in the latter most of the improvement was due to increased exports of automobiles.[22]

The impact of foreign labor on capital intensity and on the development of new technologies is difficult to measure. Many factors affect capital/labor ratios and technological developments. In the short term, using or not using foreign workers does not appear to be associated with changes in total productivity (see Tables 7.2 and 7.3). Therefore, it cannot be concluded on the basis of these data that immigration has helped or hindered the development of new production technologies or that it has adversely affected comparative advantage.

The data indicate that foreign labor, as an input, has been used in much the same way as other factors of production, such as domestic labor and capital. Each factor seems to have participated during periods of growth and idled during periods of recession in roughly the same proportions. The movement of foreign workers into or out of a sector is proportionate to the movement of citizen workers. The only significant difference between the use of foreign and citizen workers appears to be the much higher rate of foreign employment in the construction industry.[23]

The data presented in Tables 7.1 to 7.3 are still highly aggregated. The next section looks at foreign employment in selected industrial and non-industrial branches relying on firm-level data from Minsitry of Labor surveys conducted in 1967, 1973, 1976, and 1979.

Immigration and Manufacturing

The *économie concertée* of the 1950s and 1960s gradually gave way to a more competitive market economy in the 1970s and 1980s.[24] The state was forced to abandon its support for highly concentrated traditional manufacturing industries (the so-called national champions).[25] The reasons for this shift from a statist to a more liberal economic policy are linked to changes in France's position in Europe and the world economy. In the 1970s, with the rising costs of imported energy and greater competition in both domestic and foreign markets, it became increasingly expensive for the state to subsidize inefficient firms. Yet the traditional involvement of the state in both the public and private sectors—the legacy of *étatisme*—made government responsible in the eyes of the electorate for protecting jobs in declining sectors such as steel, shipbuilding, and automobiles.[26]

In addition to protecting domestic markets for French goods through subsidies and tariffs,[27] French governments in the 1970s sought to protect the labor market by suspending immigration and attempting to repatriate foreign workers. Protecting domestic markets became part of a new industrial strategy to give French firms time to adjust to changes in the world economy. Since 1973 the state had tried to promote efficient firms, while encouraging nonefficient firms to restructure and automate the production process. The difficulty with this strategy was how to improve productivity and economic efficiency without destroying the national champions and causing more unemployment. As during the period of reconstruction, when planners turned to foreign labor to increase labor supply, policymakers of the seventies hoped to use foreign workers to ease the pains of industrial restructuring.[28]

In the previous section we saw that the use of foreign labor in various sectors of the economy did not differ radically from the use of citizen labor. Now we shall take a closer look (using firm-level data) at how changes in immigration policy affected the use of foreign workers in certain industrial sectors. The analysis focuses on industrial sectors that have done poorly in terms of productivity and employment, including traditional manufacturing industries, such as steel and textiles, as well as some sectors that have done well since 1973 such as the service sector and a few selected manufacturing industries. Another criterion that was used to select industrial sectors for study is the degree of concentration of production. This is important because achieving economies of scale was the goal of French industrial policy during much of the postwar period. The most highly concentrated industries were, not surprisingly, the ones with the largest state participation.[29] Nationalized industries (steel and automobiles) became highly concentrated with only a few firms dominating production and marketing. At the other extreme were services and retail sales, which remained decentralized and without state control. A final, obvious criterion for selecting industrial sectors to study is the degree to which the sector relied on foreign labor in the postwar period.

Table 7.4 gives a breakdown of the overall levels of foreign employment and the percentage of foreign workers in the labor force for several industrial sectors. Included in this group are formerly nationalized industries with a high degree of concentration of production (steel and automobiles); nonnationalized traditional industries with a low degree of concentration (textiles); and the dynamic tertiary sectors of services and sales. The industries that were the heaviest users of foreign labor were socially and politically important, because they employed large number of workers and produced strategically important goods. The steel and auto industries began using immigrant labor during the expansionary period of the late 1950s. The tertiary sector (services and sales) became a heavy user of foreign labor during the 1960s and 1970s. The most traditional industry in this group, textiles, was not a heavy user of foreign labor. Was the degree of penetration

Table 7.4 Foreign employment in selected industrial sectors in France, 1967–1979 (thousands)

Sectors	1967	1973	1976	1979
Textiles				
Foreign emp.	56.5	63.0	54.7	50.2
(% of total)	(7.2)	(9.7)	(9.5)	(9.7)
Steel				
Foreign emp.	32.6	36.1	33.6	24.2
(% of total)	(15.6)	(16.5)	(15.1)	(13.6)
Auto				
Foreign emp.	28.3	125.9	104.0	96.9
(% of total)	(8.4)	(24.8)	(19.7)	(18.6)
Services				
Foreign emp.	62.6	137.5	152.6	—
(% of total)	(4.0)	(6.5)	(6.5)	—
Sales				
Foreign emp.	38.3	94.5	102.4	—
(% of total)	(2.4)	(5.0)	(5.2)	—

Source: Data for the textile, steel and auto industries were taken directly from the Ministry of Labor foreign manpower surveys. They include only firms with more than 10 employees. Data for the tertiary sector (services and sales) were taken from Courault, *Contribution à la théorie de l'offre de travail*, p. 682. Data for 1979 for these sectors were unavailable.

of foreign labor in these industries the result of policy decisions or market forces?

Since the beginning of industrialization in France in the nineteenth century, the textile industry has been one of the mainstays of the French economy.[30] Historically, textile production was carried out primarily by small family firms. In the postwar period the industry became increasingly concentrated in a few firms in certain regions; it has been in a state of decline since before the recessions of the 1970s.

The steel industry also was decentralized in small firms until the efforts to rationalize production under the first economic plans of the Fourth Republic.[31] In the 1970s and 1980s the industry was battered by foreign competition, and the state subsidized the entire sector (within guidelines laid down by the EC) to preserve jobs and save what was considered to be a strategic industry.

Until the recession of the early 1980s, the automobile industry fared better than other manufacturing industries.[32] This was in part the result of early investments in more efficient production techniques, such as robotics. The tertiary sector, services and sales, eventually became one of the most dynamic sectors of the French economy, and one of the biggest users of labor.[33]

Tables 7.4 and 7.5 show the evolution of foreign employment in each of these industries. To evaluate the political and economic importance of foreign/immigrant workers in each sector, we must compare industrial and immigration policy and examine how they have affected each sector. One caveat is in order concerning the selection of industries. Traditionally, the largest user of immigrant workers has been the construction industry. This is true for most labor-importing countries.[34] Immigrant labor has been widely used in this sector because of the dangerous and difficult nature of the work, and because of uncertainties in demand, which require a flexible labor force. Perhaps because of the large numbers of foreign workers in this sector and the recognition that citizen workers are likely to be unavailable for these types of jobs, the construction industry has not been the focus of political controversy. Politicians and policymakers, as well as the general public, have been more concerned with high levels of

Table 7.5 Foreign and national employment in France, 1967–1979 (average annual percentage change)

Sectors	1967–1973	1973–1976	1976–1979
Textiles			
Foreign	10.3	−15.2	−9.0
Native	−23.6	−12.5	−12.2
Steel			
Foreign	9.7	−7.4	−38.8
Native	4.1	−3.2	−21.2
Auto			
Foreign	124.8	−21.1	−7.3
Native	19.1	9.7	0.2
Services			
Foreign	119.7	11.0	—
Native	31.6	11.0	—
Sales			
Foreign	146.7	8.4	—
Native	17.5	4.0	—

Source: Ministry of Labor and INSEE.

immigrant employment in such industries as steel and automobiles. One of the principal reasons for the greater attention given to the manufacturing sector is the often militant role that foreigners have played in strikes, and the rocky relationship between trade unions and foreign workers in this sector.

Textiles

Unlike other industries, the French textile industry has received little assistance from the state to stave off the decline and disappearance of small firms. The textile industry has not figured prominently in postwar industrial policy because it was not considered by planners to be a strategically important sector.[35] Market forces and competition from newly industrialized countries forced employers to devise strategies for cutting costs. Despite the effort to cut costs, however, the industry did not rely heavily on foreign labor. Levels of foreign employment fluctuated just below 10 percent, which is slightly lower than the average levels of foreign employment in industry as a whole. In the 1960s, however, foreign labor became more prominent in this sector because of the sharp decline in total employment, caused by the movement of citizen workers out of textiles (23.6 percent, see Table 7.5).[36]

Declining overall employment in textiles was the result of changes in the international division of labor, which placed French products in direct competition with much cheaper products from the newly industrialized countries. Despite being out of favor with economic policymakers for much of the postwar period, however, the textile industry managed to hold its own against foreign competition; and its contribution to industrial production (5.5 percent) and industrial employment (10 percent) is not negligible.

Diversity and decentralization of production did not help the textile industry overcome its problems. The costs of French textiles remained high relative to those produced in developing countries. The production process remained labor intensive because the French firms were slower to adopt capital intensive techniques. One would expect, therefore, that the textile industry would be a heavy user of cheap foreign labor, but this was not the case (see Table 7.4).[37]

Even before the 1973–74 crisis, the textile industry was growing at a slower pace than industry as a whole (2.4 percent as compared to 6 percent). Investments and employment continually declined from the

1960s, and wages were lower than in other sectors, in part because of low rates of unionization. Following the downturn in 1974, domestic production of textiles declined at an annual average rate of 1.8 percent.[38] Thus we might have expected foreigners to be laid off in greater numbers than citizen workers, given the uncertain economic future and the difficulty of dismissing citizen workers after new regulations governing layoffs were adopted following the Grenelle Agreements.[39] As can be seen from Table 7.5, however, this was not the case. Foreign and national employment in this sector declined at roughly the same rate.

What strategies did employers in the textile industry pursue to avoid going out of business altogether? With the saturation of the domestic market for textiles and an inability to compete abroad because of high production costs, the prospects for French textiles were not good. The textile industry in other industrial countries faced many of the same problems. In the United States textile manufacturing benefited from cheap nonunion labor in the South, and from undocumented foreign labor in the sweatshops of San Francisco and New York. British textile producers were unable to cut production costs on two counts; expensive union labor, and a severe shortage of the investment capital that would have permitted retooling. Unlike their French counterparts, Italian textile manufacturers took advantage of decentralized production, most of which was in small firms in the informal economy, and in the form of home work. Michael Piore and Charles Sabel described the textile industry in Northern Italy as an ideal typical industry of the new industrial age—one capable of adapting quickly to the very competitive environment of the 1980s. They labeled this strategy "flexible specialization," most common to firms like Benetton. It is interesting to note that nowhere in their work, *The Second Industrial Divide,* is immigrant labor metioned as a feature of the new industrial order of the late twentieth century.[40] The Japanese eliminated inefficient textile firms through the development of new technologies and by exporting the labor intensive processes to the newly industrialized countries (the little dragons) of East Asia.[41]

At the urging of the French state, the response of textile manufacturers to the growing economic crisis was to concentrate on product lines in which they had comparative advantage. This meant a greater emphasis on expensive brands of *haute couture,* which required highly skilled labor. Such specialization, combined with an effort to export labor intensive processes, helps explain why the French textile industry did not disappear altogether, and why it did not rely heavily on foreign labor. The state, for its part, was reticent to subsidize textiles, offering limited assistance only to the strongest firms that were most likely to survive. Any protectionist measures or tax reductions, particularly during the neoliberal periods of the late 1970s and mid-1980s, were contingent upon the willingness of firms to invest in new production technologies. The neoliberal version of "indicative planning" created a disincentive for hiring foreign, or for that matter citizen, workers (see Table 7.5). The French textile industry has been made to restructure through a combination of intense market pressures and the selective allocation of protection and credit, extended by the state to eliminate inefficient firms. As a result, both foreign and national employment declined markedly.

Steel

In the 1950s and 1960s the steel industry was the showcase of the French economy. Modernizing industry to increase production of steel was one of the principal aims of the early plans. Since the crisis of the 1970s, however, the French steel industry has fallen on hard times because of foreign competition, a drop in overall demand for steel, and growing inefficiency of production. Like textiles, steel was the victim of changes in the international market. French companies found it increasingly difficult to compete with cheaper steel from Japan and the newly industrialized countries of East Asia, such as Korea and Taiwan.

The drop in domestic demand and the loss of foreign markets led to lower investments at a time when production costs continued to rise, partially as a result of increased wage costs: the workforce in the steel industry was highly unionized and dominated by the militant CGT.[42] The decline of steel became a major policy problem, first, because of the high degree of concentration of the industry both geographically and structurally; second, because it was part of the public sector; and finally, because of the militancy of its workforce, which represented 3.5 percent of industrial employment in 1976. Not until the late 1980s, following the adoption of the Single European Act in 1985 and subsequent restructuring to prepare for the single European market in 1992, did French steel finally begin to make some headway in recapturing past glory.

Foreign labor has been an important part of the workforce in the steel industry for much of its history.[43] In the 1960s and 1970s, the percentage of foreign workers employed in this industry fluctuated between 15 and 17 percent (see Table 7.4). Following the dual labor market argument, we would expect that after the 1973–74 crisis foreign workers would be the first to lose their jobs, because of their political vulnerability and lack of seniority. As can be seen from Table 7.5, levels of foreign employment rose significantly prior to the recession (9.7 percent from 1967 to 1973) and fell sharply after 1973, especially during the three-year period from 1976 to 1979 (38.8 percent). But 21.2 percent of citizen workers also lost their jobs during the same period.

Unlike the textile industry, steel continued to benefit from protectionism and subsidies; after the rationalization of the industry during the 1950s, steel production became increasingly concentrated in a few large firms. In the 1960s and early 1970s the production capacity of the steel industry was expanded at a time when other countries, such as Germany, were cutting back and concentrating on streamlining production in those branches of the industry which had comparative advantage.[44] The expansion of productive capacity in the early to mid-1970s led to an increase in the workforce, but by the late 1970s productive capacity and employment were declining rapidly. Mounting deficits in the nationalized firms forced policymakers to intervene to save jobs, although by the end of the 1970s the level of foreign and national employment in the steel industry was declining rapidly (see Table 7.5). It does not appear that efforts by the state to restructure the industry during the first years of the Giscard administration (from 1974 to 1976) saved many jobs, whether for foreign or citizen workers.

The optimism of the planners' econometric forecasts in the 1960s and early 1970s are at least partly to blame. Policymakers and politicians saw steel as a strategically important sector and a measure of national economic prowess. The expansion of production capacity created more jobs in the short term, which pleased the trade unions. As can be seen from Table 7.5, however, some of these new jobs in steel during the Pompidou period were filled by foreigners. It is interesting to note that even though steel is a nationalized industry, the government did nothing to discourage the recruitment and hiring of foreign workers during this period. French steel production was still a labor intensive process.[45] Expansion therefore meant the creation of new jobs, which the trade unions would have to defend later in the decade. It is likely, although difficult to prove, that the development of more modern production techniques was slowed by the influx of foreign labor into the steel industry during the expansionary period 1967–1973. After 1973 both foreign and citizen workers paid the price for the expansion of production capacity in this sector.

Automobiles

The French automobile industry has been the heaviest user of foreign labor in the industrial sector. On the eve of the recession in 1973, foreign workers accounted for almost one quarter of total employment in the auto industry (see Table 7.4). The expansion of foreign employment in this sector in the late 1960s and early 1970s was completely out of proportion with the growth in French employment. The use of foreign workers on the production line increased by 125 percent during this period, whereas employment of citizen workers grew by only 19 percent (see Table 7.5).[46] Such heavy use of foreign labor was unprecedented in the industrial sector. Some of the newly hired foreign workers lost their jobs in the period following the oil shock. But the drop in immigrant/foreign employment (21 percent) from 1973–1976 was marginal compared to increases in the 1960s. Employment of citizen workers after the recession continued to expand, although at a much slower rate than before.

The auto industry recovered fairly quickly from the downturn in 1973–74, as witnessed by the continued increase in levels of employment among French workers (9.7 percent from 1973 to 1976). The drop in immigrant employment and the rise in national employment indicates that citizen workers were being hired instead of foreign workers. This can be seen in the decline in the percentage of immigrants in the work force from 25 percent in 1973 to 19 percent in 1979 (see Table 7.4). One obvious explanation for this change is the stopping of worker immigration in 1974, which made it difficult to hire foreign workers. However, the auto industry continued to increase its workforce and create jobs in the late 1970s. Employment in this sector increased by a slim 0.3 percent from 1973–1979, while it decreased by 1.2 percent in manufacturing as a whole.[47] This does not mean, however, that the French auto industry escaped unscathed from changes in the international economy. In the late 1970s exports declined in the face of stiff Japanese competition in traditionally safe foreign markets such as Africa and the Middle East. Also, despite

French efforts to protect the domestic market, which was reaching the saturation point in the late 1970s, imports increased, primarily from Germany and Italy. The state took steps to protect domestic markets from Japanese competition.

The auto industry occupied a strategically important position in the economy (unlike textiles) because it remained one of the most important export industries and one of the largest users of labor and capital.[48] It is also important because of multiplier effects, that is, the large number of inputs necessary to produce an automobile means that many other firms (both downstream and upstream) are dependent on the performance of this industry. For these reasons high levels of foreign employment in the auto industry have attracted much public attention.[49] The fact that the industry was so highly concentrated and at the same time part of the public sector (many firms were, and Renault still is nationalized) contributed to the high-profile public image. The government was therefore expected to control levels of foreign employment to protect the jobs of citizen workers.

Despite pressure on the authorities from public opinion and trade unions to keep foreign employment down, foreign workers remained an attractive alternative to citizen workers for many firms because the volatility of demand for automobiles, the rapidity of model changes, and changes in production techniques require flexibility in hiring and firing workers. Also, it proved difficult to find French workers willing to accept the monotonous pace of assembly-line work.[50] Instead of substituting citizen workers, firms such as Renault developed more automated and robotized assembly plants and thereby reduced the demand for unskilled foreign labor.[51] It does not appear that the use of foreign labor in this sector has delayed the development of capital-intensive production techniques or hindered the ability of the auto industry to compete in world markets.

Throughout the manufacturing sector as a whole, foreign labor has been more prevalent in high growth sectors and the hiring and firing of foreign workers has followed closely changes in overall employment and in the national economy.

Services and Sales

The service sector is easily the most dynamic one of the French economy, at least since the 1960s. Demand for public and personal services to cater to an affluent population in a consumer society soared in the decade of the 1970s. As can be seen from Table 7.5, levels of foreign employment in the service sector increased by well over 100 percent. This is the only sector in which both foreign and national employment increased after 1973.

One of the problems with this expansion is that such jobs added little to GNP, did not help the balance of payments, or make the economy more competitive.[52] Production in this sector has few multiplier effects. In fact, the service sector soaks up capital and labor that might otherwise be invested in improving industrial production. This is particularly true of public service jobs and personal services, both of which were heavy users of foreign labor. Some services—domestic servants, all types of maintenance personnel, garbage collectors, bus drivers—were dominated by foreign workers.[53] The high visibility of service sector jobs also contributes to the public's xenophobic fear that foreigners are taking jobs away from citizen workers.

Growth of foreign employment in the service sector was (and still is) a more difficult policy problem than in other sectors. The demand for services and for immigrant workers to fill low-paying jobs has shown no sign of diminishing, while the productivity and competitiveness of industry continues to decline. Whether immigrant workers could (or should) be exported or shifted into more productive sectors is an open question. It is not certain that citizen workers can be found to replace foreign workers in such essential services as transportation, garbage collection, and others. The policy response to these questions is contingent upon the administrative capacity of the state and its ability to use immigration for making industrial policy. We already have seen that this is difficult at the national level, therefore it seems even less likely that the state would be effective in regulating foreign labor in the dynamic service sector.

Given the difficult policy choices that employers and the government have faced with regard to reorganizing industry and restructuring markets in response to changes in the international division of labor, it is important to know what factors condition the use of foreign labor in specific firms. The next section addresses this question in the framework for analysis developed in chapters 5 and 6.

Explaining Policy Outcomes at the Sectoral Level

As we saw earlier, policy change had little effect on aggregate levels of immigration and foreign employment, net of the effects of market conditions and group politics. Market and political factors far outweighed policy as determinants of immigration and the use of foreign labor. This time the statist, Marxist, and liberal arguments will be reviewed in the light of policy outcomes at the sectoral level, and the results of this analysis compared to the findings in chapter 6.

Recall that immigration and foreign employment are assumed to be a function of market conditions, groups politics (especially employers' control of worker migration), and policy. The model for immigration can therefore be written as

$$I_{kt} = b_0 + b_1 I_{kt-1} + b_2 lnMar_{t-1} + b_3 lnCon_{t-1} + b_4 Pol_{t-1}$$

and the model for foreign employment as

$$E_t = b_0 + b_1 E_{t-1} + b_2 lnMar_{t-1} + b_3 lnCon_{t-1} + b_4 Pol_{t-1}$$

where *lnMar* is a measure of labor market conditions, *lnCon* is a measure of employers' control of migration as captured by the legalization rate, and *Pol* is a measure of the interaction of policy and legalization rates. The major conceptual and methodological differences between the tests that were done in the previous chapter and the ones here is that the endogenous variables are microlevel (sectoral) outcomes, explained in terms of macrolevel structural conditions. Also, the questions are somewhat different. The statist argument is still of interest, as is the question of determining to what extent immigration and foreign employment are driven by market forces. In addition, the analysis presented here will help determine whether the state has had more success in controlling the market for foreign workers in some sectors than in others. We might expect, for example, that policy change would have a greater impact in manufacturing industries than in the service or construction sectors because of the heavy involvement of the state in manufacturing.[54]

The endogenous variables in this analysis are measures of immigration of permanent workers (*I*) and immigrant employment (*E*) at the sectoral levels. Because of the difficulty of disaggregating the ONI data on foreign workers employed in manufacturing, the industrial sector has been operationalized as a single endogenous variable. The one exception is the mining industry, which is a separate variable. The complete list of endogenous variables for immigration is as follows: mining (I_{5t}), manufacturing (I_{6t}), construction (I_{7t}), and services (I_{8t}).[55] The data on foreign employment—stocks—are more highly aggregated. Due to the difficulty of estimating stocks,[56] the sectoral data on foreign employment correspond to the major product sectors used earlier: intermediate goods (E_{2t}), capital goods (E_{3t}), consumer goods (E_{4t}), and construction (E_{5t}).[57]

The exogenous variables are identical to those used in chapter 6. The guiding hypotheses are also the same, that is, a strong state is capable of influencing outcomes, hence policy outputs (Pol) are expected to have a significant impact. We know, however, that this was not the case at the national level. If the results of the analysis of sectoral outcomes are consistent with the results of the analysis of national outcomes, then we will have more evidence against the statist theory of immigration in France. We would expect the state to have greater control over outcomes in sectors such as mining and intermediate and capital goods where the state is heavily involved in the production process. For example, the state is assumed to have greater control over hiring practices in nationalized firms. On the other hand, sectors with less state involvement, such as construction, services, and consumer goods, should not be greatly affected by policy change.

Table 7.6 gives the results of the model for immigration in each sector. A quick glance at the results reveals that, as in the analysis of national outcomes, the economic/labor market conditions have the greatest impact on levels of worker immigration in each sector. The market coefficient (b_2) is statistically significant in every sector, and the impact of the market variable is, in almost every case, double that of the other variables. Market conditions appear to have the greatest impact in the mining sector (I_{5t}), where a drop in the demand for coal greatly reduced the overall demand for labor, including immigrant labor. The next highest market coefficient is in the manufacturing sector, which again confirms the hypothesis that the use of immigrant labor in industry is primarily a conjunctural phenomenon. The smallest impact of the market variable is, as expected, in the service sector, where demand for labor has remained high, even during the recessionary period when demand for labor in the economy as a whole was dropping. Finally, the signs of the market coefficients are all in the expected direction. The negative signs indicate that when the overall supply of labor rises and the overall demand for labor falls, immigrant employment in each sector declines.

The legalization rate *Con* (the ability of employers to control worker immigration) has a statistically significant impact on levels of worker immigration in three of the four sectors. The largest impact

Table 7.6 Estimates of the political-economic model of worker immigration by four sectors, 1946–1980 (βs are in parentheses)

	Immigration of permanent workers (I)			
	(I_{5t})	(I_{6t})	(I_{7t})	(I_{8t})
b_0	9.4584[a]	5.0373[a]	5.1784[a]	1.5641[a]
b_1	0.5396[a]	0.3076[a]	0.4211[a]	0.7164[a]
	(0.4208)	(0.2996)	(0.4069)	(0.7728)
b_2	–3.1993[a]	–2.6885[a]	–1.7751[a]	–0.4820[a]
	(–0.5895)	(–0.6574)	(–0.4173)	(–0.2157)
b_3	–1.0796[a]	0.7816[a]	0.2325	0.3333[a]
	(–0.2027)	(0.1992)	(0.0569)	(0.1265)
b_4	0.0367	–0.0395	0.2131[a]	0.0400
	(0.0361)	(–0.0487)	(0.2524)	(0.1078)
adj r^2	0.5309	0.8446	0.8832	0.9696
F	8.638	40.395	55.819	176.148
Prob	0.0002	0.0001	0.0001	0.0001
df	27	29	29	22
d	2.006	2.000	1.756	1.931

[a]Significant at .05 level or better, two tail test.

is in the mining sector (I_{5t}). The negative sign for this coefficient is not surprising in view of the general decline in the mining sector beginning in the late 1950s. Employers had been cutting back on the hiring of both foreign and citizen workers. Thus greater control by employers of worker immigration led to a decline in immigrant employment in the mining sector. Employers' control over worker immigration has, on the contrary, contributed to a rise in immigrant employment in the manufacturing and the service sectors.

The change in immigration policy in 1974 had no significant impact on immigrant employment in any sector, except for the construction industry. This finding allows us to reject the hypothesis that the state had greater control over immigrant employment in those sectors where policymakers have more control over the production process. Yet in the construction industry, which is decentralized with little state control, policy change led to lower levels of immigrant employment. A provisional explanation of this result is that the ministries of Labor and the Interior are better able to supervise the use of foreign workers in the construction industry.

Our model explains the variance in immigration well in all but the mining sector (*adj.* $r^2 = 0.53$), principally because mining was in full decline long before the recession of the 1970s and the ban on recruitment of immigrant workers. The model is significant for all sectors and there is no problem with autocorrelation.

If we compare the impact of each explanatory variable within each sector (that is, the βs), we see that market conditions have by far the greatest impact on levels of immigration. The only exceptions are the construction industry, where the impact of policy change (β = 0.21) is almost half as large in absolute terms as the impact of market conditions (β = 0.42). In the service sector the effect of employers' control of worker immigration (β = 0.13) is slightly larger than half the effect of market conditions (β = 0.22).

Table 7.7 gives the estimates for the political-economic model of foreign employment by sector. Interpretation of these results must be tempered by the small number of cases; in the models for the intermediate and capital goods' sectors the levels of autocorrelation are high enough to give biased estimates.[58] In the intermediate goods

Table 7.7 Estimates of the political-economic model of foreign employment by economic sector (βs are in parentheses)

	Employment			
	(E_{2t})	(E_{3t})	(E_{4t})	(E_{5t})
b_0	3.1225[a]	14.0257[a]	12.5511[a]	13.2900[a]
b_1	0.7620[a]	0.0130	0.0069	0.0498[a]
	(0.9775)	(0.0567)	(0.0684)	(0.4845)
b_2	−0.1218	−0.5745[a]	−0.2824[a]	−0.3102[a]
	(−0.3318)	(−0.9745)	(−1.0917)	(−1.1701)
b_3	−0.0303	−0.3374	−0.1744	−0.1447
	(−0.0408)	(−0.3199)	(−0.3769)	(−0.3051)
b_4	0.0003	−0.1027[a]	−0.0337	−0.1551[a]
	(0.0580)	(−1.1513)	(−0.8604)	(−0.9230)
adj r^2	0.9779	0.8603	0.7023	0.8253
F	111.493	17.936	7.487	13.955
Prob	0.0001	0.0009	0.0114	0.0019
df	10	11	11	11
d	1.581	2.599	1.866	1.736

[a]Significant at .05 level or better, two tail test.

sector, autocorrelation is largely the result of the lagged endogenous variable, which has been entered as an exogenous variable. This variable (E_{5t-1}) is the only statistically significant exogenous variable.

The analysis for the other sectors (capital goods, consumer goods, and the construction industry) brings out a familiar pattern. The market variable is again the most significant explanatory variable. Its effects on foreign employment in each sector are roughly equal. The effects of employers' control over worker immigration are not statistically significant in any of the sectors. A more interesting result is the significance of the policy variable in the capital goods sector and the construction industry. The negative sign for these coefficients (b_4), however, means that suspension of immigration contributed to a loss of state control of immigration. This finding confirms the results from chapter 6, that the suspension of worker immigration had the opposite effect of that intended.[59]

Finally, the assessment of the weight of each coefficient within models shows that in the capital goods sector (E_{3t}) policy change had a very large negative effect on state control of foreign employment. Thus the suspension of migration actually led to the hiring of more foreign workers in this sector. The same is also true for the construction industry. This is probably a short-term effect, attributable to the decision of foreign workers who were holding temporary jobs to stay and seek permanent employment after the suspension.

Conclusion

Consistent with the Lewis-Kindleberger model, many sectors of the French economy relied heavily on immigration to increase output. Mining, construction, and steel all became heavy users of foreign labor during the Fourth Republic when immigration increased as a result of rapid economic growth. With the continued growth in the economy in the 1960s and early 1970s, other industries, such as textiles and automobiles, hired foreign workers so they could fully utilize existing productive capacity and keep pace with demand.

Immigrant/foreign labor appears to have been a structural component of the labor supply in some sectors, such as construction, autos, and services. The fact that foreign labor continued to be an important part of the work force in these sectors indicates that there was something about the nature of these jobs (low-skill, low wages, poor working conditions, and so on) that made them unacceptable to citizen workers who have experienced upward mobility—partly as a result of immigration. This finding does not, however, confirm the dual labor market hypothesis. For reasons that are outlined in the following chapter, immigrant workers did not fulfill the function of an industrial reserve army, nor have they simply added an element of flexibility to the labor market. Civil and social rights accrue to migrants, creating new legal spaces for foreigners and making it difficult to expel or repatriate them, even when they are the victims of economic hardships and unemployment.

The overriding result of the analysis of the role of immigrant labor in industrial change is that, by and large, immigrants do *not* appear to have been treated much differently in the marketplace than French workers. The rates of layoffs and unemployment among foreign workers have been higher than among citizen workers in the period after 1973, and especially after the recession of 1981–82, which also hit citizen workers in France very hard. But this does not mean that foreign workers serve as an industrial reserve army or can be used as shock absorbers in advanced capitalist societies. The evidence does not support the thesis that foreign workers, because of their political and social vulnerability, are preferred by employers over citizen workers. What the analysis in this chapter has shown is that the overall supply of and demand for labor—a market which, as a result of increasing interdependence, is highly sensitive to changes in the international economy—has the greatest impact on the use of foreign labor. When times were good and borders were relatively open, as was the case in France until the early 1970s, immigrant workers were hired in the medium and the long term. When times were bad and overall demand declining, foreign workers were laid off at somewhat higher rates than citizen workers, but most remained as job seekers, joining the ranks of the unemployed. Thus foreign workers are not much more vulnerable or more protected from market change than citizen workers. These findings reinforce the conclusions of earlier chapters, namely that restrictionist policy had only a marginal impact on levels of immigration and foreign employment. In fact policy had many unintended consequences. It proved extremely difficult, if not impossible, for the state to use foreign workers to restructure labor markets according to the dictates of the national interest, as expressed in employment and industrial policies.

In conclusion, immigrants do not appear to have played any special role in the process of industrial adjustment. The use of foreign/immigrant labor, like other productive factors, is subject to changes in the overall levels of demand, rather than to preferential hiring practices of employers or policy interventions in the economy. During the postwar period (until the 1980s), immigration has been viewed largely in economic terms. This does not mean that the state could do nothing to affect the conditions under which foreigners work, once they have entered the labor market. As with any other group of unskilled workers, improvement or deterioration of their working conditions and protection from arbitrary actions by their employers depend in large part on the willingness of the state to enforce labor laws and protect civil rights. At the beginning of the 1980s, with a surge in refugee and family immigration, immigration policy has taken on a partisan edge, provoking struggles over *citizenship and civil rights*. It is to these issues that we now turn our attention.

IV • MARKETS AND RIGHTS IN EUROPE AND THE UNITED STATES

8 ✦ Citizenship and Rights

The government of a democracy brings the notion of political rights to the level of the humblest citizens . . .
—ALEXIS DE TOCQUEVILLE, *Democracy in America*

Policymakers in a liberal polity cannot assume that foreign workers are simple commodities rather than individuals to whom civil, social, and even political rights accrue. Governments have too often failed to take into account the sociopolitical dimension of immigration. Likewise, old-fashioned push-pull arguments, which rely heavily on neoclassical economic reasoning, miss this important point and so fail to explain the persistence of immigration in the face of restrictionist policies and anti-immigrant sentiments among Western publics.

In addition to the push and pull of market forces, immigration is fueled by the rise of a new rights-based politics in the liberal democracies. This brand of politics—new in the sense that it is linked to postwar political developments primarily in the area of civil rights—is itself a function of political struggles that have generated new definitions of citizenship and membership in liberal societies. These last issues in the political economy of immigration—citizenship and humanitarianism—are closely linked.[1] We shall see how the rights of foreigners have been expanded by changes in the legal and political cultures of France, Germany, and the United States, and how these rights find expression in legislative acts, judicial rulings, and in partisan and interest-group politics.

The new brand of liberalism in the industrial democracies is linked

169

closely to the politics of civil rights, which surfaced in the United States in the 1950s and has continued in political struggles in Europe over immigrant and minority rights in the 1970s and 1980s. Rights-based liberalism goes hand-in-hand with the spread of market relations, and is closely associated with new ideas of social justice as well as individual and group entitlements.[2] The political battles over rights have given rise to new conceptions of citizenship that differ from classical "contractarian" views of the relationship between the individual and the state. The relationship has come to be defined in terms of social justice and human rights rather than in terms of contracts and consent. This new brand of liberal politics finds expression at every level of democratic polities, from legislatures and courts to parties and interest groups. It acts to constrain statist policies and helps to create new spaces for foreigners in these societies. The confluence of unregulated markets for foreign labor and the rise of rights-based politics explains the failure of restrictionist policies and the persistence of immigration. Although in Europe we have seen a nationalist backlash against immigration (and the liberal consensus), which has shifted the terms of policy debates and partisan politics, these anti-immigrant forces have failed to undermine the consensus. In the United States, by contrast, immigration continues to be treated in a liberal, nonpartisan way, as reflected in the immigration reform acts of 1986 and 1990.

To illustrate the relation between citizenship and immigration, this chapter examines the reform of immigration policy in the United States; the rise of a new politics of citizenship in France, which has a strong partisan dimension; and the *Gastarbeiter* policies in Germany, to see how the failure of these policies and the settlement of a large foreign population have helped to change traditional views of German identity and citizenship. We also shall look at how the politics of unification has altered the terms of debate over immigration and citizenship in the Federal Republic.

Markets and Rights

A shift in the arena of political conflict—from parties and legislatures to courts and administrative agencies—has led to a new emphasis on process and justice and the advent of rights-based politics in liberal states, which spill over to the international level.[3] These rights are an expression of changes in political culture. One of the clearest manifestations of the new kind of politics is to be found in the areas of immigration and citizenship, where issues of membership and rights impinge heavily upon traditional notions of nationhood and community.

The jurisprudences of France, Germany, and the United States have begun to reflect the new social and economic realities of interdependence, and changes in immigration law can be seen as another indicator of the erosion of the classical, realist conceptions of the sovereignty and autonomy of the nation-state. The new liberal-political cultures make it difficult for states to exercise sweeping, exclusionary powers with respect to aliens.[4] Cultural and legal constraints on sovereignty (at the domestic level) serve to reinforce a liberal international order, while the expansion of international markets for labor and the concomitant extension of civil rights to aliens serve as important measures of change in the political culture of the advanced industrial democracies. Of course, these developments are not without their detractors.

Intense struggles have developed in Europe in the 1970s and 1980s to recapture a lost sense of national identity. More often than not, these struggles are tinged with racist discourse. The battle over identity has been waged primarily within the confines of party politics, occasionally spilling over into the judicial arena, if not into the streets. Perhaps the most celebrated (although not the most important) development in the politics of immigration in Western Europe is the rise of extremist and xenophobic movements such as the National Front parties in Britain and France (and to a lesser extent the Republikaner party in Germany), which herald a new age of nationalist politics. These movements were built, not surprisingly, on the edifice of anti-immigrant, racist and xenophobic appeals. Their electoral successes and failures have hinged on a variety of factors, ranging from economic conditions to the nature of the party system. A strong two-party system, coupled with the "take-no-prisoners" approach of the Tory leader Margaret Thatcher, nipped anti-immigrant politics in the bud in Britain in the early 1980s. In France, however, a weaker party system, a long tradition of nationalist subcultures (on the left in the form of Jacobinism and on the right in the forms of Gaullism and a peculiarly French variety of fascism), and high unemployment combined to encourage the development of the Front National (FN) under the leadership of Jean-Marie Le Pen. In contrast, the liberal political culture of the Federal Republic of Germany has shown remarkable resilience and a well-founded aversion to ethnonationalist movements. Not until the 1980s, with the rise (and apparent fall) of the Republikaner party, did anti-immigrant and nationalist politics break through the carefully crafted party system that was designed to keep extemist movements at bay. Finally, in the United States, nativist politics have receded in the postwar period, relegated for the most part to the state and local level, in the wake of the civil rights revolution, which laid the groundwork for a new ethnic pluralism.[5] How and why has immigration been transformed from an economic and demographic issue to an issue of citizenship and membership in these liberal polities?

Defining who is an alien and who is entitled to membership in the liberal polity is no longer the exclusive prerogative of the executive, or of administrative authorities. Judges have become involved in these decisions in every liberal democracy. In the United States, the shift in the bases of immigration law is clearly a legacy of the civil rights movement, which seems to have spread to Western Europe, albeit in different institutional and cultural settings, in the 1980s.[6] Despite the important institutional differences between these countries, their immigration and citizenship laws have become similar as the contradictions and paradoxes of liberalism work themselves out in each society.

The "working out" of the contradictions of liberalism and the assertion of aliens' civil and political rights in Europe and the United States—the development of rights-based politics—have dovetailed with the development of largely unregulated markets for foreign labor. These two factors go a long way in explaining the difficulties that liberal states have faced in their attempts to regulate immigration. The dovetailing of rights and markets, however, has brought to the fore the liberal paradox, about which Karl Polanyi wrote in *The Great Transformation:* how can an individual be both a commodity in the marketplace, devoid of social and political purpose, *and* an actor in the liberal polity, entitled to civil, social, and political rights?

Citizenship and the Liberal Polity

Jean-Jacques Rousseau made a forceful argument for instilling in the individual a sense of republican virtue, civic duty, and commitment to the republican ideals of liberty and equality.[7] English liberals—John Locke and John Stuart Mill—were more attentive to the importance of maintaining a balance between the identity and self-interest of the individual and a sense of national community.[8] The French ideal of citizenship finds its origins in the French Revolution and the contractarian philosophy of Rousseau, whereas the modern Anglo-American tradition of citizenship and nationhood is more closely linked with liberal ideas of individuality and consent.[9] These two notions of citizenship, which have strongly influenced public attitudes and debates over immigration in postwar France and the United States, are universalist, republican, *and* stringently assimilationist. The German conception of citizenship, which is closely connected to the history of nation-building in the German *Reich*, is more organic, particularist, and ethnocultural than either the French or American ideas. Historically, German citizenship has found expression in the *Volksgemeinschaft* (national community), which had strong ethnic, cultural, and (in the case of the Third Reich) racist overtones.[10] How do these cultural and historical traditions affect immigration and the status of foreigners in postwar Europe and the United States?

To the skeptic traditions of nationhood and theories of citizenhip are too far removed from the practice of politics to influence public policy, and institutional and cultural practices have little to do with immigration and naturalization. If this view is correct, some of the most cherished generalizations of comparative politics are not well founded. To argue that French and German politics are historically more statist than American politics—which is heavily influenced by a liberal and pluralist tradition—may be a futile exercise that at best explains nothing, and at worst perpetuates ideological stereotypes about politics in these countries. My position is, to the contrary, that immigration and naturalization policy, as well as nationality and citizenship laws, cannot be understood without reference to political culture and theories of citizenship. In postwar Europe and the United States a new liberal view of citizenship is replacing nationalist and particularist conceptions of the relationship between the individual and the state. The contractarian theory of Rousseau and the Jacobin view of citizenshp are under great pressure in France, as a result of the influx of Muslim immigrants in the 1960s and 1970s. The English notions of contract and consent, which have been the cornerstone of citizenship in the liberal American polity, have been eroded by more expansive ideals of membership, social justice, and human rights, leading some to conclude that citizenship itself has been *devalued*.[11] The ethnocultural, German ideal of citizenship, so clearly evident in the *Volksgemeinschaft*, has given way to a new civic culture in the Federal Republic, which assiduously avoids Germanization of foreign and ethnic minorities, while maintaining a strict naturalization policy. In each of these cases we will find evidence of national traditions and differences in political culture that influence the politics of citizenship. Yet there is strong evidence of convergence in immigration and citizenship policies, which is a harbinger of a new ideal of citizenship and civic culture in the liberal democracies. This ideal finds greater expression in the work of Tocqueville than in the works of Rousseau, Locke, or Mill.[12]

Immigration brings sharply into focus institutional and cultural differences among the liberal democracies. By the same token, these differences are crucial in determining how states define who is and who is not entitled to membership in society. Several differences in the political traditions of Europe and the United States immediately stand out. The first historical difference is the stronger statist tradition of administrative and bureaucratic politics in France and Germany, compared with the more liberal, antistatist, and pluralist political culture in the United States.[13] The statist tradition has been weakened by a range of political and economic changes—such as the development of the European Community, which has had a liberalizing effect on the political economy of many European states—but it still influences the way in which France and Germany attempt to regulate immigration (see chapters 3 and 4) and define citizenship. The legal systems reflect the statist tradition. Notions of popular sovereignty that stem from the French Revolution underlie and legitimate systems of codified Roman law. Universalist principles of natural right, individualism, and consent have tended to be less important than the principle of popular sovereignty. Judges continue to play a more important role in the politics of immigration in the United States, although the role of the judiciary in defining the rights of aliens has been evolving rapidly in Europe.

Secondly, in some European states, nationalist and statist traditions have given rise to political cultures that tend to be exclusive.[14] The late development of the German state and the necessity of rapidly creating a national identity led to a narrow view of citizenship and community, which took ethnicity and kinship as the primary criteria for defining who is or is not German. The French Jacobin tradition, while universalist and expansive in terms of rights (see the Declaration of the Rights of Man *and* the Citizen) is also highly nationalist.

Jacobinism is intertwined with the history of the French nation and with struggles (since 1789) to turn internal ethnic minorities (Bretons, Corsicans, Alsacians, and others) into citizens.[15] In the United States the strong constitutional tradition—based on liberal notions of natural right, the inherent worth of the individual, and consent—has been a driving factor in the politics of immigration. But this expansive liberal tradition, which gave rise eventually to a pluralist political culture, ran head on into the social and political realties of racism— African Americans were denied citizenship until the Civil War, and they continued to be excluded from many of the benefits of political, social, and civil citizenship until the postwar civil rights revolution. The harsh assimilationist ideology of the melting pot was reflective of a narrow Anglo-Saxon view of American identity. Not until the postwar period did the constitutional tradition begin to exert a stronger influence on politics, leading to a pluralist (Tocquevillian) vision of citizenship, anchored more firmly in the civic culture.[16]

Another important institutional difference between the European and American states is that European states tend historically to be unitary rather than federal, thus masking or suppressing long-standing divisions within these societies—cleavages which may still pose a threat to national unity. The postwar West German regime represented an important break with this unitary tradition, which is still best symbolized by the "one and indivisible" French Republic. European party systems have tended to institutionalize deep-seated social cleavages along class, ethnic, or regional lines.[17] As a result, multiparty politics are more common in Europe than in the United States, and a centralizing national ideology (such as Jacobinism or the *Volksgemeinschaft*) became a necessary counterweight to centrifugal political and social forces. The unitary nature of European political systems, the parliamentary tradition (as opposed to separation of powers), and multiparty systems (usually with an element of proportional representation) have contributed to a more volatile politics of citizenship in Europe.

Finally, it is important to note that member states of the EC have ceded some of their sovereignty with respect to control of their populations and territory, thus creating the possibility of a European citizenship. As signatories to the Treaty of Rome, France and Germany must grant freedom of entry to the nationals of other member states. This is an important point of difference with the United States, which has no such treaty obligations. The effort to create a single market for capital, goods, and services in the Community by the end of 1992 has reinforced liberal tendencies with respect to the mobility of people. Although there have been discussions about the desirability of creating a North American common market, no multilateral agreements exist governing the movement of people between Canada, Mexico, and the United States.

Civil Rights and Sovereignty in the United States

If we confine our comparison of immigration and the politics of citizenship in Europe and the United States to the 1970s and 1980s, the contrasts are quite stark. Citizenship was not at the center of debates over immigration in the United States during that period because the civil rights movement and the subsequent development of a new legal culture, based on liberal and communitarian principles of social justice, had helped to pave the way for a rights-based approach to issues of citizenship and assimilation. In the late 1970s, during the presidency of Jimmy Carter, the U.S. Congress set up a commission to reconsider American immigration laws and policies (the Select Commission on Immigration and Refugee Policy). The impetus for this initiative for immigration reform was not the result of a crisis of citizenship, of national identity, or of partisan political pressures. Rather, the initiative was part of the general development of civil rights, a concern for the protection of minorities (reflected in the growing importance of judicial and administrative review in American politics), the play of organized interests, including a desire better to control illegal immigration, and the commitment of a few legislators to immigration reform.[18] The effort to reform immigration laws brought into play several prominent lobbies: organized labor, Mexican-Americans, nativist groups, and growers of perishable fruits and vegetables.[19] The major points of contention in these debates were less global than in France or Germany. Citizenship was clearly a secondary issue, as the interests of employers in procuring an adequate supply of cheap foreign labor and the desire of minority groups to protect their rights took precedence over philosophical concerns.[20]

The United States is by far the largest importer of foreign labor among the liberal/industrial democracies. What is intriguing is that in the United States, unlike in the labor-importing states of Western Europe, immigration has had an important clandestine dimension, which would seem to indicate that immigration is driven largely by market relations. Yet the American political system has come closer than European systems in reconciling markets (the commodification of foreign labor) with the rights of immigrants. For this reason the United States provides an essential point of reference for a comparative study of the political economy of immigration. Having said this, a note of caution is in order; many "traveling problems" are involved in American—European comparisons. Even though Europe and America share a common (enlightenment) culture, which values individual freedom and equality before the law, the nature of democracy and the founding myths of the American republic are quite different from those of the European republics.[21]

By virtue of its political, economic, and military prowess, the United States has become the dominant world power in the latter half of the twentieth century, which has led some to refer to the post-World War II period as *Pax Americana*.[22] If there is a hegemonic (international) system with the United States at its center, we would expect the system to be characterized by liberal institutionalism in which rights and markets play a prominent role. The history of immigration in the United States parallels the rise of American power, a developing sense of nationhood following the Civil War, and a growing awareness of what it means to be *American*. Successive waves of immigration were absorbed, in the first instance through a stringent (Anglo-Saxon) assimilationist ideology—the famous melting pot—and in the second instance through a political system characterized by a separation of powers, sufficiently decentralized to allow immigrants to find an institutional niche in which to pursue their interests. This historically occurred at the local, municipal level, through the good offices of the party boss and the party machine.[23] In the period between the two world wars, which was crucial from the standpoint of the evolution of immigration law, assertions of American identity and national sovereignty led to the adoption of some of the most restrictionist and illiberal policies in the history of the American republic, for example, the invidious National Origins Quota system. But in the postwar period the restrictive aspects of immigration law and policy gradually receded in favor of a new liberalism. Immigration since the 1950s has not provoked the crises of national identity that have been evident in Europe. To find this type of nationalist backlash, we must go back in American history to the early part of the century, when largescale immigrations of culturally and ethnically distinct groups—Chinese, Irish, Italians, and Jews—led to outbreaks of xenophobia and nativism. Historically, however, the politics of citizenship in the United States has turned on the second-class status of African Americans—from conflicts over the abolition of slavery in the nineteenth century to the civil rights movement of the 1950s and 1960s. It was the civil rights movement in particular that helped to establish a broad definition of citizenship and started the shift in immigration politics away from the assimilationist ideology of the melting pot and toward a new cultural pluralism. This ongoing pluralist settlement of citizenship issues in the United States has been reinforced by the federal courts, which play a crucial role in guaranteeing the rights of individuals, be they citizens or aliens.[24]

Unlike France and Germany, the United States after the war never made a largescale effort to recruit foreign workers, except for the *bracero* and H-2 (skilled immigrant) programs, and the Special Agricultural Worker (SAW) provision of the 1986 Immigration Reform and Control Act (IRCA). These policies were designed not for the whole-scale recruitment of foreign workers, but to manage the flow of seasonal and agricultural labor. The principal institution for implementing immigration policy in the United States, the Immigration and Naturalization Service, has not played the same role in immigration policy as the French Office des Migrations Internationales or the German Bundesanstalt für Arbeit. The latter agencies were set up specifically for the purpose of administering foreign worker programs. The INS has played a lesser role in administering worker immigration, especially after 1965, when most legal immigrants to the United States came as family members rather than workers. Although the INS has the responsibility for policing American borders, it has been (and continues to be) relatively ineffective in its efforts to control illegal worker migration.[25] The marketplace rather than the state is the driving factor behind worker immigration in the United States. A large proportion of immigration to the United States takes place through private rather than public channels, and there has been no official recruitment policy.[26]

American immigration policy reflects a strong liberal bias, both in terms of politics and economics. The American labor market has remained relatively open to foreigners throughout the postwar period, even though the 1986 IRCA included a provision for employer sanctions for the first time in American history. The act has made it more difficult for foreigners to find jobs, but available evidence indicates that it has not stemmed the flow of undocumented aliens into the

American labor market.[27] While there have been sporadic outbursts of nativist and xenophobic politics in the United States in the postwar period, especially at the state and local level, immigration has not been the most hotly debated political issue, and nativist groups have not succeeded in forcing a radical change in American policy. Even the 1986 IRCA, designed to gain greater control over illegal immigration through measures such as employer sanctions, retains many of the liberal biases of earlier policies.[28] In fact, the act contains a number of specific provisions for the protection of the civil rights of aliens, especially Hispanics, and the employer sanctions clause is subject to periodic review and may be eliminated if it is determined to be the cause of discrimination against foreign-looking job applicants. Clearly, American politicians and policymakers have not opted for radical policies of suspending immigration, even though legal and illegal immigration have reached historically high levels in the 1970s and 1980s.[29] Still, there have been some attempts to crack down, for instance, Operation Wetback in 1954 in which over a million Mexicans residing illegally in the United States were deported.

The Rise of a New Legal Culture

The American approach to regulating immigration reflects the development of a new politics of public policy, which is more adversarial and more protective of the rights of individuals and groups in the political process. Immigration policy was actually one of the last bastions of relatively unchecked executive and administrative power. As late as the 1960s, executive authorities were able to exercise sweeping exclusionary powers with respect to aliens. Since that time, however, the federal judiciary has grown increasingly active and no longer remains on the sidelines with respect to the implementation of immigration policy. As Peter Schuck demonstrates in his powerful essay on "The Transformation of Immigration Law," the reasons for the very passive role of the judiciary in earlier periods were linked to the old legal distinction between right and privilege, whereby an alien should have no inherent right to enter the territory of the United States. Entrance into American territory was a privilege which could be conferred only by the sovereign state, as represented by Congress and the President. The Congress, which has the constitutional responsibility "to establish an uniform Rule of Naturalization," in the past has delegated to the President and the Attorney General broad powers for classifiying and excluding individuals who sought to enter and reside in the United States.

The decision to vest sweeping power in the hands of the executive and one cabinet official, even for the sake of protecting the national interest, has come into conflict with new rulings in administrative and constitutional law. Schuck documents the way in which each of these traditions is linked to broader changes in American politics and political culture, from the New Deal to the civil rights movement. In the 1970s and 1980s a shift in legal culture began to transform immigration law by limiting the autonomy of administrative authorities, especially the Immigration and Naturalization Service. Schuck links the weakening of notions of national sovereignty in immigration law and policy to the changing role of the United States in the international system. The erosion of American hegemony in the postwar period, particularly in the 1960s and 1970s in the wake of the Vietnam War, found its parallel in public law, as the powers of the executive in many policy areas were increasingly constrained by the judiciary.[30] At the same time, the civil rights revolution was transforming other areas of the law. The full application of the Fourteenth and Fifteenth amendments created new procedural protections for minorities and aliens that made it more difficult for administrative authorities such as the INS to act arbitrarily.[31] Judges were emboldened to intervene in the deportation, exclusion, and detention of aliens—procedures which are statutorily defined as civil rather than criminal, which makes it more difficult for aliens to bring suit to stop the government from acting in summary fashion.

One of the practical effects of these new checks on the administrative state has been to open the American labor market to undocumented aliens, who are able to find a niche both in the marketplace and in the polity. Within the immigration bureaucracy itself, the rights of aliens are protected through the application of stricter standards of "reasonableness and fairness," which is a central feature of the mandate for immigration judges (who adjudicate under the authority and supervision of the INS, the Attorney General, and the Department of Justice).[32] Although the INS often acts as judge, jury, and executioner for undocumented aliens, it has been increasingly susceptible to political and interest group pressures, not unlike other administrative agencies.[33] Deportation procedures for undocumented aliens are fairly stringent, and it is possible for the INS to act quickly to expel them. However, more and more aliens have been successful in appealing INS rulings or in requesting political asylum, thereby delaying or stopping deportation, exclusion, and detention.[34] Such judicial review puts administrative authorities on the defensive, often bringing into conflict the civil and human rights of aliens and questions of foreign policy. At times American immigration and refugee policy has been driven more by foreign policy than by considerations of equity and justice.

The rights of aliens in the United States were expanded by the Supreme Court decision in *Plyler v. Doe,* which forced authorities in Texas to admit the children of undocumented aliens into the public school system. This decision is a good example of the impact of the new legal culture on immigration in the United States. By arguing that the innocent children of undocumented aliens should not be punished for a crime committed by their parents (residing illegally in the United States), the Court opened the way for greater restrictions and judicial review of government agencies with respect to immigrants and refugees. Schuck argues that the *Plyler v. Doe* decision does for immigration what *Brown v. Board of Education* did for civil rights and school desegregation.[35] The extension of constitutional protections to aliens residing in the United States is yet another indication of the importance of rights in setting levels of immigration and reinforcing the development of a market for foreign labor. The full impact of the new legal culture on immigration and its limiting effect on administrative authority has become apparent only in the 1980s: "until the early 1980s, it was almost inconceivable that a court would haul the government into court primarily at the behest of excludable or deportable aliens and require it to defend a policy such as that concerning EVD [Extended Voluntary Departure—the principal administrative procedure for deportation], a policy that is plainly and appropriately discretionary in nature, intimately intertwined with the most delicate and volatile aspects of our foreign policy, and reflective of political negotiation between Congress and President."[36]

By placing a stronger check on the power of government summarily to deport undocumented aliens, the federal judiciary extended basic civil rights of due process and equal protection to noncitizens, but nonetheless members—in terms of basic human rights—of American society. While the trends in adminstrative and constitutional law have been in the direction of a greater rights-based politics, there have been some reversals of liberal policy, especially in the power and willingness of immigration authorities in the United States to incarcerate aliens, pending a decision of their petition to remain. Most often, cases of imprisonment have involved asylum seekers whom the government will not trust to appear for an administrative hearing. A good example of this illiberal policy of incarcerating aliens seeking refugee status is the detention of thousands of Central Americans along the Texas border, pending a hearing before an immigration judge on their request for political asylum. The summary detention and deportation of thousands of Haitian refugees each year in South Florida is another example of attempts by immigration authorities to circumvent liberal policy constraints. Both of these policies (in Texas and Florida) have come under increasing judicial scrutiny and attack.

In 1990 the Federal Board of Immigration Appeals reversed a ruling by an immigration judge that aliens who were arrested and refused to answer questions about how and when they entered the United States could be deported immediately. The ruling essentially upheld Fifth Amendment rights against self-incrimination for aliens and shifted the burden of proof from the defendants to the government.[37] In the wake of the 1990 reform of legal immigration and the 1986 IRCA, which dealt mainly with illegal immigration, the courts have continued to expand the rights of aliens. In early 1990, the Supreme Court in *McNary v. Haitian Refugee Center* decided that the government could be sued through a class action law suit over the way the INS administered immigration policy. The suit concerned a specific provision of the 1986 IRCA, in which the government argued that Congress had intended to ban judicial review of immigration proceedings, except in the case of individual aliens who were denied amnesty. The suits brought against the INS challenged the way in which the 1986 law was being administered, arguing that INS procedures violated the spirit of the law and constitutional rights of due process. In holding for the defendants, the Court stated that "Even disregarding the risk of deportation, the impact of a denial of the opportunity for gainful employment is plainly sufficient to mandate constitutionally fair procedures in the application process."[38] By stopping arbitrary procedures for deportation and by opening the process of policy implementation to judicial review, the Court significantly expanded the rights of aliens.

In a lower court ruling early in 1991, a federal judge in San Francisco held that undocumented aliens can sue employers for discrimination under Title VII of the 1964 Civil Rights Act, thus arming immigrant workers in the United States with a potentially powerful legal weapon with which to fight discrimination in the workplace and protect their rights. Only illegal aliens covered by the amnesty provisions of the 1986 act could bring such suits, however, because other illegals would risk exposing themselves to deportation proceedings. Nevertheless, this ruling, if upheld on appeal, would extend protection for aliens from job discrimination and from the arbitrary powers of INS authorities. The ruling offers more evidence of a direct link between the civil rights revolution and the expansion of rights for aliens.[39]

Interest Groups and the Legislative Process

Apart from the role of the judiciary in protecting individual rights, there is a strong pluralist (as opposed to statist) bias in the politics of immigration in the United States. The legislative process in the United States, which is characterized by a stringent separation of powers and weakness of political parties, encourages lobbying that has led to the fragmentation of many policy debates, as interest groups line up for or against various provisions of the proposed legislation. A prime example of this aspect of the American political process is the issue of national identity cards. The frequent proposals to create a national identity card as a way of controlling illegal immigration have provoked fierce opposition from libertarian groups—such as the American Civil Liberties Union—as an unjustified invasion of privacy and an abuse of state power. Such a system of identification was put into effect in France early in this century by executive decree. Identity cards have been required for foreigners since 1917 and for French citizens since 1945.[40]

In the most recent rounds of immigration reform in the United States—the Immigration Reform and Control Act of 1986 and the 1990 act reforming legal immigration—interest group lobbying was intense.[41] Leading up to the 1986 act, fruit and vegetable growers fought successfully to preserve access to seasonal agricultural workers, while the Mexican-American Legal Defense Fund and other groups lobbied strongly for the inclusion of provisions to protect the rights of minorities against discrimination in hiring that might result from the enactment of sanctions against employers who hire undocumented workers. The adoption of employer sanctions as a central provision of immigration reform in 1986 was part of an overall strategy for controlling illegal immigration and building a political coalition between conservatives and liberals to gain passage of the legislation. Never, however, in the debate over immigration reform in the 1970s and 1980s, was consideration given to suspending immigration to the United States, in contrast to the restrictionist policies that were enacted in various European states in the mid-1970s. The suspension of worker immigration in Europe, as we saw in earlier chapters, was the result of actions taken by administrative and executive authorities in the name of the national interest. The possibility of the American President unilaterally suspending immigration is unthinkable, and indeed unconstitutional, even though the executive is given considerable discretion by Congress to administer immigration policy. A good example of this administrative discretion is the parole authority of the Attorney General for granting political asylum on an ad hoc, emergency basis. The executive, and especially the Immigration and Naturalization Service (part of the Department of Justice), must operate within the guidelines set down by Congress. If there is a dispute over the interpretation of the law, the judiciary will get involved in short order—at least this has been the case in the 1970s and 1980s. Wide-ranging legislative debates over immigration occur periodically, usually once every ten to twenty years. Yet American political parties play a very different role in debates over immigration than do parties in Europe.

Both the 1986 and the 1990 acts serve to illustrate this point. The 1990 reform of legal immigration injected a larger labor-market component into immigration law by increasing the number of slots reserved for skill-based immigration, while keeping a high priority for family immigration. The 1990 act sought to achieve a greater balance between labor market (and human capital) considerations on the one hand, and the humanitarian (family-based) dimensions of legal immigration policy on the other. In the legislative process, it was difficult to discern any clear partisan pattern, as groups lined up for or against certain aspects of the legislation. Not surprisingly, groups that have benefited most from family-based immigration (such as Hispanics and some Asian nationalities) lobbied hard to retain the bias in favor of family reunification in the 1965 act, whereas groups such as the Irish—supported by Edward Kennedy, the senior senator from Massachusetts, a state with a large Irish population—sought to create a greater mix in the distribution of visas between Asian, Latin American, and European nationalities.

American political parties are notoriously weak in their ability (or inability) to set the national political agenda.[42] Congressional debates over immigration in the past decades indicate that the majority of politicians of both political parties, and many of the leaders of these parties, view immigration as a Pandora's box, better left unopened. Yet most initiatives for immigration reform have started in Congress with pressure from various interest groups, usually without a discernible partisan dimension. European politicians of the left and right also prefer not to deal with immigration as a political issue. But given the strength of parliamentary systems and strong nationalist traditions, rightwing parties in Europe have a better chance of bringing issues such as immigration, nationality, and citizenship forcefully to the electorate. As a result of weak parties and the pluralist nature of the legislative process, immigration politics in the United States is broken down into many small issues in the course of debates over policy.

In addition to the weakness of political parties and the strength of the two-party system, the federal nature of the American political system helps to create a number of local dynamics in the politics of immigration and complicates the problem of making and enforcing national immigration policy. Federalism introduces another layer of state and local government between the national administration and the targets of regulation, that is, the migrants. Some states and localities have carried on lively debates over immigration that have led to the enactment of local legislation, such as nativist laws in California and Florida making English the official language of the state (with a small "s"). Federal authorities, and especially the Supreme Court, have been slow to react to state and local laws that discriminate against aliens, despite the clear and sweeping provision of the Fourteenth Amendment, which provides that "no state shall deny to any person within its jurisdiction the equal protection of the laws."[43] Nonetheless, as we saw in the previous discussion, a new legal culture emerged in the 1970s and 1980s, which curtailed the arbitrary powers of the states in the area of immigration. The most recent example of this limitation was the striking down by a federal court of an Arizona statute, which sought to establish English as the official language of the state of Arizona.

Both the political system and the legal culture impose increasingly severe constraints on the power of government to classify and deport aliens. This new liberalism has its roots in the civil rights movement of the 1950s and 1960s. The principal characteristic of the new politics—which has been described by some scholars as adversarial legalism—is an emphasis on social justice and rights.[44] Old notions of rights versus privilege, individual consent, national sovereignty, sovereign immunity, and other statist/realist conceptions of the relationship between the individual and the state have receded in favor of greater legal protections for the rights of groups and individuals. The judicial assault on the sovereignty and autonomy of the state has contributed significantly to the rise of immigration in the United States in the 1970s and 1980s. Conversely, it has helped to suppress the politics of citizenship (the hallmark of political struggles over civil rights in the 1950s and 1960s), as aliens find protection through the courts. Thus far, political parties and politicians (with one or two notable exceptions) have not seized upon the issue of immigration to fan the flames of nationalism. The European experience, despite the many cultural and institutional differences outlined above, shows a remarkable convergence with the American experience.

Immigration and Competing Nationalisms in France

French preoccupation with the issue of citizenship in the 1980s is a reflection of longstanding concerns over the compatibility between national unity defined in revolutionary Jacobin terms, and a growing social and cultural pluralism.[45] For most of the postwar period, immigration was looked upon and analyzed in the context of economic and demographic change. The role of foreign labor in the process of economic modernization was stressed alongside the contribution of immigration to demographic growth.[46] In the 1970s immigration became the subject of political debate, as the contribution of immigrants to economic growth receded in the collective memory. How the issue of citizenship came to the fore in the 1980s reveals some fundamental rifts and tensions that exist in French political culture. These rifts, which I describe as competing nationalisms, find expression in party politics. The judiciary has played less of a role in setting the parameters of citizenship and immigration debates in France than it did in the United States, although it would be wrong to say that French courts have been absent from these debates.

French politics emphasizes citizenship and equality before the law, whereas the current trend in American politics is to offer special protection or assistance to individuals and groups on the basis of their marginal (or minority) status. Affirmative action—the centerpiece of much of the civil rights legislation in the United States—is perhaps the best example of this difference in the politics of citizenship in France and the United States. Special recognition of minorities (to insure equality of treatment for all citizens) is anathema to the Jacobin tradition, which stresses absolute equality before the law; but special treatment of individuals and groups—affirmative action to right past wrongs—has become commonplace in American politics following the 1964 Civil Rights Act. Vulnerable individuals and marginal groups in American society, including aliens, have found protection from the arbitrary powers of the state and employers. Yet there *is* a tradition of civil rights in France. Even though the bias is clearly in favor of administrative (and executive) rather than judicial power, the 1789 Declaration of the Rights of Man and the Citizen (the centerpiece of French civil liberties) is set out in the Preamble of the Constitution of the Fifth Republic, and is judicially enforceable. But on the whole French jurisprudence derives from the contractarian views of Rousseau; it tends to regard the state as a moral being and the nation as the personification of the general will.[47]

In France the principal institution for protecting individuals against the arbitary power of the state is the Council of State, which is itself part of the administration, sitting at the pinnacle of the system of administrative courts. Hence the tradition of separation of powers, while not entirely absent in French politics, is much weaker than in the United States.[48] The Council of State has intervened on several occasions to strike down aspects of French immigration and refugee policy, because of legal inconsistencies. For example, it annulled attempts by the French government to inhibit family reunification in the late 1970s.[49] In the 1980s and 1990s the Council of State also ruled against the government in matters of immigration, ethnic, and refugee policy. In 1991, for example, the government was forced to reverse its decision to deny political asylum to a well-known Moroccan dissident. The Council ruled that the socialist government of Edith Cresson had failed to demonstrate that the dissident was a threat to French national security.

But the French judiciary is not so involved in the making and implementation of immigration policy as the judiciary in the United States. American judges can prevent the enforcement of aspects of immigration law deemed unconstitutional or inconsistent with prevailing standards of fairness, in spite of the fact that the federal judiciary traditionally has deferred to the executive, and been unwilling to interfere with the administration of immigration policy.[50]

French immigration law specifies the nature and types of restrictions on the admission of foreigners, yet certain ministries have considerable discretion to administer immigration policy, particularly the ministries of Labor (or Social Affairs) and Interior. The closest French equivalent to the INS is the Office des Migrations Internationales (OMI), formerly the Office National d'Immigration (ONI).[51] The main difference between the French OMI and the American INS is that the former has no real powers of enforcement. The policing power for immigration in France is the responsibility of the Ministry of the Interior. Most battles by special interests in France about the use of foreign labor have taken place not in the National Assembly but behind closed doors in the ministries. A prime example is the construction industry, which lobbied successfully for the lifting of restrictions on labor in its sector after the official suspension of worker immigration in 1974.[52] But despite the strength of the state in France, governments have had enormous difficulty in regulating or controlling immigration (see chapter 6).

In the 1980s the government lost control of the issue of immigration, with the rise of a new politics of citizenship and the emergence of an anti-immigrant political movement on the extreme right—the National Front. The FN represents only one side of a partisan debate over immigration that has raged throughout the 1980s and into the 1990s. This debate has brought into play various nationalisms—from Jacobinism on the left to a French version of fascism on the right—while liberals have struggled to hold the middle ground.

Citizenship and French Party Politics

In France in the 1980s the problem of immigration has come to be defined in terms of citizenship and identity, rather than demography or economics.[53] Suddenly some of the oldest themes of French political development surfaced in the course of debates over immigration, citizenship, and nationality. The republican synthesis, which was achieved with such difficulty in the Third Republic, seemingly has been threatened by the arrival in the late twentieth century of a Muslim population that is reluctant to abandon the religious and cultural dimensions of its identity in favor of a truly French identity. This political crisis in turn has led to a reopening of the church-state controversy that proved so difficult to resolve during the nineteenth century, and to a renaissance of the extreme right, which has not been so strong since the 1930s and 1940s.[54]

How could immigration have shifted so abruptly from the area of labor markets and employment to the realm of citizenship, nationality, and political participation? Coming to terms with the immigration of large ethnic minorities has entailed crises of this sort in many countries. The way they are resolved depends on political culture. As we have seen from the discussion of the American experience, the potential for a volatile politics of citizenship was blunted by the struggle over civil rights before the latest wave of Latin immigration. The conflict over the rights of individuals and groups in the United States helped to reinforce constitutional and liberal traditions, thrusting the federal judiciary into the midst of the relationship between the individual and the state.

While not of equal magnitude either in terms of numbers or the crises that it provoked, the settlement in France of the culturally and ethnically distinct Muslim minority raises many of the same questions as the presence of large ethnic minorities in the United States. In both cases political parties were crucial in determining whether integration would be a relatively smooth process, or one fraught with conflict and violence. One can trace the beginning of the political crisis over immigration in France to the SONACOTRA rent strikes of 1975–76, which demonstrated clearly that institutions which succeeded in integrating and assimilating Europeans during earlier periods would not be so successful with the Muslim and African groups.[55] One of the most important integrating forces (along with the schools) was the Communist party (PCF), which had been able to rally earlier waves of immigrants to the causes of the working class. This was true for Italian, Belgian, and Polish workers during the interwar period, and to a lesser extent European immigrant groups in the postwar period. But part of the condition of this integration was that immigrants abandon their traditional identity in favor of a new proletarian, national, and Jacobin identity.[56]

Although the PCF was having problems in its relationship with immigrant workers, especially in cities and towns controlled by Communist mayors, other political parties were faring little better, with the notable exception of the Socialist party (PS).[57] The coming to power of the left and the election of François Mitterrand in 1981 marked an important turning point in the politics of immigration. The first Socialist government of Pierre Mauroy moved quickly to carry out many of the campaign promises of the left, which included a general liberalization of politics, particularly in the areas of civil rights and civil liberties (abolition of the death penalty and stopping arbitrary search and seizure and *contrôle d'identité* by the police). The new spirit of political (if not economic) liberalism extended to foreign residents, at least insofar as rights of association and integration were concerned. In addition to giving official sanction to immigrant associations (heretofore restricted by the state), the Mauroy government, under the direction of President Mitterrand, went so far as to propose giving the right to vote in local elections to all foreigners who had resided in the country for five years. This proposal was not welcomed by the parties of the right (RPR and UDF) nor for that matter by the PCF, which was a participant in the first Socialist government.[58]

The package of measures proposed by the Mauroy government included a conditional amnesty for illegal aliens, which was enacted and carried out in 1981–82. The amnesty was designed to improve the living conditions of immigrants and to rally the new North African constituency *(le vote beur)* to the Socialist cause. The problems of assimilation were thus to be resolved through a combination of liberal measures that were accompanied by stricter control of immigration, ending once and for all the old policies of managing labor supply (and the population) by means of foreign labor and immigration. Yet while the average annual rate of immigration dropped from 200,200 during the period 1974–1980 to 160,000 for the period 1981–1987, it remained relatively high; and the foreign population reached a historical high in 1982 of 6.8 percent of the total population, slightly higher than in 1931.[59]

With the stated desire of the Socialists in the early 1980s to assimilate the foreign population while carefully regulating future immigration, statistics took on added political significance. A partisan debate raged throughout the 1980s over the counting of foreigners and the accuracy of immigration statistics.[60] In the wake of the amnesty, which was only modestly successful, and with the easing of police controls and the upsurge in Middle Eastern terrorism during the 1980s, the stage was set for a xenophobic reaction against immigration and the liberal policies of the Socialist government.[61] The vehemence of this reaction—which took the form of an ultra-nationalist and neofascist political movement, Jean-Marie Le Pen's Front National—were largely unanticipated. Partisan politics fastened onto the issues of immigration and citizenship, giving new momentum for policy reform. The political program of the FN included stopping all immigration, expelling foreign workers, and revising the nationality law (Code de la Nationalité) to make it more difficult for the state to attribute citizenship to second-generation Algerian immigrants.

As the liberal/assimilationist policies of the Socialists began to take effect, the economic situation in France was deteriorating rapidly from 1981 to 1983. Unemployment was rising among the French and foreign populations. Immigrants were hit hard by the economic recession of the early 1980s. They accounted for over 10 percent of all job seekers during this period (compared with 8–9 percent for the French population), according to the labor market statistics of the National Employment Agency (ANPE). The economic insecurity created by rising unemployment, together with a more visible, larger immigrant population were important factors in the breakthrough of the FN in the municipal elections of 1983 and the European elections of 1984.[62] At the same time, the level of political activity around the immigration issue was rising steadily from 1981 to 1983, culminating in rallies by proimmigrant, antiracist, and human rights groups such as SOS-racisme, whose leader, Harlem Désir, was to become the most prominent immigrant activist of the decade. In December 1983 François Mitterrand addressed a rally of North Africans—*marche des beurs*—at which he announced further liberalization measures, including the creation of a single identity card for foreigners valid for ten years.

Meanwhile, Socialist economic policy took a 180 degree turn in 1983, away from statist policies of nationalization and neo-Keynesian stimuli and toward more liberal policies of deregulation and economic restructuring. Immigration policy became more restrictive, but with a concerted effort on the part of the governments of Pierre Mauroy and Laurent Fabius to avoid confounding immigration with the xenophobic nationalism of the extreme right. Several conditions were attached to the new ten-year residency permit, resticting it to only a small minority of foreigners. In addition, leftwing Jacobin traditions of *laïcité* and the whole range of church-state issues began to cause problems within the PS and between it and its *beur* constituency. The opening of channels of political participation for immigrants facilitated a revival of Islam in the North African community, particularly among second generation Algerians, a minority of whom were spurred on by the militancy of fundamentalist Islamic movements in the Middle East.[63]

The reaction to Islamic militancy was not limited to an assimilationist Jacobin reflex, even though the Jacobin argument was quite prevalent among intellectuals of both the left and the right.[64] The entire debate over immigration in France shifted radically in the direction of a new nationalism. The FN and Jean-Marie Le Pen made no efforts to diguise their anti-immigrant positions, overtly expressed in terms of a sinister and antisemitic nationalism. The rallying cry of the FN, from the municipal elections of 1983 to the presidential and legislative elections of 1988, was "La France aux français!" This clarion call met with considerable electoral success (Le Pen consistently garnered around 10 percent of the vote in various elections from 1984 to 1988) and forced all political parties to redefine their positions on immigration. The brief shift to proportional representation for the legislative elections of 1986 allowed the FN to win 33 seats in the National Assembly and form its own parliamentary group, thus driving a wedge into the heart of the right, which struggled mightily with the issue of immigration and tried not to lose more votes to Le Pen without alienating its traditional liberal and republican constituencies.

The neo-Gaullist RPR under the leadership of Jacques Chirac, and the centrist UDF, under the leadership of Raymond Barre, Giscard d'Estaing, and others, clearly longed for the old days when immigration was an issue of population decline and labor supply, rather than citizenship and national identity. Nonetheless, from the European elections of 1984 into the 1990s, the RPR was forced to take a tough restrictionist stand on immigration and a nationalist stand on citizenship issues, to avoid further erosion of its conservative constituency, particularly in the south of France where alliances were struck between local RPR and FN candidates. Immigration was particularly vexing for those politicians who claimed the mantle of Gaullism because Gaullist ideology is by definition nationalist, although it is a much more benign republican nationalism than that of the FN. Nevertheless, one of the principal tenets of Gaullism was to promote and defend "une certaine idée de la France," which conjures up images of past French greatness and evokes a rather pure image of *French* identity. Even though Gaullism takes an expansive and liberal vision of the relationship between the individual and the state, it contains within it nationalistic strands that make it (and its electorate) susceptible to the xenophobic appeals of the extreme nationalist right.

As a response to the breakthrough of FN, the neo-Gaullist RPR, under the leadership of Jacques Chirac, promised during the legislative campaign of 1986 to crack down on immigration and make it more difficult for foreigners to acquire citizenship. Once in power, however, the Chirac government backed gingerly away from the promise to eliminate place of birth *(jus soli)* from French nationality law (Code de la Nationalité). The new government opted instead for limits on naturalization that would restore "value and dignity" to French citizenship. The proposed change in the law provoked a political firestorm, as liberal groups of the left and the right accused the government of acquiescing to the demands of Le Pen and the FN. The response of the government was to convene a Commission of Experts (Commission des Sages). It held public hearings on reform of the Code, only to reaffirm the relatively liberal traditions of French jurisprudence in this area, especially the commitments to elective citizenship and liberal rules of naturalization. For over a century, French citizenship had been attributed to second-generation immigrants in accordance with the *jus soli* principle of the Code. In effect, the children of foreigners born in France automatically receive French citizenship at the age of eighteen, unless they specifically reject it. This aspect of French law made it easier to assimilate second-generation immigrants.[65]

The Chirac government also proposed legislation to give greater authority to prefectoral administrations (meaning local police) to expel illegal aliens. These measures were designed to curb immigration, restrict access to citizenship, and cut down on naturalizations, which were not dramatically higher in the 1980s than in the 1970s.[66] Despite the spate of political, administrative, and intellectual activity around the issues of immigration and citizenship, no real changes were made in the law. The Chirac government withdrew its bills for restricting immigration and naturalization. Still, a clear difference remained between the positions of the right and the left on the issue of immigration in the 1980s. Socialist policies had a liberalizing effect on immigration (via the amnesty of 1981–82) and on assimilation and political participation (via new rules governing associations)—trends that picked up markedly in the 1980s. The right was constrained by pressure from the FN, which compelled the major parties (RPR and UDF) to take a tough stance with respect to future immigration and immigrant political activities.

The great citizenship debate of the 1980s and 1990s also can be seen as a response to the rise of a pluralist discourse in French politics (revealed in the catchy phrase—*le droit à la différence*).[67] On the political extremes the Jacobin, leftwing groups (primarily in the Socialist party) as well as the more insular and racist FN viewed the pluralist movement as a threat to French national unity and political identity. But why did these competing nationalisms fail to carry the day politically? Apart from having the balance of political forces in the National Assembly against them, nationalist posturing worked for the right (Chirac and the RPR) as an oppositional strategy, but failed as public policy. The reason for the failure of reform (and the more nationalist positions on immigration) lay in French political culture, which in addition to being stridently assimilationist is also universalist, voluntarist, and inclusive.

The rise of the FN and the citizenship debate brought back some of the ghosts of France's recent colonial past, especially the Algerian War. After the 1962 Evian Agreements ending the war and granting independence to Algeria, many Algerians (including the *harkis* who fought on the French side) chose to settle in France and opted for French citizenship. Their children became eligible for citizenship under Articles 23 and 44 of the Code de la Nationalité. Article 23 grants citizenship according to *jus soli* and *jus sanguinis*, that is, all persons born in France with one French parent are automatically entitled to citizenship. Article 44 allows second-generation immigrants to opt for citizenship at age eighteen. A particular problem arises for the children of Algerian nationals, because the Algerian state confers citizenship upon them automatically and requires that they complete military service in Algeria. Thus a significant proportion of the *maghrébin* population in France has dual nationality. Coincidentally, this group of second-generation immigrants reached majority (age eighteen) in 1979–80 at the moment of the Iranian Revolution and the rise of a new Islamic militancy throughout the Arab world. Since the Le Pen group contained many holdovers from the Algerian war (and the *Algérie française* movement in particular), it is not surprising that young, militant Algerians would become the target of FN propaganda and attacks.

The rightwing, nationalist critique of immigration and naturalization policies gave us some of the most memorable slogans of the 1980s: "La France aux français!" "Etre français, cela se mérite!" "Français de coeur, français de papiers"—or, in the words of Le Pen, "français de fraîche date." Despite the surge in immigration throughout the industrialized West in the 1980s, this brand of xenophobic nationalism turned out to be more or less unique to France. Neither

American nor German politics displayed a comparable partisan exploitation of immigration. The citizenship debate in France reflected a crisis of national identity which brought to the fore some of the most basic themes of French political culture and development, including *laïcité*.

Islam and the Crisis of National Identity

No event better symbolized the importance of the Jacobin tradition in French politics than the controversy in 1989 sparked by three Muslim girls in the *collège* Gabriel-Havez in Creil, north of Paris, who chose to wear traditional Islamic headscarves (*foulards* or *tchador*) into the classroom. They were expelled from the school for their refusal to remove the offending scarves, ironically by a school principal from the West Indies. In the fall of 1989, in the midst of the revolutions that were sweeping Eastern Europe, the *affaire des foulards* transfixed public opinion and the intelligentsia. Should the young women be allowed to express their cultural identity through such an overt display of religiosity in the *école laïque!* The initial position of the Socialist government, headed by Michel Rocard, was to allow the women to wear the offending scarves so long as they did not proselytize. In the meantime, the whole issue was referred to the Council of State, which sided with the Rocard government, ruling that schools (and by extension the state) cannot discriminate against individuals on the basis of their religious preferences; it is legal for students to wear religious symbols in the classroom, so long as these symbols do not interfere with the religious freedom of others. The whole episode took on great symbolic importance, as intellectuals and politicians rallied in defense of the Jacobin model of assimilation and the *école laïque*.[68] The editor of *Libération*, Serge July, summarized the event as follows: "behind the scarf is the question of immigration, behind immigration is the debate over integration, and behind integration, the question of *laïcité*. By all accounts, two notions of *laïcité* are at issue here . . . what is *laïcité*, this venerable old lady of French history? Without going back to the conflicts between Jacobins and Girondins, we can see some traditional elements of French history at work here. To simplify, we have a strict assimilationist position on the one hand, and Anglo-American ghettos promoted in the name of the 'right to be different' (*droit à la différence*), on the other."[69]

The *affaire des foulards*, like the issue of immigration itself, divided political parties and the public roughly along three lines: liberal or pluralist, Jacobin, and nationalist. It is too early to tell whether the politics of immigration and ethnicity in France in the 1990s will evolve along the lines of cultural pluralism, as has been the case in the United States in the postwar period, or whether the political system and political parties will revert to a more strident Jacobin position.[70]

Clearly, however, we have seen a rejection of nationalist and statist policies. The defeat of the Chirac reform proposals was reinforced by a consultative opinion of the Council of State, which held the proposals to be legally unacceptable. President Mitterrand himself weighed in against the proposals—a stand which could have set the stage for a constitutional confrontation between the Socialist president and the neo-Gaullist premier. Certainly, the proposed legislation would have provided an interesting test of *cohabitation* (the sharing of power between the two executives from 1986 to 1988). But the RPR and Jacques Chirac, faced with a loss of support from liberal elements of the UDF and a potential confrontation with the Socialist President, decided to withdraw the legislation.

The initiative to reform the nationality law amounted to a political debacle for the French right, which was badly divided going into the presidential elections of 1988. The candidate of the right on the second round, Jacques Chirac, was forced to retreat to a liberal/pluralist position, closer to that of Mitterrand and the Socialists. Yet he was still suspected of flirting with Le Pen and the FN. Chirac and the right went on to lose the presidential and legislative elections of 1988.

This brief history of immigration, citizenship, and French party politics in the 1980s depicts the rejection of nationalist, statist, and exclusionary policies, and a reaffirmation of a tempered liberalism. The failure of the state to regulate immigration in the 1970s was not enough to justify abandoning liberal politics and minority rights in the 1980s. Institutional and cultural constraints helped to push the government in a liberal direction. In effect the political system and culture of the Fifth Republic proved capable of surmounting the crisis.

The Repression of Nationalism in Germany

If debates over immigration and citizenship in the United States were muted by the rise of a new liberal culture, in Germany the imposition

after World War II of a republican system—built upon liberal principles of constitutionalism, federalism, and respect for civil liberties
not very different from those of the American polity—helped to repress ethnonationalism. The political culture of the Federal Republic
has shown a strong commitment to civil rights, which has turned
traditional German nationalism on its head.[71] Rather than being a
force for the *Volksgemeinschaft*, nationality laws in the Federal Republic are written so as to avoid Germanization. At the same time
the standards for naturalization reflect a concern to maintain the
standards of civic culture, developed as a result of the postwar political reforms. However, critics of German law charge that the criteria
for naturalization are so stringent that it is impossible for resident
aliens to assimilate.

The protestations of various German politicians (of the left and the
right), that Germany is not a country of immigration—*Wir sind kein
ein Wanderungsland*—indicate the extent to which Germans remain
wedded to an ethnocultural conception of the German nation. Other
contradictions run through the politics of immigration and citizenship in Germany. Heavyhanded attempts to repatriate foreign workers
(through return policies described euphemistically as "the golden
handshake") were coupled with efforts to give those foreigners who
stayed a more secure social and legal status, but not citizenship. The
rights of aliens in Germany received a boost in 1975 with the adoption
of a new Aliens Act, which superseded the Aliens Act of 1938. Even
though the new act included guarantees for the legal and social status
of resident aliens—these provisions were adopted primarily as a result
of the lobbying efforts of the German trade unions (DGB)—the act
left the legal status of foreign workers sufficiently vague as to require
constant intervention by administrative courts.[72] Hence the judiciary
became more active in ruling on individual cases, even though the
act made it clear that decisions concerning immigration should be
made by administrative authorities.

Since 1978 foreigners who have resided in Germany for five years
gained the security of an unlimited residency permit (the German
version of the American green card). German administrative authorities (at the Ministry of Labor and the Bundesanstalt für Arbeit) kept
residency and work permits separate, mainly to prevent family immigration. The federal government also sought to limit the internal
mobility of foreign residents by forcing them to live in ad-
minstratively (and economically) defined districts *(Kreis)*. But as in

other liberal countries, foreigners were protected against such heavy-handed policies by the courts.[73] Perhaps the greatest legal test of the power of the adminstrative state to decide who should and should not be admitted as a member of German society came in 1979, when the effort to deny work permits to the family members of foreign workers was thwarted by administrative and constitutional tribunals, which ruled the policy to be illegal and unconstitutional.[74] These judicial decisions were the functional equivalents of the *Plyler v. Doe* decision of the U.S. Supreme Court, and the action taken by the highest administrative court in France, the Council of State. All of these decisions are an example of the importance of judicial constraints on administrative power in the liberal state, and the prominence of humanitarianism in the debate over citizenship and rights. In the German case the discretionary power of the administration in the area of immigration has been increasingly subject to judicial supervision by administrative tribunals.[75]

The German experience is even more interesting in light of the unification in 1990 of East and West Germany. The importance of immigration in postwar social and economic development, the settlement of a large and ethnically distinct population (mostly Turks), and the absorption of the former German Democratic Republic into the Federal Republic have pushed issues of citizenship and membership into the forefront of German politics. Like France, Germany has a very distinctive concept of citizenship, which is closely linked to the historical process of constructing a German national identity. But whereas the French concept of citizenship stems from the universalist Jacobin ideals of the French Revolution, the German concept has a strong ethnocultural dimension, which was transformed into a nationalist and racist ideology during the Third Reich. The unspeakable brutality and the horrors of the Third Reich can never be erased from German history; but the legacy of National Socialism should not detract from the remarkable accomplishments of the postwar West German regime, which has created and sustained a liberal political culture. Respect for civil rights and the checks and balances of a federal political system are but two of the most prominent aspects of the new political regime.[76]

Yet despite these accomplishments, German citizenship laws have retained strong differentialist (as opposed to assimilationist) and particularist (as opposed to universalist) biases, which stand in contrast to the more expansive French and American laws. A cursory examination of these aspects of German law might lead us to expect German immigration policies to be sharply restrictionist, and refugee policies to be exclusionary. But we have seen that since the 1960s immigration has been higher in Germany than any other West European state (in numbers), and Germany has perhaps the most liberal refugee and asylum policy in Europe. How can we explain this disjuncture between high levels of immigration, liberal refugee policies, and exclusionary citizenship laws?

Even though German nationality law dates from the Wilhelmine period, postwar German governments have been careful not to promote a mythical ideal of German identity such as the *Volksgemeinshaft*. The nationality law of the Federal Republic, which dates from 1913, grants citizenship on the basis of *jus sanguinis* (kinship or blood relation), as opposed to the American and French laws which attribute citizenship on the basis of kinship and place of birth (blood and soil). For reasons that go back to the founding of the Second Reich, the German state chose to emphasize ethnicity and culture as opposed to territory in deciding who qualifies for full membership in German society. Unlike France, where the construction of a unitary state under the French kings occurred long before the flowering of the Republic, in Germany pan-Germanism and the *Volksgemeinschaft* preceded the building of the unitary state under Bismarck. The Nazis obviously used the racist, *völkisch* concepts to exclude Poles and Jews from full citizenship.[77] But, as Rogers Brubaker has pointed out, it is important to distinguish between the ethnocultural basis of nationality law during the Wilhelmine period and the ethnoracial citizenship policies of the Nazi regime.[78]

Citizenship and the Liberal Paradox

The important questions are: what has happened to the ethnocultural and racist aspects of citizenship law in postwar Germany, and did the particularist view of citizenship affect the ability of the German state to regulate immigration? One of the most paradoxical aspects of immigration policy and the politics of citizenship in the Federal Republic is that the desire to unite the German diaspora—which spread from the German Democratic Republic eastward across Eurasia into Siberia—gave rise to some peculiarly liberal provisions in the Basic Law, with respect to refugees. Article 116 of the Basic Law states that anyone who held German citizenship or was the descendant of a German citizen under the laws of the old Reich is entitled to citizenship in the Federal Republic.

This provision of the Basic Law created several new categories of German citizens: the *Vertribene,* or people expelled from former Silesia and East Prussia, now part of Poland and the Soviet Union; the *Aussiedler,* or ethnic Germans from various regions of Central and Eastern Europe; and the largest group of all, the East Germans. The constitutional provision for ethnic Germans has been interpreted liberally by the German courts to extend refugee status to many other foreigners and asylum seekers. After the *Gastarbeiter* program of the 1960s was suspended in 1973, restrictive immigration policies came in conflict with liberal refugee policies, which led to some confusion and eventually to the settlement of large numbers of foreign workers and their families. This points to a close connection between immigration and citizenship in Germany, but not what might be expected given the particularist nature of nationality law, the difficulties of naturalization, and negative public attitudes toward immigration.

Successive German governments of the right and the left have insisted that foreign workers are "guests" who should be sent back home when their services are no longer needed. Yet by the mid-1970s it was increasingly apparent that the *Gastarbeiter* policies of worker rotation were based on two important fallacies, which I have discussed at length in earlier chapters: (1) that the state can use foreign workers as shock absorbers (the German expression is *Konjuncturpuffer*); and (2) that foreign workers could easily be prevented from settling in Germany. As in France, attempts by the German government to enforce worker rotation, prevent settlement, and stop family reunification were struck down by the courts, thus facilitating the settlement of a large Turkish minority in Germany.

The paradox is that an exclusionary politics of citizenship led to an expansionist immigration policy, de facto if not de jure. German political parties, in contrast to their French counterparts, have gone to great lengths to avoid politicizing immigration policy. The reason for this is quite obvious: the felt need to repress nationalist sentiments and to avoid even the hint of the racist policies of the Third Reich. The new liberal consensus in the Federal Republic, with its emphasis on civil rights, helped to keep political discourse on the issues of immigration and citizenship within certain well-defined parameters.[79] One of the biggest problems following the suspension of guestworker programs in 1973 was how to assimilate the Turkish minority. Until 1990 German naturalization procedures made it difficult for long-term resident aliens to acquire citizenship. In 1990 these procedures were relaxed somewhat, especially for second-generation immigrants. Yet a large settler population still remains without formal citizenship.[80]

Citizenship and Party Politics

The policies of the Christian-Democratic/Liberal government in Germany, since the rise to power of Helmut Kohl in 1982, have focused on the naturalization (and assimilation) of second- and third-generation immigrants, to avoid perpetuating an isolated and marginal ethnic minority. The first Kohl government espoused the findings of a study of the problems of assimilation—known as the Kühn Report—which recommended tighter controls on immigration and changes in German law to facilitate and encourage naturalizations. The naturalization procedure itself was lengthy and complex, requiring a ten-year waiting period and clear demonstrations of assimilation, such as knowledge of German history and language.[81] The Kühn Report made strong recommendations for integrating foreigners into German society. The report, issued in 1979, went so far as to define Germany as a country of immigration, a statement which drew fire from some politicians.[82] Despite the formal support of the Social Democratic/Liberal government of Helmut Schmidt, the recommendations of the Kühn Report were largely ignored until 1990, when several important changes were made in the law governing the rights of resident aliens. The goals of the 1990 reform were to facilitate naturalization (*erleichterte Einbügerung*), especially for second-generation immigrants, and to solidify the rights of resident aliens, thereby removing many legal ambiguities concerning residency, work permits, and family reunification.[83]

Prior to this liberalization, which was spurred by the unification process and the desire on the part of the Federal government to consolidate legislation on the status of foreigners, many German politicians continued to subscribe to the old anti-immigrant position—*Wir sind kein ein Wanderungsland*. This familiar refrain affirmed the ethnocultural dimensions of German citizenship and was meant to reassure nationalist elements in German public opinion. It represented a rejection of the notion that Germany was in any way built by immigrants. But the contribution of Poles and other foreign groups to German economic development in the early decades of the twentieth century and the *Gastarbeiter* programs of the postwar period, which resulted in the settlement of a large Turkish population, belie this revision of German history. The Polish Question was replaced by the Turkish Question, and both were relegated temporarily to the political back burner in the wake of the unification of East and West Germany in 1989–90.

It would be wrong to push the analogy between Poles and Turks too far, however. There were few liberal constraints on the power of the Wilhelmine state to prevent the mass deportation of Polish workers. In the post-1948 period, under the Basic Law of the Federal Republic, Turks and other minorities have been protected from the arbitrary powers of the state. Turks have been allowed to settle with their families and to work. In essence, a de facto pluralist policy has been adopted, while the more nationalist, ethnocultural, and *völkisch* concerns with identity and citizenship have been repressed. Once again we see the importance of rights-based politics helping to suppress statist policies and nationalist sentiments, much the way we have seen in the United States. In contrast to French party politics, nationalist and xenophobic discourses have not come to the fore even in the form of oppositional strategies. A partial exception was the short-lived breakthrough of the Republikaner party in local elections (particularly in West Berlin) in the late 1980s. This political movement/party, led by a former member of the Waffen SS, Franz Schönhuber, was able to make inroads into party politics—especially in crowded urban areas like Berlin with high concentrations of immigrants—by denouncing immigration as the principal cause of housing shortages and blaming immigrants for the general deterioration in urban living standards. But the Republikaner movement was swept away by the political euphoria surrounding unification. In contrast to Le Pen and the FN, Schönhuber's and the Republikaner's anti-immigrant discourse did not take on antisemitic and ultranationalist overtones—again an indication of the extreme sensitivity to neofascist politics in the Federal Republic.

With the fading of the Turkish Question in the 1990s and the collapse of Communist regimes in Eastern Europe, a new migration issue looms on the horizon: the arrival of political and economic refugees from various regions of Central and Eastern Europe (such as the gypsies from Romania) and the influx of ethnic Germans *(Aus-*

siedler) from the East. Even though the 1990 immigration and naturalization reform cleared the way for a new *Gastarbeiter* program (if needed to sustain economic growth), the influx of immigrants from the East seems to have solved, for the foreseeable future, demographic and labor supply problems in Germany. But unification has raised the spectre of a resurgent nationalism and of new extremist politics among former Communists and neo-Nazis (such as the disaffected youth known as skinheads); yet it seems improbable that a new version of the *Volksgemeinschaft* is in the offing for a unified Germany. The stable strategic situation of the new German state in Europe and the liberal political culture of the Federal Republic have brought a greater self-confidence and self-awareness to Germans, who are more attentive to ethnic and minority politics. The emergence of an Islamic minority in Germany has not provoked a crisis of national identity (or difficulties in church-state relations) similar to that which occurred in France. The mainstream political parties and the political elite also have been determined to avoid forced Germanization of ethnic minorities; Islam, like other religions, is officially recognized by the German state.[84]

Ethnic pluralism is more in keeping with the historical tradition of religious and cultural diversity in German society that predates the *völkisch* ideologies of the Second and Third Reichs. The new federalism in postwar Germany and the conscious suppression of the nationalist and militarist ideals of the unitary Prussian state (which are held responsible for the conformism of prewar German cultures) have contributed to the development of liberalism in German politics.[85] Once again, the French experience with citizenship and ethnicity can be contrasted with the German. Turks in Germany are encouraged to maintain their cultural identity, while North Africans in France are expected to assimilate quickly and completely. The absence of a stridently assimilationist ideology in the Federal Republic can be attributed to the transitional and uncertain status of the regime itself (until 1990); and the liberal treatment of Turks and other foreign groups is an indication of a continuing hope, on the part of German authorities, that foreigners eventually will return to their countries of origin. Pluralist policies are also an indication of the desire to keep debates over immigration, ethnicity, and citizenship within the bounds of liberal discourse. Some proimmigrant groups want to encourage partial membership in German society for resident aliens—a status just short of full citizenship—but the Christian-Liberal government of the 1980s has taken the position that long-term foreign residents should naturalize. The 1990 reform stands as a testament to liberal change, even though the assimilation of some segments of German society—especially many former citizens of the moribund German Democratic Republic—to the new civic culture remains in doubt.

Citizenship and the Liberal Paradox in Europe and America

Why should the issue of citizenship be more salient in Europe than in the United States in the 1980s? At least three factors are at work, all of them related to political culture. The first factor is *historical.* Most Americans accept their multicultural society, built through the efforts of immigrants. France and Germany, in contrast, have struggled and continue to struggle with a new social and cultural pluralism, which some citizens view as incompatible with older ideals of citizenship and national community. Immigration has yet to attain the political and social legitimacy in Europe which it has enjoyed historically in the United States. The second factor, largely institutional, helps to explain the greater emphasis on citizenship in the politics of immigration in contemporary Europe. The party system in France and Germany leaves more electoral space for anti-immigrant politics; and parties play a more important role (by virtue of parliamentary traditions) in Europe in setting a national agenda for policy debates. In the context of parliamentary systems, it is easier and more tempting (from an electoral standpoint) for parties to define an issue like immigration in terms of citizenship. In the United States the political system (the legislative process in particular) has tended to break down the issue of immigration into many small issues, which conform to a myriad of interests represented in the Congress.

The third and most important factor to explain the softening of the politics of citizenship in the United States in the postwar period is the advent of a new legal culture, more expansive in granting civil and social rights to minority groups than anything we have seen in Europe. One of the fundamental problems of regulating immigration in the liberal polity is how to deal with foreign workers who, as commodities, are subject to the full force of market relations, but as individuals are entitled to certain protections by virtue of their humanity. The American polity has moved further than European polities in resolving this incongruity. The civil rights movement and the struggle to extend full citizenship to African Americans have spawned an adversarial legal culture, which places great emphasis upon procedural rights and social justice. With respect to immigration, there is thus a greater complementarity between markets and rights in the United States than in Europe. As we have seen in earlier chapters, the tendency in Europe was to try to resolve the liberal paradox (the tension between the market for foreign labor and the rights of aliens) through administrative fiat. Of course there are some important checks on the administrative power (and sovereignty) of liberal states in Europe; but these checks are not as fully institutionalized as they are in the United States, where courts play an ever larger role in administering immigration policy. Liberal constitutionalism has helped to redefine immigration policy by compelling executive and administrative authorities to alter classical conceptions of sovereignty and the national interest, and to bring them more closely in line with prevailing standards of justice and fairness in contemporary American politics.[86] Hence political development in the United States in the postwar period has been marked by a strong commitment to individual rights and equality of opportunity for citizens and noncitizens alike.[87] In Europe, where social democracy and the welfare state are more highly developed than in the United States, the use of aliens as guestworkers has created a conflict which is centered less on social (or political) rights—problems which European welfare states generally handle quite well—and more on civil rights.[88]

The political economy of immigration involves four issues: sovereignty, citizenship, labor, and humanitarianism. We have examined each of these issues in the comparative-historical context of postwar Europe and the United States. How do liberal states bring them together (if they do) in their efforts to regulate immigration? How does the issue of citizenship relate to the issues of labor and refugee migration? What we have seen in postwar Europe and the United States is that liberal states break immigration down into various types of migration—which conform roughly to my four issues—using political, social, and economic criteria. These types of migration (or migrant flows) then become targets of regulation, each requiring a special policy or set of policies.

In the 1980s European and American efforts to control immigration converged. For example, the first socialist government under François Mitterrand in 1981 enacted a special amnesty for clandestine immigrants, which resulted in the legalization *(régularisation exceptionnelle)* of almost 90,000 immigrants over roughly a two-and-a-half year period. Similarly, the American Congress in 1986 enacted a conditional amnesty that led over 1,700,000 illegal immigrants to come forward during a one-year period in 1987–88. In 1990 the German Bundestag passed a reform of immigration and naturalization law which gave greater security to resident aliens and made it easier for them to obtain German citizenship. In each case, these reforms point to a liberalization of immigration policy and politics.

Liberalization (in terms of the rights of resident aliens) has gone hand in hand with greater efforts to control illegal worker immigration. All types of worker immigration have been restricted in Europe since 1973; in the United States the 1986 IRCA instituted employer sanctions as a strategy for controlling illegal worker immigration. Restrictions on worker immigration, combined with greater civil rights for aliens and a continuing demand for foreign labor in the industrial democracies, have contributed heavily to a surge in refugee and family immigration. For humanitarian and political reasons, family immigration also has remained a fundamental feature of the overall migration picture, and increases in both refugee and family immigration have reopened the now familiar debates over the political and economic dimensions of international migration. Despite concerted efforts on the part of the industrial democracies to distinguish between immigrant workers, family members, and political refugees, these categories have proved to be in many ways artificial.

Relatives, Refugees, and Human Rights

The United States and European countries retain a relatively strong commitment to humanitarian principles in their immigration policies. When governments wavered in this commitment, political and judicial checks brought about compliance with human and civil rights. When the French authorities attempted to stop family immigration in the late 1970s, the Council of State annulled the executive order. Many times in the 1980s, particularly under the Reagan administration, when the American government tried perfunctorily to deport refugees seeking political asylum the courts intervened to provide a measure of due process and equal protection. In Germany a liberal asylum law—written into the constitution and enforced by the courts—has protected asylum seekers from deportation. These checks illustrate how difficult it is for liberal states to target those migrants that do not fit neatly into preordained categories. Simply to label some migrants as economic and others as political refugees, as has occurred with increasing frequency in Europe and the United States since the 1970s, obfuscates policy and invites judicial intervention.

Since worker immigration was suspended in Europe in 1973–74, family immigration has become one of the most prominent types of migration in Europe. In the United States legal immigration was driven by family reunifications after the landmark 1965 Immigration and Nationality Act, which not only abolished the pernicious national origin quota system but established kinship as the principal criterion for determining who should be admitted to the country as a resident alien. In the 1980s French and German governments quietly came to accept family immigration as an inevitable consequence of earlier labor immigration. In the United States a debate was joined over the issue of family immigration, leading to the 1990 reform of legal immigration. The principal opponents of relying on kinship as the basis for admission to permanent residency argued that the United States should place more emphasis on economic criteria by admitting highly skilled migrants likely to contribute immediately and in a significant way to the pool of human capital. This lobby was composed of professional economists, and employers who argued that the United States should pay more attention to building the skill base of the labor force, admitting a greater number of individuals according to human capital criteria, such as education.[89] The lobby found a sympathetic ear among some members of Congress and the Reagan administration. With the passage of the 1990 act, the level of legal immigration was raised to 700,000 per annum, with substantially more visas reserved for skilled migrants. The overall commitment to family reunification was not abandoned, however, but reinforced by the reform.

Although family immigration is one of the most important migrant flows with a humanitarian dimension, refugee migration is by far the most visible humanitarian issue in the political economy of immigration in the 1980s, not only in Europe and the United States, but in all of the Western democracies.[90] The issue of refugees and political asylum has dominated the debate over immigration in the 1990s.[91] With the passage of the 1980 Refugee Act in the United States, an effort was made to formalize rules and procedures for dealing with refugees, in part by incorporating the United Nations definition of a refugee into American law. But requiring every individual who requests political asylum to demonstrate a "well-founded fear of persecution" did not solve the problem of definition. Determining an individual's motives for migrating is already difficult. To decide whether an individual is seeking to immigrate for political or economic reasons requires the splitting of some very fine hairs. The additional fact that refugee policy in the United States has been driven by foreign policy concerns puts in relief some of the difficulties of implementing the 1980 Refugee Act. Shortly after its passage, the government was forced to confront a series of immigration crises. The decision by Fidel Castro to allow over 125,000 Cubans to emigrate from Mariel in 1980 severely tested the new policy and placed a great strain on the system that had been established for welcoming and integrating political refugees. The Mariel boat lift was followed by waves of refugees from Iran and an exodus from Southeast Asia. Even these migrations pale in comparison with the potential exodus from the Soviet Union and Eastern Europe—should the trend of relaxing exit restrictions on the peoples of these countries continue—and from Hong Kong before its unification with the People's Republic in 1997.

Early in 1989 the American government was embarrassed by its attempt to forestall Jewish immigration from the Soviet Union—a decision which was made after the refugee ceiling had been surpassed and funds appropriated for the resettlement of refugees had been exhausted. To rectify the situation, the decision was made to allow more refugees from Eastern Europe and fewer from Southeast Asia, which brought an immediate outcry from Asian refugee and human rights lobbies. The decision also had dire consequences for many of the Vietnamese "boat people," who were suddenly turned back by Thailand and other neighboring states for fear that the United States would not agree to resettle them. Here again, the liberal/humanitarian bias of American politics helped to moderate an otherwise harsh policy. The same could be said for many other refugee groups, even those from "friendly" regimes such as El Salvador and Guatemala. Gradually, American authorities have been forced to recognize, often by the courts, that many of the individuals fleeing the oppressive political situation in these countries are legitimate asylum seekers.[92] In the 1980s, however, the INS has adopted some illiberal tactics for dealing with refugees from Central America. Individuals seeking asylum are no longer allowed to apply for asylum and then go to a destination of their choice in the United States to await a decision. Beginning in 1988, the strategy of the INS was to confine these individuals in what amount to prisons along the Mexican-American border. As a result, a reverse flow of migration has occurred, with some Central Americans preferring to return to the Mexican border towns, where they fall prey to the exploitation of local Mexican gangs, rather than risk detention in the United States and possible deportation. The battle over the legality of these detention centers is being waged in the courts.

Immigration in Western Europe has been rising in the 1980s, though not as a result of any new recruitment policy or a relaxation on the part of authorities. Like other Western democracies, France and Germany have experienced an upsurge in refugee (and clandestine) immigration. Applications for political asylum in France in the 1980s show a steady increase, from roughly 20,000 at the beginning of the decade to nearly 30,000 in 1988. These figures include individuals who arrive with a visa for the express purpose of applying for political asylum (that is, their cases have been screened in advance), as well as individuals who succeed in entering the country and then decide to apply for political asylum. The criteria for deciding asylum cases in France are fairly similar to those in the United States, with the major exception that foreign policy plays less of a role in the outcome. The procedure is more administrative, with a limited possibility of appeal. Effectively, the decision of the agency in charge of refugees, the Office Français de Protection de Réfugiés et Apatrides (OFPRA) is final; hence the rate of refusal is quite high, over 60 percent. But because individuals who are refused asylum are initially notified by mail, most of them subsequently disappear, to become illegal immigrants.[93]

True to its universalist republican tradition, France is an important country of asylum, welcoming refugees from countries throughout the world. In the 1980s substantial numbers of refugees arrived from Asia, Africa, and the Middle East. Beginning in 1985, the majority of these asylum seekers came to France as tourists before requesting refugee status, a familiar pattern in other asylum countries, particularly the United States, Canada, and Germany. The breakdown by nationality of current refugee flows into France shows that roughly half are from Asia, including Indochina and the Middle East, with another forty percent from sub-Saharan Africa (refugees from Zaire have been a particularly prominent group since 1987), and the balance from Europe and Latin America. The most prominent sending countries, Vietnam, Cambodia, and Zaire, have close cultural and linguistic ties with France, if not a distinct French colonial heritage (Zaire was a Belgian colony). In a parallel trend, the connection between past American military involvement in regions such as Southeast Asia and Central America and the level of refugee migration is striking. The colonial and neocolonial adventures of both the United States and France have helped to stimulate refugee immigration. The arrival of Nicaraguans in Miami and the flight of many Salvadorans to the United States are examples of the effects of imperialism and neo-colonialism on refugee migration.

In the last decades of the twentieth century, refugee immigration has become a dominant mode of immigration in the liberal democracies. Unlike the United States, neither France nor Germany have tried to reduce their refugee policies to debates over the political economic dimensions of immigration, in part because of the refusal to link refugee and foreign policy. But given the relatively liberal attitude toward refugees throughout the European Community (Britain is an important exception) and the potential for greater migration from the countries of Eastern and Central Europe, the debate over how to categorize refugees is sure to intensify in the 1990s. This is especially true in Germany, which has the most liberal constitutional provisions for granting political asylum in Europe.

Refugee immigration illustrates better than any other type of migration the multifaceted nature of international migration and the difficulty that liberal states encounter in trying to cope with population movements. As we have seen in the case of labor migration, the attempt to reduce individuals to their economic function, which is very attractive from a policy standpoint, is ultimately a futile exercise that has the opposite effects of those intended. Any policy that rests on a fine distinction between the political and economic motives of migrants will be impossible to implement, because in a liberal-democratic setting all individuals, including foreigners, have civil and human rights. Attempts to govern such migration in a purely administrative or technical fashion also are doomed to fail. We have seen the consequences of such an approach in France, and the German case proves even more revealing. The important point is that all forms of international migration are multidimensional. It is therefore impossible, from a policy standpoint, to define the phenomenon of immigration along only one social dimension—political, economic, or humanitarian.

Conclusion

Immigration in postwar Europe provided an important source of labor for economic modernization. Yet the effects of immigration on the nation-states of Western Europe go well beyond economics and demography. Immigration exposed the strengths and weaknesses of political systems and cultures. The struggle to deal with ethnically distinct groups taxed the ability of political parties to mobilize support and aggregate interests. Nowhere was this clearer than in the case of the French Communist Party. It had successfully integrated earlier waves of European immigrants in the 1920s and 1930s—mostly Italians and Poles—but it failed ultimately with the new Muslim underclass in the 1970s and 1980s, which sought cultural recognition as much as class solidarity. Likewise the institutions of the Jacobin state were slow to adjust to the realities of a permanent settler migration in the 1970s and 1980s. Heavyhanded administrative efforts to cutoff worker immigration in 1974 resulted in a number of unintended consequences, which increased the foreign population and contributed to the insecurity and instability of immigrants. Ultimately, immigration turned the French state against itself, as the most paradoxical of administrative organs—the Council of State—annulled executive orders to stop immigration. In 1989 the Council of State intervened once again, this time on the side of the liberal policies of the Socialist government, to permit Muslim school children to wear traditional Islamic dress.

Immigration disrupted European politics by provoking a renaissance of the xenophobic, nationalist right, which in France had lain dormant since the demise of the Vichy regime. The carefully crafted political alliances of the Gaullist era were torn apart, first by the victory of the left in 1981 and subsequently by the emergence of the FN. The French party system proved incapable of handling the issue of immigration within the context of normal party politics, and the shift to proportional representation in 1985–86 gave the anti-immigrant FN a foothold in the National Assembly. It is unlikely that France has seen the end of anti-immigrant nationalism, or of immigration.

Despite the illiberal developments in France, European political systems have shown signs of adapting to the realities of social and cultural pluralism. The liberalizing influence of Socialist policies in France in the 1980s and the willingness of German authorities to recognize that Germany has become a country of immigration—as evidenced by the 1990 reform of the naturalization law—together with the political assertiveness of immigrants in both countries have created the conditions for ethnic and civil rights politics similar to the United States. The growing weight in France of the Arab vote *(vote beur)* could play a crucial role in politics, as the French political system moves closer to American-style presidential primaries. Having helped France to overcome Malthusian problems of social and economic development during the Fourth Republic, immigrants may contribute to breaking the political stalemate—*immobilisme*—of the Fifth. In Germany immigration has been rising in the late 1980s, in part as a result of the collapse of Communism in Central and Eastern Europe. Yet there is no sign of panic in German politics, as the government of the new German state looks for ways of helping the states of Eastern Europe to cope with the difficult process of transition to market economies, in part to create new markets, but also to head off economic collapse in the former Communist regimes, which would certainly be followed by largescale migrations from East to West.

As individuals whose primary goal is to find employment and create a better way of life for themselves and their families, immigrants are capable of coping with the intricacies of regulations designed to modify their behavior in one way or another. Yet in terms of politics and policy, differences in political cultures can influence the prospects for assimilation. The Jacobin nature of political culture together with an administrative approach to regulation led the French state to redefine immigration in terms of citizenship; and heavy-handed policies for regulating immigration helped to distort and politicize the issue. These statist policies produced a number of unintended consequences. Although it is difficult to establish a direct link between the policies of the 1970s and the anti-immigrant politics of the 1980s, certainly the statist approach to immigration and the stridently assimilationist culture contributed to the politicization of the issue. Politicians of the extreme right were able to prey upon the social and cultural antagonisms of class, race, and ethnicity to create an atmosphere of national crisis in the 1980s. It remains to be seen how long these antagonisms will endure, and when the French will come to terms with the new social and cultural pluralism created by the largescale North African immigration in the 1960s and 1970s.

In the United States the federal system, the stability of party politics, and the pluralist nature of the legislative process helped to fragment the issue of immigration and keep it off of the national agenda. Moreover, the political elite (if not always public opinion) regards immigration as a legitimate feature of American society and economy. Yet by far the most important political development in the United States in the postwar period is the civil rights movement, which accentuated the liberal and pluralist dimensions of American politics and reinforced the principles of equality, consent, and due process. African Americans benefit more fully from their legal rights as citizens, and greater procedural guarantees are in place to protect minority groups. Aliens have benefited from these developments in that most Americans accept cultural pluralism and view immigration as a legitimate feature of their society. But the Fourteenth Amendment and the extension of civil rights to minorities were not a panacea for solving all of the problems associated with immigration. Some aspects of the 1986 IRCA, particularly the provision for employer sanctions, indicate that American authorities are making some of the same false assumptions about regulating immigration their European counterparts made over a decade earlier. Heavyhanded administrative efforts to suppress immigration have produced some of the same unintended consequences, such as a larger and more harsh black market for labor together with increased family and refugee immigration.[94] American refugee policy has continued to link the fate of thousands, if not millions, of individuals to foreign policy considerations, while administrators try to split hairs in determining who is an economic and who is a political refugee.

Despite differences in the European and American political systems that affect their ways of regulating immigration and assimilating immigrants, these states have retained a liberal-democratic approach to immigration and citizenship. At the level of domestic and international politics, immigration has been and will continue to be one of the most controversial issues in Europe in the 1990s. If the economies of Western Europe begin to grow at a high rate, after the implementation of the Single European Act in 1993 and the expected demographic push from Africa materializes, immigration and citizenship are likely to preoccupy politicians throughout Europe into the next century. We may then see some of the debates of the 1950s and 1960s played out again, hopefully in a liberal climate.

9 ◆ Immigration and the Principles of Liberal Democracy

> *The enclosure of the individual within national boundaries is . . . one of the most reactionary trends of our time and intrinsically damaging to strivings for international integration.*
>
> —GUNNAR MYRDAL, *An International Economy*

I began this book with a relatively simple question: why has it been difficult for liberal states to regulate immigration? The difficulty indicates that previous perceptions of sovereignty and state autonomy need to be reconsidered. Immigration is a measure of interdependence, which represents a distinctive challenge to the nation-state. Yet is it not possible for liberal countries to reassert their sovereignty by closing their borders? Simply pointing out that liberal states have that power does not explain why they have not done so, in light of public opposition to immigration and the perception that continued immigration is no longer in the national interest. We have seen a nationalist backlash against immigration in Western Europe, from Britain and France to Germany and Switzerland. Even in the United States, the classical country of immigration, politicians have been compelled to try to regain control of immigration through employer sanctions. Governments in Western Europe also have implemented restrictionist policies. Yet immigration persists.

An obvious explanation for the persistence of immigration can be derived from economic theory, which has spawned numerous "push-pull" arguments. Given the inequalities among national economies, it is perfectly rational and not terribly surprising that individuals in poorer states would seek to migrate to richer states to improve their quality of life and standard of living. According to liberal trade theory, when international migration (and trade) are allowed to proceed unimpeded these inequalities will be reduced, and individuals will no longer feel compelled to move. In the interim, to understand the ebbs and flows of international migration we must study differentials (in wage rates, for example) among national economies, as well as transportation costs, information flows, and so on. But the study of market mechanics does not get us very far. Certainly it is true that gross inequalities within the international system help to create an unlimited supply of migrants. The richer states must therefore be vigilant in controlling their borders to protect citizen workers from foreign competition, to preserve the integrity of the national community, and to avoid an escalation of demands on the welfare state that might result from uncontrolled immigration. But why have the richer liberal states allowed largescale migrations at particular moments in history, and why in the postwar period has it been so difficult for these states to assert control of immigration? Push-pull arguments offer no explanation.

A second explanation for the prominence of international migration in the modern period is derived from Marxist-Leninist theories of exchange. According to this argument, migrants represent a surplus pool of labor (an industrial reserve army) which help capitalist economies overcome periodic crises. This manpower is eminently exploitable. It can be mobilized in periods of rapid growth and disbanded in periods of slack demand. This is a seductive argument that seems to account for the extraordinary economic utility of migrant labor. Some theorists have taken this argument one step further, by pointing out that foreign workers introduce a vital element of flexibility into the employment practices of capitalist firms. Foreigners can be more easily hired and fired than citizen workers. Foreign workers constitute a secondary labor market, which is unregulated, nonunionized, and cheap. Immigration therefore can be understood as a response by capitalists to the increasing regulation of national labor markets in welfare states. This regulation, in turn, is a direct consequence of political compromises that have been worked out between citizen workers, employers, and the state. By virtue of political struggles carried on through unions and socialist parties, citizen workers have obtained greater civil and social rights. They have higher wages, protections from layoffs, welfare state benefits, and greater political power.[1] These rights create imperfections in the labor market, however, and reduce the flexibility of employment in the face of economic uncertainties that are the result of the integration of world markets, the vulnerability of national economies, and increasing competition.

Immigration is one way for employers to overcome market imperfections associated with industrial democracy and the expansion of the welfare state. But one crucial assumption of the Marxist argument is that foreign workers are in effect expendable commodities or shock absorbers, who can be laid off and even deported when no longer needed. Why then has immigration persisted even after the economic crises of the 1970s and 1980s, in the face of restrictionist and statist policies designed precisely to export unemployment? The Marxist theories offer no satisfactory explanation.

Finally, the realist/statist argument is that immigration—like trade, capital flows, and other forms of international exchange—is a function of the interests of the sovereign state. Since foreigners have no rights other than those granted to them by a sovereign state, they represent an asset or commodity at the disposal of national authorities. According to this logic, the state should be capable of controlling its borders, managing its population, and using foreigners as a resource to regulate population growth, labor supply, and human capital. Statist theory uderlies European guestworker programs of the 1950s and 1960s, but fails to account for the difficulties these states encountered in managing migrant stocks and flows. The realist theory cannot solve our puzzle, although immigration policy in many states conforms to the logic of this theory.

I have offered an alternative theory of immigration. My argument is that immigration in postwar Europe and the United States can be understood only in the context of the spread of market relations, at the domestic as well as the international level, *and* in terms of the ongoing extension of rights to individuals who are not full members of the societies in which they reside. The attraction of markets (including the demand for cheap labor) and the protection given to aliens in rights-based regimes taken together explain the rise in immigration and its persistence in the face of economic crises, restrictionist policies, and nationalist (anti-immigrant) political movements.

Even though immigration in postwar Europe and the United States must be seen as a function of these liberal developments, it nonetheless poses an acute dilemma for political and economic liberals. How can a liberal society permit an individual to reside and work there without granting her the rights and privileges that accompany membership in that society? The comparative historical and empirical analyses in chapters 3, 4, and 8 examined this dilemma through the lens of immigration and citizenship policies. The way the dilemma is resolved is heavily dependent on institutional arrangements and cultural traditions. In this respect, immigration policy and the politics of citizenship provide us with a rich set of comparisons and a window through which to explore differences and similarities among liberal regimes.

The findings of the book can be divided into four categories. The first set concerns the role of foreign labor in industrial democracies. The second concerns citizenship and the way in which the French, German, and American states have struggled to resolve the liberal paradox. The solution to the paradox depends upon the institutional and cultural arrangements that define the relationship between the individual and the state and in effect determine the political and economic dimensions of immigration. The third set of findings concerns the sovereignty and autonomy of the democratic state. Some of the principal theories of international relations (realism, hegemonic stability, interdependence) and comparative politics (pluralism, corporatism, statism) were invoked in chapters 2 and 6 as a way of understanding the problem of regulating immigration in the liberal polity. The fourth category includes the theoretical and philosophical underpinnings of liberal democracy. Their unfolding in history has important implications for immigration and refugee policies in postwar Europe and the United States.

Foreign Workers and Industrial Democracy

Foreign labor played an extraordinarily important role in Europe's postwar growth. The findings in chapters 3, 4, and 5 confirm the arguments of Kindleberger and others that the process of growth is smoother (and less inflationary) with unlimited supplies of labor. Economic policymakers in France and Germany recognized this when they took steps to recruit foreign workers in the face of domestic opposition, especially from trade unions and even some skeptical employers. In Fourth Republic France immigration policy was driven by demographic as well as economic concerns; in Germany guest-workers could be brought into the labor market on a contractual basis and were expected to return to their countries of origin when their "contracts" expired. The German government moved to recruit guestworkers at the beginning of the 1960s, for macroeconomic reasons. With the construction of the Berlin Wall in 1961, West Germany was cut off from its traditional supplies of labor in Eastern and Central Europe. Since the German economy during this period was growing at a rapid pace, German policymakers recognized the inflationary dangers of a labor shortage and wished to avoid taking German manufacturing "off shore" in search of more abundant labor and lower wages—a process that was already under way in the American economy. Although there was initial skepticism on the part of trade unions (the DGB), a consensus quickly developed among German workers, employers, and the state that foreign labor was necessary to sustain high rates of (noninflationary) growth and keep jobs at home. Thus the *Gastarbeiter* program was born at the initiative of the federal state, with clear economic objectives and (unlike France) no desire to see these guestworkers become permanent settlers.

Policies of worker rotation were not successful. Guestworkers became permanent settlers, bringing their families to live with them in Germany. Only in Switzerland—with its relatively small labor force, a continuously high demand for labor, and low unemployment—were policies of worker rotation partially successful. Even in Switzerland, however, a high percentage of the foreign population has obtained permanent resident status, and immigration has become an important feature of Swiss society. By the end of the 1960s, the role of foreign labor in Western Europe had shifted from providing stopgap injections of cheap labor to becoming a permanent, structural feature of these industrial democracies. In 1968 implementation of the "freedom of movement" clause of the Treaty of Rome marked the beginning of the end of largescale movement of Italian labor into the economies of northern Europe, especially France and Germany. The 1960s also witnessed the demise of the French Empire and rapid decolonization of North Africa in particular. Decolonization stimulated new flows of Third World migration, which France had not experienced in previous periods of immigration.[2] The continued growth of European economies, after a brief recession in 1967–68, kept worker immigration at high levels. Algerians, Tunisians, and Moroccans replaced the Italians, Spanish, and (eventually) the Portuguese in the French labor market; and Turks were arriving and settling in Germany, taking the place of Italians, Greeks, and Yugoslavs. What had begun in France and Germany as a planned injection of foreign labor from the Catholic countries of Southern Europe (and the Balkans) to boost labor supplies and stem demographic decline, became an uncontrolled immigration from Muslim North Africa and Turkey. Given the strength of the West European countries' economy and their confidence in their ability to manage migrant flows, few questioned the wisdom of a large influx of foreign labor during the 1960s and early 1970s.

Rather than competing with the French and the Swiss for Southern European labor (largely Italian, Spanish, and Portuguese), German authorities and firms looked to Yugoslavia, Greece, and Turkey for the needed injection of labor for the economy in the 1960s, at a time when the French were beginning to rely more heavily on labor from Portugal and their former colonies in North Africa. In France big business came to play an increasingly important role in the recruitment process, and trade unions were unable to exercise much influence over immigration policy. The French state simply acquiesced at first in the growing appetite of firms for foreign labor. In Germany the state maintained tighter control over the recruitment of foreign workers, with contracts issued and enforced by the *Bundesantalt für Arbeit*. Although it did not control other areas of social and economic policy in Germany, the federal state was heavily involved in making and implementing labor market policy via the *Gastarbeiter* program. The DGB chose not to fight the foreign worker program because they were part of the decisionmaking process, via neocorporatist practices (such as co-determination—*Mitbestimmung*—and concerted action—*konsertierte Aktion*) and institutions (such as the coordinating committees set up within various ministries, but especially in the Ministry of Labor). The DGB did, however, fight successfully to make sure that foreign workers would not undercut the wages and working conditions of German workers.

Thus postwar immigration in Western Europe received its impetus from the state (in the form of recruitment policies) and from the market (in the form of a high demand for labor in the 1950s and 1960s). Foreign workers quickly became a structural component of growth in these societies, but they did not play the role of shock absorbers *(Konjunkturpuffer)*. When the first signs of a slowdown in Europe's postwar growth *(Wirtschaftswunder)* appeared in 1966–67, French and German administrative elites (as well as some politicians) began to question recruitment policies. A statist, administrative reflex was building to reassert control over worker migration even before the oil shock and the massive recessions of the 1970s. In Switzerland a popular reaction against immigration that had been developing for some time found its expression in the *Überfremdung* initiatives. By the beginning of the 1970s the stage was set in Europe for a test of the strength and autonomy of the administrative state, but there was as yet no indication of resurgent nationalisms. As for the guestworkers, the feeling grew among leftwing parties and politicians that these workers were being used by employers to undercut the wages and working conditions of citizen workers; meanwhile, rightwing parties and politicians were caught between liberal commitments to maintain the best possible conditions for economic growth and investment, which included access to foreign labor for many firms, and the still distant rumbles of anti-immigrant and nationalist sentiments in the electorate.

The ban on worker immigration in Europe, in the wake of the oil shock in 1973, was in keeping with the statist tradition and administrative ethos of foreign worker programs in France and Germany.[3] The suspension of guestworker programs in Germany was implemented by a Left-Liberal government headed by Willy Brandt and the SPD. In France the ban on immigration was undertaken by a Right-Liberal government under the neo-Gaullist and Republican administrations of Georges Pompidou and Valéry Giscard d'Estaing. At this point, party politics were marginal, as the official positions of the French and German (but not the Swiss) governments were that immigration was no longer needed in view of the economic slowdown.[4] Very quickly, however, the statist and economic rationalizations for stopping immigration (and exporting unemployment) gave way to cultural and ideational motives. Suddenly there was an awareness throughout the labor-importing countries of Western Europe that the area had become a region of intense immigration, and that the influx of foreigners, primarily from the Muslim regions of the Mediterranean basin, threatened the cultural integrity and national identity of West European states.

One of the most important findings of this work is that immigration is not an efficient tool for making employment or industrial policy. Immigration helped to solve manpower shortages in France in the late 1950s and head off similar shortfalls in Germany in the 1960s.[5] But the influx of foreign workers was as much the result of economic necessity as of political choice. Recruitment policies simply set the stage for a wave of immigration in Western Europe in the

1960s and early 1970s. By the mid 1970s, foreign labor had become a structural component of the labor market. Many jobs held by foreigners would not or could not be filled by citizen workers, particularly in the construction and service sectors. In addition, the probability of uprooting a worker after she had already begun to integrate into the community and lived in the country for an extended period of time was extremely low. Thus regardless of the political expediency of policies designed to encourage workers to return to their countries of origin, using foreign labor to restructure labor markets proved not to be feasible.

What does this tell us about the role of immigration in advanced industrial democracies? Clearly, market conditions had a much greater impact on levels of immigration and foreign employment than did state policies designed to regulate "stocks and flows" of foreign workers and their families. In chapter 7 we saw only marginal differences in the way foreign and citizen workers were used in the French economy, both before and after 1973. The market did not differentiate between the two inputs, and the state was unable to use immigrants effectively for making industrial or employment policy. Foreign and citizen workers were laid off roughly in proportion to their numbers in the workforce of specific sectors. Thus although immigrant workers played an important role in Europe's postwar growth, they did not help (or hinder) the process of industrial adjustment. The market was a fairly unbiased mechanism for allocating citizen and foreign labor in an industrial economy. Foreign workers in France were no more highly concentrated in low-productivity sectors than are citizen workers. Both foreign and citizen workers moved disproportionately into the service sectors of the French economy. The growth of the service sectors at the expense of manufacturing might have long-term consequences for the ability of states such as France to compete in world markets. But this is not the fault of the foreign workers.

Nonetheless, the economic crises of the 1970s turned foreign workers into pawns in political struggles over the allocation of the pains of sacrifice and industrial adjustment. Foreign workers were viewed by governments and the public alike as expendable commodities, to be used according to an economic logic and in keeping with the national interest as defined by the state. Policies were put in place to stop worker immigration and encourage (or force) foreigners to return to their countries of origin. In effect, the administrative state attempted simply to dismantle a highly developed international labor market. These policies for stopping worker immigration did not apply to citizens of the member states of the European Community, who were guaranteed freedom of mobility. The objects of restrictionist policies clearly were migrants from the Third World, especially Africa and Turkey.

Yet despite the political consensus for suspending worker immigration, statist policies for banning foreign workers, encouraging return migration, and preventing family reunifications were ineffective. In the words of one scholar, the guests had "come to stay."[6] The "failure" of these policies was closely linked to the changed relationship between individuals, groups, and the state. The first change is largely economic: the increasing integration of national economies in the postwar period, especially in the European Community, has resulted in the globalization of markets not just for capital, goods, and services, but for labor as well. It is exceedingly difficult for states simply to withdraw from these markets when participation in them is no longer convenient, or when it conflicts with the national interest. The price for withdrawal may be too high to pay, both in economic and political terms.[7] Do interdependence and the constraints of global markets mean that immigration is predominantly an economic phenomenon, driven by international systemic conditions? The findings of this study argue against such a conclusion. The expansion of civil and social rights in the liberal democracies has contributed as much if not more than the spread of market relations to increases in immigration. Once foreign workers entered labor markets in Western Europe and the United States, they were integrated quickly into the economy *and* society; and, for reasons having more to do with *liberal* than with *industrial* democracy, it was difficult to get rid of them (in hopes of exporting unemployment) for political expediency.

Citizenship and the Liberal Paradox

Rights-based politics and more expansive citizenship policies have worked to stimulate immigration and weaken the capacity of democractic states to control their borders. Under liberal constitutions foreigners have rights, and states (in their administrative guise) are constrained by constitutional norms and procedures. This was evident in France and Germany in the 1970s and 1980s, as restrictionist policies were thwarted by courts. Such developments reflect the erosion of sovereignty and nationalist notions of citizenship. Although citizenship is, in the words of Rogers Brubaker, a "last bastion of sovereignty,"[8] the French and German states, like the American state, have been pushed by domestic and international developments (civil rights groups, European integration and so on) to expand the rights of minority groups, including foreigners. New ideals of social justice— best articulated by American political theorists such as John Rawls and Michael Walzer—find expression in the politics and policies of liberal states. In effect, we have been witnessing the convergence of immigration and citizenship policies and the de facto expansion of membership, if not political citizenship, for aliens in Europe and the United States.[9]

By far the most salient example of problems of citizenship and the liberal paradox is France in the 1980s. The settlement of a large Muslim population, which began in the 1970s, has provoked a crisis in French political culture, bringing competing nationalisms to the fore. The anti-immigrant movement which has received the most attention outside of Europe is the Front National, headed by Jean-Marie Le Pen. This movement represents a peculiarly French version of fascism, with a thinly veiled racism and anti-Semitism, which mingles easily with a stridently anti-immigrant, and anti-Arab nationalism. The rallying cry of the movement in the 1980s was "la France aux français!" The FN takes as its inspiration Joan of Arc, a symbol of France's glorious and culturally pure past.

The rise of the FN (which has received around ten percent of the vote in various elections since 1983) has led to disarray among the traditional parties of the right, especially the neo-Gaullist RPR, with its own nationalist ideology encapsulated in the old Gaullist phrase, "une certaine idée de la France." But the Gaullists, like the Socialists and the Communists, also have a strong republican bent, which harkens back to the universalist, expansionist, and nationalist ideology of the French Revolution. The Jacobin position with respect to immigration, immigrants, and citizenship is that all foreign and ethnic minorities should assimilate as quickly as possible and subscribe to the ideals of French republicanism, pariculary with respect to such cherished goals as separation of church and state *(laïcité)* and the suppression of all forms of ethnic (non-French) behavior. The assertiveness of some Muslim groups and the rise of Islamic militancy in the wake of the Iranian Revolution have come into direct conflict with the Jacobin positions of the left (especially among socialist intellectuals) and of the right.

In an attempt to respond to the nationalist sentiments of the French electorate, the rightwing government of Jacques Chirac (in 1986–87) sought to reform French nationality law to make it more difficult for second-generation Algerians to acquire French citizenship. This proposed reform was defeated, largely as a result of a resurgent liberal and civil rights politics, which cuts across party lines. The French judiciary (especially the Council of State) weighed in on the side of ethnic minorities, thus contributing to a liberal (if not a pluralist) outcome. Immigration, especially refugee flows, picked up in France in the 1980s and the citizenship debate has continued. The French political system and Jacobin culture have shown increasing flexibility, despite partisan attacks on immigrants.

The politics of citizenship in Germany are less complicated than in France. Because of the experience of Third Reich, which linked German nationalism with a virulent and destructive racism, political elites and parties in the Federal Republic have been careful not to couch the issues of immigration and ethnicity in nationalist terms. Likewise the federal state has not been so openly attacked as in France for its failure to regulate immigration. Instead, German political parties have taken refuge in strict nationality laws, which (until the 1990 reform) made it very difficult for foreign residents to acquire German citizenship. Despite the 1990 reform, which facilitates naturalization for second-generation immigrants, citizenship in Germany is still based exclusively on *jus sanguinis*. Only in the latter half of the 1980s did the debate over immigration (which in the 1960s and 1970s was focused on the economic utility of foreign labor) begin to address issues of citizenship. The terms of the debate were set by the permanent settlement of a large Turkish minority and by the surge of a rightwing, political movement—the Republikaner. This movement lost its appeal (it was never great) in the wake of German unification and the end of the Cold War. The Turkish Question became less pressing than the problem of absorbing seventeen million East Germans into the society and culture of the Federal Republic. Likewise, the collapse of communism in Eastern Europe in 1989 has opened the possibility of new flows of economic migrants from Poland, Romania, and other countries of the region.

The most striking thing about immigration politics in postwar Germany is the repression of German nationalism. Despite a continuous, soul-searching debate in the press over the presence of a large foreign population—which until the reform of 1990 was blocked from naturalization by restrictive nationality laws—there has not been a highly emotional debate over national identity such as we have seen in France. This can be attributed to a repression of nationalist sentiments, especially where the civil rights of ethnic minorities are concerned, but it is also the result of a gradual legitimation of immigration and the transformation of Germany into a multicultural society. The ease with which the German state has made this transformation is due in no small part to the changes in the political system and culture of postwar Germany. The federal system of Germany has helped to fragment the issue of immigration—even though the 1990 law gives greater power to the federal government and less to the *Länder* in fixing the terms of residence for foreigners—and the party system has proved capable of withstanding assaults from the (neo-Nazi, skinhead) extremes on the volatile issues of immigration and ethnicity. Most important, however, is the development of rights-based politics and a new political and legal culture. The importance of this culture is evident, as in France and the United States, in the role played by courts in moderating statist and administrative reactions to immigration. In the words of Peter Katzenstein, "the courts have played a central role in developing and implementing [migrant worker] policy . . . On questions of political asylum . . . the position of the courts was particularly strong."[10] Once again we can see the importance of procedural and constitutional guarantees for the civil rights of marginal groups, which constrain the power and autonomy of the administrative state in the area of immigration.

In this context, it is important to make a final mention of the the prominence of rights-based politics in the United States. American immigration policy reflects an earlier and stronger resolution of the liberal paradox (rights versus markets). I attribute this to the impact of the civil rights movement, which marked the beginning of a new era in American political development. One of the least obvious consequences of the civil rights revolution was the stimulating effect that it had on immigration. By expanding civil rights and entitlements for minority groups, the Civil Rights Act of 1964 made the United States a more attractive place for foreigners, already "clamoring at the gates" because of economic opportunities.[11] The confluence of markets and rights (resolution of the liberal paradox) explains the prominence of immigration in the United States and other liberal democracies. Interestingly, it is in the area of family and refugee immigration that the greatest convergence of immigration policies takes place. The landmark Supreme Court decision in *Plyler v. Doe,* allowing the children of undocumented aliens to attend public schools, is reminiscent of similar decisions by French and German courts on the rights of aliens and their families. These decisions are indicative of a more expansive view of membership in liberal societies which derives its meaning from new ideals of social justice and human rights, rather than from narrow definitions of sovereignty and the national interest.

Even though the 1986 Immigration Reform and Control Act contains statist provisions (such as employer sanctions and a kind of guestworker program for agricultural workers—the SAW program), the thrust of immigration reform in the United States in the 1980s has been in a liberal direction. The 1990 reform of legal immigration raised the ceiling for legal immigration by incorporating a greater skill-based component into immigration policy, but without abandoning the (humanitarian) commitment to family reunification. The 1986 act contains a constitutional check whereby administrative authorities are mandated to determine within a specified period of time whether employer sanctions have caused discrimination against foreign-looking or sounding job applicants. Not surprisingly, the evidence indicates that discrimination has occurred. Therefore Congress may be compelled to repeal this aspect of the law—a type of procedural check on the power of the administrative state that is evidence of the attempt to resolve the tension between markets and rights that is so characteristic of the political economy of advanced industrial democracies.

Despite high levels of immigration in the United States in the 1970s and 1980s, there has been no sign of a national identity crisis and no new politics of citizenship. Rather, the American state has taken an expansive view of membership: a large foreign population is allowed to reside in the country without the requirement of formal citizenship. In the American case, this is most often a voluntary choice on the part of permanent residents to remain just outside the confines of political membership—a choice which represents a decline of the assimilationist spirit of earlier periods in American history.[12] In Germany resident aliens, while benefiting from many civil and social rights, face many obstacles in obtaining citizenship. In France immigration and the settlement of a large ethnic minority has provoked a full-blown crisis of national identity and a new politics of civil rights and citizenship.[13] Yet in each case the commitment to assuring the civil rights of aliens has remained strong.

International Migration, State Autonomy, and Sovereignty

Immigration strikes at the heart of controversies over the sovereignty and autonomy of the democratic state. Given the legendary powers of the French state, we might expect France to have had an advantage over other democratic states in controlling immigration. During the Fourth Republic and in the early years of the Fifth, the economic planners were able to pursue programs of economic modernization that required short-term sacrifices by some groups for the sake of long-term economic growth.[14] The Jacobin and statist traditions in France helped to insulate policymakers from pluralist group pressures, especially trade unions. Yet in the area of immigration powerful policy instruments such as a national planning agency and a highly centralized administration were not sufficient to guarantee implementation of restrictionist immigration policies.

Statist arguments suffer from a major flaw. It is possible for a democratic state to be autonomous, that is, relatively independent of groups (unions, employers, civil rights groups, and so on) in certain policy areas, yet weak in its ability to implement policy. The strong/weak state argument tends to break down altogether when we take into account the wide variations in the ability of democratic states to formulate and implement policy from one area to another. Even though the French state may have been autonomous at certain points in the postwar period and in certain policy areas, it was not strong enough to control immigration, although foreign workers were among the most politically vulnerable members of French society. In this sense the strong/weak state categories are not helpful. The ability of a state to structure or restructure markets depends more on state-society relations and market conditions than on policy instruments. A powerful and centralized administration in France could not stop immigration, because of liberal constraints that were institutional and procedural as well as economic.

It follows that strong states are not necessarily those that act independently of groups or against the tide of market conditions. Rather, state strength implies an ability to shape market incentives and minimize interference in policy implementation by a range of interest groups. Few (if any) democratic states have the power to prevent markets and groups from affecting outcomes. Such power would presuppose an ability to suppress group politics (lobbying by unions, employers, and civil rights groups), eliminate black markets for labor (illegal immigration), and insulate the national economy from international pressures. Some states have the ability, derived from neo-corporatist arrangements, to minimize the adverse effect of group politics on policy outcomes. In Germany, for example, capital and labor have a voice in policymaking. By virtue of their participation in the policy process, groups such as trade unions and employers have greater incentives to assist in the implementation of public policies.[15] France does not fall into this category, even though the administrative elite has had a relatively high degree of autonomy vis-à-vis interest groups in some policy areas in the postwar period.[16]

France experienced nationalist/partisan reactions against foreigners in the 1980s. The "state," alternately under the control of the liberal right (in the 1970s) and the liberal left (in the 1980s), has been the target of attacks by Le Pen and the National Front because of the state's inability to control immigration. Liberal politicians of the right and the left were accused of doing nothing while France was overrun by immigration from the Third World.

These domestic political crises over immigration and citizenship are in large part a reflection of changes in the international political economy. The two levels (domestic and international) are increasingly linked because of the financial and commercial integration of the global economy. American hegemony has provided an umbrella under which this process of integration has occurred. The postwar order is based not only on American power, but on liberal norms and principles which affect every facet of international relations, including migration. Liberal norms and principles include individual and human rights which migrants invoke as they seek protection from the vagaries of the marketplace and from the arbitrary power of nation-states. Liberal states have tried to regulate migration according to the realist principles of sovereignty and the national interest, yet liberalism in its rights aspect forces these states to recognize migrants as individuals. Their own cultures and institutions have compelled the liberal states to modify or abandon statist policies. It is important to recognize that these constraints are not simply ideological, but legal and institutional as well. In the international system there is a spill-over effect that leads states to act in a humanitarian way toward migrants.[17]

What weight should be given to domestic and international factors in explaining immigration? The more exchange is dependent upon power or economic relationships, the more likely it is that international systemic factors will have a dominant influence on migration.

Conversely, the more exchange is dependent upon norms, principles, and politics (as rights), the more likely it is that domestic institutional and cultural factors will dominate. With respect to migration, I have argued that domestic factors (rules of entry and exit and the rights of aliens) are dominant. Admittedly, my argument is skewed heavily in the direction of liberal states, and I have tended to ignore international migration within the nonliberal world. Less liberal countries have more leeway in their immigration policies to behave in a mercantilist and nationalist manner.[18]

On the international level have any "regimes" developed for regulating migration comparable to liberal regimes for trade and finance? My answer remains much the same. The transnational exchange of goods and services is more easily governed by market relations or by treaty: labor is not a commodity in the same sense as an automobile or a Treasury bill. In addition, states have had few incentives to cooperate in the area of migration, since each state has been able to obtain foreign labor with ease in the postwar period. The prospects for cooperation in the area of labor are further complicated by the tremendous variation in the power and position of labor at the domestic level. Trade unions, unlike banks, manufacturing associations, and other capitalist actors, do not have the power to compel the state to regulate the flow of foreign workers. The impetus for an international migration regime in Europe has come less from the pressure of citizen workers or business groups in the member states of the European Community than from public fears of a loss of national identity and community that could result from uncontrolled immigration.

Some of the member states of the EC expressed a need to cooperate, not to obtain foreign labor or to protect their domestic labor markets—even though declining populations and dynamic economies in many of these states may necessitate new labor market and immigration policies in the coming decades—but to stave off nationalist reactions among the general public against uncontrolled immigration. This concern has been heightened by the collapse of communist regimes in Eastern Europe, which has the potential to provoke a massive outflow of economic refugees from the poorer states in this region. The Schengen Agreement is evidence of a new spirit of cooperation in Western Europe with respect to immigration (and refugees). In one sense, the agreement, which promises to eliminate internal border controls within six states of the Community (France, Germany, Italy, and Benelux) by 1992, represents a liberal development in keeping with the spirit of integration fostered by the Single European Act. The elimination of internal border controls will increase the economic integration of the Community by facilitating border crossings of people, goods, and services. But the Schengen Agreement also has a strong regionalist (postnationalist) dimension. The hope is that together these six states can accomplish what they have been unable to do individually: control immigration. The desire to eliminate internal border controls, while reinforcing external controls, requires the "harmonization" of rules of entry into the common territory. It is the ambition of this group to implement new visa (and asylum) policies at the regional level. If the Schengen Agreement is fully implemented, liberal constraints will come into play at a regional level, with European institutions (such as the Court of Justice and the Court of Human Rights) involved in setting restrictions on supra-national regimes and policies. In effect, there will be a need for a European jurisprudence in this policy area. Certainly the status of foreign residents will be a major sticking point in the creation of a common European territory. Will a Turk be allowed to move from Germany to France without any restrictions? Will a Pole be free to move from Berlin to Paris? There is nothing in the current Agreement or regulations of the Community that would make this possible.[19] *But*, when rights such as freedom of movement are extended to citizens of the member states, can other members of these societies who are not citizens (only denizens) be denied equal protection?[20] The question remains open.

The important point is that international migration is a prime indicator of interdependence and of liberal-institutional developments in international relations. The European Community constitutes an important test of these developments. Other areas of the globe, particularly North America, which already has a highly developed, if unregulated, international labor market, may soon follow the example of the European Community and create a liberal regime for labor. The Canadian and American labor markets are closely connected already, and Mexican participation in the American market is a reality, *de facto* if not *de jure*. Ongoing negotiations between Mexico and the United States over a free trade agreement hold out the possibility of normalizing relations with respect to the full range of exchange between the two nations, including migration.[21]

In retrospect, it seems clear that the surge in international migration in the postwar period is due in part to embedded liberalism, which poses a dilemma for the governments of liberal states.[22] The expansion of civil and social rights since 1945 among the principal countries of immigration (for citizens as well as denizens) has contributed as much as the globalization of markets to increases in international migration. It also seems clear that states have yet to recognize the implications of embedded liberalism, since immigration policies continue to reflect mercantilist, nationalist and restrictionist biases. Or perhaps restrictionist policies are a symbolic (nationalist) response to embedded liberalism. Yet nothing short of a major political-economic upheaval that would roll back the liberal gains of the past forty years or eliminate current international inequalities seems likely to arrest the movement of individuals across national boundaries.

Immigration and Liberal Democracy

Is immigration primarily a political or an economic phenomenon? The policy response has been to classify some migrants as political and others as economic refugees. This classification ignores one of the most fundamental tenets of liberalism: the intrinsic worth of the free, rational individual. In liberal political systems the individual occupies a sacrosanct position, regardless of his or her contractual relationship with the state or society. Whether the motivation for migration is one part political and two parts economic or vice-versa should in principle make little difference to the way the individual is treated. Even though migration may begin as a response to economic incentives, it takes on a political character as soon as the migrant enters the territory (or comes under the authority) of a liberal state. Often potential migrants do not have to leave their countries of origin to come under the "moral" jurisdiction of liberal states. Postwar history is replete with examples of migrations that have been encouraged by liberal states on foreign policy and human rights grounds. Although it may be important to separate politics and economics for policy purposes, we must recognize that in a liberal system one is embedded in the other, at the domestic if not always at the international level.

Thus immigration continues to reflect a liberal paradox of rights versus markets. French, German, and American states have struggled with this paradox in particular ways. The policy response has depended heavily upon cultural and institutional norms that define the relationship between individuals and the state in each of these societies. Yet we have found considerable evidence of a convergence of immigration and refugee policies in Western Europe and the United States, despite important cultural and institutional differences. The convergence is a result of the gradual resolution of the liberal paradox, a process which involves the expansion of civil rights for aliens and other minorities in Europe and North America and the growth of an international market for labor. These developments have made immigration one of the most salient issues in international and comparative political economy.

With the approach of the twenty-first century and the revolutions that swept Eastern Europe in 1989 and the old Soviet Empire in 1991, it seems likely that the "enclosure of the individual within national boundaries" will continue to weaken, and that migration will remain a prominent feature of the international political economy. How states respond to the increasing mobility of people will tell us a great deal about the future of world politics and the prospects for a peaceful and liberal world order.

Selected Bibliography

Notes

Index

Selected Bibliography

Adler, Stephen. *International migration and dependence*. Westmead, England: Saxon House, 1977.

Aleinikoff, Thomas Alexander, and David A. Martin. *Immigration Process and Policy*. St. Paul, Minn.: West Publishing, 1985.

Archdeacon, Thomas. *Becoming American*. New York: Free Press, 1983.

Ashford, Douglas E. *Policy and Politics in France*. Philadelphia: Temple University Press, 1982.

Ath-Messaoud, Malek, and Alain Gillette. *L'Immigration algérienne en France*. Paris: Editions Entente, 1976.

Barou, Jacques. *Travailleurs africains en France*. Grenoble: Presses Universitaires de France, 1978.

Bean, Frank B., et al. *Mexican and Central American Population and U.S. Immigration Policy*. Austin: University of Texas Press, 1989.

Becker, Gary S. *Human Capital*. New York: Columbia University Press, 1975.

Beitz, Charles. *Political Theory and International Relations*. Princeton: Princeton University Press, 1979.

Bellon, Bertrand, and Jean-Marie Chevalier, eds. *L'Industrie en France*. Paris: Flammarion, 1983.

Benjamin, Roger, and Stephen L. Elkin. *The Democratic State*. Lawrence: Kansas University Press, 1985.

Berger, Suzanne. "Lame Ducks and National Champions: Industrial Policy in the Fifth Republic." In *The Fifth Republic at Twenty*. Edited by W. G. Andrews and S. Hoffmann. Albany: State University of New York Press, 1980.

——— ed. *Organizing Interests in Western Europe: Pluralism, Corporatism, and the Transformation of Politics*. New York: Cambridge University Press, 1981.

Berger, Suzanne, and Michael Piore. *Dualism and Discontinuity in Industrial Societies*. Cambridge: Cambridge University Press, 1980.

Bernard, Philippe, ed. *Les travailleurs étrangers en Europe Occidentale*. Paris: Mouton, 1976.

Berrier, Robert J. "The French Textile Industry: A Segmented Labor Market." In *Guests Come to Stay: The Effects of European Labor Migration on*

235

Sending and Receiving Countries. Edited by Rosemarie Rogers. Boulder, Co.: Westview Press, 1985.

Beth, J., et al. *Essai d'évaluation de la dépendance du système productif français à l'égard des travailleurs étrangers.* Paris: S.E.A.E., Fondation Nationale des Sciences Politiques, 1979.

Bhagwati, Jagdish N., ed. *The Brain Drain and Taxation: Theory and Empirical Analysis.* Amsterdam: North Holland, 1976.

Bideberry, Pierre. "Bilan de vingt années d'immigration 1946–1966." *Revue Française du Travail,* 2 (1967): 7–30.

────── *Le chômage des travailleurs étrangers.* Paris: Inspection Générale des Affaires Sociales, 1974.

Blanchet, Didier, and James F. Hollifield. "Problèmes de mesures de stocks de travailleurs immigrés en France." Paris: Institut National d'Etudes Démographiques, 1982.

Böhning, Wolf R. *Les conséquences économiques de l'emploi de travailleurs étrangers, concernant en particulier les marchés du travail de l'Europe Occidentale.* Paris: OECD, 1974.

────── *The Migration of Workers in the United Kingdom and European Community.* London: Oxford University Press, 1972.

────── *Studies in International Labour Migration.* London: Macmillan, 1984.

Bonacich, Edna. "The Split Labor Market: A Theory of Ethnic Antagonism." *American Journal of Sociology,* 37 (1972): 1050–87.

Bonnechère, M. "Conditions de séjour et d'emploi en France des travailleurs africains." *Revue Pratique de Droit Social,* 392 (December 1977): 379–82.

Bonnet, J-C. *Les pouvoirs publics français et l'immigration dans l'entre-deux-guerres.* Lyon: Centre D'Histoire Économique et Sociale de la Région Lyonnaise, 1976.

Borjas, George J. *Friends or Strangers: The Impact of Immigrants on the U.S. Economy.* New York: Basic Books, 1990.

Bornstein, Stephen, David Held, and Joel Kriger, eds. *The State in Capitalist Europe.* London: George Allen and Unwin, 1984.

Bourdet, Yves. "Fonction économique et rôle politique des migrants d'après les théories marxistes." *Ethnologie Française,* 7 (1977): 239–44.

Bourguignon, F., and G. Gallais-Hamono. *Choix économiques liés aux migrations internationales du travail: Le cas européen.* Paris: OECD, 1977.

Boyer, Robert. "Rapport salarial et analyses en terme de régulation." *CEPREMAP,* 8017 (June 1980), mimeo.

Braudel, Fernand. *L'Identité de la France.* Paris: Arthaud—Flammarion, 1986.

Briggs, Vernon. *Immigration Policy and the American Labor Force.* Baltimore: Johns Hopkins University Press, 1984.

Brubaker, William Rogers. *Citizenship and Nationhood in France and Germany.* Cambridge, Mass.: Harvard University Press, forthcoming.

────── ed. *Immigration and the Politics of Citizenship in Europe and North America.* Lanham, Md.: The German Marshall Fund of the United States and the University Press of America, 1989.

Bryce-LaPorte, Roy Simon, et al. *Sourcebook on the New Immigration.* New Brunswick, N.J.: Transaction Books, 1980.

Bull, Hedley. *The Anarchical Society: A Study of Order in World Politics.* New York: Columbia University Press, 1977.

Bundesanstalt für Arbeit. *Überlegungen Il zu einer vorausschauenden Arbeitsmarktpolitik.* Nürnberg: Bundesanstalt für Arbeit, 1978.

Bundesminister für Arbeit und Sozialordnung. *Vorschlage der Bund-Länder-Kommission zur Fortentwicklung einer umfassenden Konzeption der Ausländer-beschäftigungspolitik.* Bonn, 1977.

Bunel, J., and J. Saglio. "Le C.N.P.F. et la politique d'immigration." *Economie et Humanisme,* 221 (January-February 1975): 41–50.

Bunle, H. *Mouvements migratoires entre la France et l'étranger.* Paris: Imprimerie Nationale, 1943.

Bussery, H. "Incidence sur l'économie française d'une réduction durable de la main-d'oeuvre immigrée." *Economie et Statistique,* 76 (March 1976): 37–46.

Bustamante, Jorge A. "Measuring the Flows of Undocumented Immigrants." In *Mexican Migration to the United States.* Edited by Wayne A. Cornelius and Jorge A. Bustamante. La Jolla: Center for U.S.-Mexican Studies, University of California, 1989.

Calavita, Kitty. "The Immigration Policy Debate: Critical Analysis and Future Options." In *Mexican Migration to the United States.* Edited by Wayne A. Cornelius and Jorge A. Bustamante. La Jolla: Center for U.S.-Mexican Studies, University of California, 1989.

Callovi, G. "Les communautés Européennes et la migration." *Dossier Migrations,* 1 (March-April 1981): 1–4.

Cameron, David. "The Expansion of the Public Economy, a Comparative Analysis." *The American Political Science Review,* 4 (1978): 1243–61.

Caporaso, James A., ed. *A Changing International Division of Labor.* Boulder, Co.: Lynne Rienner, 1987.

Carré, Jean-Jacques, et al. *French Economic Growth.* Stanford: Stanford University Press, 1975.

Castells, Manuel. "Immigrant Workers and Class Struggles in Advanced Capitalism: The Western European Experience." *Politics and Society,* 5 (1975): 33–66.

Castles, Francis G. "How Does Politics Matter? Structure or Agency in the Determination of Public Policy Outcomes." *European Journal of Political Research,* 9 (1981): 119–32.

Castles, Stephen. *Here for Good: Western Europe's New Ethnic Minorities.* London: Pluto Press, 1984.

Castels, Stephen, and Godula Kosack. *Immigrant Workers and Class Structure in Western Europe.* London: Oxford University Press, 1973.

Chevalier, Louis. "La population étrangère en France d'après le recensement de 1962." *Population,* 19 (1964): 569–78.

Chiswick, Barry R., ed. *The Gateway: U.S. Immigration Issues and Policies.* Washington, D.C.: American Enterprise Institute, 1982.

—— "Guidelines for the Reform of Immigration Policy." *Contemporary Economic Problems.* Washington, D.C.: American Enterprise Institute, 1981.

Choucri, Nazli. *Multidisciplinary Perspectives on Population and Conflict.* Syracuse, N.Y.: Syracuse University Press, 1984.

Cohen, Stephen. *Modern Capitalist Planning: The French Model.* Berkeley: University of California Press, 1977.

Cohen, Stephen, and Peter A. Gourevitch. *France in the Troubled World Economy.* London: Butterworth Scientific, 1982.

Cohen, Stephen, and John Zysman. *Manufacturing Matters: The Myth of the Post-Industrial Economy.* New York: Basic Books, 1987.

Commissariat Général du Plan. "Premier rapport de la Commission de la Main-d'Oeuvre (October 1946)." *Documents relatifs à la première session du Conseil du Plan, 16–19 March 1946.* Paris: Imprimerie Nationale, 1946.

—— *Rapport de la Commission Emploi (Préparation du VIè Plan).* Vol. 2. Paris: Documentation Française, 1971.

—— "Rapport général de la Commission de la Main-d'Oeuvre du Vè Plan." *Revue Française du Travail,* 28 (January-March 1966): 90–132.

—— "Rapport général de la Commission de la Main-d'Oeuvre du IIIè Plan." *Revue Française du Travail,* 20 (April-June 1958): 40–73.

Commission of the European Communities. *Free Movement of Labor within the Community.* Brussels: EEC, 1977.

Cornelius, Wayne A., and Jorge A. Bustamante, eds. *Mexican Migration to the United States: Origins, Consequences, and Policy Options.* La Jolla: Center for U.S.-Mexican Studies, University of California, 1989.

Costa-Lascoux, Jacqueline. *De l'immigré au citoyen.* Paris: La Documentation Française, 1989.

Courault, Bruno. *Contribution à la théorie de l'offre de travail: le cas de l'immigration en France, 1946–1978.* Thèse pour le Doctorat d'Etat. Paris: Université de Paris I Pantheon Sorbonne, 1980.

—— "Une nouvelle série d'effectifs salariés étrangers de 1967 à 1976." *Statistiques du Travail, Supplément au Bulletin Mensuel.* 78 (1980): 59–80.

Cross, Gary S. *Immigrant Workers in Industrial France.* Philadelphia: Temple University Press, 1983.

Dahrendorf, Ralf. *Class and Class Conflict in Industrial Society.* Stanford: Stanford University Press, 1959.

Debré, Robert, and Alfred Sauvy. *Des français pour la France, le problème de la population.* Paris: Gallimard, 1946.

de Gaudemar, Jean-Paul. *Mobilité du travail et accumulation du capital.* Paris: François Maspero, 1976.

Doeringer, Peter B., and Michael J. Piore. *Internal Labor Markets and Manpower Analysis.* Lexington, Mass.: D.C. Heath, 1971.

Dohse, Knut. *Ausländische Arbeiter und bürgerlicher Staat: Genese und Funktion von staatlicher Ausländerpolitik und Ausländerrecht. Vom Kaiserreich bis zur Bundesrepublik Deutschland.* Königstein: Anton Hain, 1981.

Dworkin, R. W. *Taking Rights Seriously.* Cambridge, Mass.: Harvard University Press, 1977.

Dyson, Kenneth. *The State Tradition in Western Europe.* New York: Oxford University Press, 1980.

Easterlin, R. A. *Population, Labor Force and Long Swings in Economic Growth: The American Experience.* New York: Columbia University Press, 1968.

Eley, Geoff. "German Politics and Polish Nationality: The Dialectic of Nation-Forming in the East of Prussia." *East European Quarterly,* 18 (September 1984): 335–74.

Ehrmann, Henry. *Organized Business in France.* Princeton: Princeton University Press, 1957.

Eymard-Duvernay, François. "L'Emploi au cours du VIè Plan." *Economie et Statistique,* 74 (January 1976): 40–52.

Feldstein, Martin S. "Specification of Labor Input in the Aggregate Production Function." *Review of Economic Studies,* 44 (October 1967): 375–86.

Fogel, Walter. "Mexican Migration to the United States." In *The Gateway: U.S. Immigration Issues and Policies.* Edited by B. R. Chiswick. Washington: American Enterprise Institute, 1981.

Franz, Wolfgang. "International Factor Mobility and the Labor Market: A Macroeconomic Analysis of the German Labor Market." *Empirical Economics,* 2 (1975): 11–30.

——— "Employment Policy and Labor Supply of Foreign Workers in the Federal Republic of Germany: A Theoretical and Empirical Analysis." *Zeitschrift für die gesante Staatswissenschaft.* 137 (1981): 590–611.

Freeman, Gary P. *Immigrant Labor and Racial Conflict in Industrial Societies: The French and British Experiences, 1945–1975.* Princeton: Princeton University Press, 1979.

——— "Migration and the Political Economy of the Welfare State." *The Annals of the American Academy of Political and Social Science,* 485 (May 1986): 51–63.

Fuchs, Lawrence H. *The American Kaleidoscope: Race, Ethnicity and the Civic Culture.* Hanover, N.H.: Wesleyan University and University Press of New England, 1990.

——— "The Corpse That Would Not Die: the Immigration Reform and Control Act of 1986." *Revue Européenne des Migrations Internationales,* 6 (1990): 111–127.

Gani, Léon. *Syndicats et travailleurs immigrés.* Paris: Editions Sociales, 1972.

Garson, Jean-Pierre, and Georges Tapinos, eds. *L'Argent des immigrés. Travaux et Documents.* Paris: Presses Universitaires de France, 1981.

Garson, Jean-Pierre, and Yann Moulier. *Les clandestins et la régularisation de 1981–1982 en France.* Geneva: ILO, document de travail, May 1982.

Garson, Jean-Pierre, Roxanne Silberman, and Yann Moulier-Boutang, *Economie politique des migrations clandestines de main-d'oeuvre.* Paris: Publisud, 1986.

Gilpin, Robert. *The Political Economy of International Relations.* Princeton: Princeton University Press, 1987.

Girard, Alain, et al. "Attitudes des français à l'égard de l'immigration étrangère: nouvelle enquête d'opinion." *Population,* 29 (1974): 1015–64.

—— "Le problème démographique et l'évolution du sentiment public." *Population*, 5 (1950): 338–40.

Girard, Alain, and Jean Stoetzel. *Français et immigrés. Travaux et Documents*. Paris: Presses Universitaires de France, 1953.

Glazer, Nathan, ed. *A Clamor at the Gates: The New American Immigration*. San Francisco: ICS Press, 1985.

Goldthorpe, John, ed. *Order and Conflict in Contemporary Capitalism*. Oxford: Oxford University Press, 1984.

Gourevitch, Peter A. *Politics in Hard Times: Comparative Responses to International Economic Crises*. Ithaca, N.Y.: Cornell University Press, 1986.

—— "The Second Image Reversed: International Sources of Domestic Politics." *International Organization* 32 (Autumn 1978): 881–911.

Grillo, R. D. *Ideologies and Institutions in Urban France: The Representation of Immigrants*. Cambridge: Cambridge University Press, 1985.

Granier, R., and J. P. Marciano. "The Earnings of Immigrant Workers in France." *International Labour Review*, 111 (February 1975): 143–65.

Granotier, Bernard. *Les travailleurs immigrés en France*. Paris: François Maspero, 1973.

Green, Diane. "The Seventh Plan—The Demise of French Planning?" *West European Politics*, 1 (1978): 60–76.

Greenwood, M. J., and J. M. McDowell. "The Supply of Immigrants to the United States." In *The Gateway: U.S. Immigration Issues and Policies*. Edited by B. R. Chiswick. Washington, D.C.: American Enterprise Institute, 1982.

Hagen, William W. *Germans, Poles, and Jews: The Nationality Conflict in the Prussian East, 1772–1914*. Chicago: University of Chicago Press, 1980.

Hagmann, Hermann-Michel. *Les travailleurs étrangers: chance et tourment de la Suisse*. Lausanne: Payot, 1966.

Hailbronner, Kay. *Ausländerrecht*. Heidelberg: C. F. Müller, 1984.

Hall, Peter A. *Governing the Economy: The Politics of State Intervention in Britain and France*. New York: Oxford University Press, 1986.

Hammar, Tomas. *Democracy and the Nation-State: Aliens, Denizens, and Citizens in a World of International Migration*. Aldershot: Avebury, 1990.

—— ed. *European Immigration Policy: A Comparative Study*. New York: Cambridge University Press, 1985.

Hayward, Jack. *Private Interests and Public Policy: The Experience of the French Economic and Social Council*. London: Longmans, 1966.

Heisler, Martin. "Transnational Migration as a Small Window on the Diminished Autonomy of the Modern Democratic State." *The Annals*, 485 (May 1986): 153–66.

Heisler, Martin, and Barbara S. Heisler. "From Foreign Workers to Settlers? Transnational Migration and the Emergence of New Minorities." *The Annals*, special issue, 485 (May 1986).

Hémery, Solange, et al. *Nationalité. Collections de l'INSEE.* Série D, no. 83. Paris: INSEE, 1981.

Hénneresse, Marie-Claude. *Le patronat et la politique française d'immigration: 1945–1975,* Thèse de 3ème cycle. Paris: Institut d'Etudes Politiques, 1978.

Herbert, Ulrich. *A History of Foreign Labor in Germany.* Ann Arbor, Mich.: University of Michigan Press, 1990.

Hiemenz, U., and K. W. Schatz. *Trade in Place of Migration.* Geneva: ILO, 1979.

Hildbrandt, E. and W. Olle. *Ihr Kampf ist unser Kampf.* Offenbach: Verlag 2000, 1975.

Hobsbawm, E. J. *Nations and Nationalism since 1780.* Cambridge: Cambridge University Press, 1990.

Hoffmann, Stanley. *Duties beyond Borders.* Syracuse, N.Y.: Syracuse University Press, 1981.

——— *The State of War: Essays on the Theory and Practice of International Politics.* New York: Praeger, 1965.

——— ed. *In Search of France.* Cambridge, Mass.: Harvard University Press, 1963.

Hoffmann-Nowotny, Hans-Joachim, and Karl-Otto Hondrich, eds. *Ausländer in der Bundesrepublik Deutschland und in der Schweiz: Segregation und Integration. Eine vergleichende Untersuchung.* Frankfurt: Campus, 1982.

Hollifield, James F. "Administration and the French State." In *The State and Public Policy.* Edited by B. G. Peters and J. F. Hollifield. Forthcoming.

——— "Immigration and the French State." *Comparative Political Studies,* 23 (April 1990): 56–79.

——— "Immigration Policy in France and Germany since 1973: Outputs vs. Outcomes." *The Annals,* 485 (May 1986): 113–28.

——— "Immigration, Race and Politics." *French Politics and Society,* 13 (March 1986): 15–20.

——— "Migrants ou citoyens: la politique de l'immigration en France et aux Etats-Unis." *Revue Européenne des Migrations Internationales,* 6 (1990).

Hollifield, James F. and Yves Charbit, eds. "L'Immigration aux Etats-Unis." *Revue Européenne des Migrations Internationales,* 6 (1990).

Hollifield, James F., and George Ross, eds. *Searching for the New France.* New York: Routledge, 1991.

Holmes, Colin, ed. *Immigrants and Minorities in British Society.* London: George Allen and Unwin, 1978.

Homze, Edward L. *Foreign Labor in Nazi Germany.* Princeton: Princeton University Press, 1967.

Honekopp, Elmar, and Hans Ullman. *The Effect of Immigration on Social Structures.* Nürnberg: Institute for Labor Market Research, 1980.

Horowitz, Donald L. *The Courts and Social Policy.* Washington: Brookings Institution, 1977.

Huber, Bertold, and Klaus Unger. "Politische und rechtliche Determinaten der Ausländerbeschätigung in der Bundesrepublik Deutschland." In *Ausländer in der Bundesrepublik Deutschland und in der Schweiz*. Edited by H-J. Hoffman-Nowotny and K-O. Hondrich. Frankfurt: Campus, 1982.

International Labour Office. *International Migration 1945–1957*. Geneva: ILO, 1959.

—— *World Employment Conference Background Papers. Vol. II: International Strategies for Employment*. Geneva: ILO, 1976.

Institut National de la Statistique et des Etudes Economiques. *Le mouvement économique en France, 1949–1979. Séries longues macroéconomiques*. Paris: INSEE, 1979.

—— *Annuaires de l'INSEE. Résumé retrospectif*. Paris: INSEE, 1967.

Jaume, Lucien. *Le discours jacobin et la démocratie*. Paris: Fayard, 1988.

Johnson, Kenneth F., and Miles W. Williams. *Illegal Aliens in the Western Hemisphere*. New York: Praeger, 1981.

Journal Officiel. Paris. Various issues.

Kant, Immanuel. "On the Agreement between Politics and Morality according to the Transcendental Concept of Public Right." In *Perpetual Peace: A Philosophical Sketch. Kant's Political Writings*. Edited by Hans Reiss. Cambridge: Cambridge University Press, 1970.

Kastoryano, Riva. *Etre turque en France*. Paris: L'Harmattan, 1986.

Katzenstein, Peter J., ed. *Between Power and Plenty*. Madison: University of Wisconsin Press, 1978.

—— *Policy and Politics in West Germany*. Philadelphia: Temple University Press, 1987.

Kennedy, Paul. *The Rise and Fall of the Great Powers*. New York: Random House, 1988.

Keohane, Robert O. *After Hegemony*. Princeton: Princeton University Press, 1984.

—— "The Theory of Hegemonic Stability and Changes in International Economic Regimes, 1967–1977." In *Change in the International System*. Edited by Ole Holsti, et al. Boulder, Co.: Westview Press, 1980.

Keohane, Robert O., and Joseph S. Nye. *Power and Interdependence*. Boston: Little, Brown, 1977.

Kepel, Gilles. *Les banlieues de l'Islam*. Paris: Seuil, 1988.

Kettner, James. *The Development of American Citizenship, 1608–1870*. Chapel Hill, N.C.: University of North Carolina Press, 1978.

Kindleberger, Charles P. *Europe's Postwar Growth: The Role of Labor Supply*. Cambridge, Mass.: Harvard University Press, 1967.

Krane, Ronald, ed. *International Labor Migration in Europe*. New York: Praeger, 1979.

Krasner, Stephen D. *Defending the National Interest: Raw Materials Investment and U.S. Foreign Policy*. Princeton: Princeton University Press, 1978.

—— ed. "International Regimes." *International Organization*, 36 (Spring 1982).

Kubat, Daniel, ed. *The Politics of Migration Policies.* New York: Center for Migration Studies, 1979.

—— ed. *The Politics of Return: International Return Migration in Europe.* New York: Center for Migration Studies, 1984.

Kuisel, Richard F. *Capitalism and the State in Modern France.* Cambridge: Cambridge University Press, 1981.

Lary de Latour, Henri. "Le particularisme du contrat de travail pour les travailleurs immigrés." *Droit Social,* 5 (May 1976): 63–72.

Layton-Henry, Zig. *The Politics of Race in Britain.* London: George Allen and Unwin, 1984.

Lebon, André. "Attribution, acquisition et perte de la nationalité française: 1973–1986," *Revue Européenne des Migrations Internationales,* 1 (1987): 17–34.

—— *Les jeunes étrangers et le monde du travail.* Paris: OECD, 1981.

—— *1986–1987: Le point sur l'immigration et la présence étrangère en France.* Paris: La Documentation Française, 1988.

—— "Ressortissants communautaires et étrangers originaires des pays tiers dans l'Europe des Douze." *Revue Européenne des Migrations Internationales,* 6 (1990): 185–202.

—— "Sur une politique d'aide au retour." *Economie et Statistique,* 193 (July-August 1979): 37–46.

Lebon, André, and O. Villey. "L'immigration et la politique de la main-d'oeuvre." *Economie et Statistique,* 113 (July-August 1979): 25–80.

Le Pors, Anicet. *Immigration et développement économique et social.* Paris: Documentation Française, 1976.

Lequin, Yves, ed. *La mosaïque France: histoire des étrangers et de l'immigration.* Paris: Librarie Larousse, 1988.

Leveau, Rémy, and Dominique Schnapper. "Religion et politique: juifs et musulmans." *Revue Française de Science Politique,* 37 (December 1987).

Levine, Daniel B. et al., eds. *Immigration Statistics: A Story of Neglect.* National Academy Press, 1985.

Lewis, W. Arthur. "Economic Development with Unlimited Supplies of Labour." *The Manchester School of Economic and Social Studies* (May 1954): 139–91.

Lindblom, Charles E. *Politics and Markets: The World's Political-Economic Systems.* New York: Basic Books, 1977.

Lochak, Danièle. *Etrangers: de quels droits?* Paris: PUF, 1985.

Long, Marceau. *Etre français aujourd'hui et demain.* Vols. 1–2. Paris: La Documentation française, 1988.

McIntosh, C. Alison. "The Rise of Twentieth-Century Pronatalism." *International Journal of Politics,* 12 (Fall 1982): 42–57.

McNeill, W. H., and R. S. Adams, eds. *Human Migration, Patterns and Policies.* Bloomington: Indiana University Press, 1978.

Maillat, Denis. "Long-Term Aspects of International Migration Flows: The Experience of European Receiving Countries." In *The Future of Migration.* Edited by OECD. Paris: OECD, 1987.

Markovits, Andrei S., ed. *The Political Economy of West Germany: Modell Deutschland.* New York: Praeger, 1982.

Marrus, Michael. *Politics of Assimilation: A Study of the French Jewish Community at the Time of the Dreyfus Affair.* Oxford: Clarendon Press, 1971.

Marshall-Goldschvartz, A. J. *The Import of Labor, The Case of the Netherlands.* Rotterdam: Universitaire pers Rotterdam, 1973.

Martin, J. L. R. *Swiss Policy on Immigrant Workers and the Überfremdung Initiatives.* New Haven: Yale University Press, 1979.

Martin, Philip L. *Harvest of Confusion: Migrant Workers in U.S. Agriculture.* Boulder, Co.: Westview Press, 1988.

—— *The Unfinished Story: Turkish Labor Migration to the Federal Republic of Germany.* Geneva: ILO, 1991.

Martin, Philip L., and Doris M. Meissner. "EC-92 and Immigration Issues in Europe." Washington, D.C.: Carnegie Endowment for International Peace, August 1990.

Martin, Philip L., and Mark J. Miller. "The Quest for Control: Illegal Immigration to Western Europe." Washington, D.C.: Report to the German Marshall Fund of the United States, 1991.

Mauco, Georges. *Les étrangers en France.* Paris: Colin, 1932.

Mayer, Nonna, and Pascal Perrineau. *Le Front National à découvert.* Paris: Presses de la FNSP, 1989.

Mehrlander, Ursula. "Bundesrepublik Deutschland." In *Ausländerpolitik im Konflikt.* Edited by Ernst Gehmacher, Daniel Kubat, and Ursula Mehrlander. Bonn: Neue Gesellschaft, 1978.

Meissner, Doris M. "The Refugee Act of 1980: What Have We Learned?" *Revue Européenne des Migrations Internationales,* 6 (1990): 129–40.

Miegel, Meinhard. *Arbeitsmarkt auf Irrwegen: Zur Ausländerbeschäftigung in der Bundesrepublik.* Bonn: Bonn Aktuell, 1984.

Milkis, Sidney M. *The Modern Presidency and the Transformation of the American Party System.* New York: Oxford University Press, forthcoming.

—— "Programmatic Liberalism and the Rise of Administrative Politics in the United States." In *The State and Public Policy.* Edited by B. G. Peters and J. F. Hollifield. Forthcoming.

Miller, Mark J. *Foreign Workers in Western Europe: An Emerging Political Force.* New York: Praeger, 1981.

——. "La politique américaine de régularisation (1986–1989): Résultats et limites." *Revue Européenne des Migrations Internationales,* 6 (1990): 141–58.

Miller, Mark J., and Philip L. Martin. *Administering Foreign-Worker Programs.* Lexington, Mass.: D.C. Heath, 1982.

Milza, Pierre, ed. *Les Italiens en France de 1914 à 1940.* Rome: Ecole Française de Rome, 1981.

Ministère de l'Interieur. *Les étrangers en France.* Paris: Ministère de l'Interieur, 1981.

Ministère du Travail et de la Participation. Service des Etudes et de la

Statistique. Division de la Statistique. *Premiers résultats de l'enquête sur la main-d'oeuvre etrangère effectuée en octobre 1979*. Paris: Ministère du Travail, 1981.

Mitchell, E. J. "Explaining the International Pattern of Labor Productivity and Wages: A Production Model with Two Labor Inputs." *Review of Economics and Statistics*, 58 (November 1968): 461–69.

Morris, Milton D. *Immigration: The Beleaguered Bureaucracy*. Washington, D.C.: Brookings Institution, 1985.

Mouriaux, René and Catherine Wihtol de Wenden. "Syndicalisme français et Islam." *Revue Française de Science Politique*, 37 (December, 1987): 794–819.

Mundell, R. A. "International Trade and Factor Mobility." *American Economic Review* (June 1967): 321–37.

Mytelka, Lynn K. "In Search of a Partner: The State and the Textile Industry in France." In *France in the Troubled World Economy*. Edited by S. Cohen and P. Gourevitch. London: Butterworth Scientific, 1982.

N'guyen Van Yen, Christian. *Droit de l'immigration*. Paris: Presses Universitaires de France, Thémis, 1986.

Nicol, J. "Les incidences économiques de l'immigration." *Problèmes Économiques*, 1583 (26 July 1978): 3–7.

Noiriel, Gérard. *Le creuset français*. Paris: Seuil, 1988.

Nordlinger, Eric A. *On the Autonomy of the Democratic State*. Cambridge, Mass.: Harvard University Press, 1981.

Notter, Nikolaus. "Le statut des travailleurs étrangers en Allemagne Fédérale." *Droit Social*, 4 (April 1973): 223–30.

O'Brien, Peter. "The Civil Rights of West Germany's Migrants." *German Politics and Society*, 19 (Spring 1990): 27–40.

——— "The Paradoxical Paradigm: Turkish Migrants and German Policies." Ph.D. Dissertation, University of Wisconsin-Madison, 1988.

Offe, Claus. "The Attribution of Public Status to Interest Groups: Observations on the West German Case." In *Organising Interests in Western Europe*. Edited by Suzanne Berger. Cambridge: Cambridge University Press, 1981.

Olson, Mancur. *The Logic of Collective Action*. Cambridge, Mass.: Harvard University Press, 1965.

OECD, ed. *The Future of Migration*. Paris: OECD, 1987.

——— *SOPEMI Reports, 1974–1983*. Paris: OECD, 1974–1980.

Papademetriou, Demetrios G., and Mark J. Miller, eds. *The Unavoidable Issue: U.S. Immigration Policy in the 1980s*. Philadelphia: Institute for the Study of Human Issues, 1983.

Perlman, R. *Labor Theory*. New York: Wiley, 1969.

Piore, Michael J. *Birds of Passage: Migrant Labor in Industrial Societies*. Cambridge: Cambridge University Press, 1979.

——— "Dualism in the Labor Market: A Response to Uncertainty and Flux—The Case of France." *Revue Economique*, 19 (January, 1978): 26–48.

——— "Economic Fluctuation, Job Security, and Labour-Market Duality in

Italy, France and the United States." *Politics and Society*, 9 (1980): 379–407.

Piore, Michael J., and Charles Sabel. *The Second Industrial Divide*. Cambridge: Cambridge University Press, 1985.

Portes, Alejandro, and Robert L. Bach. *Latin Journey: Cuban and Mexican Immigrants to the United States*. Berkeley: University of California Press, 1985.

Portes, Alejandro, and John Walton. *Labor, Class, and the International System*. New York: Academic Press, 1981.

Prognos. *The Development of the EC Labor Market to 2000*. Basel: 1989.

Le rapport Calvez, "La politique de l'immigration." *Avis et Rapports du Conseil Economique et Social* (23 May 1975): 349–75.

Reiffers, Jean-Louis. *Le rôle de l'immigration des travailleurs dans la croissance de la République Fédérale d'Allemagne de 1958 à 1968*. Geneva: ILO, March 1970.

Reimers, David. *Still the Golden Door*. New York: Columbia University Press, 1985.

Reyneri, Emilio. *La Catena Migratoria*. Bologna: Il Mulino, 1979.

Richter, H. *Probleme der Anwerbung und Betreuung der Ausländischen Arbeiter aus der Sicht der deutschen Gewerkschaften*. Dusseldorf: Deutsche Gewerkschaft Bund, 1970.

Rist, R. C. *Guestworkers in Germany: The Prospects for Pluralism*. New York: Praeger, 1978.

Ritchey, P. N. "Explanations of Migration." *Annual Review of Sociology*, 2 (1976): 363–404.

Rogers, Rosemarie, ed. *Guests Come to Stay: The Effects of European Labor Migration on Sending and Receiving Countries*. Boulder, Co.: Westview Press, 1985.

Ross, George. "French Labour and Economic Change." *France in the Troubled World Economy*. Edited by S. Cohen and P. Gourevitch. London: Butterworth Scientific, 1979.

Ruggie, John Gerard. "International Regimes, Transactions, and Change: Embedded Liberalism in the Postwar Economic Order." *International Organization*, 36 (Spring 1982): 379–415.

Rybczynski, T. M. "Factor Endowment and Relative Commodity Prices." *Economica*, 22 (November 1955): 336–41.

Safran, William. "Islamization in Western Europe." *The Annals*, 485 (May 1986): 98–112.

Samuelson, Paul A. "International Trade and the Equalization of Factor Prices." *The Economic Journal* (June, 1948): 163–84.

Sassen, Saskia. *The Mobility of Labor and Capital*. Cambridge: Cambridge University Press, 1988.

Sauvy, Alfred. "Besoins et possibilités de l'immigration en France." *Population*, 2–3 (1950): 209–234.

Schain, Martin A. "Immigration and Change in the French Party System." *European Journal of Political Research*, 16 (1988): 597–621.

Schiller, Gunter. "Channelling Migration: A Review of Policy with Special

References to the Federal Republic of Germany." *International Migration Review,* 3 (1975): 335–55.

Schlaffke, Winifried, and Rudiger von Voss. *Vom Gastarbeiter zum Mitarbeiter.* Köln: Informedia Verlag-GMBH, 1982.

Schmitter, Barbara E. "Immigrants and Associations: Their Role in the Socio-Political Process of Integration in West Germany and Switzerland." *International Migration Review,* 14 (1980): 177–92.

——— "Immigration and Citizenship in West Germany and Switzerland." Ph.D. Dissertation, University of Chicago, 1979.

Schnapper, Dominique. *Juifs et israélites.* Paris: Gallimard, 1980.

Schor, Ralph. *L'Opinion française et les étrangers, 1919–1939.* Paris: Publication de la Sorbonne, 1985.

Schuck, Peter H. "The Transformation of Immigration Law." *Columbia Law Review,* 84 (January 1984): 1–90.

Schuck, Peter H., and Rogers Smith. *Citizenship without Consent.* New Haven: Yale University Press, 1985.

Secrétaire d'Etat aux Travailleurs Immigrés. *La nouvelle politique de l'immigration.* Paris: La Documentation Française, 1977.

Siegel, J. S., J. S. Passel, and J. G. Robinson. "Preliminary Review of Existing Studies of the Number of Illegal Residents in the United States." Washington, D.C.: U.S. Bureau of the Census, 1980, mimeo.

Simon, Julian. *The Economic Consequences of Immigration.* Oxford: Basil Blackwell and The Cato Institute, 1989.

Skocpol, Theda. "Bringing the State Back In." In *Bringing the State Back In.* Edited by P. Evans, D. Rueschemeyer, and T. Skocpol. Cambridge: Cambridge University Press, 1985.

Spaich, Herbert. *Fremde in Deutschland.* Weinheim and Basel: Beltz Verlag, 1981.

Spengler, Joseph J. *France Faces Depopulation.* Durham, N.C.: Duke University Press, 1979.

Spies, Ulrich. *Ausländerpolitik und Integration.* Frankfurt: Peter D. Lang, 1982.

Statistisches Bundesamt. Nürnberg. Various issues.

Straubhaar, T. "The Accession of Spain and Portugal to the EC from the Aspect of Free Movement of Labor in an Enlarged Common Labor Market." *International Migration Review,* 22 (1984): 228–38.

Suleiman, Ezra. *Politics, Power and Bureaucracy in France.* Princeton: Princeton University Press, 1974.

Tapinos, Georges. *L'Economie des migrations internationales.* Paris: Armand Colin et Fondation Nationale des Sciences Politiques, 1974.

——— "Enquête sur les perspectives des migrations à long terme en R.F.A. et en France." *Studi Emigrazione,* 50 (June 1979): 213–45.

——— "European Migration Patterns: Economic Linkages and Policy Experiences." *Studi Emigrazione* (1982): 339–57.

——— *L'Immigration étrangère en France.* Travaux et Documents. Paris: Presses Universitaires de France, 1975.

Teitelbaum, Michael S., and Jay M. Winter. *Fear of Population Decline.* Orlando, Fla.: Academic Press, 1985.

Thomas, Brinley. *Migration and Economic Growth.* Cambridge: Cambridge University Press, 1973.

Thraenhardt, Dietrich, ed. *Ausländerpolitik und Ausländerintegration in Belgien, den Niederlanden und der Bundesrepublik Deutschland.* Dusseldorf: Landeszentrale für politische Bildung, 1986.

Tomasek, Robert D. "The Migrant Problem and Pressure Group Politics." *Journal of Politics,* 23 (May 1961): 295–319.

Tribalat, Michèle. "Chronique de l'immigration: L'Immigration en Suisse." *Population,* 1 (1984): 147–76.

——— et al., *Cent ans d'immigration; étrangers d'hier, français d'aujour-d'hui.* Paris: Presses Universitaires de France, 1991.

Tripier, Maryse. "Syndicats, ouvriers français, immigration et crises." *Pluriel,* 21 (1980): 31–49.

Ucar, Ali. *Illegale Beschäftigung und Ausländerpolitik.* Berlin: Express Edition, 1983.

Unger, Klaus. *Ausländerpolitik in der Bundesrepublik Deutschland.* Saarbrücken: Verlag Breitenbach, 1978.

Vanderkamp, J. "Migration Flows, Their Determinants and the Effects of Return Migration." *Journal of Political Economy,* 79 (September 1971): 1012–31.

La Vie Economique. Berne, Various issues.

Vieuguet, André. *Français et immigrés, le combat du P.C.F.* Paris: Editions Sociales, 1975.

Villey, Olivier. "Enquête sur la main-d'oeuvre étrangère effectué en octobre 1976." *Statistiques du travail,* suppl. 78 (1980): 11–53.

——— "Le redéploiement actuel de la main-d'oeuvre étrangère passé le premier choc de la crise." *Travail et Emploi,* 8 (April-May 1981): 47–55.

Vlassenko, E., and S. Volkoff. "Les salaires des étrangers en France en 1972." *Economie et Statistique,* 70 (September 1975): 47–54.

Waltz, Kenneth. *Theory of International Politics.* Reading, Mass.: Addison-Wesley, 1979.

Walzer, Michael. *Spheres of Justice: A Defense of Pluralism and Equality.* New York: Basic Books, 1983.

Weber, Eugen. *Peasants into Frenchmen: The Modernization of Rural France 1870–1914.* Stanford: Stanford University Press, 1976.

Weil, Patrick. *La France et ses étrangers.* Paris: Calmann-Lévy, 1991.

Weiner, Myron. "International Migration and International Relations." *Population and Development Review,* 11 (September 1985): 441–55.

——— "The Political Aspects of International Migration." Paper presented at the annual meeting of the International Studies Association, London, March 30, 1989.

Weintraub, Sidney, and Chandler Stolp. "The Implications of Growing Economic Interdependence." In *The Future of Migration.* Edited by OECD. Paris: OECD, 1987.

Werner, Heinz. "Migration and Free Movement of Workers in Western Europe." In *Les travailleurs étrangers en Europe Occidentale.* Edited by P. Bernard. Paris: Mouton, 1976.

———— "Post-war Labor Migration in Western Europe, an Overview." *International Migration Review*, 24 (1986): 543–57.

Widmer, Jean-Philippe. *Le rôle de la main-d'oeuvre étrangère dans l'évolution du marché suisse du travail.* Neuchâtel: Groups d'Etudes Economiques, 1978.

Wihtol de Wenden, Catherine. *Les immigrés et la politique.* Paris: Presses de la F.N.S.P., 1988.

———— *Citoyeneté, Nationalité et Immigration.* Paris: Arcantère Editions, 1988.

Wilson, Frank Lee. *Interest Group Politics in France.* Cambridge: Cambridge University Press, 1987.

Wirtschaft und Statistik. Bonn. Various issues.

Wisniewski, J. "Travailleurs migrants dans le bâtiment et les travaux publics." *Hommes et Migrations*, 885 (June 1975): 3–19.

Young, Oran. "International Regimes: Problems of Concept Formation." *World Politics*, 32 (April 1980): 331–56.

Zolberg, Aristide R. "Contemporary Transnational Migrations in Historical Perspective." In *U.S. Immigration and Refugee Policy.* Edited by Mary M. Kritz. Lexington, Mass.: Lexington Books, 1983.

———— "International Migration in Political Perspective." *Global Trends in Migration: Theory and Research in International Population Movements.* Edited by Mary M. Kritz, Charles B. Keeley, and Silvano M. Tomasi. New York: Center for Migration Studies, 1981.

Zolberg, Aristide R., Astri Suhrke, and Sergio Aguayo. *Escape from Violence: Conflict and the Refugee Crisis in the Developing World.* New York: Oxford University Press, 1989.

Zuleeg, Manfred. "Politik der Armut und Ausländer." In *Politik der Armut und die Spaltung des Socialstaats.* Edited by Stephan Leibrried and Florian Tennstedt. Frankfurt: Suhrkamp, 1985.

Zysman, John. *Governments, Markets, and Growth.* Ithaca: Cornell University Press, 1983.

———— *Political Strategies for Industrial Order.* Berkeley: University of California Press, 1977.

Notes

1. Regulating Immigration in the Liberal Polity

1. This is true even of the United States, often described as the quintessential immigrant society where immigration constitutes one of the "founding myths" of the republic. See Lawrence Fuchs, *The American Kaleidoscope: Race, Ethnicity and the Civic Culture* (Hanover, N.H.: Wesleyan University and University Press of New England, 1990), especially the introductory chapter, in which the author discusses immigration and its relation to the civic culture.

2. This argument, discussed in greater detail in chapter 5 of this book, was made by Charles P. Kindleberger, *Europe's Postwar Growth: The Role of Labor Supply* (Cambridge, Mass.: Harvard University Press, 1967). On immigration and economic growth in the United States, see Julian Simon, *The Economic Consequences of Immigration* (Oxford: Basil Blackwell and The Cato Institute, 1989) and George J. Borjas, *Friends or Strangers: The Impact of Immigrants on the U.S. Economy* (New York: Basic Books, 1990). On Germany, see Ulrich Herbert, *A History of Foreign Labor in Germany* (Ann Arbor, Mich.: University of Michigan Press, 1990).

3. These statist trends of the 1950s and 1960s—regulation, welfare entitlements, interest group and bureaucratic politics—presumably added up to a "crisis of democracy." See Michel Crozier et al., *The Crisis of Democracy* (New York: New York University Press, 1975).

4. See Kindleberger, *Europe's Postwar Growth*, chapter 10, and Simon, *The Economic Consequences of Immigration*, especially pp. 339–344.

5. See, for example, John Rawls, *A Theory of Justice* (Cambridge, Mass.: Harvard University Press, 1971), Michael Sandel, *Liberalism and Its Critics* (New York: New York University Press, 1984), and Michael Walzer, *Spheres of Justice: A Defense of Pluralism and Equality* (New York: Basic Books, 1983).

6. Karl Polanyi, *The Great Transformation* (Boston: Beacon Press, 1944), especially chapters 4–6.

7. See the introductory chapter in Michael J. Piore, *Birds of Passage: Migrant Labor in Industrial Societies* (Cambridge: Cambridge University Press,

1979). Piore's argument is similar to the classical Marxist argument that migrant workers represent an industrial reserve army. One of the best examples of this argument is to be found in Stephen Castles and Godula Kosack, *Immigrant Workers and Class Structure in Western Europe* (London: Oxford University Press, 1985). See chapters 2, 5, and 9 for further discussion of Marxist theories of immigration.

8. For more on this point, see Robert O. Keohane and Joseph S. Nye, *Power and Interdependence* (Boston: Little, Brown, 1977), Robert Gilpin, *The Political Economy of International Relations* (Princeton: Princeton University Press, 1987), and chapter 2 of this book.

9. For a cogent and insightful discussion of the relationship between politics and economics, see Peter A. Hall, *Governing the Economy: The Politics of State Intervention in Britain and France* (New York: Oxford University Press, 1986), especially pp. 1–22.

10. See Myron Weiner, "International Migration and International Relations," *Population and Development Review* 11 (September 1985), pp. 441–455, and Aristide Zolberg, "International Migration in Political Perspective," in Mary M. Kritz, Charles B. Keely, and Silvano M. Tomasi, eds., *Global Trends in Migration: Theory and Research in International Population Movements* (New York: Center for Migration Studies, 1981), pp. 3–27.

11. See T. H. Marshall, *Class, Citizenship and Social Development* (Cambridge: Cambridge University Press, 1950), William Rogers Brubaker, *Citizenship and Nationhood in France and Germany* (Cambridge, Mass.: Harvard University Press, forthcoming), and Barbara E. Schmitter, "Immigration and Citizenship in West Germany and Switzerland" (Ph.D. diss., University of Chicago, 1979).

12. For a historical perspective on recent debates in the United States and France, see Thomas Archdeacon, *Becoming American* (New York: Free Press, 1983) and Gérard Noiriel, *Le creuset français* (Paris: Seuil, 1988), pp. 13–67.

13. For an American perspective on the relationship between immigration and citizenship, see Peter H. Schuck and Rogers Smith, *Citizenship without Consent* (New Haven: Yale University Press, 1985).

14. See Yves Lequin, ed., *La mosaïque France: histoire des étrangers et de l'immigration* (Paris: Librarie Larousse, 1988).

15. For a discussion of the "strength and autonomy" of democratic states see James F. Hollifield, "Immigration and the French State," *Comparative Political Studies* 23 (April 1990), pp. 56–79.

16. Several edited works that suffer from this problem are Daniel Kubat, ed., *The Politics of Migration Policies* (New York: Center for Migration Studies, 1979); Ronald Krane, ed., *International Labor Migration in Europe* (New York: Praeger, 1979); and Tomas Hammar, ed., *European Immigration Policy: A Comparative Study* (New York: Cambridge University Press, 1985). Among the comparative works on immigration which avoid the pitfalls of the compendium are the now classic works of Castles and Kosack, *Immigrant Workers and Class Structure in Western Europe;* Gary

P. Freeman, *Immigrant Labor and Racial Conflict in Industrial Societies: The French and British Experiences, 1945–1975* (Princeton: Princeton University Press, 1979); Mark J. Miller, *Foreign Workers in Western Europe: An Emerging Political Force* (New York: Praeger, 1981); and (on citizenship) Brubaker's *Citizenship and Nationhood.*

2. The Political Economy of International Migration

1. For further discussion of international migration and classical political economy, see Brinley Thomas, *Migration and Economic Growth* (Cambridge: Cambridge University Press, 1973), pp. 1–26.

2. On the notion of *Pax Britannica* and the emergence of Great Britain as a global power see Paul Kennedy, *The Rise and Fall of the Great Powers* (New York: Random House, 1988), especially chapters 4–6, and on the role of money and finance in this new system see Robert Gilpin, *The Political Economy of International Relations* (Princeton: Princeton University Press, 1987), pp. 118–127.

3. Steven Krasner defines international regimes as "principles, norms, rules and decision-making procedures around which actor expectations converge in a given issue-area." While I have some reservations about the notion of an international regime, the concept is useful for understanding trade and factor mobility, beginning in the middle of the nineteenth century. For further discussion of the concept, see Oran Young, "International Regimes: Problems of Concept Formation," *World Politics* 32 (April 1980), pp. 331–356, and various articles in Steven Krasner, ed., "International Regimes," *International Organization* 36 (Spring 1982), from which the quote above is taken. I would contrast the use of the term *regime* in this literature with the classical Greek concept of *politeia.* See Aristotle's discussion of regimes in Book III of *The Politics.*

4. For a discussion of the politics of international migration and the importance of the state in setting the terms of entry and exit, see Myron Weiner, "International Migration and International Relations," *Population and Development Review* 11 (September 1985), pp. 441–455, and Aristide Zolberg, "International Migration in Political Perspective," in Mary M. Kritz, Charles B. Keely, and Silvano M. Tomasi, *Global Trends in Migration: Theory and Research in International Population Movements* (New York: Center for Migration Studies, 1981), pp. 3–27. On the realist approach to international relations, see Kenneth Waltz, *Theory of International Politics* (Reading, Mass.: Addison-Wesley, 1979) and Stephen D. Krasner, *Defending the National Interest: Raw Materials Investment and U.S. Foreign Policy* (Princeton: Princeton University Press, 1978). Myron Weiner compares and contrasts the realist (or security) perspective with what he calls a "political economy" approach in Weiner, "Security, Stability and International Migration" (MIT Center for International Studies, April 1990).

5. As Myron Weiner aptly states, "migrants differ from other international transactions in one fundamental respect: migrants themselves have their

own will." Weiner, "The Political Aspects of International Migration,"paper presented at the annual meeting of the International Studies Association, London, March 30, 1989, p. 75.

6. This discussion draws upon the arguments of John G. Ruggie, "International Regimes, Transactions, and Change: Embedded Liberalism in the Postwar Economic Order," in S. Krasner, ed., "International Regimes," pp. 379–415.

7. See Thomas, *Migration and Economic Growth*, p. 1. For a realist perspective on international political economy, see Robert Gilpin, *U.S. Power and the Multinational Corporation* (New York: Basic Books, 1975). See also Steven Krasner, *Defending the National Interest*, and Wolf R. Böhning, *Studies in International Labour Migration* (London: Macmillan, 1984), pp. 3–15.

8. In *Capital* Marx argues that the "organic composition of capital" has a tendency to rise: the ratio of variable to constant capital will inevitably decline as accumulation proceeds. Since the demand for labor is dependent on the amount of variable capital, a temporarily superfluous work force is created. See Karl Marx, *Capital, Vol. I* (New York: International Publishers, 1977), pp. 628 ff. See also Jean-Paul de Gaudemar, *Mobilité du travail et accumulation du capital* (Paris: Maspero, 1976), chapter 8.

9. These arguments are presented by Rosa Luxemburg in *The Accumulation of Capital* (New York: Monthly Review Press, 1968).

10. Among the more prominent works on international migration which fall within a Marxist perspective are Stephen Adler, *International Migration and Dependence* (Westmead: Saxon House, 1977); Alejandro Portes and John Walton, *Labor, Class, and the International System* (New York: Academic Press, 1981); and Saskia Sassen, *The Mobility of Labor and Capital* (Cambridge: Cambridge University Press, 1988).

11. Two of the most influential works in this regard are Stephen Castles and Godula Kosack, *Immigrant Workers and Class Structure in Western Europe* (London: Oxford University Press, 1973), and Michael J. Piore, *Birds of Passage* (Cambridge: Cambridge University Press, 1979).

12. The dual labor-market hypothesis was developed by Michael Piore in a series of works beginning with Peter B. Doeringer and Michael J. Piore, *Internal Labor Markets and Manpower Analysis* (Lexington, Mass.: D.C. Heath, 1971). Later works include Michael Piore, "Economic Fluctuation, Job Security, and Labor-Market Duality in Italy, France and the United States," *Politics and Society* 9 (1980), pp. 379–407; Suzanne Berger and Michael J. Piore, *Dualism and Discontinuity in Industrial Societies* (Cambridge: Cambridge University Press, 1980), pp. 15–26. Other works on the political economy of immigration that rely heavily on the notion of an industrial reserve army are Manuel Castells, "Immigrant Workers and Class Struggles in Advanced Capitalism: The Western European Experience," *Politics and Society* 5 (1975), pp. 33–66; A. J. Marshall-Goldschvartz, *The Import of Labor, The Case of the Netherlands* (Rotterdam: Universitaire pers Rotterdam, 1973); de Gaudemar, *Mobilité du travail et accumulation du capital*; and Christian Mercier, *Les déracinés du*

capital (Lyon: Presses Universitaires de Lyon, 1977). For a review of Marxist theories of immigration see Yves Bourdet, "Fonction économique et rôle politique des migrants d'après les théories marxistes," *Ethnologie Française* 7 (1977), pp. 239–244.

13. See Castells, "Immigrant Workers and Class Struggles," pp. 46–55, and Edna Bonacich, "The Split Labor Market: A Theory of Ethnic Antagonism," *American Journal of Sociology* 37 (1972), pp. 1050–1087.

14. For a discussion of these concepts, see Charles P. Kindleberger and Peter Lindert, *International Economics* (Homewood, Ill.: Richard D. Irwin, 1978), pp. 62–67, 85 ff.

15. See, for example, Eli F. Heckscher, *Readings in the Theory of International Trade* (Homewood, Ill.: Richard D. Irwin, 1950); Bertil Ohlin, *Interregional and International Trade* (Cambridge, Mass.: Harvard University Press, 1933); Paul A. Samuelson, "International Trade and the Equalization of Factor Prices," *The Economic Journal* (June 1948), pp. 163–184; T. M. Rybczynski, "Factor Endowment and Relative Commodity Prices," *Economica* 22 (November 1955), pp. 336–351; and the detailed discussion of trade theory and international migration in Thomas, *Migration and Economic Growth*, chapter 2, as well as Georges Tapinos, *L'économie des migrations internationales* (Paris: Armand Colin et Presses de la F.N.S.P., 1974), pp. 197 ff.

16. See Samuelson, "International Trade and the Equalization of Factor Prices."

17. See U. Hiemenz and K. W. Schatz, *Trade in place of migration* (Geneva: International Labor Office, 1979).

18. For an application of this argument to postwar Mexican migration to the United States, see Sidney Weintraub and Chandler Stolp, "The Implications of Growing Economic Interdependence," in OECD, *The Future of Migration* (Paris: OECD, 1987).

19. One of the best accounts of this theory is offered by Gilpin in *The Political Economy of International Relations*, pp. 72–80.

20. Ibid., p. 72.

21. See Robert O. Keohane and Joseph S. Nye, *Power and Interdependence* (Boston: Little, Brown, 1977) and Robert O. Keohane, "The World Political Economy and the Crisis of Embedded Liberalism," in *Order and Conflict in Contemporary Capitalism*, ed. John H. Goldthorpe (Oxford: Oxford University Press, 1984).

22. This is the central thesis of Ruggie's article. See Ruggie, "International Regimes."

23. Reference here is to Charles Lindblom's notion of the privileged position of business. See Lindblom, *Politics and Markets* (New York: Basic Books, 1977), pp. 170–188.

24. As happens with realist theories of international relations, the change from a domestic to an international level of analysis produces a reification of the state. In the discussion that follows, I have adopted the reified conception of the state as an actor. I can then take the state (as well as individuals and groups) as the unit of analysis, and still remain faithful

to my liberal assumptions. These assumptions (of state rationality or its endeavor to maximize its self-interest) underpin rationalist and liberal theories of international relations.

25. Contemporary political theorists view rights as the cornerstone of liberal regimes. See, for example, John Rawls, *A Theory of Justice* (Cambridge, Mass.: Harvard University Press, 1971), pp. 130 ff, Ronald M. Dworkin, *Taking Rights Seriously* (Cambridge, Mass.: Harvard University Press, 1977), pp. 130–136; Michael Walzer, *Radical Principles* (New York: Basic Books, 1980), especially chapter 13; and Michael Sandel, ed., *Liberalism and Its Critics* (New York: New York University Press, 1984), especially the chapter on "Liberalism" by Dworkin (pp. 60–79) and "Justice and the Good" by Sandel (pp. 159–176). On the importance of these political theories for international relations, see Charles Beitz, *Political Theory and International Relations* (Princeton: Princeton University Press, 1979).

26. For example, "anyone within the territorial jurisdiction of the United States is entitled to the due process of law, as secured by the Constitution's Fifth and Fourteenth Amendments. As a result, before the government can deprive undocumented aliens of *fundamental rights* it must provide them with a hearing that conforms to prevailing standards of fairness." See Elizabeth Hull, *Without Justice for All: The Constitutional Rights of Aliens* (Westport, Conn.: Greenwood Press, 1985), p. 88, emphasis mine. See also Peter H. Schuck, "The Transformation of Immigration Law," *Columbia Law Review* 84 (January 1984), especially pp. 54–58, and Thomas Alexander Aleinikoff and David A. Martin, *Immigration: Process and Policy* (St. Paul, Minn.: West Publishing, 1985), pp. 61–84 and 293–314. This aspect of my liberal argument is more fully developed in chapter 8 of this book.

27. See Aristide Zolberg, Astri Suhrke, and Sergio Aguayo, *Escape from Violence: Conflict and the Refugee Crisis in the Developing World* (New York: Oxford University Press, 1989), especially chapters 9 and 10.

28. Certainly there is a strong neo-Kantian element in this argument: individual behavior and the "actions" of states are constrained by universalistic principles of reason and morality. But the notion of a rights-based regime remains an ideal type. Relations of power cannot be ignored in any study of international politics. See various essays by Kant in Hans Reiss, ed., *Kant's Political Writings* (Cambridge: Cambridge University Press, 1970), especially the argument "On the Agreement between Politics and Morality according to the Transcendental Concept of Public Right," in *Perpetual Peace: A Philosophical Sketch*, pp. 125–130. See also Beitz, *Political Theory and International Relations*, especially pp. 129–136.

29. For more on the relationship between domestic and international political systems, see the discussion by Stanley Hoffmann, *The State of War: Essays on the Theory and Practice of International Politics* (New York: Praeger, 1965), chapter 4. See also Hoffmann, *Duties beyond Borders* (Syracuse, N.Y.: Syracuse University Press, 1981), especially chapter 3 on "The Promotion of Human Rights," and Peter A. Gourevitch, "The Sec-

ond Image Reversed: International Sources of Domestic Politics," *International Organization* 32 (Autumn 1978), pp. 881–911.

30. These points follow the arguments of John Kenneth Galbraith in *The New Industrial State* (Middlesex: Penguin, 1967), especially chapter 5 on "Capital and Power."

31. One account of this process of incorporation is to be found in Ralf Dahrendorf, *Class and Class Conflict in Industrial Society* (Stanford: Stanford University Press, 1959), pp. 241–279. See also Adam Przeworski, *Capitalism and Social Democracy* (New York: Cambridge University Press, 1985).

32. A complete review of the development of international markets for labor and capital is beyond the scope of this chapter. For further discussion, see Sassen, *The Mobility of Labor and Capital*, chapters 1, 3, and 4.

33. This argument (see above) is summarized and criticized by Gilpin. For another perspective on the theory of hegemonic stability, see Robert O. Keohane, "The Theory of Hegemonic Stability and Changes in International Economic Regimes, 1967–1977," in Ole Holsti et al., *Change in the International System* (Boulder, Co.: Westview Press, 1980), and Keohane, *After Hegemony* (Princeton: Princeton University Press, 1984).

34. Again, see Hoffmann, *The State of War*, chapter 4, on the difference between domestic and international political systems.

35. For a discussion of migrations that do not fall within the North-South category, see Weiner, "The Political Aspects of International Migration." Weiner points out that migrants and refugees have the potential to become bona fide political actors, even in nonliberal regimes and areas of the world. Many of his examples are drawn from the Asian subcontinent, where ethnic strife adds another dimension to the politics of international migration. In the Middle East, ethnic solidarity among Arabs also creates a potentially new category of political actors, for example Palestinians and Egyptians in Kuwait and Saudi Arabia. See Nazli Choucri, *Multidisciplinary Perspectives on Population and Conflict* (Syracuse, N.Y.: Syracuse University Press, 1984); Janet Abu-Lughod, "Recent Migrations in the Arab World," in W. McNeill and R. Adams, eds., *Human Migrations: Patterns and Policies* (Bloomington, Ind.: Indiana University Press, 1978); and A. G. Hill, "Les travailleurs étrangers dans le Golfe," *Revue du Tiers Monde* 69 (January—March 1977), pp. 115–130.

36. Denis Maillat, "Long-Term Aspects of International Migration Flows: The Experience of European Receiving Countries," in OECD, *The Future of Migration*, p. 38, emphasis mine.

37. The 1986 IRCA created a conditional amnesty, employer sanctions, and a limited guest worker program for agriculture. See Lawrence H. Fuchs, "The Corpse That Would Not Die: the Immigration Reform and Control Act of 1986," in James Hollifield and Yves Charbit, eds., "L'Immigration aux Etats-Unis," *Revue Européenne des Migrations Internationales* 6 (1990), pp. 111–127. For a history of postwar immigration in the United States, see David Reimers, *Still the Golden Door* (New York: Columbia University Press, 1985). See also my chapter 8.

38. See, for example, Emilio Reyneri, *La catena migratoria* (Bologna: Il Mul-

ino, 1979), and Georges Tapinos, "European Migration Patterns: Economic Linkages and Policy Experiences," *Studi Emigrazione* (1982), pp. 339–357.

39. See, for example, the various essays in Rosemarie Rogers, ed., *Guests Come to Stay: The Effects of European Labor Migration on Sending and Receiving Countries* (Boulder, Co.: Westview Press, 1985); various articles in Martin Heisler and Barbara Schmitter, eds., "From Foreign Workers to Settlers? Transnational Migration and the Emergence of New Minorities," *The Annals*, 485 (May 1986); Wolf R. Böhning, *The Migration of Workers in the United Kingdom and the European Community* (London: Oxford University Press, 1972); and Böhning, *Studies in International Labor Migration* (London: Macmillan, 1984), pp. 156, 271n.

40. Many European states owe more to migration than one might think. France is the most obvious example of a country that has a relatively long history of immigration. On this point, see Gérard Noiriel, *Le creuset français* (Paris: Seuil, 1988); Lawrence H. Fuchs, *The American Kaleidoscope* (Hanover, N.H.: Wesleyan University and University Press of New England, 1990); and chapter 3 of this book.

41. See, for example, Barry R. Chiswick, ed., *The Gateway: U.S. Immigration Issues and Policies* (Washington, D.C.: American Enterprise Institute, 1982).

42. On the dimensions of illegal immigration in the United States, see Kenneth F. Johnson and Miles W. Williams, *Illegal Aliens in the Western Hemisphere* (New York: Praeger, 1981), pp. 84–105; Jorge A. Bustamante, "Measuring the Flows of Undocumented Immigrants," in Wayne A. Cornelius and Jorge A. Bustamante, eds., *Mexican Migration to the United States* (La Jolla: Center for U.S.—Mexican Studies, University of California, 1989), pp. 95–106, and Frank D. Bean et al., *Mexican and Central American Population and U.S. Immigration Policy* (Austin: University of Texas Press, 1989).

43. There are three exceptions to this generalization: the *bracero* program of the 1950s, the H-2 program, and the Special Agricultural Worker provision of the 1986 act. See Reimers, *Still the Golden Door*, chapter 2, and Böhning, *Studies in Intenational Labour Migration*, pp. 123–125.

44. See Fuchs, "The Corpse That Would Not Die," and Schuck, "The Transformation of Immigration Law."

45. In fact the inflows of foreign labor fluctuate considerably. For example, in Germany the figures went from 21,900 in 1975 to 82,600 in 1980, before dropping back again. In France they have fluctuated between 25,600 in 1975 and 96,700 in 1982, with the latter figure reflecting the effects of the amnesty offered by the first Mitterrand government. In Switzerland there has been a steady *increase* in worker migration since 1976. See Maillat, "Long-Term Aspects of International Migration Flows."

46. But, as Peter Katzenstein has pointed out, "Constitutional guarantees have increasingly been subordinated to a bureaucratic filter that checks whether reasonable grounds exist for inferring that the refugee turning up at West German borders is misusing the right to asylum for economic

and social gain. The exercise of this disretionary bureaucratic power is controlled by administrative courts." See Peter J. Katzenstein, *Policy and Politics in West Germany* (Philadelphia: Temple University Press, 1987), p. 233. See also Dietrich Thraenhardt, ed., *Ausländerpolitik und Ausländerintegration in Belgien, den Niederlanden und der Bundesrepublik Deutschland* (Dusseldorf: Landeszentrale für politische Bildung, 1986), pp. 125 ff.

47. For a comparison of citizenship and naturalization policies in Europe and the United States, see William Rogers Brubaker, ed., *Immigration and the Politics of Citizenship* (Lanham, Md.: The German Marshall Fund of the United States and the University Press of America, 1989), and chapter 8 of this book.

48. In the extension of programmatic rights to all members of American society regardless of race or national origin, the Fourteenth Amendment, guaranteeing equal protection, has played a crucial role. For more on the new rights-based politics in the United States, see Sidney Milkis, "Programmatic Liberalism and the Rise of Administrative Politics in the United States," in B. Guy Peters and James F. Hollifield, eds., *The State and Public Policy* (Boulder, Co.: Westview Press, forthcoming). See also chapter 8 of this book.

49. Some critics of American immigration politics and policies point out that the courts could do more to protect the rights of aliens. See Hull, *Without Justice for All,* pp. 151–154. Nevertheless, in a comparative perspective, the American political system and the courts in particular offer more extensive protection for aliens from the state, if not the marketplace, than other liberal democracies. See also Schuck, "The Transformation of Immigration Law"; Christian N'guyen Van Yen, *Droit de l'immigration* (Paris: Presses Universitaires de France, Thémis, 1986); Kay Hailbronner, *Ausländerrecht: ein Handbuch* (Heidelberg: C. F. Müller, 1988); and Knut Dohse, *Ausländische Arbeiter und bürgerlicher Staat: Genese und Funktion von staatlicher Ausländerpolitik und Ausländerrecht. Vom Kaiserreich bis zur Bundesrepublik Deutschland* (Königstein: Anton Hain, 1981), pp. 231–306.

50. For a more complete account of the history and politics of immigration in the United States in the postwar period, see Reimers, *Still the Golden Door* and Thomas Archdeacon, *Becoming American* (New York: Free Press, 1983). On citizenship and naturalization, see Peter Schuck and Rogers Smith, *Citizenship without Consent* (New Haven: Yale University Press, 1985), who argue for a more contractual form of citizenship than now is the case. Such a reform of naturalization policy, proposed by Schuck and Smith, would bring American policies closer to the French.

51. EC Regulation No. 1612/68 states that a worker of one member state has the right to seek employment in another member state. The only restriction is that the individual must find employment within a three-month period. This regulation does not apply to nationals of nonmember states residing in the Community. Hence the EC labor market is not fully integrated, and individuals do not have *absolute* freedom of movement. See Commission of the European Communities, *Free Movement of Labor*

within the Community (Brussels: EEC, 1977), W. R. Böhning, *The Migration of Workers in the United Kingdom and the European Community* (London: Oxford University Press, 1972), and Giuseppe Callovi, "Les Communautés Européennes et la migration," *Dossiers Migrations* 1 (March-April, 1981), pp. 1–4.

52. See T. Straubhaar, "The Accession of Spain and Portugal to the EC from the Aspect of Free Movement of Labor in an Enlarged Common Labor Market," *International Migration Review* 22 (1984), pp. 228–238; and Heinz Werner, "Post-War Labor Migration in Western Europe, an Overview," *International Migration Review* 24 (1986), pp. 543–557.

53. *Eurostat,* 1988, Table 12. For further discussion, see Heinz Werner, "Free Movement of Labour in the Single European Market," *Intereconomics* (March/April, 1990), pp. 77–81.

54. See *Eurostat* and various issues of the SOPEMI report, published annually by OECD. Unfortunately no data were given for Italy, which promises to become a major port of entry for future immigration to the European Community.

55. See especially Prognos, *The Development of the EC Labor Market to 2,000* (Basel, 1989) and ILO, *Informal Consultation Meeting on Migrants from Non-EEC Countries in the Single European Market after 1992* (Geneva, April 1989). Various options for dealing with immigration and the labor market in the Community are spelled out in Philip L. Martin and Doris Meissner, *EC-92 and Immigration Issues in Europe* (Washington, D.C.: Carnegie Endowment for International Peace, August 1990).

3. Guestworkers and the Politics of Growth

1. Rather than take great pains to distinguish between the prewar German regimes, the Third Reich, the postwar regimes (the Federal Republic and the German Democratic Republic) and the postunification Federal Republic, I have chosen simply to refer to Germany or the German case, letting the historical context convey to the reader the specific regime. Most references obviously are to the Federal Republic, meaning preunification West Germany.

2. For a discussion of immigration in the United Kingdom, see Gary P. Freeman, *Immigrant Labor and Racial Conflict in Industrial Societies* (Princeton: Princeton University Press, 1979); Zig Layton-Henry, *The Politics of Race in Britain* (London: George Allen and Unwin, 1984); and various historical essays in Colin Holmes, ed., *Immigrants and Minorities in British Society* (London: George Allen and Unwin, 1978).

3. For a discussion of the history of immigration, citizenship, and traditions of nationhood in the French and German cases, see William Rogers Brubaker, *Citizenship and Nationhood in France and Germany* (Cambridge: Mass.: Harvard University Press, forthcoming). See also David Blackbourn and Geoff Eley, eds., *The Peculiarities of German History* (Oxford: Oxford University Press, 1984); Ulrich Herbert, *A History of Foreign Labor in Germany, 1880–1980* (Ann Arbor: University of Michi-

gan Press, 1990), especially chapter 1; and for the French case see Gérard Noiriel, *Le creuset français* (Paris: Seuil, 1988), and Yves Lequin, ed., *La mosaïque France* (Paris: Larousse, 1988).

4. See H. Bunle, *Mouvements migratoires entre la France et l'étranger* (Paris: Imprimerie Nationale, 1943).

5. See Gérard Noiriel, *Ouvriers dans la société française, XIVe-XXe siècles* (Paris: Seuil, 1986), his *Le creuset,* and Lequin's *La mosaïque France,* especially "L'invasion pacifique," 335–352.

6. See Geoff Eley, "German Politics and Polish Nationality: The Dialectic of Nation-Forming in the East of Prussia," *East European Quarterly* 18 (September 1984), pp. 335–374; Klaus J. Bade, ed. *Auswanderer— Wanderarbeiter—Gastarbeiter: Bevölkerung, Arbeitsmarkt und Wanderung in Deutschland seit der Mitte des 19. Jahrhunderts* (Ostfildern: Scripta Mercaturae Verlag, 1984), vol. 1, pp. 110–134; Knut Dohse, *Ausländische Arbeiter und bürgerlicher Staat,* pp. 29–53; and Herbert Spaich, *Fremde in Deutschland: Unbequeme Kapitel unserer Geschichte* (Weinheim: Beltz, 1981). Dohse (p. 77) reports 250,000 Polish workers in Germany in 1914, fewer than in 1913.

7. On the political importance of this "marriage" see Alexander Gerschenkron, *Bread and Democracy in Germany* (Berkeley: University of California Press, 1943), especially chapter 1; Hans Rosenberg, "Political and Social Consequences of the Great Depression in Europe, 1873–1896," *Economic History Review* 13 (1943), pp. 58–73; and Barrington Moore, Jr., *Social Origins of Dictatorship and Democracy* (Boston: Beacon Press, 1966), chapters 3, 8–9.

8. Industrialization in the West drew immigrants from peripheral areas of Central and Eastern Europe. See Gustav Stolper, *German Economy, 1870—1940, Issues and Trends* (New York: Reynal and Hitchcock, 1940), p. 40.

9. See Edward L. Homze, *Foreign Labor in Nazi Germany* (Princeton: Princeton University Press, 1967) and Herbert, *A History of Foreign Labor in Germany,* chapter 4.

10. See Ralph Schor, *L'Opinion française et les étrangers, 1919—1939* (Paris: Publication de la Sorbonne, 1985), pp. 275–290; Noiriel, *Le creuset français,* pp. 189–245; Fernand Braudel, *L'Identité de la France* (Paris: Flammarion: 1986), vol. 1, pp. 27–107; and Lucien Jaume, *Le discours jacobin et la démocratie* (Paris: Fayard, 1988), pp. 389–403. Although he does not discuss the Jacobin tradition as it relates to immigration, much of Gérard Noiriel's analysis of the history of immigration is driven by a concern for the role of the state in defining who is and is not foreign, and how foreigners should be assimilated.

11. Michael Marrus, *Politics of Assimilation: A Study of the French Jewish Community at the Time of the Dreyfus Affair* (Oxford: Clarendon Press, 1971); Dominique Schnapper, *Juifs et israélites* (Paris: Gallimard, 1980); and Schnapper, "Le juif errant," in Lequin, ed., *La mosaïque France,* pp. 373–383.

12. Again, see Noiriel, *Ouvriers dans la société française,* and Noiriel,

Longwy, immigrés et prolétaires, 1880—1980 (Paris: PUF, 1984), pp. 220–226.

13. See Schor, *L'Opinion française et les étrangers*, pp. 491–510.

14. For a history of immigration in France from the 1880s to the 1930s, see Gary S. Cross, *Immigrant Workers in Industrial France* (Philadelphia: Temple University Press, 1983), especially pp. 214 ff. See also Georges Mauco, *Les étrangers en France* (Paris: Colin, 1932), and Pierre Milza, ed. *Les Italiens en France de 1914 à 1940* (Rome: Ecole Française de Rome, 1981), especially pp. 1–67, and 501–561. For an account of the politics of immigration during the interwar period see Schor, *L'Opinion française et les étrangers*. On the history of immigration policy during the interwar period see Jean-Claude Bonnet, *Les pouvoirs publics français et l'immigration dans l'entre-deux-guerres* (Lyon: Centre d'histoire économique et sociale de la région lyonnaise, 1976), especially pp. 61–185.

15. Hans-Joachim Hoffmann-Nowotny and Karl-Otto Hondrich, eds., *Ausländer in der Bundesrepublik Deutschland und in der Schweiz: Segregation und Integration. Eine vergleichende Untersuchung* (Frankfurt: Campus, 1982).

16. For an overview see Michèle Tribalat, "Chronique de l'immigration: l'immigration en Suisse," *Population* 1(1984), pp. 147–176.

17. Hoffmann-Nowotny and Hondrich, *Ausländer in der Bundesrepublik Deutschland und in der Schweiz*.

18. See Eley, "German Politics and Polish Nationality"; William W. Hagen, *Germans, Poles, and Jews: The Nationality Conflict in the Prussian East, 1772—1914* (Chicago: University of Chicago Press, 1980), pp. 60–62; Dohse, *Ausländische Arbeiter*, pp. 21–28 and 85–104; Brubaker, *Citizenship and Nationhood*, chapter 3; and Hans-Ulrich Wehler, "Die Polen in Ruhrgebiet bis 1918," in *Krisenherde des Kaiserreichs*, ed. by Hans-Ulrich Wehler (Göttingen: Vandenhoek and Ruprecht, 1970), pp. 219–236.

19. See J. L. R. Martin, *Swiss Policy on Immigrant Workers* (New Haven: Yale University Press, 1979), chapter 1.

20. See Charles P. Kindleberger, *Europe's Postwar Growth* (Cambridge, Mass.: Harvard University Press, 1967), pp. 28–36 and Peter J. Katzenstein, *Policy and Politics in West Germany* (Philadelphia: Temple University Press, 1987), chapters 3 and 5.

21. See Joseph J. Spengler, *France Faces Depopulation* (Durham, N.C.: Duke University Press, 1938).

22. On the pronatalist movement, see Alison C. McIntosh, "The Rise of Twentieth-Century Pronatalism," *International Journal of Politics* 12 (Fall, 1982): pp. 42–57, and Michael S. Teitelbaum and Jay M. Winter, *Fear of Population Decline* (Orlando: Academic Press, 1985).

23. Robert Debré and Alfred Sauvy, *Des français pour la France, le problème de la population* (Paris: Gallimard, 1946), p. 225.

24. For a good account of political development during this period, see Herbert Luethy, *France Against Herself* (New York: Praeger, 1955).

25. On the problems confronting the postwar French economy, see Charles P. Kindleberger, "The Postwar Resurgence of the French Economy,"in *In Search of France*, ed. Stanley Hoffmann (Cambridge, Mass.: Harvard University Press, 1963). Kindleberger points out the central role played by immigration in France's postwar economy.

26. See Stephen Cohen, *Modern Capitalist Planning: The French Model* (Berkeley: University of California Press, 1977), pp. 81–90, and Peter Hall, *Governing the Economy* (New York: Oxford University Press, 1986), pp. 139–191.

27. On manpower, immigration policy, and the planning process, see Georges Tapinos, *L'Immigration étrangère en France* (Paris: Presses Universitaires de France, 1975), pp. 16–18. On the question of labor productivity and internal migration, see Jean-Jacques Carré et al., *French Economic Growth* (Stanford: Stanford University Press, 1975), pp. 94 ff.

28. The corporatist elements of economic planning were not simply window dressing. They were attributable in part to the legacy of Vichy and the experiences of industrial management during the Occupation. On these points, see Cohen, *Modern Capitalist Planning*, pp. 253 ff.

29. For more on the *populationnistes'* position, see Alfred Sauvy, "Besoins et possibilités de l'immigration en France," *Population* 2–3 (1950), pp. 209–434. On trade unions and immigration during this period, see Léon Gani, *Syndicats et travailleurs immigrés* (Paris: Editions Sociales, 1972), pp. 53–54, and Milza, *Les Italiens en France*.

30. See Bonnet, *Les pouvoirs publics français et l'immigration*, pp. 89–93, and Marie-Claude Hénneresse, *Le patronat et la politique française d'immigration: 1945—1975* (Paris: Thèse, Institut d'Etudes Politiques, 1978), pp. 60–65.

31. See Dohse, *Ausländische Arbeiter* (pp. 135–230) on the creation and mandate of the Bundesantalt für Arbeit, and Meinhard Miegel, *Arbeitsmarktpolitik auf Irrwegen: Zur Ausländerbeschäftligung in der Bundesrepublik* (Bonn: Bonn Aktuell, 1984), pp. 92–109.

32. See Klaus Unger, *Ausländerpolitik in der Bundesrepublik Deutschland* (Saarbrücken: Verlag Beitenbach, 1980), pp. 113–114, and Ray C. Rist, *Guestworkers in Germany: The Prospects for Pluralism* (New York: Praeger, 1978), pp. 61–63.

33. See also International Labour Office, *International Migration 1945–1957* (Geneva: ILO, 1959).

34. See Tapinos, *L'Immigration étrangère en France*, pp. 10–36, and Bruno Courault, *Contribution à la théorie de l'offre de travail: le cas de l'immigration en France, 1946–1978* (Paris: Thèse, Université de Paris I, Panthéon Sorbonne, 1980), pp. 211–213.

35. CGP, "Premier rapport de la commission de la main-d'oeuvre (octobre 1946)" in *Documents relatifs à la première session du Conseil du Plan, 16—19 mars 1946* (Paris: Imprimerie Nationale, 1946), pp. 23, 26. See also the section on planning and economic growth in Carré et al., *French Economic Growth*, pp. 458 ff.

36. The reticence of employers to go along with the planners' designs for the economy is well documented. See, for example, Pierre Bauchet, *La planification française* (Paris: Seuil, 1966), pp. 287–290.
37. For more on immigration, industrial policy, and the sectoral distribution of immigrant workers in France, see chapter 7.
38. Hénneresse documents the gradual movement of employers toward extra-legal recruitment of foreign labor in the 1950s. See Hénneresse, *Le patronat et la politique d'immigration*, pp. 155–181.
39. See Carré et al., *French Economic Growth*, pp. 432–437.
40. See Tapinos, *L'Immigration étrangère en France*, pp. 34 ff.
41. Nonetheless, entries and departures of Algerians were tabulated by the Ministry of the Interior. On the evolution of the legal status of Algerian workers in France, see Malek Ath-Messaoud and Alain Gillette, *L'Immigration algérienne en France* (Paris: Editions Entente, 1976), pp. 40–54. On the method of counting Algerian immigrants, see Tapinos, *L'Immigration étrangère*, pp. 128–130.
42. See Alain Girard, "Le problème démographique et l'évolution du sentiment public," *Population* 5 (1950), especially pp. 338–340; and Alain Girard and Jean Stoetzel, *Français et immigrés*, Travaux et Documents, INED, Cahier no. 19 (Paris: PUF, 1953–54).
43. See Tapinos, *L'Immigration étrangère en France*, p. 40.
44. For a discussion of the relationship between decolonization, immigration, and ethnic conflict in France and Britain, see Freeman, *Immigrant Labor and Racial Conflict in Industrial Societies.*
45. On the globalization of production and its impact on the international division of labor see Robert Gilpin, *The Political Economy of International Relations* (Princeton: Princeton University Press, 1987), chapters 6 and 9, and James A. Caporaso, ed., *A Changing International Division of Labor* (Boulder, Co.: Lynne Rienner, 1987), chapter 1.
46. In France, in the initial stages of recruitment, employers felt that national labor supplies would be adequate to meet demand. In Germany employers feared that guestworkers would cause "social and economic problems." See Tapinos, *L'Immigration étrangère en France*, pp. 10–36, and Rist, *Guestworkers in Germany*, p. 125.
47. On these points, see Unger, *Ausländerpolitik*, pp. 39–47.
48. See Gani, *Syndicats et travailleurs immigrés*, and H. Richter, *Probleme der Anwerbung und Betreuung der Ausländischen Arbeiter aus der Sicht der deutschen Gewerkschaften* (Düsseldorf: Deutsche Gewerkschaft Bund, 1970).
49. On the tradition of social democracry and the social market economy, see Katzenstein, *Policy and Politics in West Germany*, pp. 86 ff., and Andrei S. Markovits, ed., *The Political Economy of West Germany: Modell Deutschland* (New York: Praeger, 1982).
50. For more on the politics of foreign worker policies during this period, see Bertold Huber and Klaus Unger, "Politische und rechtliche Determinanten der Ausländerbeschaftigung in der Bundesrepublik Deutsch-

land," in Hoffmann-Nowotny and Hondrich, eds., *Ausländer in der Bundesrepublik Deutschland und in der Schweiz*, pp. 125–194.

51. Bundesanstalt für Arbeit, *Überlegungen II zu einer vorausschauenden Arbeitsmarktpolitik* (Nürnberg: Bundesanstalt für Arbeit, 1978), pp. 75 ff. On the issue of residence and work permits in Germany see Miegel, *Arbeitsmarktpolitik*, especially pp. 95–98, and Nikolaus Notter, "Le statut des travailleurs étrangers en Allemagne Fédérale," *Droit Social* 4 (April, 1973), pp. 223–230.

52. Dohse, *Ausländische Arbeiter*, and Unger, *Ausländerpolitik*.

53. The economic successes of the Fourth Republic were due at least in part to the fiscal and monetary policies of the Pinay governments and to the application of the recommendations of the Rueff-Armand Commission, which restored a measure of competition to industry. These short-term policies complemented the efforts of planners to encourage long-term investments. See Carré et al., *French Economic Growth*, pp. 388–389, 449–450. See also Vera Lutz, *Central Planning for the Market Economy* (London: Longmans, 1969), pp. 3–5.

54. See Henry Ehrmann, *Organized Business in France* (Princeton: Princeton University Press, 1957), pp. 207–276, and Georges Lefranc, *Les organisations patronales en France* (Paris: Payot, 1976), pp. 188–207.

55. See Gani, *Syndicats et travailleurs immigrés*, pp. 44–55; Hénneresse, *Le patronat et la politique d'immigration*, pp. 124–181; and René Mouriaux, "Trade Unions, Unemployment and Regulation: 1962–1989," in James F. Hollifield and George Ross, eds., *Searching for the New France* (New York: Routledge, 1990), pp. 173–192.

56. On total labor supply see Carré et al., *French Economic Growth*, pp. 55–57. Wages in France remained relatively low during the 1950s and early 1960s, as the French labor market was more competitive than other OECD countries. Ibid., pp. 426–430.

57. Ezra N. Suleiman, *Politics, Power and Bureaucracy in France* (Princeton: Princeton University Press, 1974), pp. 352–371, and Stanley Hoffmann, "The Institutions of the Fifth Republic," in Hollifield and Ross, eds., *Searching for the New France* pp. 43–56.

58. Tapinos, *L'Immigration étrangère*, p. 53. See also Louis Chevalier, "La population étrangère en France d'après le recensement de 1962," *Population* 19 (1964), 569–578, and the CGP, "Rapport général de la Commission de la Main-d'Oeuvre (IIIè Plan)," *Revue Française du Travail* 20 (April–June 1958), pp. 40–73.

59. Gani, *Syndicats et travailleurs immigrés*, pp. 52–58, Bernard Granotier, *Les travailleurs immigrés en France* (Paris: François Maspero, 1973), pp. 266–270, as well as André Vieuguet, *Français et immigrés, le combat du P.C.F.* (Paris: Editions Sociales, 1975). The latter is more or less a tract of the PCF.

60. See Stephen Adler, *International Migration and Dependence*, especially pp. 90–121. On the legal status of various African groups in France, see M. Bonnechère, "Conditions de séjour et d'emploi en France des

travailleurs africains," *Revue Pratique de Droit Social* 392 (December 1977), pp. 379–382. See also K. Amousson, *L'immigration noire en France depuis 1945*, (Paris: Thèse, Université de Paris VIII, 1976).

61. Quoted in Gani, *Syndicats et travailleurs immigrés*, p. 68.

62. CGP, "Rapport général de la Commission de la Main-d'Oeuvre du Vè Plan," *Revue Française du Travail* 28 (January/March, 1966), pp. 90–132.

63. On the concept of an industrial reserve army and the use of foreign labor for maintaining "flexibility" in the labor market, see my discussion in chapter 2. See also Stephen Castles and Godula Kosack, *Immigrant Workers and Class Structure in Western Europe* (London: Oxford University Press, 1973), and Gani, *Syndicats et travailleurs immigrés*, pp. 68 ff.

64. See Gani, *Syndicats et travailleurs immigrés*, and various works of Michael Piore, especially *Birds of Passage* (Cambridge: Cambridge University Press, 1979), as well as Edna Bonacich, "The Split Labor Market: A Theory of Ethnic Antagonism," *American Sociological Review* 37 (1972), pp. 547–559.

65. Alain Girard et al., "Attitudes des français à l'égard de l'immigration étrangère: nouvelle enquête d'opinion," *Population* 29 (1974), pp. 1015–1064.

66. See, for example, Vieuguet, *Français et immigrés, le combat du P.C.F.*, pp. 104–145, and Granotier, *Les travailleurs immigrés en France*, pp. 238–239.

67. See Jacqueline Costa-Lascoux, *De l'immigré au citoyen* (Paris: La Documentation Française, 1989), pp. 20 ff.

68. See Stanley Hoffmann, *Decline or Renewal: France since the 1930s* (New York: Viking Press, 1974), pp. 145–184.

69. Because of certain clauses in the work contract between immigrant workers and their employers, the former were in a vulnerable position. Most notably, the work contract severely limited the mobility of the immigrant worker, who was practically forbidden to change jobs during the first year of employment in France. See Henri de Lary de Latour, "Le particularisme du contrat de travail pour les travailleurs immigrés," *Droit Social*, 5 (May 1976), pp. 63–72. Michael Piore, "Economic Fluctuation, Job Security, and Labor-Market Duality in Italy, France and the United States," *Politics and Society* 9 (1980), pp. 379–407.

70. On manpower, employment, and immigration policies during the Pompidou years, see the statement by J. Fontanet in OECD, "Manpower Policy in France," *Reviews of Manpower and Social Affairs* 12 (1973), pp. 22–28, emphasizing, as was common throughout this period, employment equilibrium and the difficulty of achieving this goal through policy manipulations of the labor market.

71. One major difference between the new and the old Gaullists is that the new went to great lengths to assuage the fears of the traditional sector. Pompidou created a ministry, headed by Jean Royer, to deal with their interests. See Suzanne Berger on the political representation of traditional interests, "Regime and Interest Representation: The French Middle Classes," in Suzanne Berger, ed., *Organizing Interests in Western Europe:*

Pluralism, Corporatism, and the Transformation of Politics (New York: Cambridge University Press, 1981), pp. 83–102.

72. The "structural" role of foreign labor in the growth process was the subject of numerous works on immigration, labor markets and labor mobility in the mid-1970s. Many of these works adopted the Marxist position that immigration and the use of foreign labor were responses to crises of capitalist production. Perhaps the best known of these works is Castles and Kosack, *Immigrant Workers and Class Structure*, particularly pp. 374 ff., as well as Manuel Castells, "Immigrant Workers and Class Struggles in Advanced Capitalism: The West European Experience," *Politics and Society*, 5 (1975), pp. 33–66, and Piore, "Economic Fluctuation, Job Security, and Labor-Market Duality." See also Jean-Paul de Gaudemar, *Mobilité du travail et accumulation du capital* (Paris: Maspero, 1976), pp. 49–51. Finally, for an application of the structural—Marxist argument to the French case, see Christian Mercier, *Les déracinés du capital* (Lyon: Presses Universitaires de Lyon, 1977).

73. Thirty glorious years refers to the unprecedented period of virtually uninterrupted growth from 1946 to 1975. See Jean Fourastié, *Les Trente glorieuses, ou la Révolution invisible de 1946 à 1975* (Paris: Fayard, 1979).

74. See the section on immigrant labor by Vidal and Sallois in CGP, *Rapport de la Commission Emploi (Préparation du VIè Plan)*, vol. 2 (Paris: Documentation Française, 1971); See also François Eymard-Duvernay, "L'Emploi au cours du VIè Plan," *Economie et Statistique* 74 (January 1976), pp. 40–42.

75. See Tapinos, *L'Immigration étrangère*, pp. 88–91.

76. It is important to note that the normal procedure for issuing executive orders is through the *Journal Officiel*.

77. In 1975 the Conseil d'Etat declared this and other attempts to regulate immigration by means of administrative decree to be inconsistent with French jurisprudence. On the important role of the Conseil d'Etat in the politics of immigration see Christian N'Guyen Van Yen, *Droit de l'immigration* (Paris: Presses Universitaires de France, 1986), pp. 112–114, and Patrick Weil, *L'analyse d'une politique publique, la politique française d'immigration: 1974–1988* (Paris: Thèse, Institut d'Etudes Politiques, 1988).

78. See J. Wisniewski, "Travailleurs migrants dans le bâtiment et les travaux publics," *Hommes et Migrations* 885 (June 1975), pp. 3–19.

79. Jacques Barou, *Travailleurs africains en France* (Grenoble: PUF, 1978), pp. 40–55. See also Bonnechère, "Conditions de séjour et d'emploi en France des travailleurs africains."

80. See Alain Girard et al., "Attitudes des français à l'égard de l'immigration étrangère"; Freeman, *Immigrant Labor and Racial Conflict*, pp. 280–283; and Mark Miller, *Foreign Workers in Western Europe: An Emerging Political Force* (New York: Praeger, 1981).

81. See Martin A. Schain, "Immigration and Change in the French Party System," *European Journal of Political Research* 16 (1988), pp. 597–621.

82. See OECD, *SOPEMI, Continuous Reporting System on Migration, Report*

for 1973 (Paris: OECD, 1974), p. 17. See also Notter, "Le statut des travailleurs étrangers en Allemagne Fédérale," and Unger, *Ausländerpolitik*, pp. 4–8.

83. See J. Bunel and J. Saglio, "Le CNPF et la politique d'immigration," *Economie et Humanisme* 221 (January/February 1975), pp. 41–50, and Hénneresse, *Le patronat et la politique française d'immigration*, p. 417.
84. Rist, *Guestworkers in Germany*, pp. 120–32.
85. See Huber and Unger, "Politische und rechtliche Determinanten der Ausländerbeschäftigung," and Stephen Castles, *Here for Good: Western Europe's New Ethnic Minorities* (London: Pluto Press, 1984).

4. Foreigners and the Politics of Recession

1. Length of residency requirements for obtaining permanent resident status in the societies of Western Europe changed frequently in the 1970s and 1980s. For a review of these and other problems associated with foreign worker programs, see Mark J. Miller and Philip L. Martin, *Administering Foreign-Worker Programs* (Lexington, Mass.: D.C. Heath, 1982).
2. In fact, the Swiss state was never committed to a suspension of guestworker programs, but to a reduction in the number of entries and a stabilization of the foreign population. See Jean-Philippe Widmer, *Le rôle de la main-d'oeuvre étrangère dans l'évolution du marché suisse du travail* (Neuchâtel: Groupes d'Etudes Economiques, 1978) and Hans-Joachim Hoffmann-Nowotny and Martin Killias, "Switzerland," in Daniel Kubat, ed., *The Politics of Migration Policies* (New York: Center for Migration Studies, 1979), p. 202.
3. Valéry Giscard d'Estaing summarizes his ambitions for transforming France into a *société décrispée* in his political testament, *Démocratie française* (Paris: Fayard, 1976).
4. See Bundesanstalt für Arbeit, *Überlegungen II zu einer vorausschauenden Arbeitsmarktpolitik* (Nürnberg: Bundesanstalt für Arbeit, 1978); also Klaus Bade, ed., *Auswanderer, Wanderarbeiter, Gastarbeiter* (Ostfildern: Scripta Mecaturae Verlag, 1984), pp. 661–665; Knut Dohse, *Ausländische Arbeiter* (Königstein: Anton Hain, 1981), pp. 309–316; and Ulrich Spies, *Ausländerpolitik und Integration* (Frankfurt: Peter D. Lang, 1982), pp. 16–21.
5. Secrétaire d'Etat aux Travailleurs Immigrés, *La nouvelle politique de l'immigration* (Paris: La Documentation Française, 1977). Exemptions, however, accounted for only 14 percent of total worker immigration controlled by ONI in 1974–75. See Hénneresse, *Le patronat et la politique d'immigration*, pp. 433–444.
6. Reference here is to the etatist tradition. See Andrew Shonfield, *Modern Capitalism* (London: Oxford University Press, 1965), pp. 71–87. See also chapter 6 of this book.
7. On this point, see Claus Offe, "The Attribution of Public Status to Interest Groups: Observations on the West German Case" in Suzanne

Berger, ed., *Organising Interests in Western Europe* (Cambridge: Cambridge University Press, 1981), pp. 123–158.

8. For a general account of changes in the German political system in the postwar period, see Klaus von Beyme, *The Political System of the Federal Republic of Germany* (Gower: Aldershot, 1983).

9. There have been other periods in French history when liberal (economic) policies were pursued, primarily during the Third Republic prior to the First World War. See Richard F. Kuisel, *Capitalism and the State in Modern France* (Cambridge: Cambridge University Press, 1981), pp. 1–30. On the demise of planning and the weakening of the *étatiste* tradition, see Diane Green, "The Seventh Plan—The Demise of French Planning?" *West European Politics* 1 (1978), pp. 60–76.

10. These measures were adopted at the urging of the new Secretary of State for Immigrant Workers, Postel-Vinay. For the complete texts of the *circulaires*, see the *Journal Officiel*, July 5, 9, and 19, 1974.

11. See Gani, *Syndicats et travailleurs immigrés*, pp. 68–69.

12. See René Mouriaux and Catherine Wihtol de Wenden, "Syndicalisme français et Islam," *Revue Française de Science Politique* 37 (December 1987), pp. 794–819. On the structural role of foreign labor in industrial production in France, see J. Nicol, "Les incidences économiques de l'immigration," *Problèmes Économiques* 1583 (26 July 1978), pp. 3–7, and D. Provent, "Le travail manuel dans la société industrielle: recherche des conditions de sa revalorisation à travers l'analyse des structures de travail et d'emploi," *Revue Française des Affaires Sociales* 2 (April-June 1976), pp. 85–144.

13. See Mark J. Miller, *Foreign Workers in Western Europe* (New York: Praeger, 1981), pp. 149–55; Tewfik Allal et al., *Situations migratoires: la fonction miroir* (Paris: Editions Galilée, 1977), pp. 111–128; and R. D. Grillo, *Ideologies and Institutions in Urban France: The Representation of Immigrants* (Cambridge: Cambridge University Press, 1985), pp. 88–140.

14. See Unger, *Ausländerpolitik*, p. 187 and Richter, *Probleme der Anwerbung und Betreuung der Ausländischen Arbeiter aus der Sicht der deutschen Gewerkschaften*. For a statistical and sociological picture of foreign workers and their families, see Friedrich Ebert Foundation, *Situation der ausländischen Arbeitnehmer und ihrer Familienangehörigen in der Bundesrepublik Deutschland* (Bonn: Bundesminister für Arbeit und Sozialordnung, 1981).

15. On the position of employers vis-à-vis the suspension of immigration, see Bunel and Saglio, "Le C.N.P.F. et la politique d'immigration," *Economie et Humanisme* 221 (January 1975), pp. 41–50. and Hénneresse, *Le patronat et la politique d'immigration*, pp. 414–484.

16. See Hénneresse, *Le patronat et la politique d'immigration*, pp. 485–510.

17. His views were outlined in a publication of the Secretary of State for Immigrant Workers, *La nouvelle politique de l'immigration*, reprinted in the Introduction to a special issue of *Droit Social* 5 (1975).

18. See the report of the Bundesminister für Arbeit und Sozialordnung, *Vorschlage der Bund-Länder-Kommission zur Fortentwicklung einer um-*

fassenden Konzeption der Ausländer-beschäftigungspolitik (Bonn, February 1977).

19. Le rapport Calvez, "La politique de l'immigration," Avis et Rapports du Conseil Economique et Social (23 May 1975), pp. 349–375.

20. See André Lebon and Olivier Villey, "L'immigration et la politique de la main-d'oeuvre," Economie et Statistique 113 (July-August 1979), pp. 25–80.

21. In the service sector in particular, undocumented immigration became more prominent after 1974. For example, the number of immigrant workers flowing into service-related firms rose from 58,800 in 1973 to 92,400 in 1979. A substantial portion of the increase was due to some form of "extra-legal" migration. See Jean-Pierre Garson and Yann Moulier, Les clandestins et la régularisation de 1981–1982 en France (Geneva: ILO, working paper, May 1982), p. 32. See also Olivier Villey, "Le redéploiement actuel de la main-d'oeuvre étrangère passé le premier choc de la crise," Travail et Emploi 8 (April-May 1981), pp. 47–55.

22. See Garson and Moulier, Les clandestins et la régularisation, pp. 43–47.

23. See Anicet Le Pors, Immigration et développement économique et social, (Paris: La Documentation Française, 1976), pp. 147–151.

24. See Hénneresse, Le patronat et la politique d'immigration, pp. 433–434.

25. Ibid., pp. 436–437.

26. It is not surprising that small businesses in the service and construction sectors were the most likely to use some form of extra-legal immigrant labor. Hénneresse, Le patronat et la politique d'immigration, pp. 439–444. See also Garson and Moulier, Les clandestins et la régularisation, pp. 43–47, and Villey, "Le redéploiement actuel de la main-d'oeuvre étrangère passé le premier choc de la crise," pp. 47–55. For a discussion of the changing role of the traditional sector in the French economy, see Suzanne Berger "Lame Ducks and National Champions: Industrial Policy in the Fifth Republic," in William G. Andrews and Stanley Hoffmann, The Impact of the Fifth Republic on France (Albany, N.Y.: SUNY Press, 1981), pp. 160–178, and Berger, "Regime and Interest Representation: The French traditional middle classes," in Berger, ed., Organizing Interests in Western Europe, pp. 83–102.

27. Unger, Ausländerpolitik and Horst Reimann and Helga Reimann, "Federal Republic of Germany," in Ronald Krane, ed., International Migration in Europe (New York: Praeger, 1979), pp. 63–87.

28. Data from the Ministry of Labor surveys of foreign manpower in France show that foreign employment declined in the manufacturing sector but rose in the service sector (11 percent increase from 1973 to 1976). In Germany, the number of foreign workers in manufacturing increased by 7 percent from 1978 to 1980. See Villey, "Le redéploiement actuel de la main-d'oeuvre étrangère," and Winfried Schlaffke and Rudiger von Voss, eds., Vom Gastarbeiter zum Mitarbeiter (Köln: Informedia Verlag-gmbh, 1982), pp. 351–355.

29. Compared to other national/regional groups, sub-Saharan migration to France remained small. See Courault, Contribution à la théorie de l'offre

de travail, pp. 300–301. On the Franco-Algerian case, see Miller and Martin, *Administering Foreign-Worker Programs,* pp. 44–48; and Adler, *International Migration and Dependence.* For a general discussion of return policies and migration, see Daniel Kubat, ed., *The Politics of Return: International Return Migration in Europe* (New York: Center for Migration Studies, 1984).

30. See Kubat, ed., *The Politics of Return* and John Vanderkamp, "Migration Flows: Their Determinants and the Effects of Return Migration," *Journal of Political Economy* 79 (September 1971), pp. 1012–1031.

31. OECD, *SOPEMI, Continuous Reporting System on Migration, Report for 1980* (Paris: OECD, 1981), p. 102. See also André Lebon, "Sur une politique d'aide au retour," *Economie et Statistique* 193 (July-August, 1979), pp. 37–46.

32. OECD, *SOPEMI* (Paris: OECD, 1984 and 1985), pp. 16–17 in the 1984 Report and page 22 in the 1985 Report. See also Kubat, ed. *The Politics of Return,* and Lebon, "Sur une politique d'aide au retour."

33. For a discussion of these measures in the French case, see Jacqueline Costa-Lascoux, *De l'immigré au citoyen* (Paris: La Documentation Française, 1989) pp. 24 ff. and Spies, *Ausländerpolitik und Integration,* pp. 147–167.

34. For an analysis and explanation of the unintended consequences of the suspension of immigration, see chapters 5–6 of this book.

35. On the impact of immigration in French urban areas, see Grillo, *Ideologies and Institutions in Urban France,* especially chapters 4–6. Ursula Mehrlander, "Bundesrepublik Deutschland," in Ernst Gehmacher, Daniel Kubat, and Ursula Mehrländer, eds., *Ausländerpolitik im Konflikt* (Bonn: Neue Gesellschaft, 1978), pp. 115–137, and Gunter Schiller, "Channelling Migration: A Review of Policy with Special References to the Federal Republic of Germany," *International Migration Review* 3 (1975), pp. 335–355.

36. See Ali Ucar, *Illegale Beschäftigung und Ausländerpolitik* (Berlin: Express Edition, 1983), pp. 15–21, and Manfred Zuleeg, "Politik der Armut und Ausländer," in Stephan Leibfried and Florian Tennstedt, eds., *Politik der Armut und die Spaltung des Socialstaats* (Frankfurt: Suhrkamp, 1985), pp. 295–308. On family immigration and other migrant flows in France and Germany after the suspension, see Georges Tapinos, "Enquête sur les perspectives des migrations à long terme en R.F.A. et en France," *Studi Emigrazione* 50 (June 1978), pp. 213–245 and Ebert Foundation, *Situation der ausländischen Arbeitnehmer und ihrer Familienangehörigen.*

37. Admissions to the labor market have been at 40,000 or above annually since 1976, according to statistics from the French Ministry of Labor.

38. The public's perception of the costs of supporting a large immigrant population, as is so often the case, may have had little bearing on the reality of immigrants' contribution to the economy. A study of the costs and benefits of immigration was carried out by Anicet Le Pors—a Communist and minister in the first Mitterrand government—who concluded

that the economic benefits of immigration far outweighed the social costs. See Le Pors, *Immigration et développement économique et social*, pp. 91–136. See also a similar study of the contribution of immigrants to economic growth in Germany by Jean-Louis Reiffers, *Le rôle de l'immigration des travailleurs dans la croissance de la République Fédérale d'Allemagne de 1958 à 1968* (Geneva: ILO, March 1970).

39. Le rapport Calvez, "La politique de l'immigration." On the historical role of the Economic and Social Council in the political process, see Jack Hayward, *Private Interests and Public Policy, the Experience of the French Economic and Social Council* (London: Longmans, 1966). For a discussion of immigration and welfare state politics, see Gary P. Freeman, "Migration and the Political Economy of the Welfare State," *The Annals* 485 (May 1986), pp. 51–63. See also Mehrländer, "Bundesrepublik Deutschland," and Schiller, "Channelling Migration."

40. See various SOPEMI reports; Zuleeg, "Politik der Armut und Ausländer"; and Pierre Bideberry, *Le chômage des travailleurs étrangers* (Paris: Inspection Générale des Affaires Sociales, 1974).

41. Anicet Le Pors, *Immigration et développement économique et social*, pp. 89–136; Mehrländer, "Bundesrepublik Deutschland"; and Grillo, *Ideologies and Institutions in Urban France*.

42. See Elmar Honekopp and Hans Ullman, *The Effect of Immigration on Social Structures* (Nürnberg: Institute for Labor Market Research, 1980). See also chapter 8 and Costa-Lascoux, *De l'immigré au citoyen*, 115–144.

43. For a review of these changes in French policy, see Costa-Lascoux, *De l'immigré au citoyen*, pp. 41 ff.

44. See the *Bundesgesetzesblatt*, part I, pp. 353 ff.

45. The new naturalization procedure is referred to as *erleichterte Einbürgerung*. For more on this and other aspects of the 1990 act, see chapter 8 of this book; F. Franz, "Der Gesetzentwurf der Bundesregierung zur Neuregelung des Ausländerrechts," *Zeitschrift für Ausläderrecht und Ausländerpolitik* 1 (1990); H. Rittstieg, "Das Ausländergesetz 90 als Einwanderungsgesetz," *Informationsbrief Ausländerrecht* 7–8 (1990); and also L. Hoffmann, *Die unvollendete Republik: Zwischen Einwanderungland und deutschem Nationalstaat* (Köln: Papyrossaverlag, 1990).

46. See Miller, *Foreign Workers in Western Europe*, pp. 147–179. Peter O'Brien, "The Paradoxical Paradigm: Turkish Migrants and German Policies" (Ph.D. diss., University of Wisconsin—Madison, 1988).

47. On the political activities of immigrants in Germany, see Unger, *Ausländerpolitik*, pp. 188–189. On the political participation of immigrants in France, see Catherine Wihtol de Wenden, *Les immigrés et la politique* (Paris: Presses de la F.N.S.P., 1988), and various articles in "Les musulmans dans la société française," special issue of *Revue Française de Science Politique* 37 (December 1987), especially Mouriaux and de Wenden, "Musulmans et prolétaires," pp. 794–819.

48. The French data on foreign population are taken from Solange Hémery et al., *Nationalité, Collections de l'INSEE* Série D, no. 83 (Paris: INSEE, 1981) and annual statistics of the Ministry of Interior. For a discussion of

the strengths and weaknesses of the French data, see Courault, *Contribution à la théorie de l'offre de travail*, Tapinos, *L'Immigration étrangère en France*, and various issues of the SOPEMI reports published by OECD. The German data on foreign population are taken from the *Statistisches Bundesamt* and the *Statistisches Jahrbuch der Bundesrepublik Deutschland*. For a discussion of the reliability of the data, see Schlaffke and von Voss, *Vom Gastarbeiter zum Mitarbeiter*, and various *SOPEMI* reports. The Swiss data were collected from *La Vie Economique*, which also gives lengthy commentary and analysis of immigration and other population statistics. See also Widmer, *Le rôle de la main-d'oeuvre étrangère*.

49. Measuring stocks of foreign workers in France is difficult. For a discussion of some of the problems, see Courault, *Contribution à la théorie de l'offre de travail*, p. 323 ff. Data for France in Figure 4.3 are based on estimates using the Ministry of Labor foreign manpower surveys, and for the years 1980–1987 the data come from INSEE annual employment surveys. See Didier Blanchet and James Hollifield, "Problèmes de mesures de stocks de travailleurs immigrés en France" (Paris, INED, 1982, mimeo). See also Bruno Courault, "Une nouvelle série d'effectifs salariés étrangers de 1967 à 1976," *Statistiques du Travail, Supplément au Bulletin Mensuel* 78 (1980), pp. 59–80, and Bruno Courault and Olivier Villey, "1,640,000 travailleurs étrangers en France en 1976," *Economie et Statistique* (July-August 1979), pp. 40–55. The German data on foreign employment were provided by the Bundesantalt für Arbeit and the Swiss data were taken from *La Vie Economique* and the OECD *SOPEMI* reports.

50. Immigration statistics for France, Germany and Switzerland were taken from the OECD *SOPEMI* reports of various years.

51. Numerous official and unofficial studies of the relationship between immigration and economic growth were conducted during the period immediately following the cutoff in immigration. All were able to document the continuing importance of foreign workers in the economy. See for example H. Bussery, "Incidence sur l'économie française d'une réduction durable de la main-d'oeuvre immigrée," *Economie et Statistique* 76 (March 1976), pp. 37–46; Pierre Bideberry, *Le chômage des travailleurs étrangers* (Paris: Inspection Générale des Affaires Sociales, 1974); also André Lebon and Xavier Jansolin, *Rapport sur l'immigration en France en 1978* (Paris: OECD, 1979), pp. 41–60.

52. According to ONI statistics, seasonal workers entered at an average annual rate of 61,000 from 1974 to 1980, compared to a rate of 40,000 for the period 1968—1973. The average annual rate of family immigration went from 20,000 for the period 1968—1973 to 25,000 for the period 1974—1980.

53. Garson and Moulier, *Les clandestins et la régularisation*, p. 6.

54. On this point, see Wolf R. Böhning, *Les conséquences économiques de l'emploi de travailleurs étrangers concernant en particulier les marchés du travail de l'Europe Occidentale* (Paris: OECD, 1974), and Emilio Reyneri, *La catena migratoria* (Bologna: Il Mulino, 1979).

55. See Tapinos, "Enquête sur les perspectives des migrations à long terme,"

pp. 216–220, 227–230. For the impact of immigration on the French and German populations, see also the various articles of Michèle Tribalat in the "Chronique de l'Immigration" of the January issues of *Population.*

56. As of 1987, France had the largest population of EC residents at 1,577,900, which accounted for 43 percent of the total foreign population. There were 1,377,600 Community residents in Germany, which was equal to 30 percent of the foreign population. See *Eurostat* and André Lebon, "Ressortissants communautaires et étrangers originaires des pays tiers dans l'Europe des Douze," *Revue Européenne des Migrations Internationales* 6 (1990), pp. 185–202.

57. See André Le Bon, *1986–1987, Le point sur l'immigration et la présence étrangère en France* (Paris: La Documentation française, April 1988).

58. On refugee policy and rights of asylum seekers in Germany, see Hailbronner, *Ausländerrecht: Ein Handbuch* (Heidelberg: C. F. Müller, 1988).

59. For more on illegal immigration in the United States and attempts to regulate it, see Michael J. White, Frank D. Bean, and Thomas J. Espenshade, "The U.S. 1986 Immigration Reform and Control Act and Undocumented Migration to the United States," *Population Research and Policy Review* 9 (May 1990), pp. 93–116, and Frank D. Bean et al., eds., *Undocumented Immigration to the United States: IRCA and the Experience of the 1980s* (Washington D.C.: Urban Institute Press, 1990).

60. See Garson and Moulier, "Les clandestins et la régularisation," and Peter Fendrich, *Federal Republic of Germany, 1980 SOPEMI Report* (Paris: OECD, 1981), and OECD, *SOPEMI 1982.*

61. See Miller and Martin, *Administering Foreign-Worker Programs* and Horst Reimann and Helga Reimann, "Federal Republic of Germany."

62. Garson and Moulier, *Les clandestins et la régularisation,* pp. 36–37.

63. Lebon, *1986–87. Le point sur l'immigration en France* and OECD, *SOPEMI 1983,* p. 12.

5. Immigration Policy and Labor

1. For a comparative study of financial systems, see John Zysman, *Governments, Markets and Growth* (Ithaca, N.Y.: Cornell University Press, 1983). On the relationship between the scarcity and power of capital, see John Kenneth Galbraith, *The New Industrial State* (Middlesex: Penguin, 1969), p. 65; and for a discussion of the "privileged position of business," see Lindblom, *Politics and Markets,* chapter 13.

2. See Robert Skildesky, "The Decline of Keynesian Politics," in Colin Crouch, ed., *State and Economy in Contemporary Capitalism* (London: Croom-Helm, 1979), pp. 55–87, and Peter A. Hall, ed., *Political Power of Economic Ideas: Keynesianism Across Nations* (Princeton: Princeton University Press, 1989). On the concept of "industrial democracy," see Dahrendorf, *Class and Class Conflict,* chapters 2, 5, and 7.

3. See Michael J. Piore and Charles F. Sable, *The Second Industrial Divide: Possibilities for Prosperity* (New York: Basic Books, 1984), chapter 10; Stephen Cohen and John Zysman, *Manufacturing Matters: The Myth of*

the Post-Industrial Economy (New York: Basic Books, 1987), chapter 9; and Peter A. Gourevitch, *Politics in Hard Times: Comparative Responses to International Economic Crises* (Ithaca, N.Y.: Cornell University Press, 1986), chapter 5.

4. See Peter A. Hall, *Governing the Economy* (New York: Oxford University Press, 1986), pp. 192–226.

5. See, for example, Douglas A. Hibbs, "Industrial Conflict in Advanced Industrial Societies," *American Political Science Review* (September 1976), pp. 1033–58. In fact, trade unions in France have been much weaker than in Germany and Britain.

6. See Zysman, *Governments, Markets, and Growth*, especially chapter 2; also Cohen and Zysman, *Manufacturing Matters*.

7. Note that there are two variants of this argument: the dual labor-market version suggests that foreign workers are likely to be laid off in an economic downturn because of their political and social vulnerability (see the various works of Michael Piore); the other version is that the demand for foreign labor is unrelated to business cycles. According to the latter version, the special characteristics of foreign labor make it attractive irrespective of market conditions. See Castells, "Immigrant Workers and Class Struggle," *Politics and Society* 5 (1975), p. 44: "We thus want to argue that immigration is not a conjunctural phenomenon linked to the manpower needs of expanding economies but a structural tendency characteristic of the current phase of monopoly capitalism." See chapter 2 for a discussion of the Marxist arguments.

8. See W. Arthur Lewis, "Economic Development with Unlimited Supplies of Labor," *The Manchester School of Economic and Social Studies* (May 1954), pp. 139–191, and Simon, *Economic Consequences of Immigration*.

9. Charles P. Kindleberger, *Europe's Postwar Growth* (Cambridge, Mass.: Harvard University Press, 1967), chapter 1.

10. Ibid., p. 8. See also B. Courault, *Contribution à la théorie de l'offre de travail* (Paris: Sorbonne, 1980), pp. 66–83, and Georges Tapinos, *L'Economie des migrations internationales* (Paris: Armand Colin, 1974), pp. 142–146.

11. See Hall, *Governing the Economy*, pp. 70–80.

12. On labor supply and economic growth in France, see Kindleberger, *Europe's Postwar Growth*, pp. 57–68. On the role of foreign labor in Germany and Switzerland, see respectively W. Schlaffke and R. von Voss, *Vom Gastarbeiter zum Mitarbeiter* (Köln: Informedia verlags, 1982) and Jean-Philippe Widmer, *Le rôle de la main-d'oeuvre étrangère dans l'évolution du marché suisse du travail* (Neuchâtel: Groupes d'Etudes Economiques, 1978), especially chapter 1.

13. Since the Industrial Revolution, immigrants have contributed to the expansion of production and employment in Europe and the United States. For the historical evidence see Brinley Thomas, *Migration and Economic Growth* (Cambridge: Cambridge University Press, 1973), pp. 83 ff., and R. A. Easterlin, *Population, Labor Force and Long Swings in Economic Growth: The American Experience* (New York: Columbia University

Press, 1968), pp. 148–153. For a discussion of the relationship between unemployment and immigration, see Tapinos, *L'Economie des migrations internationales*, p. 164.

14. From 1960 to 1981, the female labor force in France grew at an average annual rate of 1.6 percent; whereas in France, Germany and Switzerland, the yearly average of the total labor force as a percentage of population from ages 15 to 64 from 1960 to 1981 was respectively 67.7, 68.9, and 76.0. The average annual unemployment rate from 1960 to 1981 in France was 3.2 percent; in Germany it was 1.8 percent; in Switzerland it was too small to measure. These figures give some indication of the much higher employment rates in Switzerland, as opposed to France and Germany. See OECD, *Historical Statistics 1960—1981* (Paris: OECD, 1983).

15. See Widmer, *Le rôle de la main-d'oeuvre étrangère* and Hermann-Michel Hagmann, *Les travailleurs étrangers: chance et tourment de la Suisse* (Lausanne: Payot, 1966).

16. This is a basic assumption in labor economics; see Richard Perlman, *Labor Theory* (New York: Wiley, 1969), pp. 7–11.

17. For a discussion of the use of production functions to derive demand for productive factors, see Belton M. Fleisher, *Labor Economics* (Englewood Cliffs, N.J.: Prentice-Hall, 1970), pp. 119–121. See also INSEE, "Fonctions de production et de demande de facteurs," *Annales de l'INSEE* 38–39 (April-September 1980), pp. 40–75.

18. See Martin S. Feldstein, "Specification of Labor Input in the Aggregate Production Function," *Review of Economic Studies* 44 (October 1967), pp. 375–386, and E. J. Mitchell, "Explaining the International Pattern of Labor Productivity and Wages: A Production Model with Two Labor Inputs," *Review of Economics and Statistics* 58 (November 1968), pp. 461–469.

19. Jean-Louis Reiffers, *Le rôle de l'immigration des travailleurs dans la croissance de la République Fédérale d'Allemagne de 1958 à 1968* (Geneva: ILO, March 1970), pp. 91, 106 ff.

20. For a study of the effects of the use of foreign labor on the performance of various European economies, see F. Bourguignon and G. Gallais-Hamono, *Choix économiques liés aux migrations internationales du travail: Le cas européen* (Paris: OECD, Centre de Développement, 1977). See also chapter 7 of this book.

21. For an account of the effects of regulation on factor choice, see Robert Boyer, "Rapport salarial et analyses en terme de régulation," *CEPREMAP* 8017 (June 1980), mimeo.

22. While it is possible to obtain some data on immigrants' wages in Europe, such data are too highly aggregated and collected at irregular intervals. Nevertheless, these data have been used for generalizations about the costs of foreign labor. Such generalizations can be misleading, however, when other variables affecting wages such as seniority are not taken into account. On wage rates among foreign workers in France, see R. Granier and J. P. Marciano, "The Earnings of Immigrant Workers in France,"

International Labour Review 111 (February 1975), pp. 143–165; E. Vlassenko and S. Volkoff, "Les salaires des étrangers en France en 1972," *Economie et Statistique* 70 (September 1975), pp. 47–54; and C.E.R.C., "Qui sont les salariés les plus mal payés," *Documents du C.E.R.C.*, suppl. 50 (Paris: Documentation Française, November 1979), pp. 1–53.

23. See Philip L. Martin, *Harvest of Confusion: Migrant Workers in U.S. Agriculture* (Boulder, Co.: Westview Press, 1988).

24. The discussion draws on a variety of works dealing with the role of foreign labor in the process of economic growth. Some of these works include: Kindleberger, *Europe's Postwar Growth*, pp. 6 ff.; Robert E. B. Lucas, "The Supply-of-Immigrants Function and Taxation of Immigrants' Income," in Jagdish N. Bhagwati, ed., *The Brain Drain and Taxation: Theory and Empirical Analysis* (Amsterdam: North-Holland, 1976), pp. 63–82; Michael J. Greenwood and John M. McDowell, "The Supply of Immigrants to the United States," in Barry R. Chiswick, ed., *The Gateway: U.S. Immigration Issues and Policies* (Washington, D.C.: American Enterprise Institute, 1982), pp. 54–85; Wolfgang Franz, "Employment Policy and Labor Supply of Foreign Workers in the Federal Republic of Germany: A Theoretical and Empirical Analysis," *Zeitschrift für die gesamte Staatswissenschaft* 137 (1981), pp. 590–611; Courault, *Contribution à la théorie de l'offre de travail*; Reiffers, *Le rôle de l'immigration des travailleurs*; and Vernon Briggs, *Immigration Policy and the American Labor Force* (Baltimore: Johns Hopkins University Press, 1984).

25. See Kindleberger, *Europe's Postwar Growth*, pp. 57–68, Jean-Jacques Carré et al., *French Economic Growth* (Stanford: Stanford University Press, 1975), pp. 229 ff., and Franz, "Employment Policy and Labor Supply."

26. Hall, *Governing the Economy*, pp. 139 ff.

27. In fact, Germany began to use Italian labor in the late 1950s. At this point, however, Italian workers were covered by the Treaty of Rome, which offered greater freedom of movement for EC workers. See W. Franz, "International Factor Mobility and the Labor Market: A Macroeconomic Analysis of the German Labor Market," *Empirical Economics* 2 (1975), pp. 11–30. In France a good portion of the increase in labor supply from 1946–1966 came from the repatriation of French colonists, especially in 1962 from Algeria (*les pieds noirs*). See Georges Tapinos, *L'Immigration étrangère en France* (Paris: Presses Universitaires de France, 1975) p. 55, and Pierre Bideberry, "Bilan de vingt années d'immigration 1946–1966," *Revue Française du Travail* 2 (1967), pp. 7–30.

28. Kindleberger, *Europe's Postwar Growth*, p. 8.

29. For a review of the rights of French workers under the Grenelle Agreements, see the various articles in *Droit Social* 6 (June 1975).

30. See Piore, "Dualism in the Labor Market: A Response to Uncertainty and Flux: The Case of France," *Revue Economique* 19 (January 1978), pp. 26–48.

31. The total labor force as a percentage of population from ages 15 to 64

declined in France (from 68.1 in the period 1960—1967 to 67.4 in the period 1968—1973), in Germany (from 70.4 to 69.2), and in Switzerland (from 78.5 to 77.5). OECD, *Historical Statistics*, Table 2.6.

32. See Mancur Olson, *The Rise and Decline of Nations* (New Haven: Yale University Press, 1982), pp. 203–204, and Skidelsky, "The Decline of Keynesian Politics."

33. On the overall problem of assimilation in Germany, see Ray C. Rist, *Guestworkers in Germany* (New York: Praeger, 1978), pp. 245–246; on the suspension and policies of assimilation in Switzerland, see H. J. Hoffmann-Nowotny and Martin Killias, "Switzerland," in Daniel Kubat, ed., *Politics of Migration Policies* (New York: Center for Migration Studies, 1978), pp. 202–203. On the French case, see Michel de Guillenschmidt, "Une évolution libérale de la politique des naturalisations," *Droit Social* 5 (May 1976), pp. 188–189, and J. Costa-Lascoux, *De l'immigré au citoyen* (Paris: Documentation Française, 1989), pp. 71–114.

34. See Wayne A. Cornelius, "The United States Demand for Mexican Labor," in W. Cornelius and J. Bustamante, eds., *Mexican Migration to the United States* (La Jolla: Center for U.S. Mexican Studies, 1990); Barry R. Chiswick, "Guidelines for the Reform of Immigration Policy," *Contemporary Economic Problems* (Washington, D.C.: American Enterprise Institute, 1981), p. 322; Simon, *Economic Consequences of Immigration*, pp. 307–336; Carmel Samut, "L'Immigration clandestine en France depuis les circulaires Fontanet, Marcellin et Gorse," in *Les travailleurs étrangers en Europe Occidentale* (Actes du colloque organisé par la commission nationale pour les études interethniques, June 5–7, 1974), pp. 379–387; and Garson and Moulier, *Les clandestins et la régularisation*, p. 6.

35. The notion of interest groups invoked here is similar to that used in Gabriel A. Almond, "A Comparative Study of Interest Groups and the Political Process," *American Political Science Review* 52 (March 1958), pp. 270–282.

36. This point is similar to the argument about distributional conflict made by Olson in *The Rise and Decline of Nations*, pp. 41–47.

37. The state and state actions are here defined primarily in Weberian terms as an administrative structure in society, which has its own motivations and area of expertise. See, for example, Max Weber, *Economy and Society* (Berkeley: University of California Press, 1978), vol. 2, pp. 950–960.

38. Policy can only affect markets at the margins. However, in a mixed economy this marginal influence can be very important. It is the degree of marginality that is important and must be defined. See Lindblom, *Politics and Markets*, especially pp. 170–188, Francis G. Castles, "How Does Politics Matter?: Structure or Agency in the Determination of Public Policy Outcomes," *European Journal of Political Research* 9 (1981), pp. 119–132, and various essays in Charles S. Maier, ed., *Changing Boundaries of the Political* (Cambridge: Cambridge University Press, 1987), especially the introduction by Maier and chapter 11, "Problems of Political Economy after the Postwar Period," by John Goldthorpe.

6. Immigration and the French State

1. Ezra Suleiman in *Politics, Power and Bureaucracy* (Princeton: Princeton University Press, 1974) cites this traditional (Jacobin or Tocquevillian) view of the French state "as the sole guardian of the public interest" tending to "deny any virtue to group behavior in the political process," p. 319. Although Suleiman disagrees with this view on empirical grounds, he admits that it is widely held, especially by French political elites.

2. On the latter point, see Martin Heisler, "Transnational Migration as a Small Window on the Diminished Autonomy of the Modern Democratic State," in Barbara and Martin Heisler, *The Annals* (May 1986), pp. 153–166.

3. See, for example, Eric Nordlinger, *On the Autonomy of the Democratic State* (Cambridge, Mass.: Harvard University Press, 1981); Peter Evans, et al., *Bringing the State Back In* (Cambridge: Cambridge University Press, 1985), especially the introductory essay by Theda Skocpol; Roger Benjamin and Stephen Elkin, *The Democratic State* (Lawrence, Kansas: University of Kansas Press, 1985); and B. Guy Peters and James Hollifield, eds., *The State and Public Policy* (Boulder, Co.: Westview Press, forthcoming).

4. For a discussion of some of these concepts, see Peter Hall, *Governing the Economy* (New York: Oxford University Press, 1986), pp. 15–20; Francis G. Castles, "How Does Politics Matter? Structure or Agency in the Determination of Public Policy Outcomes." *European Journal of Political Research* 9 (1981), pp. 119–132; and Peter J. Katzenstein, ed., *Between Power and Plenty* (Madison: University of Wisconsin Press, 1978), especially the conclusion.

5. Reference here is to Michel Crozier, et al., *The Crisis of Democracy* (New York: New York University Press, 1975).

6. See Mancur Olson, *The Logic of Collective Action* (Cambridge, Mass: Harvard University Press, 1965), and James Buchanan and Gordon Tullock, *The Calculus of Consent* (Ann Arbor: University of Michigan Press, 1967).

7. Theda Skocpol seems to make this distinction in her essay, "Bringing the State Back In," in Evans, et al., *Bringing the State Back In*, and Ezra Suleiman clearly recognizes its importance in his introduction to *Private Power and Centralization* (Princeton: Princeton University Press, 1987); but they did not make it a central feature of their analysis.

8. This definition of autonomy is roughly equivalent to Nordlinger's type I state autonomy: a situation "in which public officials translate their preferences into authoritative actions when state-society preferences are divergent." Eric Nordlinger, *On the Autonomy of the Democratic State*, p. 118. He tends to downplay the possiblity of this type of autonomy, however, falling back instead on a more pluralist interpretation of policymaking in democratic states.

9. See Jack Hayward, *The One and Indivisible French Republic* (New York: Norton, 1973); Ezra Suleiman, "The French Bureaucracy and Its Students:

Toward the Desanctification of the State," *World Politics* 23 (1970), 121–170; Suleiman, *Private Power and Centralization;* Peter Hall, *Governing the Economy,* chapters 6–8, and James Hollifield, "Administration and the French State," in Peters and Hollifield, eds., *The State and Public Policy.*

10. See Charles Kindleberger, "The Postwar Resurgence of the French Economy," pp. 118–154, in S. Hoffmann, ed., *In Search of France* (Cambridge, Mass.: Harvard University Press, 1963), and Andrew Shonfield, *Modern Capitalism* (London: Oxford University Press, 1965), pp. 121–150.

11. See J. Zysman, *Political Strategies for Industrial Order* (Berkeley: University of California Press, 1977).

12. Diane Green,"The Seventh Plan—The Demise of French Planning," *West European Politics* 1 (1978), pp. 60–76.

13. See Olson, *The Logic of Collective Action,* pp. 53–65.

14. Nordlinger foresees this possibility in his typology of state-society relationships. In areas of controversy, however, such convergence of political and social interests is unlikely, because were everything working so nicely, state intervention probably would not be necessary in the first place. Nordlinger, *On the Autonomy of the Democratic State,* p. 28.

15. This is *the* major argument in Mancur Olson's *The Rise and Decline of Nations* (New Haven: Yale University Press, 1982), pp. 47–53.

16. On this point, see Robert O. Keohane and Joseph S. Nye, *Power and Interdependence* (Boston: Little, Brown, 1977), pp. 9–19.

17. See Crozier et al., *The Crisis of Democracy,* and Olson, *The Logic of Collective Action.*

18. See Philippe Schmitter and Gerhard Lehmbruch, *Trends toward Corporatist Intermediation* (Beverly Hills: Sage, 1979), and David Cameron, "Social Democracy, Corporatism, Labor Quiescence, and the Representation of Economic Interests in Advanced Capitalist Society," pp. 143–178 in John Goldthorpe, ed., *Order and Conflict in Contemporary Capitalism* (Oxford: Oxford University Press, 1984).

19. See Peter Lange, George Ross, and Maurizio Vannicelli, eds., *Unions, Change and Crisis: French and Italian Union Strategy and the Political Economy, 1945–1980* (London: George Allen and Unwin), particularly the chapter by Ross; and Peter Hall, "Patterns of Economic Policy: An Organisational Approach," pp. 21–53 in S. Bornstein, David Held, and Joel Krieger, *The State in Capitalist Europe* (London: George Allen and Unwin, 1984).

20. For a comparative and historical view of the development of the administrative state in France, see James F. Hollifield, "Administration and the French State," in Peters and Hollifield, eds., *The State and Public Policy.*

21. Algerians and some West Africans have been treated very differently from other "foreign" groups. The Algerians, whose numbers are considerable, benefited from their special colonial status, which gave them virtually complete freedom of movement before and after the granting of independence in 1962. Algerian migration was unilaterally suspended by the Algerian government in 1973 (in principle). However, Algerians contin-

ued to arrive in significant numbers after this date. West Africans, who also benefited from their colonial status, are much less numerous than other "foreign" groups. Despite these caveats, the entry data, collected by the OMI (formerly ONI) are quite reliable.

22. See Didier Blanchet and James F. Hollifield, "Problèmes de mesures de stocks de travailleurs immigrés en France" (Paris: Institut National d'Etudes Démographiques, 1982), mimeo.

23. INSEE, *Annuaires Statistiques de la France* (Paris: INSEE, 1949–1987).

24. The year 1974 was declared as missing because that was when policy changed from a relatively open system of recruitment to one of suspension *(politique d'arrêt)*.

25. On the calculation and interpretation of interaction effects in a multivariate time-series model, see H. H. Kelejian and W. E. Oates, *Introduction to Econometrics: Principles and Applications* (New York: Harper and Row, 1974).

26. The terms I_{kt-1} and E_{t-1} are the lagged endogenous variables entered as exogenous variables to control for any possible effects of serial correlation. On the merit of using this technique, see Kelejian and Oates, *Introduction to Econometrics*, pp. 192–199. The inclusion of the lagged endogenous variable will lead to an inflated r^2. For further discussion of the problems of serial correlation and the dangers of biased estimates when using lagged endogenous variables, see Douglas A. Hibbs, "Problems of Statistical Estimation and Causal Inference in Time—Series Models," in Herbert Costner, ed., *Sociological Methodology, 1973–1974* (San Francisco: Josey—Bass, 1974), pp. 252–308.

27. The decision to use a simple one-year lag, as opposed to some form of a distributed lag, is based on the assumption that going to a more complex function will not increase the explanatory power of the model. An Almon lag was in fact tried with these data, and it did not increase the power or significance of the model. For a discussion of the use of lagged exogenous variables, see Kelejian and Oates, *Introduction to Econometrics*, pp. 145–158.

28. Note that we can recover the recruitment function for immigration

$$I_{kt} = b_0 + b_1 I_{kt-1} + b_2 \ln Mar_{t-1} + b_3 \ln Con_{t-1},$$

whereas the suspension function can be written as

$$I_{kt} = b_0 + b_1 I_{kt-1} + b_2 \ln Mar_{t-1} + (b_3 + b_4) \ln Con_{t-1}.$$

Thus a positive sign for the policy coefficient indicates an increase in state control after 1974, and a negative sign indicates a loss of control.

29. This finding conforms to Nordlinger's type III state autonomy, in which the preferences of state and society converge. See Nordlinger, *On the Autonomy of the Democratic State*, pp. 74 ff.

7. Immigration and Industrial Policy in France

1. Again, see C. P. Kindleberger, *Europe's Postwar Growth* (Cambridge, Mass.: Harvard University Press, 1966), p. 12.

2. On French industrial policy, see John Zysman, *Political Strategies for Industrial Order* (Berkeley: University of California Press, 1977), Alain Lipietz, "Governing the Economy in the Face of International Challenge: From National Developmentalism to National Crisis," and René Mouriaux, "Trade Unions, Unemployment, and Regulation: 1962–1989," both in J. Hollifield and G. Ross, eds., *Searching for the New France* (New York: Routledge, 1991), pp. 17–42, and 173–192.

3. See Gary P. Freeman, *Immigrant Labor and Racial Conflict* (Princeton: Princeton University Press, 1979), pp. 173–215, Ray C. Rist, *Guestworkers in Germany* (New York: Praeger, 1978), pp. 116–120, and chapter 4 of this book.

4. At least three works in French have attempted to evaluate the sectoral impact of immigration and changes in the use of foreign workers across industries. See Anicet Le Pors, *Immigration et développement économique et social* (Paris: Documentation Française, 1976), J. Beth et al., *Essai d'évaluation de la dépendance du système productif français à l'égard des travailleurs étrangers* (Paris: S.E.A.E., Fondation Nationale des Sciences Politiques, 1979), and Bruno Courault, *Contribution à la théorie de l'offre de travail* (Paris: Sorbonne, 1980), especially pp. 327–372.

5. One of the most difficult methodological problems faced by a sectoral study of the French economy is that of defining the sectors and finding ways of matching old and new sectoral classifications. For a good discussion of some of these difficulties with respect to immigration and foreign employment, see Bruno Courault, "Une nouvelle série d'effectifs salariés étrangers de 1967 à 1976," *Statistiques du Travail, suppl.* 78 (1980), pp. 59–80. See also Didier Blanchet and James Hollifield, "Problèmes de mesures de stocks de travailleurs étrangers" (Paris, INED, 1982, mimeo).

6. See in particular Le Pors, *Immigration et développement économique et social.* See also F. Bourguignon and G. Gallais-Hamono, *Choix économiques liés aux migrations internationales de main-d'oeuvre* (Paris: OECD, 1977).

7. See S. Cohen, *Modern Capitalist Planning* (Berkeley: University of California Press, 1977), pp. 81–154 and C. Gruson, *Origines et espoirs de la planification française* (Paris: Dunod, 1968).

8. Employment in the auto industry was growing at an average annual rate of 2 percent in the decade from 1959 to 1968, compared to 0.6 percent for industry and 0.5 percent for the work force as a whole. Investments, as a ratio of value added, expanded by 17—21 percent during this period. See Laurent de Mautort, "L'automobile, la nécessaire consolidation des acquis," in Bertrand Bellon and Jean-Marie Chevalier, eds., *L'industrie en France* (Paris: Flammarion, 1983), pp. 202, 210.

9. On this point, see J-J. Carré et al., *French Economic Growth* (Stanford: Stanford University Press, 1975), p. 266. See also Steven Warnecke and Ezra Suleiman, eds., *European Industrial Policy* (New York: Praeger, 1975), pp. 23–30.

10. For a comparison of rates of economic growth in France since the nineteenth century, see Carré et al., *French Economic Growth*, chapter 1, and

Richard Kuisel, *Capitalism and the State in Modern France* (Cambridge: Cambridge University Press, 1981).

11. Carré et al., *French Economic Growth*, pp. 39–41, 229–230, 235–236. For an analysis of these problems see Bourguignon and Gallais-Hamono, *Choix économiques*, pp. 42 ff.

12. On the opposition of the communists to immigration during this period see Léon Gani, *Syndicats et travailleurs immigrés en France* (Paris: Editions Sociales, 1972), and Bernard Granotier, *Les travailleurs immigrés en France* (Paris: François Maspero, 1973), pp. 260–274. For an account of change in the unions attitudes towards immigrant/foreign workers in the period after 1974, see Mark Miller, *Foreign Workers in Western Europe* (New York: Praeger, 1981) and Maryse Tripier, "Syndicats, ouvriers français, immigration et crises," *Pluriel* 21 (1980), pp. 31–49.

13. See Gani, *Syndicats et travailleurs immigrés*, pp. 53–54 and chapter 3 of this book.

14. For an account of the performance of the French economy during this period see Carré et al., *French Economic Growth*, pp. 408 ff.

15. This is the argument made by Michael Piore in "Economic Fluctuation, Job Security, and Labor-Market Duality," *Politics and Society* 4 (1980), pp. 390–398.

16. In 1973 a clear majority of Frenchmen (54 percent) considered immigration a serious problem. An overwhelming number (71 percent) expected the state to do something to prevent an increase in the number of foreign workers. See Freeman, *Immigrant Labor and Racial Conflict*, p. 266.

17. Reference here is to the *circulaires* Marcellin, Fontanet, and Gorse. See chapters 3 and 4 of this book for more details.

18. W. R. Böhning argues that, at a certain point in the migratory process, immigration becomes a self-perpetuating phenomenon. See Böhning, *Conséquences économiques de l'emploi de travailleurs étrangers* (Paris: OECD, 1974), pp. 43–158.

19. The aggregate sectoral classifications used throughout this analysis are taken from the 1973 classificatory scheme (NAP—Nomenclature d'Activités et de Produits). Unfortunately, it was not possible to breakdown these sectors further. The *intermediate goods* sector includes such industries as minerals, metals, glass, petrochemicals, paper, and rubber. The *capital goods* sector includes all types of machinery and durable goods such as electronics, automobiles, shipbuilding, and arms. The *consumer goods* sector includes pharmaceuticals, textiles and apparel, leather goods, furniture, printed materials. Finally, *construction* includes the building industry and public works. See INSEE, *Le mouvement économique en France* (Paris: INSEE, 1979), pp. 12–13.

20. For definitions of the measures of productivity and investment used here see ibid., pp. 36, 83.

21. If we could control for seniority, it is highly probable that the decline in immigrant employment after 1973 would be roughly equal to the decline in employment among citizen workers.

22. The ratio for the auto industry during the period 1974—1979 was 2.12.

23. This is in large part the result of the need for unskilled workers to perform difficult and often dangerous jobs. On this point, see Le Pors, *Immigration et développement économique et social*, pp. 139–151.

24. "Concertation" was the term used by Etienne Hirsh, the second director of the Planning Commission—he was a violinist—to describe the politics of economic management in the early years of the Fourth Republic. See Cohen, *Modern Capitalist Planning*, pp. 67–68.

25. See Suzanne Berger, "Lame Ducks and National Champions," in W. Andrews and S. Hoffmann, *The Fifth Republic at Twenty* (Albany, N.Y.: SUNY Press, 1980), pp. 292–310, Zysman, *Political Strategies for Industrial Order*, and Peter Hall, *Governing the Economy* (New York: Oxford University Press, 1986), chapters 6–7.

26. See Alain Lipietz, *Mirages and Miracles* (London: Verso, 1987).

27. On protectionism in France, see Warnecke and Suleiman, *European Industrial Policy*, pp. 23, 234.

28. The most blatant attempt by the state to use foreign workers to solve the problem of unemployment was the so-called "return policy," which was designed to pay foreign workers to leave the country. See A. Lebon, "Sur une politique d'aide au retour," *Economie et Statistique* 193 (July-August 1979), pp. 37–46.

29. See Douglas E. Ashford, *Politics and Policy in France* (Philadelphia: Temple University Press, 1982), pp. 146–186, Zysman, *Political Strategies*, chapter 1, and Warnecke and Suleiman, *Industrial Policies*, pp. 25–40. Steel was among the most concentrated industries; textiles were among the least concentrated. For a measure of the evolution of industrial structure, see Carré et al., *French Economic Growth*, pp. 163 ff.

30. See Laurent Benzoni, "Le textile, une industrie d'avenir," in Bellon and Chevalier, eds., *L'Industrie en France*, pp. 90–120; and L. K. Mytelka, "In Search of a Partner: The State and the Textile Industry in France," in Stephen Cohen and Peter Gourevitch, *France in the Troubled World Economy* (London: Butterworth Scientific, 1982), pp. 132–150.

31. See Arezki Dahmani, "La sidérurgie, le poids de l'assistance permanente," in Bellon and Chevalier, eds., *L'Industrie en France*, pp. 124–156.

32. See Laurent de Mautort, "L'Automobile, la nécessaire consolidation des acquis," in ibid.

33. On the dramatic rise of the tertiary sector and its importance in the postwar French economy see Stephen Cohen, "Twenty Years of the Gaullist Economy," in Andrews and Hoffmann, eds., *The Fifth Republic at Twenty*, pp. 247–248.

34. On this point see Le Pors, *Immigration et développement économique et social*, pp. 139–151.

35. On this point, see Mytelka, "In Search of a Partner," in Cohen and Gourevitch, eds., *France in the Troubled World Economy*, p. 132. Even during the recent crisis period (1973—1974), textiles received only 3.7 percent of subsidies to industry. Benzoni, "Le textile," p. 117n.

36. On the substitution of foreign for citizen workers in the textile industry, see Courault, *Contribution à la théorie de l'offre de travail*, p. 350.

37. It is interesting to contrast the French textile industry with the sweatshop industries in the United States. See M. Piore, *Birds of Passage* (Cambridge: Cambridge University Press, 1979), p. 100, and Robert J. Berrier, "The French Textile Industry: A Segmented Labor Market," in R. Rogers, ed., *Guests Come to Stay* (Boulder, Co.: Westview Press, 1985).

38. See Benzoni, "Le textile," pp. 103–109.

39. See Piore, "Economic Fluctuation, Job Security, and Labor-Market Duality," pp. 390–398.

40. See M. Piore and C. Sable, *The Second Industrial Divide* (Cambridge: Cambridge University Press, 1985), pp. 205, 213–216, 226–229.

41. Ibid., pp. 213–216, 223–226. For a comparative study of the textile industry, see Frederick Clairmonte and John Cavanagh, *The World in Their Web: Dynamics of Textile Multinationals* (Cambridge: Cambridge University Press, 1982).

42. On the unions approach to changes in industrial policy in the 1970s, see George Ross, "French Labor and Economic Change," in Cohen and Gourevitch, eds., *France in the Troubled World Economy*, pp. 151–179.

43. See G. Noiriel, *Longwy, immigrés et prolétaires* (Paris: Seuil, 1986).

44. See Benjamin Stora, *Crise, puissance, perspectives de la sidérurgie mondiale* (Paris: Editions Economica, 1978), and Jean Baumier, *La fin des maîtres de forge* (Paris: Plon, 1981).

45. Dahmani, "La sidérurgie," pp. 149–150.

46. On the various uses of immigrant labor in the automobile industry, see Le Pors, *Immigration et développement économique et social*, pp. 151–158. On the distribution of foreign labor in German industry, see W. Schlaffke and R. von Voss, *Vom Gastarbeiter zum Mitarbeiter* (Köln: Informedia verlags, 1982).

47. See de Mautort, "L'Automobile," p. 202.

48. Ibid., pp. 202—203, 210.

49. An executive joked with me in an interview that "the primary product of Renault is sociology, not automobiles!"

50. J. Beth et al., in *Essai d'évaluation de la dépendance du système productif français à l'égard des travailleurs étrangers*, demonstrate using input-output analyses the degree of dependence on foreign labor of various sectors of the economy. The automobile sector, according to their analysis, was highly dependent on foreign workers. See also Le Pors, *Immigration et développement économique et social*, pp. 153–158.

51. Le Pors, *Immigration et développement*, pp. 155–156.

52. Piore and Sabel argue that Western economies have evolved in the direction of smaller, more competitive and more efficient firms, many of which can be found in the service sector. See Piore and Sabel, *The Second Industrial Divide*, chapters 10–11.

53. On the movement of foreign workers into the service sector after 1973, see Olivier Villey, "Le redéploiement actuel de la main-d'oeuvre étrangère passé le premier choc de la crise," *Travail et Emploi* 8 (April-May 1981), pp. 47–55.

54. The involvement of the state may take the form of nationalization (for

example in mining, steel, and automobiles) or the selective allocation of credit, otherwise known as indicative planning. See Cohen, *Modern Capitalist Planning*, pp. 130–135, and Hall, *Governing the Economy*, chapter 6.

55. All of these data were taken from the annual statistical reports of the ONI (now OMI).

56. See Blanchet and Hollifield, "Problèmes de mesures."

57. See note 19 for a breakdown of the various industrial branches included in each of these sectors.

58. See H. Kelejian and W. Oates, *Introduction to Econometrics* (New York: Harper and Row, 1974) on interpreting the Durbin-Watson statistic, pp. 200–206.

59. For an explanation of how to calculate and interpret interaction effects, see notes 25–28 in chapter 6.

8. Citizenship and Rights

1. See my discussion of issues in the political economy of immigration in the introductory chapter of this book.

2. See my discussion of rights-based regimes in chapter 2 of this book.

3. On this point, see R. Shep Melnick, *Regulation and the Courts* (Washington, D.C.: Brookings Institution, 1983), Donald L. Horowitz, *The Courts and Social Policy* (Washington, D.C.: Brookings Institution, 1977), Sidney Milkis, "Programmatic Liberalism and the Rise of Administrative Politics in the United States," in B. Guy Peters and James F. Hollifield, *The State and Public Policy* (Boulder, Co.: Westview Press, forthcoming), and chapter 2 of this book.

4. For an analysis and critique of the expansion of social membership that the new liberal culture has spawned, see Peter Schuck and Rogers Smith, *Citizenship without Consent* (New Haven: Yale University Press, 1985), especially pp. 116–121.

5. See Thomas Archdeacon, *Becoming American* (New York: Free Press, 1983), and Archdeacon, "Melting Pot or Cultural Pluralism? Changing Views of American Ethnicity," in James F. Hollifield and Yves Charbit, "L'Immigration aux Etats-Unis," *Revue Européenne des Migrations Internationales* 6 (1990), pp. 11–28.

6. See Peter Schuck, "The Transformation of Immigration Law," *Columbia Law Review* 84 (January 1984), pp. 1–90, Christian N'guyen Van Yen, *Droit de l'immigration*, (Paris: Presses Universitaires de France, 1986), and Kay Hailbronner, *Ausländerrecht* (Heidelberg: C. F. Müller, 1984).

7. See, for example, Jean-Jacques Rousseau, *The Government of Poland* (New York: Bobbs-Merrill, 1972), p. 19, and various passages from *A Discourse on Political Economy*, (New York: Dutton, 1973), pp. 173 ff.

8. See, for example, John Stuart Mill, *On Liberty* (London: Dent, 1972), p. 143. John Locke, the preeminent rational theorist, seeks a way around the potential conflicts between the individual and society by tying the interests of the individual—preserving his liberty, property, and so on—to

those of the state. See Locke, *The Second Treatise of Government* (New York: Bobbs-Merrill, 1952), p. 73.

9. See James Kettner, *The Development of American Citizenship, 1608–1870* (Chapel Hill: University of North Carolina Press, 1978) and Jacques Godechot, *La Grande Nation: L'expansion révolutionnaire de la France dans le monde de 1789 à 1799* (Paris: Aubier Montaigne, 1983).

10. For further discussion and analysis of these comparative conceptions of citizenship, see William Rogers Brubaker, ed., *Immigration and the Politics of Citizenship in Europe and North America* (Lanham, Md.: The German Marshall Fund of the United States and the University Press of America, 1989), pp. 67–79, and Brubaker, *Citizenship and Nationhood in France and Germany* (Cambridge, Mass.: Harvard University Press, forthcoming).

11. See Schuck and Smith, *Citizenship without Consent.*

12. See the quote from *Democracy in America* at the beginning of this chapter.

13. On the importance of the statist tradition in Europe, see Kenneth Dyson, *The State Tradition in Western Europe* (New York: Oxford University Press, 1980).

14. On nationalist traditions in Europe, see E. J. Hobsbawm, *Nations and Nationalism since 1780: Programme, Myth, Reality* (Cambridge: Cambridge University Press, 1990).

15. Fernand Braudel, *L'identité de la France* (Paris: Arthaud—Flammarion, 1986), Eugen Weber, *Peasants into Frenchmen: The Modernization of Rural France 1870—1914* (Stanford: Stanford University Press, 1976).

16. See Archdeacon, *Becoming American,* and Lawrence H. Fuchs, *The American Kaleidoscope: Race, Ethnicity and the Civic Culture* (Hanover, N.H.: Wesleyan University and University Press of New England, 1990).

17. For a discussion, see Seymour M. Lipset and Stein Rokkan, *Party Systems and Voter Alignments* (New York: Free Press, 1967), introduction, and Richard Hofstader, *The Idea of a Party System: The Rise of Legitimate Opposition in the United States, 1780—1840* (Berkeley: University of California Press, 1969), especially chapter 6.

18. On the importance of civil rights and the development of procedural protections for minority groups, see Sidney Milkis, "Programmatic Liberalism," Richard B. Stewart, "The Reformation of American Adminstrative Law," *Harvard Law Review* 88 (1975), pp. 1669, 1805 and Janet A. Gilroy, "Administrative Review in a System of Conflicting Values," *Law and Social Inquiry* 13 (Summer 1988), pp. 515–579.

19. For more on the impetus for reform, see Fuchs, "The Corpse That Would Not Die: The Immigration Reform and Control Act of 1986," in Hollifield and Charbit, eds., "L'Immigration aux Etats-Unis," pp. 111–128. Throughout the postwar period immigration reform has been debated in the context of interest group politics. See R. D. Tomasek, "The Migrant Problem and Pressure Group Politics," *Journal of Politics* 23 (May 1961), pp. 295–319.

20. Issues of citizenship and the civic culture have been raised by some

scholars who prefer a more contractarian citizenship and naturalization policy. See Schuck and Smith, *Citizenship Without Consent*. Professors Schuck and Smith argue that allowing large numbers of individuals to reside in the United States as resident aliens without citizenship is detrimental to the civic culture.

21. For example, the liberal constitutionalism of the founders of the American republic can be contrasted with the Jacobin ideals of the French revolutionaries. See Patrice Higonnet, *Sister Republics: The Origins of French and American Republicanism* (Cambridge, Mass.: Harvard University Press, 1988), and Simon Schama's *Citizens* (New York: Random House, 1990).

22. See Paul Kennedy, *The Rise and Fall of the Great Powers* (New York: Random House, 1988), and Robert Gilpin, *Political Economy of International Relations* (Princeton: Princeton University Press, 1987).

23. See Thomas Archdeacon, *Becoming American*, David Reimers, *Still the Golden Door* (New York: Columbia University Press, 1985), and Fuchs, *American Kaleidoscope*.

24. In the United States the struggle over citizenship and political participation pitted liberal constitutional principles embodied in the Fourteenth Amendment (due process, equal protection) and federal authorities, especially judges, against entrenched regional (and racist) interests determined to keep "foreigners" (in this case African Americans) out of the political process. See Kettner, *Development of American Citizenship*; James Hollifield, "Migrants ou citoyens: La Politique de l'immigration en France et aux Etats-Unis" in Hollifield and Charbit, "L'Immigration aux Etats-Unis," pp. 159–181; and Schuck, "The Transformation," pp. 66–72.

25. A polemic has raged over the issue of control of illegal immigration and the effectiveness of the INS, especially since the 1986 act, which provided for a limited amnesty that was supposed to slow the rate of illegal immigration. See Milton D. Morris, *Immigration: The Beleaguered Bureaucracy* (Washington, D.C.: Brookings Institution, 1985), Mark J. Miller, "La politique américaine de régularisation (1986—1989): résultats et limites," in Hollifield and Charbit, "L'Immigration aux Etats-Unis," pp. 141–158, and Kitty Calavita, "The Immigration Policy Debate: Critical Analysis and Future Options," in Wayne A. Cornelius and Jorge A. Bustamante, *Mexican Immigration to the United States* (La Jolla: Center for U.S.—Mexican Studies, University of California, 1989), pp. 151–177.

26. According to census estimates, for the decade from 1970 to 1980 a total of 4,370,000 legal immigrants, refugees, and parolees entered the country, along with 1,517,000 undocumented immigrants. Even these conservative estimates show that over 25 percent of all immigration to the United States during this decade was illegal—a figure that is likely to be much higher during the current decade. See Daniel B. Levine, Kenneth Hill, and Robert Warren, *Immigration Statistics: A Story of Neglect* (National Academy Press, 1985), pp. 18–20.

27. Although it is too early to know the full impact of the 1986 reforms, initial evidence indicates that illegal worker migration continues at

roughly the same rate as before the reforms. See Wayne Cornelius,"The U.S. Demand for Mexican Labor," in Cornelius and Bustamante, *Mexican Immigration,* and George J. Borjas, *Friends or Strangers: The Impact of Immigrants on the U.S. Economy* (New York: Basic Books, 1990).

28. See Miller, "La politique américaine de régularisation," and Fuchs, "The Corpse That Would Not Die."
29. See Leon Bouvier, "Immigration, changement démographique et la mosaïque américaine," in Hollifield and Charbit, "L'Immigration aux Etats-Unis,"pp. 45–58.
30. See Schuck, "The Transformation," pp. 35–73, T. Alexander Aleinikoff and David A. Martin, *Immigration Process and Policy* (St. Paul, Minn.: West Publishing, 1985), pp. 61–80, Robert O. Keohane, *After Hegemony* (Princeton: Princeton University Press, 1984), chapters 8 and 9, and Martin M. Shapiro, *Who Guards the Guardians: Judicial Control of Administration* (Athens, Ga.: University of Georgia Press, 1988).
31. Schuck, "The Transformation," pp. 54–73, and Aleinikoff and Martin, *Immigration Process and Policy,* pp. 433–463, 562–569.
32. Immigration judges are not as independent from political manipulation as administrative judges in Europe. See Aleinikoff and Martin, *Immigration Process and Policy,* pp. 244–252, *et passim,* Schuck, "The Transformation" p. 30, Gilroy, "Administrative Review and Conflicting Values," p. 552, and Guy Braibant, *Le droit administratif français* (Paris: Presses de la FNSP et Dalloz, 1988), pp. 418–427.
33. See Schuck, "The Transformation," p. 49, Stewart, "The Reformation of Administrative Law," Morris, *Immigration: The Beleaguered Bureaucracy,* pp. 27–33 and 136–137, and Melnick, *Regulation and the Courts,* pp. 155–192.
34. See Morris, *Immigration: The Beleaguered Bureaucracy,* Schuck, "The Transformation," pp. 62–66, and Aleinikoff and Martin, *Immigration Process and Policy,* pp. 348 ff.
35. See Schuck, "The Transformation," p. 54, and Aleinikoff and Martin, *Immigration Process and Policy,* p. 309.
36. Schuck, "The Transformation," p. 62.
37. "U.S. Loses Mass Deportation Case," *New York Times,* October 7, 1990.
38. "Justices Allow Lawsuits in Amnesty Procedures," *New York Times,* February 21, 1991.
39. "Judge Upholds Rights of Undocumented Aliens," *New York Times,* March 6, 1991.
40. See Gérard Noiriel, *Le cruset français* (Paris: Seuil, 1988), p. 71.
41. See Fuchs, "The Corpse That Would Not Die."
42. The weakness of parties in the United States is linked to the growth of an administrative state centered on the executive—the presidency, as it emerged during the New Deal era. See Sidney M. Milkis, *The Modern Presidency and the Transformation of the American Party System* (New York: Oxford University Press, forthcoming).
43. See Elizabeth Hull, *Without Justice for All: The Constitutional Rights of Aliens* (Westport, Ct.: Greenwood Press, 1985), pp. 39–46.

44. Cf. Milkis, "Programmatic Liberalism" and Melnick, *Regulation and the Courts.*

45. See Noiriel, *Le creuset français,* passim, and Catherine Wihtol de Wenden, *Citoyeneté, Nationalité et Immigration* (Paris: Arcantère Editions, 1988).

46. See Georges Tapinos, *L'immigration étrangère en France* (Paris: Presses Universitaires de France, 1975) and Tapinos, "Une approche démographique," in Yves Lequin, ed., *La mosaïque France: histoire des étrangers et de l'immigration* (Paris: Larousse, 1988), pp. 429–446. See also James F. Hollifield, "Immigration and Modernization," in James F. Hollifield and George Ross, eds., *Searching for the New France* (New York: Routledge, 1991), pp. 113–135.

47. See Braibant, *Le droit administratif,* p. 50, and M. Hauriou, *Précis de droit constitutionnel* (Paris: Sirey, 1923).

48. For more on the power of the administrative state in France, see James F. Hollifield, "Administration and the French State" in Peters and Hollifield, eds., *The State and Public Policy.* See also Jack Hayward, *The One and Indivisible French Republic* (New York: W. W. Norton, 1973) pp. 116 ff.

49. See N'guyen Van Yen, *Droit de l'immigration,* pp. 112–114, and Patrick Weil, *L'Analyse d'une politique publique: la politique française d'immigration* (Paris: Institut d'Etudes Politiques, 1988).

50. The doctrine of sovereign immunity, as well as the courts' interpretation of the constitutional separation of powers, come into play here. See Schuck, "The Transformation," pp. 14–18, 58–62, and Hull, *Without Justice for All,* pp. 148–151.

51. Note the subtle but important name change (in 1986), which is supposed to reflect the new mission of the institution: managing the flow of foreigners across French borders, rather than helping to recruit and settle foreigners. See chapters 3 and 4 of this book.

52. See Marie-Claude Hénneresse, *Le patronat et la politique française d'immigration* (Paris: Institut d'Etudes Politiques, 1978), pp. 60–65.

53. For a classic depiction of the Jacobin position on citizenship, see Rousseau, *Government of Poland,* p. 19. See also Godechot, *La Grande Nation,* Lucien Jaume, *Le discours jacobin et la démocratie* (Paris: Fayard, 1988), and James F. Hollifield, "Jacobinism: Moribund or at Bay?" Paper presented at the 1987 Annual Meeting of the American Political Science Association, Chicago, Ill.

54. For a discussion of the "republican synthesis" and the problems of French political development, see Stanley Hoffmann, "Paradoxes of the French Political Community," in Hoffmann, ed., *In Search of France* (Cambridge, Mass.: Harvard University Press, 1963), pp. 1–117.

55. See Mark J. Miller, *Foreign Workers in Western Europe, An Emerging Political Force* (New York: Praeger, 1981), and R. D. Grillo, *Ideologies and Institutions in Urban France: The Representation of Immigrants* (Cambridge: Cambridge University Press, 1985), pp. 51–66, 281–301.

56. See Gary P. Freeman, *Immigrant Labor and Racial Conflict in Industrial*

Societies: The French and British Experience, 1945–1975 (Princeton: Princeton University Press, 1979). See also Catherine Wihtol de Wenden, *Les immigrés et la politique* (Paris: Presses de la FNSP, 1988).

57. See Martin A. Schain, "Immigration and Change in the French Party System," *European Journal of Political Research* 16 (1988), pp. 597–621; Grillo, *Ideologies and Institutions in Urban France*, pp. 258 ff; and William Safran, "Islamization in Western Europe: Political Consequences and Historical Parallels," in Martin O. Heisler and Barbara Schmitter Heisler, eds., "From Foreign Workers to Settlers?" *The Annals* 485 (May 1986), pp. 98–112.

58. From a comparative standpoint, it is important to note that the impetus for a stronger rights-based immigration policy in France came not from the legal system but from a political party—the Socialists. On this point, see Jacqueline Costa-Lascoux, *De l'immigré au citoyen* (Paris: Documentation Française, 1989), pp. 31 ff.

59. See chapters 3 and 4, as well as Hollifield, "Immigration and Modernization," p. 116.

60. Not surprisingly, this polemic was joined by rightwing scholars, some with close ties to the FN. See Philippe Bourcier de Carbon and Pierre Chaunu, "Un génocide statistique: on recherche 1,893,000 étrangers disparus dans les ordinateurs de l'INED," *Histoire, Economie et Société* 1(1986). For a more dispassionate account of the evolution of immigration and the foreign population in the 1980s, see the various "Chroniques de l'immigration" by Michèle Tribalat in the January issues of *Population*.

61. Over a three year period, from 1981 to 1984, 88,492 were admitted to permanent resident status as a result of the amnesty. For a discussion of the effects of the amnesty and other measures on the rate of immigration and naturalization, see André Lebon, "Attribution, acquisition et perte de la nationalité française: un bilan, 1973–1986," *Revue Européenne des Migrations Internationales* 1 (1987), pp. 17–34; and Lebon, *1986–1987, Le point sur l'immigration et la présence étrangère en France*, (Paris: Documentation Française, 1988), pp. 31–38.

62. See Nonna Mayer and Pascal Perrineau, *Le Front National à découvert* (Paris: Presses de la FNSP, 1989), Edwy Plenel and Alain Rollat, eds., *L'Effet Le Pen* (Paris: Editions de la Découverte, 1984), and James F. Hollifield, "Immigration, Race and Politics," *French Politics and Society* 13 (March 1986), pp. 15–20.

63. See Gilles Kepel, *Les banlieues de l'Islam* (Paris: Seuil, 1988), and Riva Kastoryano, *Etre turque en France* (Paris: L'Harmattan, 1986).

64. For a discussion of the immigrant problem from the standpoint of religion and politics, see Rémy Leveau and Dominique Schnapper, "Religion et politique: Juifs et musulmans," *Revue Française de Science Politique* 37 (December 1987).

65. French citizenship law and naturalization procedures take into account a variety of factors, including kinship *(jus sanguinis)*, birthplace *(jus solis)*, length of residence, colonial connections, marriage with a French national, and services rendered to the country. See the report presented

by Marceau Long to the Prime Minister on the proceedings of the Commission on Nationality, *Etre français aujourd'hui et demain*, vols. 1–2 (Paris: Documentation Française, 1988). For further discussion and analysis of French citizenship law, see Brubaker, ed., *Immigration and the Politics of Citizenship*, pp. 99–128, and Costa-Lascoux, *De l'immigré au citoyen*, pp. 115 ff. See also Danièle Lochak, *Etrangers: de quels droits?* (Paris: PUF, 1985).

66. Although French naturalization statistics are sketchy, particularly for the period prior to the 1980s, when citizenship became such a big political issue, figures given by the Direction de la Population et des Migrations of the Ministry of Labor and Social Affairs show that from 1973 through 1987 the numbers have ranged from a low of 33,616 in 1973 to a high of 60,677 in 1985, before falling back to 41,754 in 1987—hardly a dramatic increase. See Costa-Lascoux, *De l'immigré au citoyen*, p. 121, and Lebon, *Le point sur l'immigration et la présence étrangère en France*, pp. 31–38.

67. See, for example, Judith Vichniac, "French Socialists and *Droit à la différence*," *French Politics and Society* 9 (Winter 1991), pp. 40–57.

68. The most famous initiative in this regard was taken by a group of five intellectuals, including Alain Finkielkraut and Régis Debray, who, in an open letter to the Minister of Education, Lionel Jospin, warned that the year of the Bicentennial of the French Revolution might become the "Munich de l'école républicaine." See *Le Nouvel Observateur*, 2–8 November 1989, p. 30.

69. Serge July, editorial, "La Ligne de Crète," in *Libération*, 6 November 1989, p. 7. My translation.

70. Interviewing a high government official charged with immigration affairs in 1986, I posed a question concerning policy towards ethnic minorities. At the very mention of the issue of ethnicity, the official, showing great consternation, stated simply: "Monsieur, en France nous sommes tous républicains."

71. See Peter O'Brien, "The Paradoxical Paradigm: Turkish Migrants and German Policies" (Ph.D. Dissertation, University of Wisconsin-Madison, 1988), and O'Brien, "The Civil Rights of West Germany's Migrants," *German Politics and Society* 19 (Spring 1990), pp. 27–40.

72. Hailbronner, *Ausländerrecht*, and Katzenstein, *Policy and Politics in West Germany*, pp. 228–234. See also Eckart Hildebrandt and Werner Olle, *Ihr Kampf ist unser Kampf* (Offenbach: Verlag 2000, 1975), pp. 135–154.

73. Ulrich Spies, *Ausländerpolitik und Integration* (Frankfurt: Peter D. Lang, 1982), pp. 95–134, and Klaus Unger, *Ausländerpolitik in der Bundesrepublik Deutschland* (Saarbrücken, Verlag Breitenbach), pp. 154–165.

74. See, for example, Hailbronner, *Ausländerrecht*, and Ali Ucar, *Illegale Beschäftigung und Ausländerpolitik* (Berlin: Express Edition, 1982), pp. 33–38.

75. See Manfred Zuleeg, "Politik der Armut und Ausländer," in Stephan Leibfried and Florian Tennstedt, eds., *Politik der Armut und die Spaltung des Sozialstaats* (Frankfurt: Suhrkamp, 1985), pp. 295–308; Ucar, *Illegale Beschäftigung*; and Unger, *Ausländerpolitik*, pp. 122 ff.

76. See David P. Conradt, *The German Polity* (New York: Longman, 1989), chapters 3 and 8.
77. On this point see William W. Hagen, *Germans, Poles, and Jews: The Nationality Conflict in the Prussian East, 1772–1914* (Chicago: University of Chicago Press, 1980), and Edward L. Homze, *Foreign Labor in Nazi Germany* (Princeton: Princeton University Press, 1967).
78. For an excellent, historical analysis of German citizenship and traditions of nationhood, see Brubaker, *Citizenship and Nationhood*, especially chapters 3, 7, and 9.
79. See O'Brien, *The Paradoxical Paradigm*, and Unger, *Auslaenderpolitik*, pp. 13–38.
80. On the size of the foreign population in Germany, see chapters 3 and 4.
81. Bertold Huber and Klaus Unger, "Politische und rechtliche Determinaten der Ausländerbeschätigung in der Bundesrepublik Deutschland," in Hans-Joachim Hoffmann-Nowotny and Karl-Otto Hondrich, eds., *Ausländer in der Bundesrepublik Deutschland und in der Schweiz: Segregation und Integration* (Frankfurt: Campus, 1982), pp. 124–194.
82. See Spies, *Ausländerpolitik und Integration*, pp. 35–44, and Katzenstein, *Policy and Politics in West Germany*, pp. 240–242.
83. See the *Bundesgesetzblatt*, part I, no. 34 (July 14, 1990), pp. 1354 ff.
84. This acceptance of Islam can be contrasted with the crisis in church-state relations provoked by immigration in France. See Kepel, *Les banlieues de l'Islam* and the discussion of *laïcité* above.
85. For a historical and sociological discussion of German political development, see Ralf Dahrendorf, *Society and Democracy in Germany* (Garden City, N.Y.: Doubleday, 1967).
86. On the "constitutionalizing" of immigration law and policy in the United States, see the powerful article of Peter Schuck, "The Transformation of Immigration Law," p. 62 ff. For a less sanguine interpretation of the evolution of immigration law, see Hull, *Without Justice for All*. See also Shapiro, *Who Guards the Guardians*, for an account of judicial constraints on the administrative state.
87. On this last point, see James Q. Wilson, *American Government* (Lexington, Mass.: D.C. Heath, 1989), pp. 489 ff.
88. On the issue of social citizenship, immigration, and the welfare state in Europe, see Gary P. Freeman, "Migration and the Political Economy of the Welfare State," in Heisler and Heisler, "From Foreign Workers to Settlers," pp. 51–63.
89. On the concept of human capital, see Gary Becker, *Human Capital* (New York: Columbia University Press, 1975). On the importance of human capital considerations in American immigration policy, see Barry R. Chiswick, ed., *The Gateway: U.S. Immigration Issues and Policies* (Washington, D.C.: American Enterprise Institute, 1982), and Julian Simon, *The Economic Consequences of Immigration* (Oxford: Basil Blackwell and The Cato Institute, 1989). Unlike Chiswick, Simon takes the position that legal immigration should be increased and that no strict selection according to human capital criteria should be imposed.
90. Like the Europeans and the Americans, the Japanese have begun to expe-

rience some of the same political and policy dilemmas with respect to international migration, especially from South and Southeast Asia. How the Japanese state copes with these dilemmas will be a true test of the liberal foundations of the regime.

91. See Aristide R. Zolberg, Astri Suhrke, and Sergio Arguayo, *Escape from Violence: Conflict and Refugee Crisis in the Developing World* (New York: Oxford University Press, 1989) and Yossi Schain, *The Frontier of Loyalty* (Boulder, Co.: Westview Press, 1988).

92. See Schuck, "The Transformation," pp. 39 ff., and Doris M. Meissner, "The Refugee Act of 1980: What Have We Learned," in Hollifield and Charbit, "L'Immigration aux Etats-Unis," pp. 129–140.

93. See Lebon, *Le point sur l'immigration,* pp. 19–21.

94. For evidence, see Wayne A. Cornelius, "Les entreprises et les industries californiennes dépendantes des immigrants mexicains," in Hollifield and Charbit, eds., "L'Immigration aux Etats-Unis," pp. 71–92.

9. Immigration and the Principles of Liberal Democracy

1. See Ralf Dahrendorf, *Class and Class Conflict in Industrial Society,* on "industrial democracy," pp. 257 ff, and chapter 5 of this book.

2. On the importance of this point, see Gary P. Freeman, *Immigrant Labor and Racial Conflict in Industrial Society* (Princeton: Princeton University Press, 1979).

3. See Mark J. Miller and Philip L. Martin, *Administering Foreign-Worker Programs* (Lexington, Mass.: D.C. Heath, 1982).

4. In Switzerland political pressure had been building for a suspension of foreign worker programs since the mid-1960s. See Hans-Joachim Hoffmann-Nowotny, "Switzerland," in Tomas Hammar, ed., *European Immigration Policy: A Comparative Study* (Cambridge: Cambridge University Press, 1985), pp. 206–236. But Swiss authorities were committed to maintaining access to foreign labor while attempting to stabilize the foreign population.

5. This is Charles Kindleberger's central point in *Europe's Postwar Growth* (Cambridge, Mass.: Harvard University Press, 1966).

6. See Rosemarie Rogers, ed., *Guests Come to Stay* (Boulder, Co.: Westview Press, 1985).

7. This finding is consistent with the arguments of Robert O. Keohane and Joseph S. Nye, *Power and Interdependence* (Boston: Little, Brown, 1977).

8. See W. Rogers Brubaker, *Citizenship and Nationhood in France and Germany* (Cambridge, Mass.: Harvard University Press, forthcoming), p. 388.

9. The best account of these changes in the American case is to be found in Schuck, "The Transformation of Immigration Law," *Columbia Law Review* 84 (January 1984), pp. 1–90. On immigration and rights-based politics in Europe, see especially chapter 8 of this book.

10. See Katzenstein, *Policy and Politics in West Germany,* p. 234.

11. See Nathan Glazer, ed., *A Clamor at the Gates: The New American*

Immigration (San Francisco: ICS Press, 1985), David Reimers, *Still the Golden Door* (New York: Columbia University Press, 1985), and George Borjas, *Friends or Strangers* (New York: Basic Books, 1990).

12. See Schuck and Smith, *Citizenship without Consent.*

13. See Brubaker, *Citizenship and Nationhood in France and Germany.*

14. See Andrew Shonfield on the "étatiste" tradition in *Modern Capitalism* (London: Oxford University Press, 1965), pp. 71 ff., and Peter A. Hall, *Governing the Economy* (New York: Oxford University and Polity Press), pp. 164 ff.

15. States that have consistently (and successfully) pursued such policymaking strategies tend to be the smaller, homogeneous, social democracies of Western Europe, such as Sweden, Austria, Norway, and Denmark. For a discussion of the impact of corporatism on politics and public policy in the smaller democracies, see Peter Katzenstein, *Corporatism and Change: Austria, Switzerland and the Politics of Industry* (Ithaca, N.Y.: Cornell University Press, 1984).

16. On this point, see, for example, Frank Lee Wilson, *Interest Group Politics in France* (Cambridge: Cambridge University Press, 1987).

17. Obviously this is not true in every instance. But a recent event on the high seas can serve to illustrate the point. A U.S. Navy captain was court martialed for refusing to pick up a sinking boatload of Vietnamese refugees in the South China Sea.

18. See Myron Weiner, "The Political Aspects of International Migration," paper presented at the annual meeting of the International Studies Association, London, March 1989, and Weiner, *Sons of the Soil: Migration and Ethnic Conflict in India* (Princeton: Princeton University Press).

19. On this point, see Giuseppe Callovi, "Regulating Immigration in the European Community, Effects of the Single European Act," paper presented at the Seventh International Conference of Europeanists, Washington, D.C., March 23–25, 1990.

20. On the notion of citizens and denizens, see Tomas Hammar, *Democracy and the Nation-State: Aliens, Denizens, and Citizens in a World of International Migration* (Aldershot: Avebury, 1990) and W. Rogers Brubaker, "Membership without Citizenship: The Economic and Social Rights of Noncitizens," in Brubaker, ed., *Immigration and the Politics of Citizenship* (Lanham, Md.: The German Marshall Fund and the University Press of America), pp. 145–162.

21. See, for example, Cornelius and Bustamante, eds., *Mexican Immigration to the United States,* and Borjas, *Friends or Strangers.*

22. See Ruggie, "International Regimes, Transactions, and Change: Embedded Liberalism in the Postwar Economic Order," *International Organization* 36 (Spring 1982), pp. 379–415.

Index

Adenauer, Konrad, 51
Adversarial legalism, 185–186, 205
Affirmative action, 186
Africa, 30, 40, 66, 157, 209, 213, 222
African-Americans, 177–178, 205
Agence Nationale Pour L'Emploi
  (ANPE), 133, 136
Agriculture, 47, 53, 59, 69, 76, 80, 109,
  178, 183
Algeria: immigration, 57–58, 61–62,
  66–68, 191, 194, 218, 224; return
  migration, 82–83; War, 57, 61, 194
Algérie française, 194
Aliens Act, German, 1938 and 1975, 197
Alsacians, 175
American Civil Liberties Union
  (ACLU), 183
Amnesty: for illegal aliens in France,
  91, 93, 190, 193, 205–206; in United
  States, 182–183, 206
Anarchy, State of, 25–26
Antisemitism, 192, 202, 223
Arizona, 185
Asia, 32, 154–155, 184, 208–209
Assimilation, 83–88, 116, 173, 188, 190,
  195
Asylum, political, 8, 11, 28, 35, 39,
  92–93, 179–183, 187, 193, 200,
  206–210, 225, 229. See also Refugees
Aussiedler (ethnic Germans), 35, 200,
  202–203
Australia, 6, 15, 32
Automobile industry, 144, 149–150,
  157–158, 164
Autonomy: of democratic states, 9, 17,
  124, 171, 214, 227–228; definition of,

126; of the administrative state, 110,
  117–118, 180, 220, 225; of the French
  state, 139–140

Baby-boom, 145
Balkans, 219
Banking. See Capital markets, Finance
Barre, Raymond, 192
Basic Law, 35, 93, 200, 202; Articles 16
  and 113, 93; Article 116, 199, 206
Bauer, Otto, 22
Beirat, 119
Belgium, 15, 38–39, 46, 48–49
Benelux, 229
Bennetton, 154
Berlin, 86, 202
Berlin Wall, 52, 59, 90
Beurs, 190–191, 212. See also Algeria,
  Immigration
Bismarck, Otto von, 47, 199
Boat people, 208
Bracero, 16, 178
Brandt, Willy, 70, 75, 220
Bretons, 175
Bretton Woods, 26–27.
Brixton riots, 120
Brown v. Board of Education, 181
Brubaker, William Rogers, 199, 223
Buchanan, James, 125
Bundesanstalt für Arbeit (BA-Federal
  Labor Office), 54, 60–61, 178, 197, 219
Bundestag, 87, 206
Bundesvereinigung Deutscher
  Arbeitgeberverbände (BDA-German
  Employers Association), 52, 81
Business. See Employers

Business, privileged position of, 100, 129, 219

California, 185
Cambodia, 210
Canada, 6, 15, 176, 209, 230
Capital goods sector, 147, 161, 283n19
Capital intensity, 148
Capital markets, 99–102
Castells, Manuel, 131, 137
Castro, Fidel, 208
Central America, 92, 182, 208, 210
China, 15, 25, 208
Chinese Exclusion Act, 36
Chirac, Jacques, 77, 192–194, 196, 224
Christian Democratic Union (CDU), 51, 201
Church and state, in France, 188, 191, 223
Church groups, German, 84
Circulaires, 77; Fontanet, 68–69; Gorse, 69; Marcellin, 69
Citizenship, 169–213, 222–227; colonialism and, 15; immigration and, 11, 16, 34, 170–172, 176–206, 228; liberal paradox and, 204–206; politics and policies of: European, 175–176; French, 16–17, 35, 48, 172–175, 186–196, 223–224; German, 16, 35, 50, 87, 172–175, 196–204, 224–225; U.S., 16, 35–36, 172–186, 225–226; rights and, 13, 121, 123, 169–213, 222–226; sovereignty and, 222–223
Civic culture. *See* Culture, civic
Civil rights. *See* Rights, civil
Civil Rights Act, 1964 U.S., 182, 186, 225
Civil Rights Movement, U.S., 172, 175–178, 180, 183–185, 206, 213, 225
Civil society, 5
Civil War, U.S., 175, 177
Cobb-Douglas production function, 106
Code de la Nationalité (nationality law), France, 191, 193, 194
Cohabitation, 195
Colbertist tradition. *See* Etatiste tradition
Cold War, 30–31, 224
Colonialism, 15, 19, 20, 22–23, 57–58, 61–63, 194, 210
Commissariat Général du Plan

(CGP-National Planning Commission) 53, 65, 88, 127
Commission des Sages, 183
Communists, (German), 203
Communism, collapse of, 224
Communist Party, French. *See* French Communist Party (PCF)
Comparative advantage, 106–107, 149, 154, 156
Comparative analysis, 13–17, 106, 217
Comparative political economy, 13–14, 125, 177, 232
Comparative politics, 173
Concentration of production, 150, 155–156, 158
Concertation *(économie concertée)*, 149, 284n24
Confédération Française Démocratique du Travail (CFDT-French Democratic Confederation of Labor), 63, 68, 88
Confédération Française des Travailleurs Chrétiens (CFTC-French Confederation of Christian Workers), 52, 55
Confédération Générale des Petites et Moyennes Entreprises (GGPME), 79, 81
Confédération Générale du Travail (CGT-General Confederation of Labor), 52, 55, 59, 62, 63, 78, 120, 155
Congress, U.S., 176, 179, 181–182, 184, 204, 206–207, 226
Conseil Economique et Social (CES), 80, 85, 119
Conseil National du Patronat Français (CNPF), 79
Constitution, French, 187
Constitution, German. *See* Basic Law
Constitution, U.S., 180, 182
Constitutionalism, 11, 27–29, 35–36, 84, 86–87, 96, 99, 117, 132, 175, 177–178, 181, 189, 197, 205, 210, 222, 225
Construction Industry, 15, 68, 79, 142–145, 149, 152, 160–161, 164, 188, 221
Consumer goods sector, 147, 161, 283n19
Contrôle d'identité, 190
Coordinating Committee *(Koordinierungskreis*, German Ministry of Labor), 80

Corn Laws, 19
Corporatism (neocorporatism), 51, 54, 60, 76, 117, 119, 129, 219, 228
Corsicans, 175
Cost-benefit analysis, 143
Council of State *(Conseil d'Etat)*, 187, 195–197, 206, 210, 224
Cresson, Edith, 187
Croizat, Ambroise, 57
Cultural pluralism, 37, 171–172, 178, 186, 196, 203–204, 211–212, 225.
Culture, 11, 177, 228; civic, 4, 174–176, 204; legal, 8, 176, 179–183, 204, 225; political, 8, 13, 16, 170–171, 173–175, 180, 186, 189, 194–199, 203–204, 211–212, 224–225

de Gaulle, Charles, 52, 54
de Tocqueville, Aléxis, 169, 174–175
Debré, Michel, 145
Debré, Robert, 53
Declaration of the Rights of Man and the Citizen, 174, 187. *See also* Constitution, French
Democratic states: theories of, 125; *See also* Autonomy of; Strength of
Democratic theory. *See* Autonomy and Strength of democratic states
Demography, 92, 95. *See also* population
Dependency theory, 22
Deportation procedures, U.S., 180, 182–183
Deregulation, 5, 142
Désir, Harlem, 191
Deutscher Gewerkschaftsbund (DGB-Federation of German Trade Unions), 52, 59, 79, 88, 197, 218–219
Dijoud, Paul, 79
Direction de la Population at des Migrations (DPM), 64, 81
Discrimination, 35, 76, 109, 179, 183, 185, 195, 226
Dreyfus Affair, 48
Droit à la différence, 193, 195
Dual labor markets: 23–24; demand for foreign labor and, 7–8, 91, 94, 96, 102, 105, 115, 146, 156; Marxist theory and, 23–24, 131; regulation and, 105, 146; unemployment and, 102, 131, 156, 275n7
Dual nationality, 194

Due process, 13, 28, 132, 181, 206, 256n26. *See also* Constitutionalism

East Asia, 154, 155
Eastern Europe: emigration from, 35, 93, 208, 210, 212, 224; refugees from, 93, 208, 210; revolutions in, 212, 224, 232, as source of labor, 40, 52, 218
East-West migration, 30, 35, 202–203, 208, 212. *See also* Eastern Europe
Ehrhard, Ludwig, 51
El Salvador, 208, 210
Employer sanctions, 33, 67, 93, 115, 118, 128–129, 178, 183, 213–214, 217
Employers associations, 79, 81, 139
Employment policy, 13, 94
Enclaves, ethnic and immigrant, 79, 84, 86
Enclosure Acts, 19
English, as an official language, 185
Entitlements, 5, 105, 110, 113, 115, 117–119, 121, 125, 170, 225
Equal protection, 181, 206. *See also* Constitutionalism
Equality before the law, 177, 186–187
Equality of opportunity, 205
Erleichterte Einbügerung, 201. *See also* Naturalization
Etatiste tradition, 77, 126, 139. *See also* Statism
Ethnic pluralism. *See* Cultural pluralism
Ethnic politics, 84–88
Ethnoculturalism, 173, 197–198, 199, 201, 202
Ethnonationalism, 172, 197, 199
European Community, 37–40; border controls in, 15, 38; citizenship and, 40, 230; creation of, 144, 174, 175; freedom of movement in, 38–39, 176, 222, 230; immigration in, 25, 37–40, 91, 92, 229; as an international regime, 9, 37–40; refugees and, 210; steel production and, 151
European Court of Human Rights, 40, 230
European Court of Justice, 40, 230
Evian Agreements, 194
Extended Voluntary Departure (EVD) 181. *See also* Deportation

Federation for American Immigration Reform (FAIR), 8

Fabius, Laurent, 191
Factor-price equalization, 24–25, 31
Family immigration, 83–86, 206–207, 225; explanation of, 138; in France, 66, 83–86, 133, 138, 187; in Germany, 83–86, 201; human rights and, 11, 187; labor markets and, 91, 116; in U.S., 207
Family reunification, 11, 33, 35, 60, 83–88, 95, 116, 138, 184, 187, 200–201, 207, 222, 226
Fascism, 53, 171, 188, 190, 201–202, 223
Federal Board of Immigration Appeals, U.S., 182
Federalism, 175, 185, 197, 203
Fédération Nationale du Bâtiment (FNB), 68, 79, 160–161, 164, 188, 221
Fifth Amendment (U.S. Constitution), 180, 182, 256n26.
Fifth Republic (France), 62, 77, 127, 134, 187, 196, 212, 227
Finance, 102
Flexible specialization, 154
Florida, 182, 185
Foreign policy, 15, 181, 209, 213, 231
Foreign worker policy. See Gastarbeiter
Foulards, Affaire des, 195–196
Fourteenth Amendment (U.S. Constitution), 180, 185, 213, 256n26, 259n48, 288n24
Fourth Republic (France), 51, 52, 54, 56–59, 61–62, 77, 81, 127, 134, 146, 149, 151, 164, 212, 217, 227
France, chapters 3–9, passim
Franco-Algerian Accords, 82
Freedom of Movement (clause of Treaty of Rome), 38, 259n51. See also European Community
French Communist Party (PCF), 48, 58, 78, 120, 189, 211, 223
French Revolution, 48, 173–174, 198, 223
Fundamentalism, Islamic, 191, 194. See also Islam

Gastarbeiter (Guestworkers), 45–73, 88–94, 218–219; economic growth and, 4, 45–73, 202; in Germany, 4, 16, 55, 58–61, 70–73, 76–77, 170, 200, 218–219; naturalization of, 87; policy failure and, 70–73, 88–94, 170, 216; recruitment of, 32, 55; social policy for, 85–88; in Switzerland, 4, 16, 70–73, 218
Gaullism, 61–70, 145, 171, 192, 211, 223
General Agreement on Tariffs and Trade (GATT), 26, 30
German Democratic Republic, 198–199, 204, 260n1
Germanization, 197, 203
Germany, chapters 3–5, 8–9, passim
Gilpin, Robert, 25
Giscard d'Estaing, Valéry, 70, 75, 77, 156, 192, 220
Golden handshake, Germany, 197
Great Britain (England): colonial legacy of, 14–15; European Community and, 38, 210; Hong Kong and, 28; liberalism/neoliberalism in, 4–5, 100–101, 172; migration in history of, 19–20, 46
Great Depression, 30, 49
Greece, 15, 32, 38, 40, 60, 83, 218–219
Grenelle Agreements, 65, 80, 113, 145–146, 154
Guatemala, 208
Guestworkers. See Gastarbeiter
Gypsies, 202

H-2 program, U.S., 178
Haitian refugees, 10, 182
Harkis, 61, 194
Harmonization, of policy in E.C., 230
Haute couture, 154
Hegemonic stability, 25–27, 30, 177, 180, 228
Hénneresse, Marie-Claude, 81
Hispanics, 179, 184
Hitler, Adolph, 48
Home work, 154
Hong Kong, 28, 208
Housing policy, 79, 202
Human capital theory, 34, 202, 216
Human rights. See Rights, human

Illegal immigration: control of, 6, 15, 33, 39, 92, 178, 206; European integration and, 39; in France, 92; measure of, 33; in U.S., 6, 12, 33, 109, 176–178
Immigration and Nationality Act (1965), U.S., 207
Immigration and Naturalization Service (INS), 178, 180, 182–184, 209

Immigration judges, U.S., 180, 289n30
Immigration Reform Act, U.S. 1990, 5, 170, 182, 183, 184, 226
Immigration Reform and Control Act (IRCA), U.S. 1986, 5, 33, 170, 178–179, 182–183, 184, 206, 213, 226
Imperialism, 22
Implementation (of immigration policy), 124–140, 179, 227–228
Indochina. *See* Southeast Asia
Industrial adjustment, 142, 148, 221
Industrial democracy: citizenship and, 169, 171, 176, 206, 216, 217–222; labor markets and, 100, 102, 108, 110–125, 128–129, 130; liberalism and, 5, 9, 11, 13–15, 18, 29, 32, 41
Industrial policies, 17, 101, 127, 141–166, 220–221
Industrial Reserve Army, 22, 75, 131, 140, 215
Industrial Revolution, 10, 275n13
Inflation, 50, 56, 71, 104–117, 217
Informal economy, 154
Input-output analysis, 143
Interaction analysis, 122, 136
Interdependence, 5, 9, 18, 26, 41, 129, 171, 214, 222, 230
Interest group politics, 78–94, 117–121
Intermediate goods sector, 16, 283n19
Interministerial Committee on Immigration (France), 62
International division of labor, 153, 159
International Labor Office (ILO), 8
International Monetary Fund (IMF), 26, 30
International political economy, 10, 19–20, 22, 41, 228, 232
International regime, 9, 20, 26, 37–40, 229, 253n3.
International relations, 5, 21–41, 217, 228
International system, 14, 20, 25, 30–32, 117, 215
Investment, 101
Iranian Revolution, 194, 223
Irish, 20, 46, 177, 184
Islam: in France, 67, 173, 195–196, 223; and German citizenship debate, 203; and restrictionism, 72, 75, 189–196, 211, 219–220, 223
Italy, 15, 32, 38, 40, 46, 48–49, 55, 60, 66, 145, 158, 211, 218, 229

Jacobinism, 48, 61, 134, 171, 174, 175, 186–196, 198, 212, 223–224, 227
Japan, 6, 15, 25, 101, 154–155, 157–158
Jeanneney, J. M., 63
Jews: in Germany, 199; in U.S., 177, 208
Joan of Arc, 223
Judicial review, 174, 176, 181, 182
July, Serge, 195
Junkers, 47
Jus sanguinis, 16, 35, 194, 199, 224
Jus soli: 16, 35, 193–194

Katzenstein, Peter, 225
Kennedy, Edward, 184
Keohane, Robert O., 26
Keynesian policy, 71, 74, 100, 113, 141, 191
Kindleberger, Charles P., 25, 45, 95, 106, 112, 127, 217
Kohl, Helmut, 201
Konjuncturpuffer (shock absorbers), 200, 219
Konsertierte Aktion (concerted action), 219
Korea, 15, 56, 155
Krasner, Steven, 21
Kreis, 197
Kühn Report, 201

Labor, 11, 15, 21, 36, 99–109, 217; markets, 33, chapters 3–5, *passim;* migration, 33. *See also* dual labor markets
Labor unions. *See* Trade unions
Laïcité (secularism, France), 188, 191, 195, 223
Länder (German states), 77, 87, 225
Latin America, 15, 30, 92, 210
Le Pen, Jean-Marie, 171, 190–192, 196, 202, 223, 228
Legal (documented) immigration, 6, 90, 178, 182, 184, 207, 226, 288n2
Legalization rate (*taux de regularisation*, France), 52, 61, 66, 134, 136, 160–161, 206
Lenin, V. I., 22, 215
Lewis-Kindleberger Model, 104–117, 143, 164
Liberal democracy. *See* Liberalism
Liberal paradox. *See* Liberalism, paradox of
Liberalism, 3, 4–17, 24–25, 94–96,

121–122, 139, 231–232; economic,
104–109; embedded, 26–28, 36,
230–231, 254n6; paradox of, 7, 171,
205, 217, 222–227, 231; rights-based,
18, 169–213, 216, 222–227; test of,
134–140, 160, 169–213
Libération, 195
Lindblom, Charles, 99
Locke, John, 172, 174
Luxembourg, 39
Luxemburg, Rosa, 22

Macroeconomic policies, 100, 141, 218
Maghrébin population, (France) 194. *See
also* North Africa, Algeria
Malthusianism, 57, 212
Manpower policy, 62, 65. *See also*
Human capital theory
Manpower shortages, 82, 96, 220
Manufacturing sector, 141–142,
144–145, 149–159, 160
Marginal product of labor, 107–117
Mariel boatlift, 208
Marshall Plan, 56
Marx, Karl, 22
Marxist theory, 22–24, 94, 96, 102, 131,
134–140, 147, 160, 215–216. *See also*
Industrial reserve army
Mauroy, Pierre, 189, 191
McNary v. Haitian Refugee Center, 182
Mediterranean basin, 38, 220
Melting pot, 177–178
Mercantilism, 24, 229, 231
Mexican-American Legal Defense Fund
(MALDF), 183
Mexico, 15, 16, 37, 176, 230
Miami, 210
Microeconomic theory, 107–108, 125
Middle East, 15, 32, 92, 157, 191, 209
Migratory chain, 33
Mill, John Stuart, 6, 19, 24, 172, 174
Mining industry, 72, 82, 142, 144, 160,
162, 164
Mitbestimmung (codetermination) 60,
219
Mitterrand, François, 91, 93, 189–191,
205
Monetarism, 141
Monnet plan, 53, 56–57, 144
Morocco, 63, 82, 92, 218
Multiculturalism, 204, 225
Multiplier effects, 158–159

Muslims. *See* Islam
Myrdal, Gunnar, 214

Nation-state, 10, 19, 171, 211, 214, 228
National Assembly, 188, 192, 194, 211
National Front (France), 8, 77, 86, 120,
171, 188, 190–192, 194, 196, 202, 211,
223, 228
National identity, 4, 8, 11–12, 16, 31,
46, 67, 171, 195–196, 225–226, 229
National identity cards, 183
National interest, 20, 22, 31, 72, 74–75,
94, 109, 125, 130, 205, 214, 222, 226,
228
National origins quota system, 36, 177,
207
Nationalism, 3–4, 10, 31, 95, 170, 220;
competing conceptions of, in France,
186–196, 223; repression of, in
Germany, 196–204, 224
Nationality, 13, 35; American, 207;
French, 191–196; German, 87, 173,
185, 188–189, 197–201, 206, 211,
224–225. *See also* Dual nationality
Nativism (U.S.), 172, 178, 185
Naturalization, 16, 35, 45, 50, 64,
87–88, 172, 173, 180, 193–194, 197,
200–202, 206, 211, 224–225
Nazi Party, 48, 50, 198–199
Neoinstitutionalism, 125–126
Neo-Nazis, 203, 225
Neoliberalism, 4–5, 155
Netherlands, 15, 38–39
New Deal 5, 80
New Zealand, 6
Newly Industrialized Countries (NICs),
153
Nicaragua, 210
North Africa, 15, 32, 58, 61, 66, 67, 75,
82, 190–191, 203, 212, 218
North America, 32, 37, 230
North American Free Trade Area
(NAFTA), 176, 230
North-South relations, 30, 38–39,
257n35.
Nye, Joseph S., 26

Office Français de Protection de
Refugiés et Apatrides (OFPRA), 209
Office des Migrations Internationales
(OMI), 160, 178, 188, 281n21,

290n51. *See also* Office National d'Immigration (ONI)

Office National d'Immigration (ONI), 54–69, 81, 91, 136, 160, 188, 281n21, 290n51. *See also* Office des Migrations Internationales (OMI)

Oil Embargo, OPEC, 33, 70, 75, 100, 113, 130, 141, 220

Olson, Mancur, 125, 127

Operation Wetback, 179

Organization for Economic Cooperation and Development (OECD), 5, 27, 32, 101–102

Pareto optimality, 112–116

Parole authority (U.S. Attorney General), 179–180, 184

Party system, 171, 175, 185–185, 204, 211, 225

Pax Americana, 30, 177

Pax Britannica, 20, 26

People's Republic of China. *See* China

Persian Gulf, 32

Pieds noirs, 61

Piore, Michael, 7–8, 23, 113, 131, 154

Planning (economic), 53, 56–57, 127, 144, 155

Pluralism, 17, 117, 125–126, 129–131, 173–175, 183–186, 193, 202–204, 211–213, 217, 224, 227. *See also* Cultural pluralism

Plyler v. Doe, 181, 197, 226

Poland, 40, 46–47, 48–49, 199, 202, 218, 224

Polanyi, Karl, 7, 26, 27, 172

Polish Question, 202

Political participation, 87–88, 190, 191

Political system, 13, 16, 29, 35, 45, 101, 117, 127–129, 175, 204, 213; American, 177, 185; French, 196, 211–212; German, 76–77, 198

Pompidou, Georges, 65–66, 69–70, 75, 146–147, 220

Popular sovereignty, 174

Population, 14–15, 19–23, 37–40, 45, 47, 116, 216, 229, 276n14; Algerian, 68; foreign, 33–34, 49–58, 61, 63–73, 88–92, 105, 130, 133–134, 190–193, 201; and Marxist theory, 22–23; and *populationnisme*, 53–58; and pronatalism, 51, 53; and realist theory, 19–20, 216; surplus, 22–23

Portes, Alejandro, 23

Portugal, 32, 38, 40, 63, 66–68, 82, 92, 145, 219

Presidency, U.S., 179, 181, 184

Production capacity, 156–157

Production function, 105

Profits, 104–117

Pronatalism, 51, 53, 58, 145

Proportional representation, 192

Protectionism, 39, 149, 155–156

Prussia, 46–47, 200, 203

Push-pull, 14, 25, 132, 169, 213, 214–215

Quotas. *See* National origins quota system

Rassemblement Pour la République (RPR), 190, 192, 194, 223

Rawls, John, 6, 223

Reagan, Ronald, 5, 206–207

Realism, 20–22, 25, 171, 216, 228

Reconstruction (economic), 50–58

Recruitment fees, 71

Refugee Act (1980, U.S.), 207–208

Refugees, 10, 11, 12, 28, 92–93, 116, 206–210, 224. *See also* asylum, political

Regionalism (post-nationalism), 37, 230

Régularisation, 57, 62, 67–68, 93, 134, 206

Reiffers, Jean-Louis, 105–106

Renault, 158

Repatriation, 16, 77, 82–83, 100, 115, 221

Republican synthesis, 188, 290n54. *See also* Third Republic

Republikaner, 8, 77, 120, 171–172, 202, 224

Resettlement, 208

Residency permits, German, 197, 201

Restrictionism, 5–6, 39, 74–96, 116, 130, 184, 222, 231

Ricardo, David, 19

Rights: 3, 6–7, 9, 11–13, 21, 26–40, 105, 113, 117–119, 125, 140, 169–216, 222–225; civil, 6, 28, 36–41, 84, 86, 121, 164–166, 222–226; confluence of markets and, 28, 170, 225; human, 13, 27, 31–36, 39–40, 84, 173, 181, 226, 228; interaction of markets and, 13–14, 29, 131; of association, 69, 87, 190, 193; of employment in EC, 38,

Rights (continued)
259n51; of residence, 15, 60, 87, 191,
197, 201; political (voting), 6, 10, 84,
87, 134, 190; programmatic, 6,
259n48; property, 26, 29; social, 6, 41,
86, 222, 226; versus markets, 10,
27–29, 225–226, 231–232. See also
Liberalism
Rocard, Michel, 195
Roman law, 174
Romania, 202, 224
Rousseau, Jean-Jacques, 172–173
Ruggie, John G., 26, 27, 31

SOS-racisme, 191
Sabel, Charles, 154
Sales, 151–152, 158–159
Salvadorans, 210
Samuelson, Paul, 24
San Francisco, 182
Sauvy, Alfred, 53
Scale effect, 107–108
Schengen Agreement, 39, 229, 230
Schmidt, Helmut, 201
Schönhuber, Franz, 202
Schuck, Peter H., 179, 180–181
Seasonal immigration, 8, 12, 33, 34, 59,
66, 76, 80, 91–92, 133, 138
Second Empire, 46
Second-generation immigrants, 85–86,
88, 191–193, 201, 224
Second Reich, 199, 203
Sectoral Analysis, 141–166
Select Commission on Immigration and
Refugee Policy (U.S.), 176
Separation of powers, 177, 183, 188
Service sector, 15, 95, 145, 151–152,
158–159, 164, 221
Shipbuilding, 149
Shonfield, Andrew, 124, 127
Siberia, 199
Silesia, 47, 200
Single European Act, 39, 155, 213,
229–230
Skinheads, 203, 225. See also Neo-Nazis
Slavery, 178
Smith, Adam, 19, 24
Social democracy, 58–61, 70–71, 114,
205. See also Social market economy
Social Democratic Party (SPD), 60, 70,
75, 201, 220
Social market economy, 58–61

Social mobility, 115, 165
Social services, 83–88
Socialist Party, 79, 189, 194, 196, 211
Société Générale d'Immigration (SGI),
49, 52, 62
SONACOTRA rent strikes, 85, 120, 189
South-North migration, 30, 38
South Asia, 32
Southeast Asia, 15, 30, 92, 208–210
Sovereign immunity, 186
Sovereignty, 5, 9, 10, 20, 37–38, 205,
214, 226–231
Soviet Union, 35, 40, 208, 232
Spain, 15, 32, 37–38, 40, 49, 66, 83, 92,
145, 218
Special Agricultural Worker (SAW)
Program, 178, 226
Statism: and citizenship, 174, 225; and
immigration policy, 32–37; and
industrial policy in France, 160–161;
and policy implementation in France,
130–132, 134–140; and recruitment of
foreign labor, 51–58, 226–228; and
restrictionist policies, 92, 114–115,
212, 216, 219, 222, 226–228; and the
issue of sovereignty, 226–228. See
also Realism
Steel sector, 149, 150–151, 152,
155–157, 164
Strength (capacity) of democratic states,
17–18, 118, 124, 126–129, 134,
139–140, 220, 227
Subsidies, 156
Substitution effect, 107–108
Supreme Court, U.S., 182, 185, 197
Sweatshops, 154
Sweden, 15
Switzerland: chapters 3–5, passim;
economic growth and labor supply in,
103–105, 111, 114; and recruitment of
foreign labor, 46, 49–50, 55, 58, 111,
218; and restrictionist policies, 88,
114; and the Überfremdung, 3–4, 220
Symbolic politics, 139–140, 195, 231

Taiwan, 155
Tapinos, Georges, 57
Terrorism, 190
Texas, 181–182
Textiles, 151–155
Thailand, 208
Thatcher, Margaret, 4, 171

Third Reich, 61, 173, 198, 200, 203, 224, 260n1.
Third Republic, 48–50, 53, 188
Third World, 14, 15, 32, 69, 72, 125, 218, 222, 228
Time-series analysis, 121, 133–135
Trade, free, 5, 19, 230; theory of, 24–25, 31, 38, 129, 215
Trade unions: and labor market policies, 100, 118, 128; and recruitment of foreign labor, 52–68, 217–218; and restrictionism, 78–94, 158, 228
Treaty of Rome, 37, 175, 218
Tunisia, 63, 92, 218
Turkey, 32, 35, 60, 63, 66, 75, 83, 93, 201, 203, 218–219, 222, 224
Turkish Question, 202–203, 224

Überfremdung, 3, 8, 16, 50, 74, 120, 220
Underclass, 211
Unemployment, 33, 72–73, 85–86, 104–117, 191
Unification (German), 87, 170, 198, 201–202, 203, 224
Union pour la Démocratie Française (UDF), 190, 193, 196
Unionization (rates of), 153–155
United Nations, 8, 208
United States: chapter 8, *passim*; civil rights in, 176–186, 225–226; in comparative perspective, 14–16; federalism in, 84–85; illegal immigration in, 93; liberal policies in, 33–36; 231–232; pluralist tradition in,

172–174, 204; position of labor in, 100–101; restrictionism in, 5–6

Vertribene (displaced and/or expelled persons), 52, 200
Vichy, 53, 211
Vietnam, 57, 208, 210
Vietnam War, 180
Völkisch concept, 199, 202–203
Volksgemeinschaft (national community), 173, 175, 197, 199, 202–203
Voting. *See* Rights, political

Waffen SS, 202
Wages, 104–117, *passim*
Walzer, Michael, 6, 223
Weimar Republic, 48
Welfare state, 6–7, 61, 64, 75, 84–85, 99, 205, 215–216
West Africa, 63, 66, 68, 82, 135
Wirtschaftswunder, 4, 219
Work permits, 60, 63, 68–70, 76, 84–87, 92, 133, 197–198, 201
World politics, 232
World systems theory, 22–23
World War I, 47, 49
World War II, 47–48, 90

Xenophobia. *See* racism

Yugoslavia, 32, 60, 63, 66, 218–219

Zaire, 209–210
Zysman, John, 127